CONTEMPORARY CLINICAL PSYCHOLOGY

CONTEMPORARY CLINICAL PSYCHOLOGY

HERBERT GOLDENBERG

California State University, Los Angeles

BROOKS/COLE PUBLISHING COMPANY
Monterey, California
A Division of Wadsworth Publishing Company, Inc.

ISBN: 0-8185-0068-9
L.C. Catalog Card No.: 72-92045
Printed in the United States of America
2 3 4 5 6 7 8 9 10—77 76 75 74

This book was edited by Mara Niels and designed by Jane Mitchell. It was typeset by The Heffernan Press, Inc., Worcester, Massachusetts, and printed and bound by Kingsport Press, Kingsport, Tennessee.

Preface

Contemporary Clinical Psychology has two main objectives. The first is to unify the scientific and professional aspects of clinical psychology. My simultaneous experiences as an academician and practitioner have kept me keenly aware of potential rifts between colleagues whose primary commitment is to either clinical research or clinical practice. While all agree that both the scientific and professional aspects of the field need to be more closely related, this book is one of the few works to do so.

The second main objective is to provide a comprehensive overview of the field. So much is happening in current clinical research and practice that the student, as well as the individual clinician, may lose sight of the whole picture because of his specialized and sometimes necessarily narrowed view. Therefore, this book includes: (1) traditional areas of clinical psychology, such as psychodiagnostic testing and individual psychotherapy, and descriptions and evaluations of recent developments in these areas; (2) material on research and practice in many emerging areas; and (3) such relatively new developments as community mental health, crisis intervention, brief therapies, family therapy, and the encounter movement, which all point to new directions in clinical psychology.

In discussing many of the central, controversial issues of contemporary clinical psychology, I have adopted an advocacy approach—arguing first from one side of the question and then from the other side—to present as much information with as little bias as possible. I hope the reader will be sufficiently stimulated to clarify for himself just where he stands.

I wish to thank a number of colleagues who have helped me along the way with the wisdom and generosity of their comments in reviewing various portions and earlier drafts of the book. They include James Bieri,

University of Texas, Austin; David Galinsky, University of North Carolina; Jaques W. Kaswan, Ohio State University; Joseph Lyons, University of California, Davis; David Martin, University of Manitoba; and Joseph C. Speisman, Boston University.

My sincerest critic, whose honesty, intelligence, and straightforwardness I cherish, is my wife, Dr. Irene Goldenberg. Her initial encouragement, continued interest, and support over several years have sustained me through the writing of this book. Her ability, also, to provide me with emotional nourishment while at the same time providing the same for her patients, students, and our children, Philip, Erica, and Karen, is truly extraordinary.

Herbert Goldenberg

Contents

PART I *The Profession of Clinical Psychology* 1

1 **THE CLINICAL PSYCHOLOGIST—SCHOLAR AND PRACTITIONER** 3

What Clinical Psychologists Do 4
Two Professional Roles 8
The Clinical Psychologist as Research Scientist 9
Evaluation of the Academic-Research Model 25
The Clinical Psychologist as Practitioner 29
Evaluation of the Medical Model 35

2 **ROOTS OF CONTEMPORARY CLINICAL PSYCHOLOGY** 43

The Legacy of Experimental Research 44
The Measurement of Individual Differences 45
The Impact of Psychiatry 47
The Humanitarian Movement 50
The Development of Clinical Psychology 52

3 **ISSUES IN PROFESSIONAL PREPARATION AND PROFESSIONAL PRACTICE** 66

Graduate Training in Clinical Psychology 68
Alternate Proposals for Graduate Training in Clinical Psychology 79
Aspects of Professional Practice 89

PART **II** *Contemporary Clinical Psychology—*
Practice and Research   105

4   CLINICAL JUDGMENT IN DIAGNOSIS
AND ASSESSMENT   107

The Nature of Psychiatric Diagnosis   107
The Process of Clinical Judgment   126

5   PROBLEMS AND TECHNIQUES OF
PSYCHOLOGICAL ASSESSMENT   144

Psychodiagnostic Testing   145
The Assessment of Intelligence   154
The Assessment of Organic Brain Dysfunction   164
Projective Techniques in Personality Assessment   170
Objective Methods in Personality Assessment   184

6   PARAMETERS OF INDIVIDUAL PSYCHOTHERAPY
AND PSYCHOANALYSIS   191

The Common Core and Course of Psychotherapy   194
The Special Characteristics of Child Psychotherapy   195
Dimensions for Categorizing Systems of Psychotherapy
198
The Process of Individual Psychotherapy   201
The Effectiveness of Psychotherapy   213
Psychoanalysis   219
Evaluation of Psychoanalysis   231

7   BEHAVIOR MODIFICATION AND THE
PHENOMENOLOGICAL THERAPIES   238

Behavior Modification   238
Evaluation of Behavior Modification   256
The Phenomenological Therapies   265
An Overview of Major Approaches to Psychotherapy   282
Evaluation of the Phenomenological Therapies   284

PART **III** *New Directions in*
Clinical Psychology   291

8   COMMUNITY MENTAL HEALTH   293

Mental Health's Third Revolution   294

Historical Antecedents of Community Mental Health Practices   296
Community Mental Health Centers   300
The Practice of Community Mental Health   304
Research in Community Mental Health   315
Evaluation of the Community Mental Health Approach   331

9   CRISIS INTERVENTION AND OTHER BRIEF PSYCHOTHERAPIES   341

Crisis Theory   342
Crisis Intervention   344
Brief Psychotherapies   361

10   FAMILY THERAPY, GROUP THERAPY, AND THE ENCOUNTER MOVEMENT   371

Family Therapy   372
Group Therapy and the Encounter Movement   389

REFERENCES   409

NAME INDEX   441

SUBJECT INDEX   448

CONTEMPORARY
CLINICAL
PSYCHOLOGY

PART I The Profession of Clinical Psychology

CHAPTER 1

The Clinical Psychologist—Scholar and Practitioner

The specialty of clinical psychology may be defined as that branch of psychology which deals with the search for and the application of psychological principles aimed at understanding the uniqueness of the individual client or patient, reducing his personal distress, and helping him to function more meaningfully and effectively. Both the scientific and professional aspects are deliberately given equal billing in such a definition. The clinical psychologist, educated in graduate programs that usually are part of the arts and sciences faculties of universities, inevitably is imbued with a research-oriented viewpoint. Whether he ever engages in any original research during his professional career, the research orientation in the curriculum encourages an inquiring attitude that leads to questioning and objectively evaluating new clinical techniques. At a point in clinical psychology's development when new, innovative approaches abound, some more sensational than sound, it is especially important for the clinical psychologist to be influenced by scientific evidence, not swept along from one fad to the next. At the same time, he must be committed to understanding and respecting the uniqueness of his individual patient or client as well as to his professional responsibility to help prevent, alleviate, or remove that individual's emotional distress. As renowned atomic physicist J. Robert Oppenheimer (1956) put it in discussing the disciplines of physics and psychology:

> We are both faced with the problem of the need to keep intact the purity of academic and abstract research, and, at the same time, to nourish and be nourished by practice.

This chapter begins with an overview of what clinical psychologists do and the sources of their data. Then clinical psychologists' two roles and each role's theoretical rationale are described: first, the research scientist and the academic–research model, the basis for his work; next, the practitioner and his medical model. The discussion of the academic–research model includes the main areas of current research. Following the discussion of each role and its theoretical model, arguments for and against each model are presented.

WHAT CLINICAL PSYCHOLOGISTS DO

The activities of today's clinical psychologists are considerably broader than those of their predecessors. Forty years ago, most clinical psychologists worked primarily with children's problems in university or community clinics or in institutions such as those for the physically handicapped or the feebleminded. Many were trained only to the master's level. Their major responsibility was psychological testing, usually to measure intellectual ability and deficit. Twenty years ago, in the postwar years, the emphasis shifted to include personality testing and psychotherapy with adults, usually in a medical setting such as a psychiatric hospital or in an outpatient clinic. Clinical psychologists were expected to be trained to the Ph.D. level, including internship at a field work station.

Present-day psychologists are harder to categorize; they are mostly Ph.D.-trained individuals working in a variety of settings including the following *places:* (1) university psychology departments as teachers and researchers; (2) psychiatric hospitals or outpatient clinics performing research and providing clinical services; (3) community mental health centers; (4) university student health centers; (5) child guidance centers; (6) private practice as individuals or in group practice; (7) public and private schools; (8) state youth authority agencies; (9) city juvenile halls; (10) prisons; (11) medical schools; (12) conciliation courts; (13) probation departments; and (14) industry, as industrial management consultants.

The *problems* these clinical psychologists might deal with include: (1) social and interpersonal problems; (2) sexual problems; (3) marital problems; (4) vocational problems; (5) school adjustment problems; (6) speech pathology; (7) problems arising from delinquency, alcoholism, drug addiction; (8) problems arising from organic brain dysfunction; and many others.

Clinical psychologists work with individuals of all ages. For example: (1) infants—perhaps evaluating them for signs of mental retardation, with or without accompanying brain damage; (2) preschool children—identifying the gifted, the emotionally disturbed, or consulting in Head Start programs; (3) school-age children—helping them with learning and behavior problems or perhaps working with a high school drug-abuse program; (4) young adults—vocational guidance, premarital counseling; (5) parents—child-rearing problems, marital problems; and (6) the elderly—geriatric or retirement problems. In addition to working with individuals, today's clinical psychologist frequently finds that working with groups of disturbed people, including entire families, may be even more effective in bringing about constructive personality and behavioral changes.

The *clinical services* clinical psychologists provide include: (1) psychological testing and interviewing to assess or diagnose personality, intelligence, achievement, aptitude, and behavior; (2) counseling and psychotherapy with individuals, couples, families, or groups; (3) research into various aspects of personality development and functioning, etiology of psychopathology, modes of treatment, and so on; (4) selecting, training, and supervising nonprofessionals such as mental health aides or Peace Corps volunteers; and (5) community consultation with community agencies to develop programs to prevent emotional disorders.

SOURCES OF CLINICAL DATA

Like all psychologists, clinical psychologists are interested in systematically and scientifically observing and measuring an individual's behavior, in order to describe it more clearly and understand it better. Then they can more accurately judge, assess, and predict the future behavior of specific individuals, which they are often asked to do. Is Patient A a good prospect for group therapy? Would Patient B improve more quickly if treated alone or with his family? Can Patient C handle his current crisis or will he need to be hospitalized? What is the prognosis for Patient D, who has been labeled a paranoid schizophrenic? Does Patient E, a slow learner, need to be placed in a special class? Are Patient F's physical symptoms psychogenically caused? What is the type and extent of Patient G's impairment from a head injury received in an automobile accident?

It would be ideal if such decisions, all of which involve predictions of future behavior, were based on a set of established, highly reliable, valid measures. Unfortunately, they are not. Instead, they derive from objective test scores as well as subjective impressions based on the intuitive skill and experienced judgment of the practitioner. All clinicians use one or more of the following methods to arrive at their clinical judgments.

This is summarized in notes

1. **The anamnesis or case history.** The anamnesis is similar to a diagnostic examination performed by a physician; the patient usually gives this information during an early interview. Such interviews tend to be highly structured—the patient answers specific questions about the history of his complaint and about his life before the onset of his disturbance: his medical, developmental, family, and social history; the history of his sexual adjustment; and an educational and work history. In psychiatric hospitals and clinics, a psychiatric social worker may gather this information. When other informants (friends, relatives, employers) supply additional data, the broader term *case history* is used.

2. **The clinical interactive interview.** The clinical interactive interview is sometimes used when the case history is taken, and sometimes it is used separately; it is an attempt to obtain data about the patient without formal questions and answers. Some clinicians prefer to interact freely with the patient and to use whatever material emerges from such an unstructured transaction as their primary data. Such interviews tend to be ahistorical in nature, emphasizing the patient's here-and-now situation rather than the past. They frequently focus on the pattern of communication, verbal and nonverbal, between the participants. The formal case history interview has a diagnostic purpose and ends once all the necessary diagnostic information is obtained. In contrast, the clinical interactive interview begins at the initial session and continues throughout the ensuing therapy; the diagnostic and treatment processes are not separated.

3. **Psychological testing.** Sometimes psychological tests are diagnostic (to identify mental retardation, organic brain damage, schizophrenia) and sometimes they are used more broadly to describe, understand, and evaluate an individual's attributes and personality characteristics. Well constructed tests are apt to be carefully standardized, highly reliable and valid, and have an objective scoring system. In addition, the clinical psychologist adds his intuitive skills and experienced judgment for a more complete analysis of the test data. He tries to be alert to the interpersonal relationship developing between himself and the patient during testing.

Formal test procedures during which the clinician asks questions are sometimes like a structured interview.

4. Observation. Systematic observation, in either the experimental laboratory or the psychological clinic, is basic to extending our understanding of behavior. In a clinical setting, the psychologist relies on his observations of the patient's overt behavior to: (1) provide information that cannot be obtained through direct questioning; (2) evaluate how appropriate and consistent the patient's verbal communication is to his nonverbal communication; and (3) draw inferences regarding the underlying inner state, feelings, and motivations which produce the patient's behavior. For example, rather than conduct a formal clinical interview with a child, the clinician might observe him in his classroom to see how he interacts with other children, whether he initiates tasks or follows another child's leadership, or how he copes with such frustration as losing a game or misspelling a word. The clinician testing a young child would also be alert to how he separates from his mother in the waiting room, how he deals with a stranger (the psychologist), how he uses dolls, games, and toys in the psychologist's office, and how quickly he becomes fatigued or distracted. In the case of a hospitalized patient with schizophrenia (a behavior disorder characterized primarily by a withdrawal from reality), the clinician might want to observe the patient's behavior in the ward, whether he sits isolated or chooses the company of others, how he reacts to visitors and doctors, whether he appears disoriented, not knowing who or where he is, or whether he appears to be responding to auditory or visual hallucinations and seems preoccupied with inner fantasies and thoughts.

5. Home visits. Psychologists have tended to obtain data in the laboratory or the consultation room rather than in the natural habitat of a particular behavior. Because they study people in such artificial settings, both the experimentalists and the clinicians may develop a somewhat distorted or one-sided view of human behavior. As a rule, clinical psychologists do not make home visits, although social workers and public health nurses traditionally have done so. However, some clinicians have begun to make occasional or regular visits to the home, where they can see the patient and his family in their natural, everyday roles and relationships to one another. This approach seems to have had good results in treating schizophrenics in their homes together with their families (Friedman, Boszormenyi–Nagy, Jungreis, Lincoln, Mitchell, Sonne, Speck, & Spivak, 1965).

6. Patient records. School records, records of previous hospitalization, and records of previous testing and psychotherapy are often useful to the clinician. The patient (or his parents, in the case of a child) must first sign a release so other agencies can provide the clinician with his confidential records. Once he has these records, the clinician might be better able to make before- and after-treatment comparisons or better plot the development of particular significant trends in the patient's behavior. In addition, records often help him by supplying an independent impression of the patient, which he can then compare with his own impression.

7. Personal documents. Personal documents may be either first-person or third-person accounts of various aspects of the patient's life. The value of such documents for psychological analysis was first pointed out by Gordon Allport (1942), a social psychologist interested in studying personality. First-person documents include letters, diaries, stories, or autobiographical material spontaneously produced by the patient. Third-person accounts usually refer to biographical material and are probably of secondary value. The veracity of the material in first-person documents is of less significance to the clinician than the revelation of how his patient perceived his world at the time he produced the document. In assessing the value of documents, the clinician might wish to determine: (1) the motivation behind the communication (catharsis, justification for past behavior, atonement, or exhibitionism); and (2) the nature of the audience for whom the document was originally intended. In clinical situations, the content of such documents sometimes reveals previously hidden aspects of the patient's world, and may be especially useful with withdrawn, resistant, or inarticulate individuals.

TWO PROFESSIONAL ROLES

Many professional clinical psychologists choose a career in clinical research, while others commit themselves to clinical practice. For example, while researchers might be interested in gathering experimental data in order to help formulate a theory of personality development, practitioners might be more interested in applying principles of good child-rearing practices to an emotionally disturbed family who has requested professional help. The researcher's orientation is that of a problem-finder, looking for areas of study that need experimental exploration. The practitioner, on the other hand, is more apt to focus on problem solving, basing his clinical interventions on the results of research or his own or others' experience with patients.

While generally trained to carry out both roles, clinical psychologists usually identify themselves with either the scientist or practitioner role, rarely both. The remainder of this chapter will pit the researcher against the practitioner, minimizing their collaboration or cooperation, giving the pros and cons of both positions. At times, this will result in a somewhat slanted picture of clinical psychology that will be corrected as the reader proceeds.

THE CLINICAL PSYCHOLOGIST AS RESEARCH SCIENTIST

As a result of his training in research methodology, the clinical psychologist is better equipped to carry out clinical research than any of his mental health colleagues, including psychoanalysts, psychiatrists, psychiatric social workers, or public health nurses. Ideally, then, he should combine his commitment to scientific inquiry with his commitment to the performance of clinical services, producing the unique professional who is sometimes called the scientist among clinicians (other mental health workers) and the clinician among scientists (other behavioral scientists). Schofield (1964), among others, has argued that the design and execution of research into the causes and treatment of major mental illnesses requires the full-time efforts not only of clinical psychologists, but of all mental health professionals. To the extent that circumstances force them into purely service roles, they are prevented from generating research studies that could lead to improved, more effective services. Schofield has pointed out the inefficiency of what he calls "therapeutic conversation" with individual patients unless such individual psychotherapy is part of a true research endeavor.

To repeat, the ideal situation would have the clinical psychologist function as a scientist–professional. Indeed, there are a number of important collaborative efforts by researchers and clinical practitioners. Dollard and Miller (1950) attempted with considerable success to integrate learning theory, which has emerged from the experimental laboratory, with psychoanalysis, a product of the consultation room. G. A. Kelly (1955), a clinician, used experimentally derived knowledge regarding the effects of an individual's perceptions of his behavior to formulate a clinical theory of personality based on seeing the world through personal constructs that are unique for each individual. More recently, the increasing popularity of behavior modification techniques (see Chapter 7) among many psychologists, clinicians as well as experimentalists, stems at least in part from the approach's clinical application of learning principles derived from the psychology laboratory.

THE ACADEMIC–RESEARCH MODEL

Scientific inquiry is the keystone of every psychologist's formal education. He is taught to assume a detached and objective attitude in his investigative research and to take nothing for granted without experimental verification. He learns to design rigorous experiments with careful controls and to analyze his results with the appropriate precise quantitative measures. The ultimate aim is to contribute to theory by producing hypotheses which themselves will continue to undergo further scientific scrutiny.

The student learns to distrust subjective attitudes based on one individual's personal experiences or generalized from too few cases. Judgments based on intuition (clinical hunches) carry little weight with the scientist. Experimental psychologists are generally impatient with the practicing clinician who is satisfied that his particular techniques of assessment or psychotherapy are effective without researching the validity of his assumptions. The clinician has the scientific obligation, experimentalists reason, to study precisely what is producing the results he is obtaining and to experiment with other techniques that may produce even better results. They argue further that the practicing clinician should make his theoretical views explicit by examining his assumptions, seeking consistency in his hypotheses, and attempting systematization and higher-order generalizations (Rotter, 1954). Only then can he create new theories, new hypotheses, and new ways of organizing his data in order to continue to improve his skills and practices.

Perhaps a sample of current clinical research might best illustrate the activities in which clinical psychologists participate. Although a far from exhaustive list, at least six areas of current clinical research into human behavior can be delineated: (1) personality; (2) psychopathology; (3) relationship of social factors and psychopathology; (4) the biochemistry and genetics of psychopathology; (5) clinical assessment of individuals; and (6) psychotherapy.

Research in personality. As Murphy (1968) notes, "everything in psychology is directly related to the study of personality." Yet most research efforts to study personality have been fraught with difficulties, particularly in their attempts to fathom the complexities of any person's individuality. Allport (1937) has suggested that the study of personality can be furthered by taking both an idiographic and nomothetic approach to the individual. The *idiographic* approach sees the individual as a legitimate object of scientific inquiry, while the nomothetic approach searches for general laws of personality growth and functions common to all human beings. Studies of personal documents (Allport, 1942) and detailed accounts of individual biographies (White, 1952; Evans, 1950) reflect an idiographic orientation that aims to understand and perhaps predict the behavior of an individual. Such conclusions, in a clinical setting, have such immediate usefulness as assessing the patient's suicidal or homicidal risk or predicting his response to psychotherapy. Diagnostic methods in clinical psychology have been influenced by the idiographic approach, especially in trying to ascertain the unique set of factors that account for the patient's present psychopathology. Basic to the *nomothetic* approach is the principle that general laws of personality development and functioning apply to all people. Principles of personality growth, such as the psychoanalytic formulations regarding psychosexual development (Freud, 1938) or Erikson's (1963) view of the personal and social crises occurring throughout the "eight ages of man," follow from the nomothetic approach. Nomothetic generalizations about personality and behavior contribute to scientific theory and understanding.

Escalona's (1968) research on the roots of individuality in infancy is an example of the idiographic approach to such studies. She studied the behavior patterns of normal infants between the ages of 4 and 32 weeks through detailed observational records, home visits, developmental test protocols, activity level ratings, filmed records, and pediatric examinations. In addition, questionnaires and interviews with the mother and other family members produced a wealth of data on the origins in infancy of individual differences. The nomothetic approach has been used in various longitudinal studies of children from birth to maturity. Gesell at the Yale Study Center (Gesell, Amatruda, Castner, & Thompson, 1939) and Bayley (1956) at Berkeley (the Berkeley Growth Study) have been pioneers in studying the typical physical, intellectual, social, and personality growth patterns over time.

The research clinician may use various cross-cultural, developmental, clinical, and experimental techniques in order to study personality scientifically. A particularly challenging problem lies in relating research results to the complex human situation with which the clinical practitioner must deal. As Kogan (1966) has suggested, the challenge is to develop concepts and variables that meet scientific criteria such as clarity of definition, communicability, objectivity, and measurability, and also are relevant to the needs, goals, and interests of clinical practice.

Research in psychopathology. Just as it is difficult to agree on what constitutes normal behavior (Mowrer, 1954), so there is no agreement in research literature on what may be considered psychopathology or mental illness. Specifically, it is still not clear whether mental illness is a unitary concept or whether a number of different disorders are simply grouped together for convenience. In addition, there remains the problem of determining at what point deviant behavior ceases being considered normal and becomes abnormal. Also unresolved is the issue of who should determine another person's mental state and what criteria he should use. Finally, a major controversy is whether mental illness stems from a chronic condition triggered by exposure to stress or whether it is essentially an acute state resulting from an abrupt break in a previously normally functioning person.

Considering these difficulties in simply agreeing on what constitutes psychopathology, it is not surprising that research in this area has been uneven in quality. Many researchers have compared the performance of psychopathological and normal groups, although frequently the criteria for inclusion in one or the other group are unsatisfactory. Scott (1958) has reviewed these criteria, as reported by various research investigators, and has concluded that most researchers assume an individual is mentally ill if he is under psychiatric treatment, particularly if he is hospitalized in a psychiatric institution. Objections to this assumption are many: (1) psychiatric diagnosis is frequently unreliable (see p. 121) with similar patients receiving different diagnoses by different psychiatrists; (2) this assumption limits the size of the mentally ill population to the number of available psychiatrists and psychiatric hospital beds; (3) many individuals outside hospitals may show signs of mental illness while many individuals in hospitals are in various stages of recovery and may in effect show fewer signs; (4) admission rates and criteria for hospitalization vary enormously from community to community, thus possibly giving the false impression that the rate of mental illness is higher or lower in one community or another; and (5) hospital record-keeping is not standardized, adding to the overall confusion.

Research in psychopathology has moved away from its previous emphasis on the individual case history to a more scientific biopsychological base (Maher, 1970). Dramatic breakthroughs in such fields as genetics, neurophysiology, and psychopharmacology, plus the refinement of actuarial and epidemiological techniques, have considerably influenced the direction of current research in psychopathology. At least six approaches to the study of psychopathology can be differentiated: (1) clinical; (2) actuarial; (3) experimental; (4) biological; (5) social-cultural; and (6) developmental (Palmer & Goldstein, 1966).

Clinical studies are likely to observe individuals or their families in depth over a sustained period of time in order to uncover their feelings, attitudes, and fantasies, which are not usually discernible by the casual or superficial observer. The *actuarial* approach is more concerned with data on large aggregates of individuals and leads to hypotheses regarding the occurrence, etiology, or prognosis for certain sets of disorders. *Experimental* studies with psychiatric patients are likely to formulate hypotheses based on clinical studies and test these through the usual experimental methods, or perhaps through some exploratory studies. The *biological* perspective concentrates on the anatomical or physiological causes or concomitants of psychopathology. On the other hand, *social-cultural* research into mental illness is likely to stress the relationship of the individual's deviant behavior to his socioeconomic status, his race, his ethnic group, or his subculture. Finally, *developmental* studies of psychopathology have focused on the child, the family grouping, or perhaps on the attitudes of parents of mentally ill adult patients.

A number of experimental studies, such as those of Shakow (1963) and his co-workers, have extended over several decades. Shakow has carefully studied and compared the laboratory performance of schizophrenic and normal subjects on a wide variety of tasks in a laboratory setting. Responses ranging from reaction times of simple reflexes to the complexities of group behavior involving cooperation and competition have been catalogued. This is a good example of using the carefully controlled conditions of the laboratory to isolate specific characteristics more difficult to measure and understand in the more complex clinical situation.

Still another approach, that of *experimental psychopathology,* has attempted to study a psychopathological phenomenon by attempting to create it under laboratory conditions. There a careful study can be made of the exact conditions under which the behavior develops in order to test ways of treating or otherwise counteracting the condition. Many early studies were carried out on animals, such as the work of Masserman (1943) with cats. Masserman produced experimental neuroses in cats by first training them to reach for food in a box, and then from time to time sending out an electric shock or unexpected air blast when they entered the box. Not knowing what to expect when entering the box, the cats developed disorganized behavior—crouching, trembling, sweating, breathing rapidly—and showed increased pulse rate and blood pressure. These symptoms are similar to human anxiety reactions. Interestingly, Masserman found the cats lost some of their anxiety symptoms when they were fed small amounts of alcohol. However, when the alcohol effects wore off the anxiety returned. Once again, the experimental analogue is meant to generalize to behavior outside the laboratory and to extrapolate from animals to humans.

Research into the relation of social factors and psychopathology. Interdisciplinary teams of behavioral scientists, including clinical research psychologists, have undertaken studies of various aspects of the relationship of social class and mental illness (Srole, Langner, Michael, Opler, & Rennie, 1961; Langner & Michael, 1963; Myers & Bean, 1968). All confirm Hollingshead and Redlich's (1958) original findings of definite social class differences in: (1) the type of mental illness developed; (2) the prevalence of mental illness; (3) the reactions to the presence of mental illness in a family member; and (4) the place, type, and length of treatment. Basing their conclusions on a sample of New Haven, Connecticut, residents involved in psychiatric treatment, Hollingshead and Redlich found that the lower the social class the higher the proportion of psychiatric patients (schizophrenia is nine times higher among the lowest group than the highest).

However, when a lower-class person becomes psychotic, he is committed to a usually overcrowded, understaffed hospital. If he is fortunate enough to be admitted to a low-cost psychiatric clinic, he is likely to be seen by the least experienced staff psychiatrist. If, further, he is seen for psychotherapy, his psychiatrist is likely to misunderstand his cultural values and to find him unpleasant to work with as a patient. In contrast, the higher the social position, the more likely the patient and his family are to recognize the disturbance and know where to go for treatment. They are most likely to see a psychiatrist in private practice or in a private psychiatric hospital. Whereas the more privileged persons are likely to undergo psychoanalysis, the poorer patient is more apt to be treated by directive means or organic therapy (that is, drugs or electroconvulsive shock treatment). Figure 1 shows the relative proportions of psychotic and neurotic patients as a function of social class. Classes I–II are the people with the highest social position (business and professional leaders) while Class V includes people with the lowest social position (semiskilled and unskilled laborers). While people in the upper social classes are more commonly diagnosed as neurotic, the overwhelming proportion of lower-class psychiatric patients are diagnosed as psychotic.

Myers and Bean (1968), in a follow-up research study of Hollingshead and Redlich's original sample of over 1500 patients, confirm that, a decade later, social class remains a decisive factor in the outcome of psychiatric treatment as well as adjustment to the community. The higher the social class, the less likely the patients are to be hospitalized 10 years after the original study. If readmitted, the chances of hospital discharge are greater for higher-status persons not only for first discharge but for any subsequent discharge following readmission. Since lower-status persons, once readmitted, are less likely to be discharged as quickly, there is a piling-up of patients in the hospital as social-class status decreases. (Typically, state hospitals tend to be populated by the poor.)

Research in biochemical and genetic factors in psychopathology. Another line of clinical research has looked at biochemical and genetic factors to determine if certain individuals may be biologically or constitutionally more vulnerable to psychopathology than others. If so, this may explain why certain individuals develop behavior disorders while others exposed to the same environment do not.

One particularly challenging approach has been the effort to discover

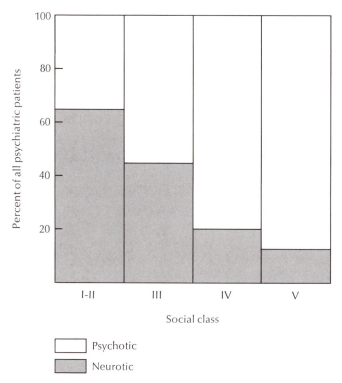

Figure 1. The relative proportion of psychotic and neurotic patients in each social class. (After Hollingshead & Redlich, 1958.)

a biochemical etiology to mental disorders, particularly schizophrenia. Kety (1959) has noted that numerous sources of error are inherent in such undertakings, making their conclusions open to question. For example, there is little evidence that all forms of schizophrenia have a common etiology. Therefore, a researcher must include in his experimental design some recognition that he might be dealing with a number of different mental disorders which nevertheless share common symptoms. In addition, since most of the biochemical research is likely to be carried out on chronic patients hospitalized over long periods in crowded and possibly unhygienic institutions, there is the possibility of chronic infection and nutritional deficiencies obscuring the results. Furthermore, such hospitalized patients are likely to have received some previous treatment, possibly producing biochemical changes that may then be mistakenly attributed to the presence of the schizophrenic disorder.

In all such studies, since behavioral and biochemical events are so closely integrated in any individual, it is difficult to ascertain whether any of the unique biochemical factors in schizophrenics are the cause or the effect of the condition. Thus, while some evidence suggests that psychotics do differ from normal individuals along certain biochemical dimensions (Russell, 1965), proof that biochemical factors are involved in the etiology of these disorders remains unsubstantiated. Even if biochemical differences are characteristic of individuals with mental disorders, there is little proof that they represent either the cause or the effect of the disorder; in fact, both may be the consequence of some other condition or set of conditions.

The problem of control over the multitude of potentially relevant variables is enormous. Many escape control, while others may simply defy control. The typical research design matches schizophrenics with a normal control group for as many factors as possible except the one under study: the presence of schizophrenia. However, such a *cross-sectional* approach, while tempting because of its simplicity, is limited in usefulness because of the difficulty in controlling the previously mentioned possible sources of error. According to Reiss (1958), there are enormous daily variations in the biochemistry of some schizophrenics, so any single statistic, even if based on extensive research, is useless. Relatively few studies have a *longitudinal* research design, collecting sequential data on individuals. Such a promising approach would permit each individual to serve as his own control; it would correlate biochemical changes in him with changes in his clinical state over a period of time. It would solve some of the research design problems of patient heterogeneity, groups unmatched on all relevant factors, or previous history of treatment for some individuals and not others, obscuring the overall results (Durell & Schildkraut, 1966).

Despite inconclusive results to date, strong interest and vigorous investigation continue in this area of research. New knowledge and the development of new biochemical techniques have encouraged many to expect a breakthrough once the tremendous problems of methodological research design are overcome. The collaborative efforts of various scientific disciplines is encouraging. This same kind of collaboration is going on in the field of behavior genetics, which is concerned with the hereditary correlates of behavior. Particularly relevant is the effort by geneticists, biochemists, experimental and clinical psychologists, together, to study the possible hereditary basis of psychopathology, particularly schizophrenia. There are sufficient data available to indicate that the rate of schizophrenia is higher in families in which at least one other member has been diagnosed as a schizophrenic. Schizophrenic women are very likely to have schizophrenic children (Mednick & Schulsinger, 1965). While children of a schizophrenic parent have incidence rates of schizophrenia from five to ten percent, the incidence of schizophrenia in the general population is less than 1 percent.

The interpretation of the conclusions from these studies in behavior genetics remains controversial. As in other areas where the nature–nurture question exists (for example, the role of heredity and environment in intelligence), many psychologists have accounted for these results by insisting that they prove only that members of a family share the same environment. To deal with this issue, studies have been carried out on parents and children who were separated early in the child's life, by comparing the incidence of schizophrenia in the children and their families. In this regard, many researchers have conducted their investigations in Denmark, a relatively small country with excellent record-keeping procedures. Kety, Rosenthal, Wender, and Schulsinger (1968) studied the records of over 5000 Danish children given up for nonfamilial adoption at an early age between 1924 and 1947. Those adoptees who had subsequently been hospitalized in a psychiatric institution were matched, case by case, to a control group of adoptees who had no psychiatric history. All adoptive and biological families were also identified, and data regarding any history of their psychiatric hospitalization were included. Results indicated a significantly greater number of related schizophrenic disorders among the biological relatives of schizophrenic adoptees than of the normal adoptees. Among the adoptive relatives, there was no appreciable difference between the two groups; environmentalist theories would have predicted a higher incidence of schizophrenia among the adoptive parents of the schizophrenic adoptees. Results supported the genetic theory, which suggests a hereditary transmission of schizophrenia.

An interesting new methodological design involves a longitudinal high-risk technique aimed at predicting (and perhaps being useful in preventing) the development of schizophrenia. Mednick and McNeil (1968) have pointed out certain difficulties inherent in the usual methods of studying schizophrenia. The method of observing hospitalized schizophrenics and inferring the causes of their behavior is questionable, since it is often impossible to separate which behavior is caused by the disorder and which reflects the effects of institutionalization. The method of observing schizophrenics with their families also has serious drawbacks, since it is difficult to determine if the strain in their interpersonal relationships helps produce the schizophrenic condition or is the result of living with a schizophrenic individual. Finally, the method of examining childhood histories and birth and school records may be useful but often yields unreliable, incomplete data. Instead, Mednick and McNeil suggest studying children who are likely to become schizophrenic (that is, children who have chronically and severely schizophrenic mothers), gathering data on them before any develop schizophrenia. Again using the data available in Denmark, Mednick and his colleagues began in 1962 to identify and examine extensively over 200 high-risk children and over 100 matched low-risk children of normal mothers. Their plan is to follow these individuals over 15 to 20 years. When some appreciable number of them becomes schizophrenic or otherwise deviant, they plan to reexamine their original 1962 data to: (1) determine if early premorbid characteristics distinguished those who developed disorders from those who did not; (2) investigate the interaction of such characteristics with life circumstances; and (3) plot these factors as they change from the time of the first examination to the time of the schizophrenic breakdown. In addition to comparing outcomes for high-risk and low-risk children, comparisons can also be made in the high-risk group between those who eventually become schizophrenic and those who either do not or who become otherwise deviant. In this way, Mednick and his colleagues hope to begin to determine possible causes of schizophrenia against which treatment and prevention programs can begin. Early results appear to show serious pregnancy or birth complication damage in the history of those who have already become mentally ill, suggesting that such difficulties may trigger or exacerbate some genetic vulnerability in such individuals (Mednick, 1971).

Research in clinical assessment. Clinical psychologists' use of assessment techniques, particularly psychological tests, reached its peak in the decade following World War II. With emphasis on providing clinical diagnostic services, however, little effort was devoted to research regarding the accuracy or usefulness of the various test instruments. New tests proliferated and at times appeared to be used with little regard to their reliability, validity, standardization, or applicability to those specific individuals being assessed. Theoretical assumptions underlying some tests were taken at face value, frequently unchallenged. The accuracy of the test instruments themselves was overvalued by some clinicians, giving their test reports an undeserved impression of ultimate truth in describing a person's psychodynamics. Frequently these reports were so filled with psychological jargon, grandiose conclusions, or vaguely described attributes found in all people that their usefulness was limited. Differences in the skills, experiences, and levels of sophistication of the clinicians using the tests frequently were overlooked in accepting their conclusions.

Considerable clinical research in the last 15 years has been directed at: (1) developing objective test scoring systems and computerizing processing of personality test data; (2) establishing tables of test norms (for adolescents, adults, the elderly) based on the collection of large samples of test responses; (3) empirically validating the meaning of particular test signs and patterns; and (4) developing more carefully constructed and standardized tests.

The traditional practice of relying primarily on the psychologist's personal clinical sensitivity, experience, and intuition in the interpretation of test data has been repeatedly challenged by a number of psychologists, beginning with Meehl in 1954 (see p. 130). While clinicians clearly have certain unduplicable powers, the individual clinician's efforts frequently produce results that are little better, if at all better, than can be produced by statistical methods in the hands of a clerk, or better yet, a machine such as a computer.

Automated test interpretations are becoming more common, particularly on objective personality tests[1] like the Minnesota Multiphasic Personality Inventory (see sample computer print-out on p. 189). The MMPI, by presenting 566 items to be answered "true" or "false" and to be scored on several scales, lends itself easily to a coded profile. In turn, the computer can read the profile code and print out a personality description

[1] An objective personality test is a method of assessing personality by keeping the interpretation as free from any examiner bias as possible. The administration, scoring, and test interpretation follow specific rules. Ideally, different examiners administering the same test to the same individual will produce the same results. The computer interpretation of the MMPI is discussed in greater detail on p. 185 and is introduced at this point only to suggest a current area of research in clinical assessment.

previously fed into it corresponding to that code. Since Meehl's paper, MMPI scales have multiplied at such a rate that it would be impractical for any clinician to score them all. Moreover, the research related to the original MMPI scales has grown so complex that no clinician would be able to keep it all in mind when interpreting the usual MMPI profile (Dreger, 1966). Considerable clinical research in recent years has been devoted to developing personality descriptions matched to different coded profiles, as well as to developing new clinical scales (identifying suicidal tendencies, delinquency tendencies, readiness for psychotherapy). Automated techniques have freed the clinician from the time-consuming job of test administration, scoring, analysis, and report writing. In addition, they provide an independent, unbiased source of information regarding his client. With such data, together with other information—from interviews, nonautomated tests, observations, knowledge of client history, and so on—he can make more reliable clinical decisions.

Test reliability and validity has been a continuing problem for research workers, particularly with projective techniques[2] such as the Rorschach, Thematic Apperception, Draw-A-Person, and Sentence Completion Tests, where the multitude of possible responses makes it more likely that the clinician may misinterpret the test's results. In the past 15 years, considerable research effort has gone into developing objective scoring systems for projective techniques. For example, Holtzman, Thorpe, Swartz, and Herron (1961) have developed a new set of inkblots similar to the Rorschach blots but easier to administer and score objectively. In addition, norms are available for children and adults. The test is made more reliable because two equivalent forms are available so that the patient is not given the same form twice. Finally, a group method of administration is available and computer scoring is possible.

Research in psychotherapy. Psychotherapy, a process aimed at achieving positive behavioral and personality changes in another individual, has interested clinicians for almost 100 years. Yet few organized research studies were undertaken before 1940. Long dominated by psychiatry, the

[2] A projective technique is a personality test in which the stimuli material is deliberately made relatively unstructured (as in Rorschach inkblots) and therefore open to various interpretations by the patient. The underlying assumption is that he will perceive and organize the ambiguous, potentially affect-laden stimuli by projecting his own needs, fantasies, and conflicts into his interpretation of the test materials. A fuller discussion on personality assessment through the use of projective techniques appears on p. 170.

ethics of medicine were carried over into psychotherapeutic work; privacy and privileged communication between doctor and patient were considered inviolable, and this interaction was thus off limits to the research investigator. Also, the busy psychotherapist had little time for, and usually little training or interest in, research. Some of the available data came from summary reports of overall treatment results of hospitalized patients. In these reports of group results, statistical charts listed the proportion of patients who had recovered, were much improved, improved, or not improved after treatment (Landis, 1938). Unfortunately, data presented in this form are not very meaningful since they fail to provide specific information on the exact nature of the patient population. Data on patients hospitalized for different lengths of time with different diagnoses and different forms of treatment are commonly grouped together. Consequently, it is not clear how long each patient received treatment or whether other forms of organic treatment were used in conjunction with psychotherapy. Most reports of this nature also fail to provide a baseline comparison with a control group receiving no treatment. Thus, with the data thrown together in such a way, the results are inevitably confusing and open to various interpretations.

Perhaps the main drawback to such a shotgun approach is the hidden assumption that psychotherapy itself is a unitary phenomenon, which experience indicates it is not. As Truax and Carkhuff (1964) point out, to ask the question, "Is psychotherapy indeed therapeutic?" and then go about answering such a question in the traditional way is very much like the pharmacologist asking the question, "Is chemotherapy (drug therapy) therapeutic?" and then researching it by randomly giving unknown kinds of drugs in unknown quantities to one group of patients with various complaints and no drugs to another similar group. Psychotherapy research has all too often proceeded in this naive way.

Carl Rogers' 1942 publication, *Counseling and Psychotherapy,* marked a turning point in psychotherapy research. For the first time, Rogers went beyond the usual case history summary followed by a summary account of treatment. Instead, he provided a verbatim, phonographically recorded account of one individual's entire counseling process. Thus avoiding any editing reflecting the bias or vested interest of the therapist, the unabridged data were available for research analysis. Of equal importance, this courageous, undefensive act made it clear that the consultation room was not sacred, that the client's anonymity could still be protected by giving him a fictitious name, and that the live, ongoing therapeutic process could be researched.

Rogers has continued to be instrumental in collecting and analyzing the empirical data of psychotherapy and in encouraging his colleagues and students to study the process of psychotherapy as they would any other psychological phenomenon. In the early 1950s at the University of Chicago Counseling Center, Rogers studied the effect of client-centered therapy by first forming two matched groups from the individuals applying there for psychotherapy. After some initial pretherapy testing, members of the experimental group began individual psychotherapy, while the members of the control group were asked to wait 60 days before seeing a counselor. At the end of 60 days, the members of both groups were tested to compare the results of the therapy with any changes in members of the control group of equally motivated clients who received no therapy. All clients were also tested in follow-up studies. The results supported Rogers' view that those clients receiving therapy judged their real selves in closer agreement with their idealized selves than did their matched control-group clients. Among other innovations in evaluating the outcome of psychotherapy, Rogers and his group have used periodic therapeutic ratings, client self-ratings, Q sorts[3] of items of personality description rated before and after treatment, and physiological indices of anxiety as therapy proceeded. A summary of the early research dealing with client-centered therapy has been reported by Rogers and Dymond (1954). The extensive research project on psychotherapy with schizophrenics carried out by Rogers and his colleagues (Rogers, Gendlin, Kiesler, & Truax, 1967) shows his continued commitment to research.

In the 1960s, advocates of behavior therapy (sometimes called behavior modification) began to publish research papers on their approach to psychotherapy. Essentially, this approach (see Chapter 7) involves the application of learning theory principles, such as conditioning and reinforcement, to shape or modify an individual's maladaptive behavior. With

---

[3] A Q sort is an assessment technique in which a client may evaluate himself by sorting a number of statements regarding personality, usually typed on separate cards, into piles ranging from those statements most characteristic of himself to those least characteristic. A variation of this technique is for the therapist to make similar ratings of the client at various stages of psychotherapy.

such strong links to the academic research laboratory, it is not surprising that so much of current research on treatment of individuals in and out of psychiatric hospital settings is being carried on by behavior therapists.

Research on psychotherapy can be divided into two large categories: *outcome research* and *process research*. The former focuses on the effect of therapy on personality and behavior change, the latter on what psycho-therapy is all about, by studying and measuring what actually takes place in an ongoing, moment-to-moment therapeutic relationship. Most clinicians are especially interested in evaluating the effectiveness of psychotherapy based on outcome research (see p. 213).

Both categories usually attempt to determine whether any particular therapeutic approach is successful and which approach is most effective for which type of patient or type of problem. There are several major problems:

> The major problems that must be faced by any attempt to evaluate psy-chotherapy are that we are dealing with a treatment modality that has not been defined, the effects of which are presumed to require a long period of treatment, and the evaluation of which demands long-term follow-up. Furthermore, the treatment procedures are designed to modify conditions where the spontaneous recovery rate is considerable and the means of evaluating recovery controversial. Even fairly strong treatment effects might easily be swamped by the heterogeneity of subject popu-lation and the inevitable effects of intercurrent changes in life situations [Fiske et al., 1970, p. 727].

Ideally, the research clinician should design research so two groups are matched on relevant criteria—an experimental group receiving treat-ment and a no-treatment control group. The question of whether these controls, equally motivated, will not seek professional or lay help else-where remains a thorny problem. He must evaluate the ethics of keeping people in need of help (the control group) from receiving such help at least until after the experiment. He must decide which aspects of the complexities of human behavior he is measuring, always cognizant that in the process he may lose the essence of the person or overlook less obvious but nevertheless significant changes that result from treatment. Certain variables are thus simply not controllable in psychotherapy re-search. The researcher also must determine how he will measure personality and behavior change, who will judge such change, over how long a period of time, and so on. Above all, any research on the outcome of psychotherapy must take into account that therapists vary in background, personality, life experiences, attitudes, ability, and motivation; patients vary in diagnosis, severity of problems, resistance to change, ability to communicate verbally, and their understanding of or trust in the psychotherapeutic process; techniques of treatment vary, even among therapists with the same theoretical orientations.

EVALUATION OF THE ACADEMIC–RESEARCH MODEL

ARGUMENTS FOR THE ACADEMIC–RESEARCH MODEL

1. Clinical psychologists are primarily psychologists and clinicians only secondarily. As psychologists, their interests and goals should contribute to developing the general theory of psychological science. They should use their research training to produce testable hypotheses to account for the phenomena they see in their clients or patients. Only through such a process can higher-order generalizations and conceptualizations concerning human behavior emerge.

2. The development of new clinical methods depends on research. We must not continue to rely on assessment methods that have proved to be of dubious value or on psychotherapeutic techniques that elude scientific inquiry. The public has been oversold on both. New clinical methods should be based on: (a) a solid, broad, theoretical understanding of normal personality development, factors determining the development of psychopathology or disordered behavior, and how such behavior can most usefully be assessed and treated; and (b) empirical evidence gathered through research into these factors, as predicted by the theories.

3. The clinician must be able to make a sophisticated appraisal of theories and techniques advanced by colleagues. Thinking in theoretical terms furnishes the clinician with an additional tool for making evaluations in areas where experimental evidence is missing or is perhaps extremely difficult to obtain. Beyond theoretical considerations, the clinician who can evaluate new techniques remains open to new ideas. He continues to learn and grow professionally as he attempts to understand, explain, and test his clinical data in new ways.

Wolman (1965) points out that certain theoretical questions are not answerable in the usual way—that is, "Do people have a self-system (Sullivan) or do they have an id-ego-superego system (Freud)?" Instead, a more sophisticated appraisal of new theories should resolve the question, "Which hypothetical system is more consistent, is more in agreement with the established body of empirical data, explains more facts, and thus is heuristically more fruitful and methodologically more convenient [p. 19]?"

4. **Research techniques have advanced beyond the traditional manipulation of experimental variables and need to advance still further.** Practicing clinicians can use modifications of current research methodology. Such methods as field studies, participant observation, survey techniques, and critical incident techniques can be used to study problems not feasible for laboratory investigation (Hoch, Ross, & Winder, 1966). Practitioners prematurely dismiss research efforts as wasteful and irrelevant to their work because they incorrectly equate research with formal experimental studies. Yet the practicing clinician, from his clinical observations and hunches, is in the best position to help the researcher pinpoint relevant areas for study.

5. **Clinical psychology's major link with general psychology is through research.** If this link were broken, clinical psychology would risk simply training technicians who are cut off from the nourishment of new ideas founded in general psychological theory, and general psychology would receive no feedback from outside the laboratory and would tend to become insular. Both would suffer.

All psychology has as its subject matter the study of behavior. Knowledge is advanced through a cross-fertilization of ideas and methods among the various disciplines and fields in psychology. Rather than break away, clinical psychology should strengthen its ties to general psychology through research. The result should be a synergistic one, with the overall benefits to both resulting in more than the sum of individual efforts.

6. **Of all the members of the mental health profession, clinical psychologists have the best training in research methodology.** In working with colleagues, such competence should be used in designing and evaluating existing programs in hospitals, clinics, or schools. In addition, the traditional question-posing attitude of the researcher is a useful counterbal-

ance for other professionals trained in the service orientation of medicine, social work, public health nursing, or education.

Psychologists, particularly those participating in new programs such as community mental health (see Chapter 8), have an obligation to use their research outlook and skills to plan, execute, and evaluate new programs in order to determine whether they accomplish their intended purposes in the most effective way.

ARGUMENTS AGAINST THE ACADEMIC–RESEARCH MODEL

1. The model does not represent what most clinical psychologists actually do. Surveys by Kelly (1961a) and more recently Goldschmid, Stein, Weissman, and Sorrells (1969) have questioned clinical psychologists about their professional activities (see p. 66); their results show that they are increasingly functioning in nonacademic positions and carrying out nonresearch activities such as psychotherapy and community consultation. The academic-research model seems to be out of step with the professional service orientation of the majority of clinical psychologists.

2. Most practicing clinicians have neither the time, the interest, nor the skill to carry out research. Their education and training has, at best, made them consumers rather than producers of research. At worst, they see little if any relationship between what appears in psychological journals and the issues of their daily practice. Moreover, those in private practice, especially, are under no external pressure to publish or in other ways make public their professional activities. Without such motivation, few practicing clinicians contribute articles to scientific journals, even those journals devoted to clinical psychology. The modal publication rate for graduates of clinical training programs during their first decade after graduation is zero, despite the heavy emphasis in such programs on research (Levy, 1962).

3. Graduate-school research training appears inapplicable to clinical problems. In their zeal to train clinicians as general psychologists and later as specialists, psychology departments have downgraded clinical work. Nonclinical professors (and sometimes even clinical professors) tend to dismiss psychotherapy as failing to meet scientific criteria and therefore as unworthy of scientific inquiry. Graduate-school research training often deals with the problems and methods of the laboratory only. To many practicing clinical psychologists, research means rigorous experimental methodology and sophisticated statistical analyses of problems that appear trivial and unrelated to clinical practice. These clinicians question the value of quantitative research dictated by methodology rather than content—research that produces statistically significant results that they see as irrelevant.

4. **If research is defined more broadly than the traditional laboratory experiment, today's clinical psychologists are participating in research.** Research, if defined as any exploration that contributes to knowledge or involves scholarly inquiry, is what practicing clinicians do in their daily practice. The case-study method, for example, focuses on the individual and aims at discovering and generating hypotheses about him. Such hypotheses may form the basis for theorizing about human behavior in general. As such, its contribution to science may be considerable.

5. **The style, approach to problems, and general orientation of the clinician and researcher are basically incompatible.** The clinician attempts to obtain a broad, comprehensive view of behavior, while the researcher is interested in a small, manageable segment of behavior. The clinician is concerned with action, the researcher with knowledge. The clinician involves himself in the relationship while the researcher strives to avoid bias by intervening as little as possible. The clinician wants to know everything important about a person, while the researcher is content to know less if what he knows is exact (Holt, 1965). In short, the two roles call for differences in outlook, style, and emphasis.

6. **Since clinical psychology is an art, not a science, the emphasis in training should be on developing intuition and clinical sensitivities, not learning sterile research skills.** Clinical judgment is based on the subjective experience and carefully developed intuitive skills of the practitioner. He cannot always make the basis for his judgment explicit to others, and sometimes he himself cannot explain what he senses or feels is happening in the relationship with his client. In any event, scientific laws are of little value and offer him scant guidance. He must learn through practice how to deal with the irrational, the unconscious, the symbolic.

Berenda (1957) has questioned whether clinical psychology is a science. He characterizes the scientist as traditionally committed to the methodological viewpoint that stresses the objective, impersonal, mathematical, and precise while deemphasizing the creative, imaginative, emotional aspects of man, about which clinical work concerns itself. To do so, however, Berenda argues, is to ignore the fact that science itself is a human activity and that today's established theories may be tomorrow's myths. Modern physics, for example, increasingly questions so-called natural physical laws, absolute truths, objective reality. As Oppenheimer (1956) cautions, "the worst of all possible misunderstandings would be that psychology be influenced to model itself after a physics which is not there anymore, which has been quite outdated [p. 134]."

THE CLINICAL PSYCHOLOGIST AS PRACTITIONER

Many students are initially attracted to psychology because they are fascinated by human behavior. Whether for intellectual or more personal reasons, such students look forward with great interest to the study of human motives and conflicts. If they contemplate a career as clinical psychologists, they are likely to see themselves as professionals performing clinical services for individuals, much like the students wishing to become physicians. Many students of this kind are far more interested in technique than theory. Research takes a backseat to the action, glamour, and excitement they expect to result from the practice of clinical psychology.

Such a student often is quickly disappointed and frustrated that the university's objectives do not seem to coincide with his own. The university, he discovers, is prepared to educate him through a long sequence of courses leading to the Ph.D. degree, which emphasizes competence to carry out original research. Any clinical or professional training he hopes to receive must be superimposed on an already rigorous and demanding training program as an academic–research scientist.

Moreover, the clinical student is subjected to conflicting value systems. He is sometimes taught clinical techniques in the practical courses as if their efficacy and validity were beyond question, but in the research seminar he is confronted with data that seriously undermine any faith in these techniques. Garfield (1966) has noted that most students resolve such dissonance between the research and the practitioner model by tending to identify with one of the models and repudiating the other.

After the university, other conflicts loom when the graduate student receives his internship training. Such training is likely to begin at a large psychiatric hospital or outpatient clinic. There the staff psychologist, unlike the clinical professor at the university, is apt to see himself as a professional psychologist whose primary obligation is to answer the pressing need for clinical services and only secondarily to do research. The excitement and immediate relevance of the staff psychologist's work are particularly appealing to those students whose initial attraction to psychology was based on carrying out just such clinical services. Real patients who have real symptoms are being treated by these psychologists, whose academic credentials confer the title, prestige, and privileges of a doctor engaged in the treatment of sick people.

The terminology used by such a clinical practitioner is clearly medical. His place of employment, whether a psychiatric hospital, an outpatient clinic, a day-treatment center, or a community mental health center, is dominated by the medical profession. He performs an ancillary medical service, frequently as a member of a psychiatric team.[4] He often becomes indistinguishable in function (if not in status) from the psychiatrist, a medically trained professional. Both deal with suffering, disability, mental illness, psychopathology—all terms which indicate that certain behavior can be labeled as due to a sickness requiring medical attention and treatment. Both serve in the role of healers helping a patient achieve mental health and well-being.

Just as when he faced conflicting value systems in school, the graduate student is now apt to find himself identifying either with his research-oriented professors who do little if any clinical practice or with the staff psychologists who do little if any research.

THE MEDICAL MODEL

The medical model is an orientation borrowed from medicine and used to conceptualize disordered or maladaptive behavior, its cause or etiology, and its treatment or modification. The professional clinical psychologist who adopts such a model, like the psychiatrist, defines his role as diagnosing, treating, and preventing mental illness.

This use of the medical model rests on certain assumptions:

[4] The team is by now a traditional relationship among mental health professionals, especially in psychiatric hospitals. It is led by a psychiatrist (an M.D.) and characteristically includes a psychologist and social worker. Occasionally others, such as public health nurses, are included.

1. The individual manifesting disordered or maladaptive behavior is sick—that is, he is showing signs of mental illness.

2. The symptoms of his mental illness can be observed and categorized just like any symptom of physical illness.

3. The illness is due to some underlying agents or processes existing within the patient.

4. His present disordered behavior results from different processes and experiences than does "normal" behavior in well individuals.

5. His illness has a more or less specific etiology, very likely stemming from emotional disturbances of early childhood.

6. Once the etiology is found and correctly diagnosed, treatment can begin, leading to a cure.

The American Psychiatric Association (1952, 1968) has given official credence to this medical viewpoint by adopting the *Diagnostic and Statistical Manual of Mental Disorders*. First published in 1952, a 1968 revision made the original classification system more consistent with that of the World Health Organization International Classification of Diseases (Spitzer & Wilson, 1969).

Mental disorders, like physical disorders, are considered health problems and are treated similarly. The physician attempts to understand the disorder in his patient (a sick person). Presented with his patient's aberrant behavior (symptoms), the physician is likely to take a more or less elaborate case history in order to pinpoint more exactly the specific cause or etiology of the problem. Since different diseases may nevertheless manifest many identical symptoms (fever, headaches), the physician is careful to look beyond the symptoms and to learn as much as he can about the fundamental disease process itself. Whether he looks for bodily lesions or suspects viral or bacterial invasion or other abnormal conditions, he is always interested in more than the overt symptoms themselves. He attempts to isolate and label the symptoms to understand better whatever underlying cause produced the illness. Thus, rather than treating the symptoms directly, he concentrates first on correctly diagnosing the condition. Once the etiological agent is determined, specific treatment can be directed toward its elimination. Once eliminated, the overt symptoms should disappear.[5]

[5] Maher (1970) has pointed out that medical practitioners actually use several disease models in thinking about bodily disorders. The model described above is one of them, which Maher would classify as the medical "infectious-disease" model.

The physician need not explain to the patient the exact nature of the illness. If special laboratory work (perhaps X rays or blood analysis) is done, the physician uses these results to aid in his diagnosis; he need not disclose the laboratory findings to his patient. If the physician decides to use medication in his treatment, he need not explain or justify his decision to his patient. In fact, he writes the order in a foreign, technical language —sometimes illegibly at that—which generally is beyond the patient's comprehension. The patient simply acts as a courier, bringing the prescription to the pharmacist without questioning the doctor's orders. Throughout the process, the physician is the authority; he is assumed to know more about the patient's malady than the patient himself. The doctor is not likely to discuss himself with the patient.

Psychiatrists and psychologists with such a medical orientation are likely to be concerned with the patient's problems or overt maladaptive behavior only as they relate to his real problem—the underlying conflicts which have produced his present symptoms. Putting aside for the moment the problem which brought the patient into treatment, considerable effort is likely to go toward uncovering those early traumas or unresolved past conflicts whose manifestation constitutes the present symptoms. Psychoanalysis, in particular, typifies such a search for early childhood fixations.

The medically oriented clinician, particularly if he has a psychoanalytic viewpoint, is likely to look to the past to understand the present. While relying primarily on his own observations and verbal communication with the patient, he may order psychological tests as an aid to diagnosis, just as the physician might order laboratory work from ancillary workers. Once he has made a diagnosis, the therapist is not likely to reveal such information to his patient. Instead, he brings to bear his theoretical understanding of the dynamics of such a condition, his technique of treatment, and his knowledge of the individual to help uncover, interpret, and work through the patient's real problems. He, too, is likely to have more insight into his patient's personality dynamics than does the patient, at least initially. Table 1 compares the medical model and the academic–research model.

The clinician with a medical service orientation is thus engaged in two traditional functions: diagnosis and treatment.

Diagnosis. The clinician's steps in arriving at a diagnosis can be speci-

Table 1. Comparison of academic-research and medical models in clinical psychology

MODEL	ROLE	COUNTER-ROLE	PATTERNED AFTER	METHOD-OLOGY	PURPOSES
Academic-research	Scientist	Subject	Physics; experimental psychology	Search for scientific laws	Further scientific inquiry; build theory
Medical	Healer	Patient	Medicine	Search for underlying causes	Service; health; cure underlying disease; reduce symptoms

fied as follows regardless of his specialty, whether medical or nonmedical (Gough, 1971).

1. Listening to the patient's statement of his problem or complaint.

2. Gathering data relevant to the complaint through: (a) observation; (b) compiling a case history; (c) learning the patient's family background; and (d) carefully describing the symptoms and their history, location, periodicity, and so on.

3. Perhaps testing to verify the symptoms and determine more exactly what other symptoms are involved.

4. Forming certain hypotheses to explain the complaint.

5. Checking the implications of his hypotheses against the observations and, if necessary, gathering new observations.

6. Making a diagnosis. In most cases, the diagnosis tells enough about the disorder so it is possible to make a prognosis, or forecast, regarding the probable outcome of the disorder.

7. Designing and carrying out a treatment strategy.

The goal of diagnosis is to permit selection of the treatment most beneficial to the patient. For many years the clinical psychologist's main role was to help the psychiatrist arrive at a diagnosis; in a few hospitals or agencies today, this remains his only function. He has thus served the psychiatrist in an ancillary role acknowledged by both. The psychologist felt familiar and comfortable with his psychological test batteries, and the physician was familiar with utilizing paramedical professionals (laboratory technicians, for example) to supply him with data on which to base his diagnosis.

As clinical psychologists advanced in developing psychodiagnostic techniques, and as the climate in psychiatric hospitals became more receptive to their services, their role in the diagnostic effort became greater. Shortly after World War II when the demand for new clinical psychologists in hospitals was at its peak, Thorne (1948) distinguished at least 10 objectives of psychodiagnosis to which the clinical psychologist could make a significant contribution:

1. Demonstrating the etiological factors.
2. Differentiating between organic and functional disorders.
3. Discovering the personality reaction of the organism to the disorder.
4. Evaluating the degree of organic and functional disability.
5. Estimating the extent and intensity of the morbid process in relation to actuarial data concerning type and severity.
6. Determining a prognosis or probable course.
7. Providing a rational basis for specific psychotherapy.
8. Providing a rational basis for discussing the case with patients and relatives.
9. Providing a scientific basis for classification and statistical analysis of data.
10. Formulating a dynamic hypothesis concerning the nature of the pathological process and the mechanisms whereby therapeutic effects are explained.

Treatment. The service-oriented clinical psychologist is again likely to follow the medical model in treating his patient. Greenblatt and Levinson (1967), psychiatrist and psychologist, respectively, suggest four goals for the therapist, in descending order of importance: "(1) as far as possible, do no harm (that is, weigh the hazards of intervention against the perils of restraint); (2) relieve suffering; (3) assist the natural healing processes toward recovery; and (4) prolong life [p. 23]." This view is clearly medical and, according to the authors, is consistent with current efforts to bring psychotherapy into the orbit of scientific medicine.

Psychotherapy literally means treatment of the mind. Psychoanalysis in particular has influenced many psychiatrists and clinical psychologists to think of the process as a healing one, a term that is at the core of medical practice. Psychotherapy will be discussed in detail in Chapters 6, 7, 9, and 10.

EVALUATION OF THE MEDICAL MODEL

ARGUMENTS FOR THE MEDICAL MODEL

1. The medical model's service orientation has immediate social usefulness. The need for clinical services is great and immediate. As these services are extended into the community or into new federal and local programs, the demand for such services will increase even further. Rather than remain shielded from the problems of the real world, the professional clinical psychologist has an obligation to practice his specialty and offer his services to the public. Medicare is an example of recent legislation that suddenly makes available a large new group of consumers of mental health services. All medical and ancillary workers should respond to such new demands.

2. The medical model places the clinical psychologist with a service orientation in an actual clinical situation where he can study deviant behavior at first hand. This, in turn, contributes to psychology's understanding of normal behavior. Rather than speculate from afar about behavior disorders or carry out laboratory research that fails to deal fully with the behavioral complexities involved, this clinician works in the crucible of psychopathology. Most theories concerning personality development and deviation have come from clinicians working with patients: Freud (1938), Adler (1925), Jung (1928), Horney (1950), Fromm (1947), Sullivan (1953), May (with Angel & Ellenberger, 1958), Wolpe (1958), Erikson (1963), and others. In contrast, no nonclinical theories provide such a comprehensive view of behavior and development, nor do they have such widespread applicability.

3. The medical model provides a frame of reference by which severe psychopathology is more easily recognized and understood. Psychological disturbances, no less than physical disturbances, constitute a form of illness. Psychologists should acknowledge that they must help sick people instead of retreating to feeble nonjudgmental attitudes concerning the normality or abnormality of their patients' behavior.

Ausubel (1961) points out that the term *disease* generally includes "any marked deviation, physical, mental, or behavioral, from normally desirable standards of structural and functional integrity [p. 71]." Certainly patients with extreme or severely incapacitating symptoms such as delusions or hallucinations, whether physical or psychogenic in origin, qualify as being ill by this definition.

Whether because of the magnitude of stress involved or because of susceptibility to ordinary degrees of stress, some individuals respond with sufficiently maladaptive and deviant behavior that their reactions are considered abnormal. This holds true for both physical and mental illness. Psychologists need to be alert to underlying psychological pathology as much as physicians must be alert to underlying physical pathology. Both must recognize disease when they see it in order to determine its causes and begin treatment.

4. The medical model provides the basis for a common set of experiences with related disciplines. These common experiences allow for a cross-fertilization of ideas and sharing of observations and clinical experiences. As a result, theoretical and practical advances in the diagnosis and treatment of psychopathology can come about. The place of clinical psychologists is secure, both in traditional medical institutions and newer agencies such as community mental health centers that have a public health orientation. Not only has clinical psychology been influenced by medicine; clinical psychology has also influenced medicine in these settings. The heightened interest among psychologists in behavior modification, a therapeutic program based on learning-theory principles from general psychology, has changed orthodox ways of dealing with hard-to-reach autistic or schizophrenic children (Lovaas, Schaeffer, & Simmons, 1965). Similar techniques—so-called token-economy programs (Ayllon & Azrin, 1968)—have been used in psychiatric hospitals and institutions for the mentally retarded. In such programs,[6] patients earn token rewards (such as chips or stamps) for desirable behavior, resulting in much improved overall functioning in a great many cases of previously hard-to-reach patients.

Certain interdisciplinary centers have been established—the Menninger Foundation in Topeka, Kansas, the Austen Riggs Center in Stockbridge, Massachusetts—where members of related mental health disciplines are encouraged to carry out clinical services and research while discussing theoretical as well as professional concerns. Departments of

---

[6] These techniques will be discussed in greater detail in Chapter 7, but are mentioned here only to illustrate the influence of clinical psychology upon standard medical and/or hospital practice.

psychiatry in traditional medical schools have been influenced to change in the direction of broader study of behavioral sciences.

Recent federally funded Community Mental Health Centers, despite their essentially medical orientation, specify that program directors be chosen on the basis of competence and skill rather than their professional discipline. According to Yolles (1966), former director of the National Institute of Mental Health, clinical psychologists in particular represent the bridge between the medical, behavioral, and social sciences.

5. The private practice of clinical psychology, a relatively new phenomenon, is based on the ethical and professional model established by the independent medical practitioner. The private practitioner functions as an autonomous professional dealing with patients. His relationship to them is confidential, and he enjoys privileged communications. He assumes responsibilities for his work with patients, for which he charges a fee. He has pressed for reimbursements from insurance companies to help his patients receive the same coverage as for medical help. The Internal Revenue Service recognizes his fees as a medical deduction for taxpayers. He is usually licensed by his state and often certified by the American Board of Professional Psychology, again like his medical counterpart. He adheres to the Code of Ethics established by the American Psychological Association.

The clinical psychologist in private practice functions almost like a psychiatrist, except he cannot prescribe medication. His relationships with patients, his professional problems, his reading material, the professional meetings he attends, and his personal friends and professional colleagues are apt to be more similar to those of the psychiatrist than to those of the nonclinical, nonprivate-practice psychologist.

ARGUMENTS AGAINST THE MEDICAL MODEL

1. The traditional medical emphasis on disease is negative and serves to obscure the search for positive strengths in people. Sharma (1968) views the medical model as "fallout from the scientific era." He suggests that with the advent of the scientific and industrial revolution during the eighteenth century, there was a corresponding expectation that increased scientific knowledge in medicine would be more effective in controlling deviant behavior than the previous reliance on theology. While certainly more progressive and humane than previous demonic explanations, this sickness explanation resulted in deviant behavior coming under medical influence, management, and ultimate control. Sharma points out, however, that this consequence was the result of a social development rather than based on any real scientific discovery or breakthrough in medicine.

George Albee, a recent president of the American Psychological Association, has been particularly critical of what he calls the "search for and excision of weakness" orientation of medicine being applied to emotionally disturbed people (1969). He finds several reasons why the model has persisted, however. First, it remains more convincing than explanations based on sin or demons. Also, some early success in linking mental illness to physical causes (for example, finding that the syphilitic infection of the brain causes paresis, an organic psychosis or severe mental disorder) has convinced certain scientists that other such links exist but simply have not been isolated yet. Albee (1968) also points out that the illness explanation justifies hospitalizing disturbed people, thus effectively ostracizing them from society. Here he is joined by Szasz (1963), a critic of present involuntary hospitalization practices. Szasz decries the fact. that society has found no more decent solution to an all-too-human problem of living than involuntary confinement in a mental hospital.

Psychoanalytic treatment, too, has perpetuated the traditional medical view of a relationship between a detached, objective, healthy analyst and his troubled patient. Philosophically, psychoanalytic theory tends to see man as weak, conflict-laden, and governed by rudimentary instincts over which he has little control and which place him in a continual struggle with society. Carkhuff and Berenson (1967) credit traditional psychoanalytic theory with offering the most comprehensive insights into "the psychodynamics of the sick man." At the same time, these authors note that psychoanalytic theory and practice, with its chilling view of people as victims of destructive motives fending off tragedy and pain, leaves little room for the possibility of high levels of pleasure, joy, or creativity.

2. The model is predicated on accepting the concept of mental illness, which itself is outdated, scientifically worthless, and socially harmful.

Mowrer (1960), a psychologist, and Szasz (1960, 1961), a psychiatrist, were among the first to question the legitimacy of applying the illness label to emotional and behavioral problems. Mowrer's position is that many psychologists who were attracted to psychoanalytic treatment early in this century were too eager to accept psychoanalytic theory prematurely and embrace it as a science before it had been adequately tested. One consequence of such acceptance, according to Mowrer, was accepting the premise that "the neurotically disturbed person is basically sick"—a position he believes we must now repudiate. Mowrer urges that psychology "get out [from] under the penumbra of medicine" and regard behavior disorders as manifestations of a moral crisis rather than illness.

Szasz (1960, 1961) believes the concept of mental illness has outlived whatever usefulness it might have had at one time and now functions merely as a convenient myth. Szasz's widely circulated article (1960) and book, *The Myth of Mental Illness* (1961), have been instrumental in crystallizing dissatisfactions and providing a slogan for many psychologists (and some psychiatrists) who are disenchanted with the medical view.

In Szasz's view, mental illness is a myth because: (1) it implies the problem stems from the existence of a physical or organic disorder while in reality it is the result of an individual's distorted belief system (for example, a belief that people are plotting against him); and (2) the diagnosis is based on a subjective judgment of another's conduct, using as the basis for comparison the belief system of the observer and the society in which they live. Such evaluative psychiatric statements as "excessive repression" or "acting out" are thus used to judge the mental health or illness of others, using the judge's standards for what exceeds the normal range of behavior.

Szasz believes the myth persists because it serves to "disguise and thus make more palatable the bitter pill of moral conflicts in human relations [Szasz, 1960, p. 118]." He is careful to acknowledge diseases of the brain (neurological defect or trauma) as legitimate illness, while challenging the concept of mental illness that implies diseases of the mind. He believes the phenomena we call mental illness are not the result of a struggle for biological survival but rather expressions of man's struggle with the problems of how he should live. Behavioral symptoms and other manifestations reflect *problems in living* (Szasz's term) and are not manifestations of disease.

Szasz sees the behaviorally disordered as deviating from ethical and psychosocial norms. Yet, the remedy is sought in terms of traditional medical measures. Szasz, like Mowrer, believes man must accept responsibility and be accountable for his behavior. Not every form of suffering is illness. Szasz's point is not that neurotics with problems in living are accountable for their situation and thus should be condemned, but rather that humane treatment should not rest on such fallacious and misleading grounds as attributing their behavior to a so-called illness. The latter is not only a feeble excuse but is harmful in that it robs the individual of the recognition that he must take responsibility for his own life.

3. The current and prospective manpower shortage in the mental health field is a direct consequence of the medical model. So long as there exists an emphasis on caring for mentally sick people and making them well, all mental health legislation will be written so as to give the highest priority to beds, nursing care, medical research, diagnosis, and treatment (Albee, 1966). The nature of the model dictates the proliferation of institutional structures that society believes will deliver the necessary care. Those institutions (hospitals, clinics, day-treatment centers) in turn dictate the kind of medical and paramedical professionals needed for staff positions. Continuing to insist on psychological services available only through existing institutions is doomed to produce an inevitable shortage of manpower and a consequent curtailment of clinical services in a period when those services are being sought by more and more troubled individuals. In addition, if the medical model for treating behavioral disorders were as universally accepted as it is for treating medical problems, it would seem reasonable to tolerate a manpower shortage. But many critics feel that existing institutions are operating with outdated, incorrect assumptions and that they are creating demand based on these assumptions. Therefore, it is especially important to challenge the medical model so we can channel our resources into more productive directions.

Albee (1968) gives several recent examples of the enormously increased demand for clinical services at the same time that too few psychiatrists, clinical psychologists, and social workers are being trained to meet present clinical needs. Labor unions, for example, continue to negotiate contracts including outpatient psychiatric care for their members and their families. Albee notes that a recent United Auto Workers' contract alone has suddenly made two and one-half million people eligible for such benefits! To these figures must be added the tremendous increase in eligibility for outpatient mental health care brought about by the federal Medicare program for the elderly or state Medicaid programs for the poor, to say nothing of various other federal programs begun under the War on Poverty banner.

As if these prospects for making mental health services available were not discouraging enough, Albee goes on to note the 2000 new comprehensive mental health centers promised by the National Institute of Mental Health by 1980, all of which must be staffed by medical and ancillary personnel!

Albee believes that one way to begin dealing with the manpower issue is to construct a new conceptual model to replace the hampering medical model. Rather than psychology emulating medicine, he proposes a model based on the principles of developmental psychology and learning theory from the psychology laboratory. The new model would permit individuals with abbreviated but more pragmatic and relevant training to work in the field of behavioral disorders (rather than in the field of mental illness). He also proposes that research and clinical services be carried out in university-sponsored psychological centers rather than in traditional medically dominated centers where psychologists lack independence and where they have adopted the values, language, and manners of psychiatrists (Albee, 1967). Rather than aiming, negatively, at reducing mental illness, Albee's model stresses maximizing human effectiveness.

4. The traditional dyadic doctor–patient psychotherapeutic relationship is inefficient and unresponsive to public welfare. The classical concern with individual patients by a psychotherapist (psychiatrist, clinical psychologist, social worker) is a model of professional functioning that is being challenged more and more. As Hobbs (1963), another former president of the American Psychological Association, sees it, "a profession that is built on a 50-minute hour of a one-to-one relationship between therapist and client . . . is living on borrowed time [p. 3]." It certainly deals with only a small number of individuals during a professional lifetime. Moreover, it fails to acknowledge the needs of the larger community. By concentrating on traditional doctor–patient relationships, primarily with white middle-class populations, psychologists have reduced their effectiveness in dealing with the nonmiddle-class individuals who present the major problems of mental health in this country.

5. Clinical psychology cannot become a truly autonomous discipline until it disengages from the medical model. So long as clinical psychologists continue to function in another profession's arena (hospitals, clinics), so long as they adhere to a "me too" philosophy regarding mental health and mental illness, so long as they continue to emulate psychiatrists and neglect the theories and approaches of general psychological science, they can never be independent or maximize their own unique role and function. Worse still, they "feed and perpetuate" unjust social and legal practices, while ignoring solutions to the interpersonal, ethical, and educational problems of their clients (Balance, Hirschfield, & Bringmann, 1970). Albee (1966) sees no alternative but to disengage from the institutions and practices that buttress and support this unacceptable medical model.

CHAPTER 2 *Roots of Contemporary Clinical Psychology*

Clinical psychology formally began as a separate profession approximately 75 years ago when Lightner Witmer founded the first psychological clinic at the University of Pennsylvania in 1896. It was Witmer (1907) who coined the term *clinical psychology*, referring to an applied branch of psychology that he proposed be established to study, individually, children whose physical defects or retardation might interfere with their school progress. Witmer also proposed opening a psychological clinic along with a training school in order to diagnose and treat the special problems of these children and at the same time provide practical training for educators, physicians, social workers, and psychologists.

Witmer's dual approach was that of clinician and scientist. His clinical method consisted of studying the individual school child (frequently the retarded child), particularly his physical and mental abilities and deficits, and then prescribing a remedial or therapeutic program. Accurate diagnosis played an important part in Witmer's approach. He was careful to include all the medical and educational data available on the child to ascertain whether the learning difficulty was due to physical causes or inadequate educational techniques. Once determined to his satisfaction, Witmer began a retraining program individually fitted to the child's unique form of learning defect.

Despite an initial lack of response from his psychological colleagues, Witmer's impact on the future direction of clinical psychology has been sizeable.[1] It was he who: (1) pointed the way to the psychological study

[1] Ironically, Witmer's efforts have been minimized or overlooked by many contemporary clinical psychologists, despite his pioneering work in establishing the profession. Shakow

of children; (2) emphasized the diagnosis of educationally retarded children who were suspected of intellectual subnormality; (3) established a multidisciplinary psychological clinic that became the model for similar clinics in other universities; (4) helped lay the groundwork for such new professions as school psychology, the remedial teaching specialty, and speech pathology; and (5) established field work experiences to supplement the usual academic training.

Before proceeding further, let us briefly explore the four main historical roots of the profession: (1) experimental research; (2) measurement of individual differences; (3) the development of the related profession of psychiatry; and (4) the influence of the humanitarian movement. In each area, the contributions of several key historical figures to various branches of contemporary clinical psychology will be described. Following this discussion, we will resume our brief historical survey of the development of clinical psychology until the present.

THE LEGACY OF EXPERIMENTAL RESEARCH

The academic and laboratory beginnings of psychology are themselves not much older than the professional beginnings of clinical psychology. Less than 100 years ago in 1879, Wilhelm Wundt (1832–1920) founded the first psychological laboratory at Leipzig, helping psychology gain recognition as an independent science. Wundt emphasized the experimental method and insisted that psychology, a "new domain of science," avoid metaphysical assumptions of any kind. Instead, Wundt believed psychology to be the science of consciousness, with its subject matter to be immediate experience as it is directly and subjectively experienced by an observer. Observations and experimentation, still among the major sources of data in psychology, stem from Wundt's early work. Wundt,

(1948) suggests that Witmer may have been out of step with the developing professional *Zeitgeist.* While Witmer's clinic's concern with educational problems led to contact with schools or institutions for the feebleminded, later clinics' concern with personality problems and social pathology (William Healy's Behavior Clinic in Chicago, for example) led to contact with psychiatric groups and social agencies. In Shakow's view, Witmer incorrectly estimated the future direction of clinical psychology. It is an interesting commentary on the cyclical nature of history that Milgram (1970) recently lamented clinical psychology's move in the direction of mental health and adult psychiatry. He urged clinicians to return to their psycho-educational beginnings, offering their services to the entire educational enterprise—teachers, students, administrators, and parents.

rigidly systematic, can be considered the first modern psychologist— founder of the first psychology laboratory, editor of the first psychology journal, synthesizer of research findings, classifier of seemingly diverse data, quantifier, pursuer of laws pertaining to the human mind. Wundt's definitions of psychology's content and methods continue to influence modern psychologists; even today, clinical psychologists, like all other psychologists, are taught to emulate the experimenter with the detached, objective attitude who carries out carefully controlled, rigorous experiments searching for verifiable laws of human behavior.

Ivan Pavlov (1849–1936), the Russian physiologist, has also enormously influenced clinical psychology. Unlike Wundt, who was concerned with the data of consciousness, Pavlov studied the connection between behavior and environmental stimuli. He began investigating conditioned reflexes in dogs in 1899, demonstrating how learning by conditioning could take place if a bell or tuning fork rang when food was presented. By repeating this procedure, the dog ultimately learned to respond (by salivating) to the tuning fork alone (see Figure 2). Pavlov's great contribution was to demonstrate with a simple, objective, experimental technique that complex behavior could be analyzed and controlled in the laboratory. Moreover, the method was entirely objective, since Pavlov was interested in the animal's behavior, not what could be inferred to have transpired in the animal's mind. Pavlov was also interested in abnormal behavior; in the last decade of his life, he designed a series of experiments in which he produced an experimental neurosis in an animal. His work, along with American psychologist Edward Thorndike's studies, inspired many later psychologists to pursue the objective description and analysis of behavior. Curiously, the impact of Pavlov's studies has been felt more in behavioristic psychology than in physiology. The recent revival of interest in developing behavior modification programs for changing or eliminating undesirable or maladaptive behavior stems from Pavlov's and Thorndike's early work.

THE MEASUREMENT OF INDIVIDUAL DIFFERENCES

Charles Darwin (1809–1882), naturalist and biologist, created a scientific revolution with his theory of evolution by natural selection. Among Darwin's major contributions especially relevant to future scientists was the careful, painstaking way he collected and organized the large-scale,

Figure 2. Pavlov's experimental apparatus for demonstrating classical conditioning of the salivary response in dogs. Each drop of saliva, passing through an opening in the dog's cheek, activates a stylus that records the secretion on a revolving drum outside the dog's chamber.

detailed record of evidence to support his hypotheses. Darwin's work particularly influenced the emerging field of psychology, which was striving to become an exact, quantitative science. Darwin helped shape psychology in the direction of biology generally; more specifically, he influenced psychologists to understand mental processes in terms of their function in an organism's adaptation to the world.

Signs of Darwin's effect on the new science of psychology were plentiful. His theory of evolution provided the groundwork for interest in animal psychology. Equally stimulating has been the impact of a comparative viewpoint in psychology stemming from Darwin's work on the continuity in reasoning between humans and higher animals as well as the similarity in bodily and facial expressions of emotion. Darwin began studies in child psychology—for example, infant development and language development —as well as studies of group behavior. Beck and Molish (1959) even suggest that Darwin's work be credited as representing the beginning of scientific clinical psychology.

Darwin's theory of evolution emphasized variation among individuals. Offspring differ from their parents, receiving a random combination of genes from each parent. Those who inherit variations that are advantageous to adaptation are more likely to survive and to increase the likelihood that their offspring, too, will possess the variation and survive, thus increasing the number of individuals with that variation. This theory stimulated Darwin's cousin, Sir Francis Galton (1822–1911), to study individual variations in men, particularly differences in hereditary makeup. Galton, a gentleman scientist trained in medicine but with a broad interest in all the sciences, set out to prove that eminence runs in families with a frequency that could not be explained on an environmental basis. He first collected data on the family trees of eminent scientists, jurists, authors, and others in order to show that genius was inherited. Noting an enormous variation in physical and mental characteristics among individuals, which he attributed to heredity, Galton found it necessary to develop a set of psychological measurements to study, quantitatively, the individual differences he was obtaining. While his conclusions have been subject to considerable criticism, Galton's inventiveness contributed a great deal to modern clinical psychology. Among those contributions were: (1) the focus on the individual; (2) the development of quantitative mental measurements; (3) the statistical analysis of psychological data; (4) the invention of mental tests such as the word-association test, the first experimental attempt to study and measure an individual's associated thoughts; (5) the development of the questionnaire method; and (6) the use of the free-association method to demonstrate the significance of childhood memories on adult life.

THE IMPACT OF PSYCHIATRY

Aberrant, disordered behavior has characterized certain individuals since the beginning of recorded history. Until the sixteenth century, insanity continued to be explained as the work of demons and witches, and behaviorally disordered individuals were kept in monasteries and prisons. Slowly, a more enlightened attitude emerged, and hospitals (or asylums, as they were then called) were established. However, these early asylums were little more than penal institutions into which the insane were herded and treated in a most inhumane manner. Toward the end of the eighteenth century, Phillippe Pinel (1745–1826), the French physician and reformer who has been called the father of scientific psychiatry, and Benjamin Rush (1745–1813), the first American psychiatrist, began to make an impact on the medical and psychiatric thinking of their time. Both were aided by the growing social movements for humanitarian reform.

Shortly after the French Revolution, Pinel was placed in charge of a large Parisian asylum. Liberal and humanitarian in outlook, Pinel soon proposed that the chains be removed from asylum inmates. Grudgingly given permission by the Revolutionary Commune, Pinel instituted a number of reforms while improving living conditions in the asylum. At the same time, Pinel tried to make psychiatry more scientific by keeping more accurate hospital records, taking case histories on inmates, and attempting some classification system of mental illness (Reisman, 1966). Although Pinel attempted some forms of physical treatment, psychiatry's role remained primarily that of custodian rather than healer.

Modern psychiatry began in the United States shortly after the American Revolutionary War when Benjamin Rush, a physician in that war, joined the staff of Pennsylvania Hospital in Philadelphia in 1783. Like Pinel, Rush took a humane view of the mentally ill. Through speeches and newspaper articles, he managed to get public support to establish a separate ward for mental patients in 1796. His efforts at scientific systematization of psychiatry resulted in his 1812 treatise, *Medical Inquiries and Diseases of the Mind,* the first and only American textbook on mental illness for the next 70 years (Lewis, 1959). However, it was not until well into the nineteenth century that public mental hospitals began to be established in any number in the United States. In 1844, a group of superintendents of hospitals for the mentally ill met to form an organization that today is known as the American Psychiatric Association. That same year, the *American Journal of Insanity* (now the *American Journal of Psychiatry*) became the first English-language journal devoted to the study of mental illness.

Despite the growing awareness of the problems of mental illness, little effort was made to discover the underlying causes of such disorders. Instead, description and classification, both important in establishing a scientific basis for ordering incoming data, took precedence. Emil Kraepelin (1855–1926), a German psychiatrist, spent years gathering thousands of case histories from which he developed his classification of mental illnesses by symptomatology as well as the course of the illness. Kraepelin, a thorough organicist, classified mental illnesses as though they were similar to physical diseases (Alexander & Selesnick, 1966). Neuroses and psychoses were classified as *functional* mental diseases (having a psychological origin) and *organic* mental diseases (due to physical pathology), such as paresis due to syphilis. Kraepelin believed each disease had a predestined outcome and had little if anything to do with individual personality or life experiences. Certain mental diseases like dementia praecox (now known as schizophrenia) were believed by Kraepelin to be incurable. Kraepelin's classification scheme exerted an enormous influence on later psychiatric classification systems (see Chapter 4) and on attitudes of psychiatrists and clinical psychologists for many years to come regarding treatment of individuals classified as schizophrenic.[2]

The treatment of neurosis was another matter. Jean Charcot (1825–1893), a French neurologist, believing neuroses to have an organic basis, began to demonstrate that hypnosis could relieve the symptoms of hysteria, a form of neurosis in which bodily ailments such as paralysis or blindness appeared without any organic pathology. Physicians from all over Europe flocked to see Charcot's dramatic demonstrations of producing and removing physical symptoms in hysterical patients through hypnosis. Charcot ultimately realized that hysteria was not due to organic damage to the nervous system, but he was unable to formulate an adequate psychological explanation. That task was left to one of Charcot's students, Sigmund Freud.

Sigmund Freud (1856–1939), trained in neurology, was also interested in hysteria and had traveled from his native Vienna to Paris to study with Charcot. Once back in Vienna, Freud attempted hypnosis with hysterical patients but found the technique did not produce the permanent relief of symptoms he was seeking. Through an evolutionary sequence of therapeutic techniques, described in greater detail on p. 220, the so-called talking cure of psychoanalysis developed. Freud's discoveries, including the importance of unconscious, instinctual forces in human behavior, trans-

---

[2] So persistent was this attitude that it was only about 30 years ago that Frieda Fromm–Reichmann (1942) was able to report that contrary to classical psychiatric thinking, she was able to establish "interpersonal contact" with schizophrenics and begin to understand their communications.

formed psychiatry from a relatively static and descriptive branch of medicine to a vital force concerned with uncovering the causes of human suffering. His psychoanalytic treatment provided the first comprehensive, psychological set of therapeutic procedures for relieving such suffering. His relevance to the emerging field of clinical psychology, although not apparent at the time, proved ultimately to be monumental. His persistent probing into uncharted areas of the human psyche, his intellectual courage in the face of professional scorn, his emphasis on the individual patient's uniqueness, his stress on uncovering and understanding the significance of early life experiences on adult psychopathology, as well as his contribution to the theory of normal personality development all mark his work as a turning point in our understanding of human behavior.

THE HUMANITARIAN MOVEMENT

In the eighteenth-century asylum, inmates were subjected to unspeakable hardships—chains, irons, collars, darkened cells, solitary confinement, filth, and starvation. Inmates wandered about naked, driven from place to place like mad dogs and subjected to whippings like vagrants and rogues. At Old Bedlam in England, a physician would visit once a year to prescribe treatment, which usually consisted of periodic blood-letting and purges. At smaller private institutions, it was not unusual for a physician to visit once in ten years to prescribe treatment for the next decade (Reisman, 1966).

The Enlightenment saw the birth of humanistic movements, accelerated especially by the rapid rise of democracy in the New World and parts of Europe. At about the time that Pinel began his humanitarian reforms in France, English tea merchant William Tuke (1732–1822), horrified at conditions in asylums he visited, induced the Society of Friends, of which he was a member, to establish a retreat under his guidance at York, in the English countryside. Rather than operating as a prison, the York Retreat provided a simple, tranquil Quaker atmosphere where patients were given good food, exercise, and recreation and were treated with respect and dignity. Instead of bleeding and purges, Tuke administered "moral treatment," consisting of encouragement, kindness, and routine work. This Quaker hospital or retreat served as a model for other such institutions around the world—for example, the Hartford Retreat in Hartford, Connecticut. Tuke and his small group of Quakers also influenced the public to develop more enlightened attitudes toward mental illness, including the belief that such illness was ultimately curable.

Despite some advances in the care of mental patients in various parts of the world, hospital care in general was deplorable. Physical restraints on patients were commonly used, and hospitals were crowded and filthy. Once again, a group of reformers, largely lay people, set about seeking humane treatment for patients. In the United States, the most celebrated and certainly the most effective reformer was Dorothea Dix (1802–1887), a New England schoolteacher. While teaching Sunday school to female prisoners, she became aware that mentally ill patients were often housed with criminals, and both were treated brutally. Visiting every jail and alms-house in Massachusetts, she became increasingly outraged at the conditions she found. As a result, she sent a vivid report to the Massachusetts Legislature, insisting that reforms be carried out. Successful in Massachusetts, Dorothea Dix continued to travel throughout the world for the next 40 years, crusading for greater public awareness of the need for humane and adequate treatment and facilities for criminals, the mentally ill, and the mentally deficient. Many millions of dollars were raised as a result of her appeals. In addition, she badgered hospital superintendents to allow her to inspect their buildings, and then, by appealing to the appropriate state legislature, forced them to give decent medical care to their patients. As a result of her personal activities, 32 mental hospitals, among them St. Elizabeth's Hospital in Washington, D. C., were built or enlarged in the United States alone. Truly a remarkable person and an extraordinarily influential reformer, she was cited by the United States Congress in 1901 as ''among the noblest examples of humanity in all history [Karnosh & Zucker, 1945].''

One more recent influence has been the development of the mental hygiene movement. The term *mental hygiene* refers to the promotion of mental health and the prevention of mental illness. This movement was founded by Clifford Beers (1876–1943) and came about as a result of Beers' book, *A Mind That Found Itself* (1908), an account of his experiences as a patient in various mental hospitals. Beers experienced several break-downs after graduating from Yale and was hospitalized in private sani-tariums and state hospitals in Connecticut, receiving the then prevailing treatment of restraints and isolation. Upon his eventual release after several years of hospitalization, Beers was determined to inform the public how it felt to be mentally ill and to arouse a movement to reform existing evils in the hospital treatment programs. Beers' book, as Bromberg (1959) notes, proved to be "the shot heard 'round the world," the catalyst that finally forced an indifferent public to become aware of some of the problems of mental illness and to demand changes in patient care. Enlisting the aid of William James, the eminent psychologist, and Adolf Meyer, the leading psychiatrist in the United States, Beers helped form a National Committee for Mental Hygiene. He remained secretary of that organization for 30 years, helping to focus public attention on the standards of care for the mentally ill, promoting measures for the prevention of mental illness, and trying to remove the stigma from mental illness. The organization and its successor, the National Association for Mental Health, have been instrumental in providing public support for further study and research into mental illness. Their persistent lobbying resulted in the post-World War II establishment of the *National Institute of Mental Health* in Washington, D. C., a federally sponsored research and training center for the study of mental illness.

THE DEVELOPMENT OF CONTEMPORARY CLINICAL PSYCHOLOGY

THE FIRST GENERATION

The history of clinical psychology begins in the early 1900s when the first generation of clinical psychologists developed (Watson, 1953). In the 1890s, the following events paved the way for this development: (1) William James published his *Principles of Psychology* (1890), considered a major source of ideas reaching into all realms of pure and applied psychology; (2) Sigmund Freud published an early paper on hysteria (1893), thus introducing the psychodynamic approach to understanding and treating abnormal behavior; (3) Lightner Witmer, a student of Wundt's, founded the first psychological clinic in the United States at the University of Pennsylvania in 1896; and (4) a small group of about 30 psychologists, at the invitation of G. Stanley Hall, met at Clark University to found the American Psychological Association in 1892.

The early psychologists functioned primarily in academic settings; it is no coincidence that Witmer's early efforts to develop what he called a clinical method in psychology emerged from the psychological laboratory of a university. However, while most psychologists around 1900 concerned themselves with formulating general laws regarding such matters as sensation and perception, Witmer was more interested in clinically applying the developing methods of psychological laboratories to individual problems.

Other psychologists, too, were becoming interested in the study of the individual. Following the tradition begun by Galton, they tried to develop tests to measure individual differences in ability, such as intelligence. James Cattell (1860–1944), an American, had been Wundt's first laboratory assistant at Leipzig and Galton's assistant in London for several months. Combining the two influences—experimental psychology and individual differences—Cattell introduced the first battery of psychological tests in the United States in 1894 when he attempted to appraise the mental abilities of incoming freshmen at Columbia University (Cattell & Ferrand, 1896). Cattell mainly tested sensory and perceptual responses, which proved to be poor predictors of academic achievement. Nevertheless, Cattell helped a developing branch of psychology loosen its ties to the laboratory and helped turn it to the solution of practical problems by using mental and physical tests.

A more successful attempt to develop psychological tests of intelligence, soon to become an important impetus to the growth of clinical psychology, came from the work of Alfred Binet (1857–1911). Binet, a French psychologist, had carried out a long series of psychological studies with children in the classroom in the 1890s, carefully noting how they showed signs of using their higher mental processes. Like Galton and Cattell, Binet was interested in developing tests for measuring intelligence. However, while Galton and Cattell looked at physiological and perceptual tests borrowed from the laboratory to gauge intelligence, Binet's approach was more simple and clinically oriented to the real classroom situation. He set about isolating different mental functions—such as memory, attention, or comprehension—and then studying how children with different degrees of skills in these functions operated. Assuming that a combination of these functions composes intelligence, Binet could then develop test items in each function and use the overall score as a measure of intelligence. In 1904, Binet was commissioned to study the special educational problems of mentally defective children in Paris. Some sort of examination was necessary to certify that these children could not benefit from ordinary classroom instruction. Not wanting to rely on subjective impressions, Binet and Theodore Simon, a physician, sought a more objective, practical, diagnostic method for measuring the degree of intellectual deficiency. The result was the 1905 Binet–Simon Scale, including 30 tasks of increasing degrees of complexity that would provide a crude means of differentiating normal and mentally deficient children. Later revisions in 1908 and 1911 introduced refinements, including a measure of mental age, to aid in classifying intelligence.

The scale was soon translated and adapted in the United States by Henry Goddard (1910), director of the Research Laboratory and Training School for mentally deficient children at Vineland, New Jersey. Lewis Terman, professor of education at Stanford University, published his Stanford Revision of the Binet–Simon Scale in 1916. Carefully standardized on 2100 children and 180 adults, Terman's revision extended the age range of the test from three years through adulthood, included items more suitable to American children, and used the concept of intelligence quotient (IQ) to measure the relationship between the subject's mental and chronological ages. In addition, Terman proposed a classification system (ranging from feeblemindedness to genius) based on IQ scores (Terman, 1916). Terman's revision[3] became so widely used as an individual test of intelligence in the United States that for many years the major task assigned to clinical psychologists was the administration of the Stanford–Binet test (Watson, 1953) (see Figure 3).

Psychological testing was just the impetus clinical psychology needed to grow and begin to gain public acceptance. Psychologists were beginning to use the Stanford–Binet and similar tests of intelligence and other functions in a variety of clinical situations, as were schools, children's homes, juvenile courts, reformatories, and prisons. Child-guidance clinics were opened for the first time around 1909, staffed by psychiatrists and occasionally also clinical psychologists. William Healy, a psychiatrist who had studied with William James, founded the Juvenile Psychopathic Institute (now known as the Institute for Juvenile Research) in Chicago, a forerunner of later child-guidance clinics. Healy's clinic treated delinquent children, whom Healy and his staff studied with psychological tests and various research techniques. By 1917, Healy had moved to Boston and established the Judge Baker Guidance Center devoted to diagnostic evaluations and treatment of delinquent children.

By 1910, however, psychiatry and clinical psychology had made little more than passing contact with each other. A number of other clinics had

---

[3] Later revisions (Terman & Merrill, 1937, 1960) have continued to improve the 1916 scale through improved standardized procedures, the removal of out-of-date content, the use of more adequate methods of test construction, and increased reliability and validity.

Figure 3. The 1960 Stanford–Binet test materials. Note the set of familiar toy objects and printed pictures, especially useful in testing young children. (Munn-Fernald-Fernald: *Introduction to Psychology,* Houghton Mifflin Company, 1969. Reprinted by permission of the publisher.)

opened after Witmer opened the first psychological clinic, but treatment of mentally ill patients was considered the exclusive province of the psychiatrist. Psychologists worked mainly in university clinics rather than in hospitals or in independent private practice and concentrated on testing and guidance of children with learning difficulties. Psychoanalysis found little acceptance among most psychologists, particularly those in academic settings. Among psychiatrists in the United States, few looked favorably on psychoanalytic treatment, although Healy was beginning to apply psychoanalytic methods to the problems of delinquency. For this first generation of clinical psychologists, applying the newly developed psychological tests was the major professional activity. The ability to administer and interpret the various versions of the Binet Scales was considered for many years to come as synonymous with clinical psychology (Louttit, 1939).

THE SECOND GENERATION

As the concept of applied psychology began to become accepted, internship training was instituted in mental hospitals and training schools for the mentally retarded in an effort to supplement the academic course work of psychology students. In addition, psychological laboratories devoted to research, formerly housed exclusively in universities, were established in these settings. When the United States entered World War I in 1917, the sudden influx of Army recruits necessitated development of some methods to group and classify them according to their abilities. The U. S. Army Medical Department turned to leading American psychologists (including Robert Yerkes and Lewis Terman) to develop group-administered intelligence tests as well as tests of neuroticism that would screen out those recruits with psychological problems. The Army Alpha, a verbal intelligence test, and the Army Beta, an intelligence test not requiring reading ability, were constructed and have continued in use, in revised form, for many years. Over two million soldiers were tested during the brief wartime period.

For the first time, academic psychologists, prepared or not, were called to help with real, pressing problems. It was the first of many similar situations in which psychologists have been asked to help solve immediate problems even though psychology's stage of development might provide only unreliable answers. The science versus service conflict, which would plague future generations of psychologists, had begun. Mental testing had clearly become the domain of the clinical psychologist, although he was reluctant to apply these services to areas other than education. Tests to appraise personality or gauge the extent of mental illness were yet to be developed. But the profession of clinical psychology was developing some identifiable signs.

The demand for testing greatly accelerated after the war. Various tests of intelligence, achievement, and vocational aptitude were developed and used in schools, industry, prisons, mental hospitals, and the new child-guidance clinics. This branch of psychology was rapidly becoming entirely service-oriented—too rapidly for some APA leaders, who resisted this direction. For a brief period (1917–1919), some members of this second generation of clinical psychologists, interested in the clinical application of psychology, banded together and rebelled at APA's insistence on keeping psychology a pure science. They formed a splinter group, the American Association of Clinical Psychologists. Their pressure was sufficiently strong that after two years they were welcomed back to APA, becoming that organization's first division, the Clinical Psychology Section (Symonds, 1946).

On another front, some medical groups were hostile to this new profession because they felt clinical psychologists were invading their professional territory, especially in diagnosing mental disorders and mental retardation. In their view, these conditions indicated medical problems that required the special skills of a qualified physician or at least his supervision of a clinical psychologist. Conflicts in professional roles, status, and responsibilities were inevitable as the two professions' areas of interest and competence overlapped. Although a number of conferences and joint American Psychological Association/American Psychiatric Association committees have attempted to resolve the conflict (see p. 92), some antagonism continues even today, although the picture is probably best described now as a truce and mutual acceptance of co-existence.

In the 1920s, two theoretical systems, behaviorism and Gestalt psychology, began to gain supporters among psychologists. Wundt's system, known as structuralism, had emphasized studying elements of consciousness in order to understand the structure of the mind. His system relied on a subject's introspection of his experiences and sensations for its data. Critics such as William James and John Dewey, influenced by Darwin's theory of evolution, proposed an alternate theory that came to be known as functionalism. The functionalists were more interested in how the mind worked—how it helped an individual adapt to a changing environment —than in how it was structured. Behaviorist John Watson (1919) carried the point a step further when he urged that psychologists abandon the concept of mind to the philosophers and concentrate instead on the study of behavior. Behavior, he argued, was more tangible, more easily measured, and required fewer inferences than did the concept of the mind's workings. Particularly relevant to clinical psychology was the early demonstration by Watson and Rayner (1920) of the use of conditioning techniques, first reported by Pavlov, to develop a phobia in a child. Clinicians became interested in the development of children's phobic reactions, reasoning that if fears could be acquired through conditioning, they might also be eliminated in the same way.

Gestalt psychology, originating in Germany in the 1920s, was brought to the United States in the 1930s by its founders Max Wertheimer, Wolfgang Köhler, and Kurt Koffka. The structuralists had insisted that all experience be analyzed according to its basic components—sensations, images, feelings, and so on. The Gestaltists, like the behaviorists, opposed this view, considering it too atomistic. Unlike the behaviorists, however, they were interested in the organization of perception and in studying the higher mental processes. Gestalt psychology had several ramifications for contemporary clinical psychology. It stressed that understanding of a patient is enhanced by learning about his unique perceptions of the world (see Chapter 7). Another early Gestaltist, social psychologist Kurt Lewin (1890–1947), helped found group dynamics and can be considered the father of sensitivity training and various other innovations in group therapy (see Chapter 10).

The 1930s saw clinical psychology veer from its earlier direction of primarily measuring intellectual ability and school achievement in children. These activities were still important, but psychologists expanded into diagnostic work with adults, usually in mental hospitals. In addition, psychological testing itself was expanding, augmented by the introduction of personality tests. The Rorschach Inkblot Test, named after its originator, Swiss psychiatrist Hermann Rorschach, had been introduced after World War I (Rorschach, 1921). However, it received little attention in the United States until Samuel Beck (1930) used the Rorschach technique in research on feeblemindedness. Later, Henry Murray and his colleagues at the Harvard Psychological Clinic carried out clinical and experimental research on 50 college-age men (Murray, 1938) using many innovative techniques, including the Thematic Apperception Test introduced three years earlier (Morgan & Murray, 1935).

During the late 1930s, psychoanalysis began to make an impact on American clinical psychology. In part this was due to the large migration of European psychologists and psychiatrists who came to this country to escape the Nazi regime. Psychoanalytic in their orientation and with a widespread interest in personality development, their influence on American psychologists was to deemphasize testing intellectual ability and emphasize the study of personality theory, especially psychoanalysis. Many clinical psychologists became interested in practicing psychoanalysis, although American psychoanalysts offered such training only to members of the medical profession. However, Freud (1927) maintained that so-called lay analysis (that is, psychoanalysis practiced by a non-physician) was not only acceptable, but desirable. In Freud's opinion, psychoanalysis, which he developed, was more a part of psychology than a branch of medicine.

THE THIRD GENERATION

World War II and its aftermath were the years of perhaps the greatest growth to date for clinical psychology. During the war itself, 1500 psychologists served in the Armed Forces (Andrews & Dreese, 1948), making significant contribution to such applied problems as selection, evaluation, and job placement of draftees, morale maintenance, studying human factors in equipment design, as well as involving themselves in the treatment of a large number of mental patients in Army hospitals. More clinical psychologists were moving into the area of individual and group psychotherapy. Significantly, in 1942, Carl Rogers' influential book *Counseling and Psychotherapy* was published. In his book, Rogers proposed a system of nondirective therapy that soon attracted much attention. Rogers, a clinical psychologist, offered other psychologists an alternative to Freudian psychoanalysis along with the appealing suggestion that research in psychotherapy was possible.

Although about three times as many psychologists engaged in clinical work after the war as in the prewar period (Andrews & Dreese, 1948), the supply still could not keep up with the demand. Both the Veterans Administration and the United States Public Health Service gave the universities considerable financial support immediately after the war in order to encourage the development of extensive clinical training programs at the Ph.D. level. At the same time, graduate students at the universities were supported by working at Veterans Administration facilities, thus gaining practical experience as well as performing a service to the woefully inadequately staffed VA hospitals and clinics. By 1951, the Veterans Administration had become the largest single employer of clinical psychologists in the United States.

This third generation of clinical psychologists differed from their predecessors in many ways. Because of the enormous government undertaking in establishing training programs, they were better trained as practitioners—in diagnosis, psychotherapy, and research—than any previous group of psychologists. In addition, the postwar demand for clinical services helped shift emphasis from children's problems to those of adults; the psychologist's educational function was being replaced by a clinical one. Projective techniques were widely used psychodiagnostic test instruments. Testing now involved searching for the patient's personality characteristics, the possible extent of his brain damage, or his predicted response to psychotherapy rather than merely calculating his IQ. A conference on clinical training in Boulder, Colorado (Raimy, 1950), attended by representatives of university psychology departments and training institutions, underscored the image of the clinical psychologist as a scientist–professional, giving equal emphasis to research and practice in his training.

Despite the expansion of clinical services and the increased acceptance of clinical psychologists engaging in psychotherapy, many clinicians were becoming increasingly restless about their second-class status in regard to psychiatrists and were looking to the American Psychological Association for support and guidance. The APA has traditionally recoiled from dealing with nonacademic professional problems, despite growing recognition of a responsibility to the public to establish standards. The Clinical Psychology Section of APA, established as a concession in 1919, disbanded in frustration in 1937 and formed a new organization, the American Association of Applied Psychology (Symonds, 1946). Thus two psychological organizations coexisted for a time, one dedicated to the advancement of psychology as a science, the other to psychology as a profession. Finally in 1945 a new APA constitution was drawn up, the two groups merged, and the objective of the new APA became "to advance psychology as a science and as a means of promoting human welfare." Division 12 became the clinical division of APA.

Edwin G. Boring, a psychologist who himself had lived through much of the history of psychology and had contributed much to its appreciation, perhaps best summed up this post-war period when he characterized clinical psychology as

> . . . rejected by its academic parents, faring forth to make its fortune, capturing the VA, and coming home with untold wealth to surround its

amazed parents with the luxury and the responsibility of a new way of living [Boring, 1948, p. 79].

The 1950s were years of professional consolidation for clinical psychology. After experience in hospital and mental hygiene clinic work, many psychologists were anxious to begin private practice for the first time. Many found the practice of psychotherapy more personally and professionally rewarding than testing, to say nothing of its increased financial compensation. They enjoyed the status, responsibility, and independence of being a doctor. But they were risking censure from their nonclinical colleagues who were becoming alarmed at this swift venture into full-time professional work, as well as from psychiatrists who were also critical of "upstart" clinical psychologists who weren't content "to know their place."

It seemed a logical step to urge state legislatures to pass licensing or certification laws,[4] both to recognize the profession's status and respectability and to protect the public from untrained, unqualified practitioners whom the public had no other way of differentiating from qualified ones. Here again there was considerable opposition from the medical profession, although some sort of regulation certifying professional competence now exists in every state. In addition, psychologists attempted to regulate themselves by: (1) adopting a Code of Ethical Standards of Psychologists (APA, 1953); and (2) establishing a certifying board, similar to medical specialty boards, called the American Board of Examiners in Professional Psychology, designed to issue diplomas certifying professional competence in three applied areas—clinical, counseling, and industrial psychology. (In 1969, a fourth specialty, school psychology, was added.) Licensing and certification laws, the code of ethics, and the certifying board are discussed in greater detail in Chapter 3.

Of particular significance to clinical psychology and the entire field of mental health was the report of a five-year study undertaken by the Joint Commission on Mental Illness and Health (1961). This group was created by Congress in 1955 through the Mental Health Study Act. It was

---

[4] A license is a permit to practice clinical psychology, including psychotherapy. To be certified as a psychologist means only that the title "psychologist" may be used by those so certified, but does not restrict others from offering the identical services so long as they do not hold themselves out to the public for a fee as "psychologists." Henderson and Hildreth (1965) draw the analogy of both to Pure Food and Drug Acts which are designed to protect the consumer from dangerous or inferior commodities.

charged with evaluating: (1) the extent of mental illness in the United States; (2) the resources available for research as well as treatment and care of the mentally ill; and (3) future needs in the field.

Noting the shortage of trained mental health professionals, the Commission's report urged the launching of a national manpower recruitment program at both the professional and subprofessional level. Psychologists, among others, were encouraged to train laymen (teachers, attendants, clergymen, public health nurses, volunteers) to become mental health counselors who would engage in early detection of mental illness and do short-term psychotherapy. Taking up the challenge, one early study reported considerable success in training a group of mature housewives, who had no previous professional experience, to practice psychotherapy under supervision (Rioch, Elkes, Flint, Usdansky, Newman, & Silber, 1963).

The Commission's report represents a landmark in the history of mental health care in the United States. The Commission was composed of representatives from all the mental health disciplines, including clinical psychology. Their final report to Congress, *Action for Mental Health* (1961), made recommendations that led to legislation committing the federal and state governments, in partnership, to create broad community mental health programs. These programs, described in greater detail in Chapter 8, were designed to supplement traditional hospital and clinic services by reaching out into the community to such groups as the poor and underprivileged who up to then had benefited little from established mental health programs. In addition to recommending that treatment facilities be improved and expanded, the Commission urged greater attention to the prevention of mental disorders through research into those biological and social factors that jeopardize mental health. The Commission's report challenged clinical psychology to reassess its traditional roles and purposes in the light of such new responsibilities.

THE PRESENT GENERATION

The 1970s find the present, fourth generation of clinical psychologists engaged in four sets of activities: diagnosis and assessment, clinical research, psychotherapy, and community consultation.

The diagnosis of psychopathology has given way, for many clinicians, to the assessment of an individual's psychological strengths as well as his weaknesses. Psychological tests, particularly projective techniques—such an important part of clinical psychology up to the late 1950s—have now taken a backseat to: (1) other more direct, interpersonal, confrontation-style assessment procedures; or (2) objective assessment procedures such as the Minnesota Multiphasic Personality Inventory (see p. 185), often with computerized interpretations. Clinical research, as indicated in Chapter 1, has become a broad, multidisciplinary enterprise, with the potential to increase collaboration between practitioner and researcher in certain areas such as behavior modification. Clinical psychologists continue to spend much of their time as psychotherapists; today there is little or no challenge to their right or competence to do so. As community consultants to various agencies aimed at improving the welfare of the community at large in an effort to prevent the development of mental disorders, today's clinical psychologists are taking on a new, exciting role.

Despite these apparent achievements, certain professional and scientific problems remain to be resolved:

1. The demand for clinical services is greater than ever and the mental health field clearly suffers from a serious manpower shortage, yet a number of prominent psychology departments at major universities have seriously curtailed or in some cases dropped their clinical training programs.

2. The professional breach between the science and applied areas of psychology in many cases remains as wide as ever, despite the peace pact that reunited both groups in 1945. Some clinicians continue to insist that APA does not represent its views with sufficient vigor, while some experimentalists believe too much of APA's energies are devoted to professional problems like legislation and insurance reimbursements.

3. Within clinical psychology itself, the place of psychological testing, synonymous with clinical psychology since its beginnings, remains uncertain. Some clinicians maintain that their unique contribution to a clinical appraisal stems from their skill in test interpretation. Others believe that research has shown many tests to be of inconclusive validity, which makes their continued use questionable. Still others argue that to accept identification as psychometricians is to acknowledge lower status to other mental health professionals, which they refuse to do.

4. Private practice of psychotherapy by qualified psychologists is approved by the American Psychological Association but is still controversial. Academicians are concerned about (and perhaps somewhat jealous of) the practitioner's income and freedom from responsibility to publish his

findings or conduct his work scientifically. Clinicians, on the other hand, are sometimes scornful of published research that appears to them to be unrelated to the real-life problems they treat daily.

5. The efficacy and relevance of individual psychotherapy continues to be debated. The traditionally slow, reconstructive, uncovering form of psychotherapy is being challenged, both by here-and-now, encounter-oriented therapists and behavior modifiers using conditioning techniques recommended by academic, experimental psychology.

6. The established views on the etiology of mental disturbances, influenced greatly for the past 40 years by psychoanalysis, are under attack. Man's problems stem from something more than intrapsychic conflict, according to those who look for social, interpersonal, biochemical, or genetic explanations. Considerable research is still necessary in this area.

7. Man's problems are interpersonal in nature and arise from communication difficulties, according to some clinical psychologists. If this is, indeed, the case, then individual psychotherapy needs to be supplemented or, in some cases, replaced by group therapy or family therapy (or perhaps some other alternatives) to deal more realistically with resolving such problems.

8. More and more clinicians are becoming disenchanted with the medical model and its search for past causes and explanations, as well as its insistence on the therapist retaining a detached, aloof, healthy role in dealing with a patient's psychopathology. However, no new comparable model is yet acceptable to the majority of clinicians.

9. New, briefer therapeutic methods directed toward individuals in crisis—such as a suicide attempt, imminent marital breakup, or job loss —are needed to replace long-term psychotherapy, especially in clinics with long waiting lists.

10. Treatment programs reaching low-income populations in their own community must be developed. Clinical psychologists need to learn new roles and new ways of reaching such individuals to replace the customary procedures whereby therapists wait for patients to come to them.

11. Methods must be developed to train nonprofessionals to increase the manpower pool of mental health workers.

12. Long-term, basic research into the means of preventing mental illness is necessary if any significant inroads are to be made into the problems of psychopathology.

Clearly, efforts to resolve these issues call for considerable ingenuity in research methodology, bold and resourceful therapeutic programs, and a sense of responsibility to the public as well as to the profession. Today's clinical psychologist, like his predecessors, can hardly afford to be complacent.

CHAPTER 3 *Issues in Professional Preparation and Professional Practice*

All fields of psychology are rapidly becoming more service oriented. While academicians traditionally have been concerned with theory and method without regard to direct applicability, they frequently are confronted by graduate students who want training that will equip them for successful postdoctoral work in an applied field of psychology. Nor is this phenomenon restricted to clinical psychology alone. Tryon (1963) points out that the professionalization of experimental psychology is now suddenly on the rise; industry and the military services have found the laboratory methods and experimental logic of this discipline useful in solving some of their problems. Tryon's 1962 survey of occupational affiliations of American Psychological Association members indicates psychologists in nonacademic positions had begun to outnumber those in academic positions, in sharp contrast to the past. Specifically, Tryon's data reveal the following for APA members:

	1940	1959	1962
In academic occupations	75%	52%	47%
In nonacademic occupations	25%	48%	53%

Within clinical psychology, Kelly's (1961a) survey of the activities of members of the clinical division of APA (Division 12) supports Tryon's contention. Kelly found that almost half (45 percent) of the approximately

1000 respondents reported their primary work setting[1] to be medical in nature—general hospitals, mental hospitals, or clinics. Private practice was the primary work setting of 17 percent of the respondents. A smaller proportion of clinical psychologists was distributed among city, state, and federal agencies, courts, correction institutions, industry, schools, residential treatment centers, or hospitals for the mentally retarded. Universities and colleges accounted for only 20 percent of the total sample. Combining the responses of those indicating primary, secondary, and tertiary appointments for each type of setting, the following results were obtained: (1) nearly three-quarters of all respondents were affiliated with medical settings; (2) slightly over half of the respondents listed private practice as one of their professional activities; (3) forty percent of the respondents held full-time or part-time faculty positions with colleges or universities.

A more recent study (Goldschmid et al., 1969) suggests the continuing professionalization of clinical psychology. Their survey of Division 12 members finds private practice the single most frequent setting for clinical psychologists. The largest proportion of respondents (28 percent) listed private practice as their primary work setting, with an equal proportion engaged in part-time private practice. Affiliation with medical settings appears to have decreased significantly since Kelly's earlier study, while affiliation with colleges or universities appears to have remained about the same. Community consultation is occupying a significant portion of the clinical psychologist's time now, and significantly, clinical services take the most professional time, followed by teaching and then by research.

The APA has tried to respond to this growing professionalization. When it merged with the American Association of Applied Psychology in 1945, APA began to represent both the scientific and professional aspects of psychology. Almost immediately, this new organization was forced to contend with the explosive postwar demands for clinical services. No formal training program in clinical psychology existed in universities before 1946 (Kelly, 1961b). Few guidelines were available for creating a responsible, and in many ways unique, profession. Willing or not, prepared or not, APA leaders suddenly found themselves being called on to: (1)

---

[1] A characteristic of the contemporary clinical psychologist is his participation in several work settings during the course of an ordinary work week. Goldschmid, Stein, Weissman, and Sorrells (1969) report that a clinical psychologist seldom spends more than one-third of his time in any one activity.

formulate a recommended university program for training clinical psychologists; (2) evaluate the staffs and hurriedly organized university psychology department programs coming into existence so the Veterans Administration might have a list of approved programs from which to select trainees for internship training; (3) develop working relationships with other professions, particularly the related and sometimes competitive profession of psychiatry; (4) draw up a code of ethics for the practice of psychology in all of its specialties; (5) establish a procedure for certifying the competence of individual psychologists to perform professional services; and (6) coordinate the legislative battles in various states over licensing and certification for clinical psychologists.

GRADUATE TRAINING IN CLINICAL PSYCHOLOGY

THE SHAKOW REPORT

Perhaps more than any other individual, David Shakow has been influential in providing the philosophy and shaping the direction of clinical training in the United States since World War II. Long associated with Worcester State Hospital as chief psychologist and director of psychological research, Shakow pioneered positions on clinical training and professional functioning that remain the basis for most graduate education and field work training even today. A collection of Shakow's writings, representing his 40-year odyssey, has appeared recently (Shakow, 1969). Its title, *Clinical Psychology as Science and Profession,* reflects his continued insistence on equal emphasis on both aspects of clinical psychology.

As far back as 1942, when APA membership totalled 3231 and only 127 Ph.D.s were awarded in psychology in the United States, Shakow already envisioned the need for clinical psychologists to be trained at the doctoral level. He recommended—and supported in a detailed rationale—a graduate curriculum of four years, including internship during the third year and a return to the university for a fourth year to complete the dissertation and make arrangements for psychoanalytic treatment, if not completed earlier. Shakow's paper also dealt with candidate selection and evaluation in graduate school as well as the need for postdoctoral training. Such was Shakow's foresight that he even proposed the establishment of a specialty board (later established by APA as the American Board of Examiners in Professional Psychology) to certify competence in the practice of clinical psychology (Shakow, 1942).

In 1947, Carl Rogers, then president of APA, asked Shakow to become chairman of a committee on training in clinical psychology. The committee, composed of many of the distinguished leaders in postwar clinical psychology, presented their report, "Recommended Graduate Training Program in Clinical Psychology," to the 1947 APA convention (Shakow, Hilgard, Kelly, Luckey, Sanford, & Shaffer, 1947). The Shakow Report was adopted as a policy document by APA and soon became APA's standard for evaluating psychology department clinical programs.

Shakow's thinking, as revealed in earlier papers, is apparent in the 1947 report, which emphasizes both the scientific and professional aspects of clinical psychology. The clinical psychologist is seen first and foremost as a psychologist, with a viewpoint and core of knowledge and training common to all psychologists. To that is added clinical training in diagnosis, therapy, and research. The report recommended that clinical experience in the form of an internship be combined with academic training in a four-year graduate program. Such training was designed to equip clinical psychologists not only to develop professional skills in the application of psychological knowledge but also to carry out research to advance psychology as a science. Rather than initiate a new degree objective, the Ph.D. degree, with its traditional emphasis on research, would be retained, confirming the clinical psychologist's commitment to research.

The Shakow Report also recommended how to select graduate students. In addition to academic promise, such personal qualifications as the ability to establish effective interpersonal relationships, self-insight, and a sense of responsibility were suggested as relevant. Other recommendations included a description of the desired undergraduate preparation, areas of emphasis in graduate training, and an ideal internship program. Finally, the report listed the recommended sequence of professional development after earning the Ph.D.: membership in Division 12 of APA followed by legal certification or licensing after an additional postdoctoral year of supervised experience. After five years of experience, the clinical psychologist was thought ready to be examined for diplomate status by the then newly created American Board of Examiners in Professional Psychology.

THE BOULDER CONFERENCE

The Shakow Report set the tone for the 1949 Boulder Conference on Training in Clinical Psychology. The conference's 1947 report had called for centering clinical training in university psychology departments to ensure the same basic graduate education for clinical students as for those in other fields of psychology. By 1949, 42 university departments had developed graduate programs in clinical psychology. Many felt that a national conference would be desirable so representatives from the various universities and other interested groups might compare experiences, discuss issues involved in clinical training, and engage in some long-range planning of future training programs. The specific impetus came from the Veterans Administration and the United States Public Health Service: they asked the APA to name the universities that already had satisfactory training programs, to formulate training programs for universities that lacked them, and to establish a procedure of accreditation.[2] As a result, a two-week conference on clinical training took place in Boulder, Colorado, in August 1949 (Raimy, 1950). Seventy-one participants represented universities and field-training installations.

In general, this conference endorsed the principles of training and curriculum construction recommended by the Shakow Report. The so-called Boulder model that emerged from the conference was the scientist–professional model, with equal weight on research and practice in the training of clinical psychologists. The conferees insisted that research training was necessary because clinical psychologists were likely to be responsible for the execution and direction of research, and service clinicians would need to be able to assess new clinical techniques.

The core curriculum of the Shakow Report was approved, as were its recommendations that students be educated to approach psychological problems in a scientific manner, using psychological theory and scientific methodology. Internship under careful supervision was supported, with the student returning to the university to complete his doctoral dissertation. Only those with a doctorate in clinical psychology were to

---

[2] A list of APA-approved doctoral programs now appears yearly in the *American Psychologist*. Such approval is based on recommendations of the APA Education and Training Board. In 1969, 73 universities were given full approval for their programs in clinical psychology, while nine were given provisional approval for new programs. In addition, 21 universities were given approval for their counseling psychology programs, with one provisionally approved program (APA, 1970).

qualify for the title "clinical psychologist," although the report acknowledged the need for lower-level practitioners—subdoctoral psychological technicians with at least two years' training, including supervised field experience.

Professional ethics were discussed, particularly timely because many newly trained clinical psychologists were facing unfamiliar public responsibilities. Education in professional ethics as well as the ethics of professional interaction was agreed to be essential.

Training in psychotherapy was recommended for all students in doctoral programs in clinical psychology. It was recommended that such training be provided in courses reflecting basic principles of psychodynamics and also in carefully supervised experiences in practical clinical situations rather than through mere technical courses stressing techniques of psychotherapy.[3] Further technical skills were to be received in supervised postdoctoral training. The conference took a dim view of private practice for psychologists. Rather, it strongly recommended that psychologists collaborate with physicians, particularly in dealing with such problems as differential diagnosis,[4] organic disease, or psychosomatic problems.

The Boulder Conference represents a milestone in the development of clinical psychology. A standard for graduate education was established and endorsed by the major university psychology departments engaged in clinical training. Clinical psychologists henceforth were expected to earn a doctorate. That doctorate would be the traditional university-awarded Ph.D. rather than any new degree, such as Doctor of Psychology, as some had suggested. Training programs would remain under university control, but an APA committee on accreditation would evaluate such programs and publish their findings. The APA Education and Training Board, with a Committee on Evaluation, was established for this purpose. Of all the resolutions adopted at the Conference, perhaps the endorsement of the scientist–professional model had the most significant impact on clinical training and practice in the next two decades.

[3] Some delegates to the conference were apparently somewhat uncertain, skeptical, and even cynical about psychotherapy. Lehner, one of the delegates, summarized one group's deliberations as follows: "I am afraid that in spite of our efforts we have left therapy as an undefined technique which is applied to unspecified problems with non-predictable outcome. For this technique we recommend rigorous training [Lehner, 1952]."

[4] A differential diagnosis determines that a specific disease exists by identifying the significant symptom(s) that distinguish it from other diseases that have similar symptoms.

THE SCIENTIST–PROFESSIONAL MODEL

The interface between science and practice, while most apparent in the field of clinical psychology, also exists in other areas such as counseling psychology, school psychology, and industrial psychology. In each of these areas, the scientist–professional model has come to represent the ideal, especially for those psychologists associated with the university. The model assumes a psychologist trained for research as well as service; he is expected to devote a substantial share of his time to professional practice as well as to make use of his research training to evaluate established theories and techniques, to advance new methods, and to keep himself as well as his profession aware of new developments. Unlike some professions where practitioners develop technical skills but fail to produce or even consume current research, the psychologist as scientist–professional has the unique opportunity to integrate both, thereby continuing his personal and professional growth. So established has this model become, reaffirmed in one training conference after another, that both aspects are an integral part of the American Board of Examiners in Professional Psychology's requirements in evaluating competence.

The clinical psychologist as a rigorously trained, professionally skilled, science-valuing person retains widespread appeal for many psychologists. Gelfand and Kelly (1960) believe the clinical psychologist can best maintain his relevance in new areas of community mental health by building on this model. Wiens (1969), having examined other training models, concludes that the viability and growth of clinical psychology is due to the scientist–professional model. Looking to the future, Wiens believes clinical students should not be trained for specific professional roles or in specific clinical techniques since these continue to change with time. Rather, he applauds the present university emphasis on training in scientific methodology, with specific techniques and procedures to be learned postdoctorally on the job, as required in specific unique job situations.

On the other hand, some psychologists have begun to challenge the appropriateness, practicality, and realism of the scientist–professional model. Cook (1958, 1965), while supporting the model philosophically, has questioned whether it has worked out in practice. He acknowledges the increase in research from clinical settings, but points out that most psychologists in those settings perform only service functions. In a much quoted report, Levy (1962) suggests that efforts to produce research-oriented professionals have not produced the expected results. His follow-up study through 1960 of clinical psychologists receiving their doctorates between 1948–1953 found close to 30 percent had no publications to their credit, about 20 percent had one publication, and that 10 percent of the group accounted for almost half of the total output of the overall group. Thus, despite the strong research emphasis during their education, most practicing clinical psychologists publish no research at all.[5] These findings tend to support the results of Kelly's (1961a) survey of Division 12 members, in which only one-tenth of the respondents were occupied primarily in research and only one-fourth reported any research activities.

Clinicians have increasingly discussed the strain inherent in maintaining the dual scientist–professional role. Those interested in performing clinical services report inadequate university preparation in clinical techniques such as psychodiagnosis, psychotherapy, or consultation. Many urge the university to provide more actual clinical experience in their doctoral programs, rather than forcing them to look for such training in postdoctoral programs. Forty recent clinical alumni of the University of Michigan (1962) made a number of proposals based on their own clinical training and postdoctoral experiences. Among other recommendations, they urged a flexible administrative policy within the university, including custom-tailoring, as far as possible, programs to the needs, interests, and skills of individual students. Thus, for the student with research proclivities, these leanings should be cultivated along with some exposure to clinical practice to sensitize him to relevant research problems. For clinically oriented students, service training should be stressed along with some training in research. In essence, most of the Michigan alumni seemed to favor maintaining the established plan for the university—providing training in both the research and practical aspects of clinical psychology, so long as each individual was not expected to be equally committed and proficient in both areas.

Others have proposed the more radical solution of divorcing clinical training from the established university psychology departments. Rodgers (1964) and, more recently, Albee (1970) have argued that academic and

---

[5] Winder (1963) has challenged Levy's conclusions by saying that the term *research-oriented* in fact includes a wider group than just those who publish research. He notes that the university must offer different training, even within the same program, for students who show different areas of special competence. Some students can contribute to the field of mental health through service, some through research, still others through both. In other words, Winder suggests that research-consumers whose psychological services are influenced by relevant research are as research-oriented as research-producers.

professional training are incompatible, inevitably producing strain unless divorced. Rodgers insists that differences in academic and professional goals demand different training strategies. The basic scientist's goal is to ask prototypical questions and seek generalizable answers. The applied scientist's goal is to seek usable answers to questions about specific rather than prototypic events. Clinicians, unlike researchers, are likely to investigate a single, perhaps unique, case, with little regard for generalization. Rodgers suggests the incompatibility between academic or basic psychology and applied or professional psychology can best be settled if each area were permitted to go its own way, pursuing its own goals with less confusion and conflict. Albee, in his 1970 APA presidential address, declared that such basic differences exist within psychology that "only drastic changes can save the profession of clinical psychology [Albee, 1970, p. 42]." He describes science as open, its knowledge public, while professions are characterized as guarding its secrets. Albee sees the scientist–professional model as unworkable, since it is incompatible, simultaneously, to be scientific (subjecting techniques and theories to public scrutiny) and professional (dealing with private events and restrained by humane and ethical considerations from manipulating people experimentally). Rather than perpetuate the scientist–professional model supported by the university psychology department, Albee suggests consideration of other options. For example, he proposes a second option—establishing a separate professional school of psychology. A third possibility proposed by Albee is to move clinical training away from the university psychology department to an established professional school—medical school, school of social work, or school of education. Albee's fourth choice is the most drastic—abandon clinical psychology as a separate field and encourage psychology departments to return to their historic role of preparing scholars to do the basic research that would be applied by other professions. Albee is so alarmed about the strain resulting from the incompatibility of the role of scientist and professional that he predicts the coexistence of an American Scientific Psychological Association and an American Professional Psychological Association within 10 to 15 years.

LATER TRAINING CONFERENCES AND THEIR AFTERMATH

The 1949 Boulder model, underscoring clinical psychology's simultaneous existence in two worlds—the academic-scientific and the clinical-professional—has been sustained at a number of subsequent national training conferences and has continued to be the basis for most current university training programs in clinical psychology. By 1955, it was time to: (1) review the policies and procedures derived from the Boulder Conference; (2) relate developing specializations such as counseling and school psychology to clinical psychology; and (3) make recommendations regarding the training needs of clinical students in the community mental health programs on the horizon. A brief four-day conference took place at Stanford University (in contrast to the two-week conference at Boulder), again attended by leaders of clinical training programs, some of whom by now were graduates of programs initiated after World War II.

The Stanford Conference (Strother, 1957) made no recommendations and provided no new direction, except perhaps to recognize that community mental health programs would greatly increase demands for clinical services on the part of various mental health professions. Research on the nature and treatment of mental illness was stressed along with the general viewpoint that professional training be broadened to provide preparation for a diversity of later roles in the community. Kelly (1961b), a delegate to both conferences, reports fewer pressing issues and much less animated discussion at Stanford than at Boulder. If anything, Kelly believes participants were too complacent about the established scientist–professional model. As a result, he reported little enthusiasm for changing the role of future clinical psychologists, involving, as it inevitably would, changes in courses, field work, and staff orientation. Kelly lamented that this young profession seemed to have matured too rapidly into a conservative adult, unwilling to accept new challenges. Elsewhere (Kelly, 1961a) he observed that earlier hopes—that psychologists would bring to the mental health field a set of critical attitudes and research skills needed to develop new knowledge—have not been fulfilled. He warned psychologists that their complacency made them prone to adopt uncritically the current developments of other disciplines such as psychiatry and social work.

In 1958, an eight-day conference on graduate education in psychology was held in Miami Beach (Roe, 1959). Almost ten years after Boulder, society had made unanticipated demands on clinical psychology, and new, applied specialties had been added. Was the scientist–professional model still appropriate for all psychologists? The Miami Beach conference took a conservative view regarding change. Psychology departments were urged to continue to stress research training. There was a return to an older training idea that subdoctoral-level students be taught skills (junior college teaching, interviewing, testing, report writing) without the broad background and research training the conference unequivocally supported for doctoral-level training. A common core of subject matter for all psychology was supported so psychologists in all specialties would have a common bond. However, each university psychology department was to establish the curriculum that would best fit the needs of its programs, students, and the capacities of its faculty. The issue of a professional doctoral degree was raised again at the Miami conference, and once again the Ph.D. was retained by strong consensus.

By the early 1960s, practicing clinicians' dissatisfaction with the scientist–professional role had become more rampant. Some agreed that this model's inherent role contradictions resulted in neither a good scientist nor a good clinician. Another contradiction—between the nature of university training and the nature of the practicing clinician's professional work—resulted in alienation of the practitioner from science and research. Finally, the status, glamour, and financial reward of independent private practice held great appeal, and the service-oriented clinician was likely to find most satisfaction in the most unscientific part of his professional repertoire, psychotherapy.

The University of Michigan clinical alumni (1962) were alarmed that clinical psychology programs were being deemphasized at many universities. They particularly disagreed with the Miami conference's recommendation of increased use of subdoctoral clinicians. They rejected the idea of only postdoctoral specialization, particularly since such programs are scarce. Instead, they argued to strengthen doctoral programs by providing more direct professional clinical experiences.

APA tried to respond to the frustrations of many clinicians, but its slow pace proved all the more frustrating for some. APA created a Board of Professional Affairs (along with a Board of Scientific Affairs) in 1957 specifically to deal with professional issues. Since then, the BPA has discussed a wide variety of topics relevant to clinical psychology—health insurance reimbursements for psychotherapy, state regulation of clinical practice, relations between psychology and allied professions, ethics, private practice, and standards for institutional employment of psychologists in service roles (McMillan, 1970).

Particularly germane to the issue of education and training in all the applied areas of psychology was the report of the APA Committee on the

Scientific and Professional Aims of Psychology chaired by Kenneth E. Clark (APA, 1965). It urged that training in the applied areas be substantially strengthened if psychologists in those areas were to be adequately trained for their professional tasks. One possible solution was to establish alternate training programs and degrees, possibly within a new professional school offering a Doctor of Psychology (Psy.D.) degree. While at present that degree would be limited to psychologists and psychotherapists, in the future it might be appropriate for other areas of applied psychology—community mental health, school psychology, counseling, and industrial psychology.

THE CHICAGO CONFERENCE ON PROFESSIONAL PREPARATION

The Clark Committee's radical recommendation of a new doctoral program was in the minds of conferees as they gathered for the 1965 Chicago Conference on the Professional Preparation of Clinical Psychologists. Conferees were also aware of discontent with university training in clinical psychology among members of various local clinical groups around the country. Spearheaded by the Clinical Division of the New York State Psychological Association and the Los Angeles Society of Clinical Psychologists, these groups had insisted that: (1) the Chicago Conference include participants who were practicing professionals (in private practice, in institutional settings, in industry) as well as the customary participants from existing university programs; (2) the Conference consider the model of the clinical psychologist as a "fully-functioning professional person [LASCP, 1964]" (see p. 91); and (3) the Conference consider the education and training as well as the recruitment, selection, and motivation of student candidates appropriate to such a model.

Approximately 100 psychologists met for a week in Chicago. The conferees represented a broad spectrum of backgrounds, experiences, interests, roles, and responsibilities. Four models for doctoral training were considered: (1) the scientist–professional model; (2) the professional psychologist, a clinician broadly trained in a variety of diagnostic, remedial, and preventive procedures; (3) the psychologist–psychotherapist, trained for a career in full-time practice of psychotherapy; and (4) the research clinician, trained for a career of research on problems in clinical psychology. The location of doctoral training and alternate degrees were examined. Among the locations considered were; (1) university psychology departments; (2) professional schools; (3) clinical centers, medical or nonmedical, connected to the university or not. In addition, the level of training appropriate to various functions of clinical psychologists was considered: (1) postdoctoral; (2) doctoral; (3) subdoctoral; and (4) undergraduate.

This conference continued the official endorsement of the scientist–professional model while encouraging diversification of training opportunities to allow different students to build on different interests in their professional preparation (Hoch, Ross, & Winder, 1966). Both the psychologist–psychotherapist and the research clinician models were rejected as too narrow a conception of the clinician's role. The conferees agreed that competence in any single professional function, whether psychotherapy, research, or psychodiagnosis, does not constitute clinical psychology. The professional psychologist model, an outgrowth of the Clark Committee Report, was given serious consideration. Unwilling to reject the model, the conferees voted to encourage innovation should university psychology departments wish it; they were interested in how one such Doctor of Psychology program at the University of Illinois would fare (see p. 82).

The conferees recognized that doctoral training in clinical psychology would be improved by presenting students with more adequate role models —that is, if practitioners as well as academicians were the professors. To that end, university departments were encouraged to offer faculty positions to clinicians whose professional roles were distributed over all of the scientist–professional continuum, including clinical practice.

The Chicago Conference fully endorsed the establishment of psychological service centers as ideal settings for clinical training. Consistent with some of Albee's proposals, such centers would be administered by psychologists (emphasizing a psychological rather than medical viewpoint), have a close association with universities, and be set up to serve a broad range of populations with a variety of psychological problems. Students at various levels of training would gain experience to supplement their clinical course work. Psychologists from various fields would be encouraged to work side by side on common problems. Giving unqualified support for such centers to be under the control and guidance of psychologists, the Conference thereby "endorse[d] psychology as an independent, fully responsible profession [Hoch et al. 1966, p. 86]."

Training in research and practice was supported. Research approaches were broadened to include techniques and methods peculiar to the clinician, to be carried out in natural settings as well as the laboratory. The Chicago Conference was much more positive about training in psychotherapy than the Boulder Conference had been 16 years before. Psychotherapy training was considered essential in the preparation of the clinical psychologist; such training should go beyond the customary one-to-one relationships between therapist and client to include training in new methods such as behavior modification, in working with groups and in the community, and in developing competence in new subspecialties such as clinical child psychology.

Postdoctoral training was considered necessary for a specialty area or for advanced training. University psychology departments were encouraged to offer postdoctoral training to supplement doctoral training—to enhance and expand skills learned up to that level—but not to make up for deficiencies in training at the doctoral level. Subdoctoral training was encouraged as a means to meet manpower needs, assuming such programs maintained a high level of quality. Clinical psychologists also were encouraged to participate in training nonprofessionals. However, the Chicago Conference was opposed to training clinical psychologists only to the master's level, as well as to giving consolation master's degrees to students who dropped out of doctoral programs in clinical psychology. In regard to undergraduate education, neglected in previous conferences, the Chicago Conference encouraged expanding the curriculum to include training in psychological assessment, group leadership, field work, interviewing, and experimentation and statistical analysis—some of the basic skills of psychology. The Conference cautioned that such training at the baccalaureate level in no way implied competence in professional activities which require much more extensive preparation and training.

ALTERNATE PROPOSALS FOR GRADUATE TRAINING IN CLINICAL PSYCHOLOGY

THE MEDICALLY ALLIED DOCTOR OF PSYCHOTHERAPY PROGRAM

Before World War II was over, psychoanalyst Lawrence Kubie foresaw increased demands for mental health services. Despite the enormous expansion in training facilities for all the mental health professions after the war, he remained convinced the supply could never keep pace with demands. What was needed, according to Kubie (1946), was the creation of a new discipline with a unique curriculum and training program, designed to produce competent practitioners of psychodiagnosis and psychotherapy more quickly than today's psychiatry and clinical psychology schools do. This discipline, according to Kubie, should ultimately have its own professional school and its own special doctoral degree, signaling membership in a new profession. At various times Kubie has suggested different names for the new professional degree, indicating its foundations in medicine and psychology: a doctorate in Psychological Medicine (Kubie, 1949), in Medical Psychology (Kubie, 1954), or more recently (Kubie, 1970), the Doctor of Psychotherapy, which emphasizes the primary role and professional activity of the new degree's recipient.

Kubie sees the lengthy, costly present form of medical training as an unnecessary prerequisite for the practice of psychotherapy. However, he believes students in the new profession need some grounding in basic medical science and tradition, as well as relevant aspects of hospital practice, in addition to training in the behavioral sciences and psychotherapy. Consequently, he proposes that the most appropriate institutional setting for such training be a university with a medical school and teaching hospital, strong departments in all the behavioral sciences, and a school of social work. Beginning with an interdisciplinary program involving all these groups, Kubie proposes that the new discipline's own graduate professional school would eventually take over training as a corps of specially trained teachers became available.

Detailed plans for curricula have been laid out by Kubie, including this one:

1. Basic medical sciences.
2. Behavioral sciences, especially clinical psychology, but also relevant aspects of social psychology, sociology, and cultural anthropology.
3. Emphasis on genetic development: physical, physiological and psychological, both normal and abnormal.
4. Statistics and research methodology.
5. Psychopathology, psychodiagnosis, and psychodynamics.
6. All relevant forms of therapy, with special emphasis on psychotherapeutic methods, including psychoanalysis.
7. Psychotherapy for the student.[6]

[6] Shakow made the same proposal in an early paper (Shakow, 1942). While most of

8. A graded sequence of clinical experience, including brief periods of work as attendant, clinical clerk, psychological tester, and social worker. In later years, students would gain clinical experience treating a broad spectrum of patients, under supervision [Holt, 1969].

The total length of training would be seven to nine years beyond the baccalaureate degree, about the same as present doctoral training, but Kubie argues that this program would bring individuals to a higher level of competence, similar to today's postdoctoral level. Members of the new profession would be licensed by state boards.

Kubie's plan for an autonomous profession of psychotherapy appeals more to students than to directors of psychiatric or clinical psychology programs, who have given it a cool reception since it was first suggested 20 years ago. Many students who wish to become psychotherapists feel the university is a detour that requires them to take courses irrelevant to their goal. Many are hesitant to admit clinical interests for fear of being rejected from graduate school as being insufficiently scientific in outlook. Once admitted to graduate work, many continue to hide their interests in clinical practice, some to the point where that initial interest atrophies and disappears. For many, graduate school becomes an obstacle course rather than an opportunity to pursue their true career interests. Kubie proposes that students interested in psychotherapy openly pursue it, supported and trained by a faculty with similar commitments. In reality, psychotherapy is becoming a separate profession anyway, with little to distinguish professional functions, despite marked differences in training.

On the other hand, there are serious objections to Kubie's plan. Physicians have argued that graduates of such professional schools might confuse the public into thinking they were physicians although they would lack the proper medical training or legal sanctions for prescribing medication, handling hospitalization, or carrying out other medical activities. Psychologists have criticized the plan as being too tied to a medical model, particularly a psychoanalytic one, which they find outdated. Many

his suggestions have been incorporated into existing university training programs in clinical psychology, the seventh item has not been adopted, perhaps reflecting the university's attitude toward psychotherapy or its belief that the suggestion's execution is not feasible.

critics believe psychotherapy is too narrow a base on which to form a profession—a conclusion also reached at the Chicago Conference. Some argue that mental health problems in this country can never be solved by simply producing more therapists; a preventive approach is necessary, and any new profession should devote itself to prevention rather than individual treatment.

THE DOCTOR OF PSYCHOLOGY (PSY.D.) PROGRAM WITHIN A PSYCHOLOGY DEPARTMENT

Rather than create a new profession that would require much groundbreaking, psychology departments might commit themselves to training clinicians at the highest levels of professional competence, free of both medical and the usual academic constraints. It is an open secret that many Ph.D.s become primarily or even exclusively practitioners despite the university's heavy investment in training them in research methodology. In addition, the public wants the practicing clinicians' services. Consequently, a more realistic and honest approach might be to train those clinical students interested in becoming service-oriented clinical psychologists to be just that. The Psychology Department at the University of Illinois has launched such a program—the usual Ph.D. degree program is for those interested in a research career and the Psy.D. degree program is for those interested in a professional career of clinical service (Peterson, 1968).

Efforts to proceed with a new professional degree program follow from certain inadequacies in the present training of clinical psychologists for professional practice. Current training programs leading to the Ph.D. are too lengthy. This is especially true in clinical psychology, where the student receives all of the usual graduate training to prepare him as a scientist, to which must be added the additional training to provide professional preparation. As a consequence, professional training is usually inadequate or downgraded, or perhaps put off to postdoctoral years, where it may never be obtained. In addition, current programs tend to select students who show promise as research scientists. Sometimes the student unable to master advanced statistics or experimental design is dropped from a graduate program despite his interest and competence in the area of clinical service.

Advocates of the professional degree program point out that the scientist–professional model, cherished since the Boulder Conference, has failed to fulfill its promise of producing the unique clinician, equally scientist and professional. Actually, data from surveys such as Levy's (1962) suggest that the interests of clinical psychologists are distributed bimodally, indicating a tendency to pursue a career in practice or research, but rarely in both. The Illinois position is that no feasible reconstruction of current Ph.D. programs is likely to change the fact that by tradition the Ph.D. is a scholarly degree, deeply ingrained in academic values, and designed to prepare graduates for a lifetime career of creative activity and research, usually in association with a teaching career at a university. However, the university does offer a number of professional doctoral degrees (in medicine, dentistry, engineering, education, business administration, public health) which do provide academic preparation for professional practice. The Psy.D. is meant to be such a professional degree.

The Illinois program frankly recognizes that some clinical students have a strong interest in professional service and little interest in research, while others hold the reverse priorities. Each deserves to be trained as effectively as possible toward achieving his goal. The professionally oriented student deserves the same status and acceptance within the university that the research-oriented student receives. He is less likely to get such recognition in many current programs where clinical psychology is denigrated as unscientific and unscholarly.

Under the Illinois plan, in progress since 1968, students are to be selected by the usual intellectual criteria, but in addition, admittance is to be determined by interest, by "psychosocial competence," or by indications of commitment to public service, such as voluntary participation in state hospital programs or the Peace Corps. Once admitted to the clinical psychology program, the student need not decide which option—research or service—he will pursue until the second year of his four-year program. Throughout the graduate program, there is a common core of course work and practical experience in clinical psychology for all students, in addition to specialized courses unique to either the Ph.D. or Psy.D. program.

The curriculum as currently planned (Peterson, 1968) is as follows:

First Year: A common core of courses for all clinical students, including a proseminar in general psychology, an introduction to clinical psychology, training in quantitative methods and research design, and courses in personality theory and behavior disorders.

Second Year: A common core of courses, including behavior assessment, social development, and behavior modification. Ph.D. candidates to begin research work on master's thesis. Psy.D. candidates to take courses in basic medicine, community psychology, educational counseling, and the special education of exceptional children.

Third Year: All students to complete a common practicum in clinical psychology and two laboratory courses in clinical psychology, ordinarily in individual psychotherapy and in behavioral desensitization procedures. Ph.D. candidates to engage in research and complete work in minor field. Psy.D. candidates to begin clerkship in field agency and enroll in additional clinical laboratories (e.g. assessment, group therapy, community action) as well as courses in the diagnosis and remediation of learning disabilities.

Fourth Year: Ph.D. candidates to complete dissertation. Psy.D. candidates to complete full-time internship, with varying proportions of time in clinics or hospitals with children and adults.

Recognizing that the student's interest may change or that he may desire to have the best of both training programs (and both doctoral degrees), the Illinois plan provides for graduates of the Ph.D. program to obtain a postdoctoral internship and additional laboratory training in clinical procedures over two years to earn the Psy.D. degree. Doctors of Psychology who want to obtain the Ph.D. can do so after two additional years of study that include conducting thesis research.

Professional sanction for the Psy.D. has come from the Education and Training Board (APA, 1970), which granted the Illinois program provisional approval pending its anticipated meeting of APA full-accreditation criteria in the next several years. The Chicago Conference also gave the Illinois program some encouragement to launch the program on an experimental basis. The Illinois plan is consistent with the recommendations of the Clark Committee (APA, 1965). The Psy.D. graduate will probably qualify for state licenses throughout the country. The Illinois plan has received support from those who advocate a professional degree earned from an established and respected source—the university psychology department—while challenging the Kubie plan as too medical in orientation and built on the too-narrow base of psychotherapy.

On the other hand, many clinicians have been skeptical and cautious, if not sometimes suspicious, of the Illinois plan for psychology departments to offer two types of graduate programs and two degrees. The following arguments have been mustered against such a plan: (1) the Psy. D. program is likely to acquire second-class status in the eyes of faculty, students, and the public; (2) the fact that support for the alternate doctorate comes from the unlikely quarter of academic psychology is suspect as being perhaps a device for shunting aside the bothersome problem of professional training in clinical psychology; (3) the profession of clinical psychology is in a state of flux, with new roles and practices emerging, making this a particularly inappropriate time to create a new profession with activities that are only dimly foreseeable at present and whose present clinical skills may soon be obsolete; (4) two parallel programs, producing two different degrees, will tend to separate clinical practice from the rest of psychology even further, thus cutting the profession off from its scientific roots; (5) expert practitioners, necessary in a professional degree program, are likely to find it as difficult to be appointed and later promoted at the university as is the case now of competent clinical professors who do not publish research findings; and (6) future graduates of such programs are likely to be stigmatized because of their different degree and different training.

THE AUTONOMOUS PROFESSIONAL SCHOOL PROGRAM

The polarization within psychology between scientists and practitioners that Albee (1970) described (see p. 73) is demonstrated by some major universities: they have abandoned their doctoral programs for training clinical psychologists altogether, returning to their traditional task of producing research scientists. Other universities have tended to dilute what professional training they offer, or to relegate such training to the postdoctoral years. Many academicians, like Coffey (1970), have concluded that while the scientist–professional model has certain merits, it is basically unrealistic in practice and therefore obsolete. Here he is joined by a recently formed militant group of professional psychologists, the National Council on Graduate Education in Psychology (Matulef & Rothenberg, 1968). This group represents a coalition of psychologists who have been lobbying within APA for the upgrading of psychology's national commitment to the professional preparation of future psychologists. The Council has been particularly critical of what they consider the inadequacies of current professional training programs, of APA's accreditation structure and criteria, and of APA's lack of responsiveness to professional and societal needs. They urge APA to take a more active part in developing clinical psychology into an independent profession. Responding to what they consider a crisis in clinical training, NCGEP suggests the immediate development of a university professional school to train service-oriented graduate students to work in clinical, counseling, and community psychology (Matulef & Rothenberg, 1969). Another possibility is to establish an independent professional school developed, administered, and staffed by professionals within the community and sponsored by professional organizations at the state or local level. One such school, the California School of Professional Psychology, opened in 1970, and two others, in New York and New Jersey, are being developed.

The California School of Professional Psychology (CSPP), sponsored by the California State Psychological Association, challenges two assumptions on which professional clinical training has been based for 25 years —that existing Ph.D. programs, with some curriculum modifications, are appropriate vehicles for clinical training, and that these programs are most appropriately staffed and administered by academic departments of psychology. Instead, the California School is built on two different assumptions: (1) that equally effective, if not more effective, programs of professional training can be based on a curriculum integrated with practical experiences at all levels, beginning with the A.A. degree as the basis for a paraprofessional cadre on through to the Ph.D.; and (2) that these new programs are most appropriately administered and planned by faculties of professional psychologists, whether the professional school is established in a university setting or operates autonomously in the community (Pottharst, 1970).

Reversing the usual priorities, CSPP proposes that training be made more consistent with professional practice by training psychologists to be professionals first and scientists second, clinicians to be clinicians first and researchers second. Moreover, such training is considered to be best provided by a faculty made up of knowledgeable, experienced psychologists actually doing professional work in various settings. In addition, the California School proposes to integrate subdoctoral and doctoral training in an effort, neglected at the university, to train paraprofessionals (as well as professionals) for community intervention programs. Finally, use of various training settings is planned—comprehensive mental health centers, correctional settings, schools, psychological service centers, group practices—in contrast to existing training programs at the university which for the most part continue to use predominantly medical and/or psychiatric settings for their students' internships.

That the California School of Professional Psychology intends to be more than a school for psychotherapists is apparent immediately from the proposed curriculum. Far more than a clinical program alone, CSPP stresses its comprehensive program of instruction in all of professional psychology, including such areas of specialization as assessment, clinical, community, counseling, industrial, school, and social psychology. Four degree programs are planned, making for flexible career exit and reentry points: (1) the A.A. degree, qualifying the recipient to function as a skilled sub- or paraprofessional; (2) the B.A. degree, making one eligible for advanced training; (3) the M.A. degree, qualifying one as a competent craftsman in a psychological specialty, capable of working with minimum general supervision; and (4) the Ph.D. degree, based on course work, supervised professional work in one major and two minor specialties, and a completed doctoral dissertation, qualifying him for independent professional work in his chosen specialties (CSPP, 1970).

The curriculum is a sequential program built around seven major areas in each year of study:

1. Field experience in professional psychology—includes a variety of institutional settings: educational, occupational, religious, medical, judicial, economic. Advanced students to perform professional services under supervision in an internship program in schools, hospitals, community agencies, and so on.
2. Theory courses—includes principles of developmental, abnormal, and social psychology, biochemistry and the physical sciences, historical and contemporary issues in psychology. Advanced students to study theories of clinical assessment, counseling, and psychotherapy, as well as small-group theory with special reference to family and group therapy.
3. Culture and society—includes community organization, economic theory, and a study of American institutions and government. Study of Afro–American, Mexican–American, Jewish, and Oriental cultures. Cross-cultural and social-class concepts of mental health and illness. Psychological aspects of current social issues. Cultural anthropology.
4. Scientific, scholarly investigation—includes fundamentals of professional and scientific communication, statistics and measurement, data

gathering and analysis, philosophy of science, research design, techniques of program evaluation, computer technology, individual research projects (including dissertation for Ph.D. candidates).

5. Professional skills and issues—includes principles of professional conduct and ethics, theory and techniques of supervision, including advanced graduate students supervising A.A. candidates. Advanced seminars in special topics in professional psychology—geriatrics, forensic psychology, epidemiology.

6. Humanities and the arts—includes conversational fluency in a foreign language. Folk culture, children's art, contemporary adolescent subculture. Cultural history of the U.S. Study of myths and symbolism, expressive techniques, body movements, psychodrama. Analysis of contemporary art, music, and literature as related to psychology. Selected problems in philosophy.

7. Personal growth—includes participation in group processes related to field work experiences, group therapy, and individual psychotherapy.

The above curriculum suggests that the California School does not intend to sacrifice breadth or excellence for practicality; rather, it aims to provide a new realistic model of training, steeped in the humanities, social sciences, and education. Its ultimate purpose is to prepare the independently functioning Ph.D. professional psychologist while integrating such training with the preparation of paraprofessionals to meet this country's mental health needs (Joint Commission on Mental Illness and Health, 1961). Rather than offer a new doctoral degree, the Ph.D. is retained since it has traditionally been the highest degree in psychology and because CSPP graduates will presumably have completed considerable work in scientific investigations, including the doctoral dissertation. Pottharst (1970) suggests that CSPP Ph.D.s will have the research capacity to carry out scientific investigations more relevant to clinical practice or professional problems than Ph.D.s educated to be scientist–professionals.

The professional school of psychology, a challenging and exciting innovation in training, is not without its critics. Many of the same arguments mustered against the Illinois plan have been cited—graduates will acquire second-class status, the scientific and professional aspects of psychology will be polarized even further, the launching of such a program now is inappropriate. In addition, some are alarmed that the structure of a professional school inevitably makes for a narrow trade school–type education, rather than producing the broad generalist needed to create new future programs. Others have questioned whether clinical psychology, at this stage of its development, has accumulated enough knowledge to develop a strictly professional program. Many are uneasy about moving training outside established psychology departments, even more so outside the university itself. Critics contend that such a move robs the student of the stimulation of rich resources of other departments in the university. Most of these critics believe the technical education of the professional-school graduate is so limited, stereotypic, and problem-centered that he is not likely to be responsive to changing conditions in society.

Many questions have been raised about training paraprofessionals in a school of psychology. While acknowledging the need for such people to increase the manpower pool, critics fear that since paraprofessionals would receive some training in psychology, the public might confuse them with professionals, which would lower the quality of professional services. State certification and licensing laws at present require the doctorate; these would need to be changed. Social regulation by the public is difficult to achieve at best, particularly for licensed practitioners in private practice; attempting to regulate paraprofessionals who might enter private practice under more relaxed laws would be all the more difficult.

Perhaps the strongest criticism, certainly the most emotionally charged one, involves the move to create a professional school independent of the university. The practical problem of continuous funding and accreditation must be met. Beyond that, many psychologists show considerable uneasiness about loosening ties with the traditional academic structure of the university. Some critics have challenged the Ph.D. as the ultimate degree of such a program, claiming that that degree is properly reserved for the demonstration of creative activity and scholarship. Bard (1970), for one, prefers the Illinois plan of two separate doctoral degrees as offering a clearer distinction between scholarship and practice as well as providing greater flexibility should a graduate of one program wish, with additional training, to engage also in the other.

ASPECTS OF PROFESSIONAL PRACTICE

Post-World War II demands for clinical services helped force APA to face up to the problems of professionalism. In addition to offering guidelines for establishing university programs offering professional training, APA was asked to deal with issues concerning professional practice. One immediate problem concerned the need for greater clarity about psychology's relation to psychiatry. A related problem dealt with efforts to achieve state-by-state legislation governing psychological practice, since such efforts tended to arouse opposition from medical and psychiatric groups. Within psychology itself, public protection demanded some self-regulatory procedures such as a code of ethical practice and methods to certify professional competence.

CRITERIA OF A GOOD PROFESSION

By 1951, it was clear to Fillmore Sanford, then executive secretary of APA, that "the professionalization of psychology is our big problem [Sanford, 1951, p. 667]." His sampling of the membership revealed that the vast majority of respondents listed the major problems facing APA as legislation, training standards, interprofessional relations, public relations, intraprofessional cleavages, and psychology's need to contribute to social goals. All of these problems, according to Sanford, were related to the general problems of psychology's growth as a profession.

Sanford attempted to describe the characteristics of a good profession as a guideline for how the emerging profession of psychology might develop in its own way, without necessarily emulating older, better established professions. Sanford's criteria, with slight modification, were later adopted in an official APA statement concerning a good profession: "a profession that will make its maximum contribution to society, one that will allow each psychologist, whatever his particular field of interest and competence, to work at his best, and one that will permit any individual possessed of humanistic and democratic values a justifiable pride in his profession [APA, 1954, p. 4]."

The following are APA's goals for psychology:

1. A good profession guides its practices and policies by a sense of social responsibility.
2. A good profession will devote relatively little of its energy to "guild" functions, to the building of its own in-group strength, and relatively much of its energy to serving its social functions.

3. A good profession will not represent itself as able to render services outside its demonstrable competence.
4. A good profession has a code of ethics designed primarily to protect the client and only secondarily to protect the members of the profession.
5. A good profession will find its unique pattern of competences and focus its efforts on carrying out those functions for which it is best equipped.
6. A good profession will engage in rational and cooperative relations with other professions having related or overlapping competences and common purposes.
7. A good profession will be characterized by an adaptive balance among efforts devoted to research, to teaching, and to application.
8. A good profession will maintain good channels of communication among the "discoverers," the teachers, and the appliers of knowledge.
9. A good profession is free of nonfunctional entrance requirements.
10. A good profession is one in which preparatory training is validly related to the ultimate function of the members of the profession.
11. A good profession will guard against adopting any technique or theory as the final solution to its problems.
12. A good profession is one whose members are socially and financially accessible to the public.
13. A good profession is a free profession [APA, 1954, p. 4].

THE FULLY FUNCTIONING PROFESSIONAL PERSON

By the 1960s, most practicing clinicians felt less self-conscious about their professional status than Sanford's earlier statement implied. Having banded together into various local clinical societies around the country, many were beginning to insist that APA pay more attention to both the professional preparation and the professional practice of clinical psychology. In particular, the Los Angeles Society of Clinical Psychologists (1964) called for a consideration of the clinical psychologist as a "fully functioning professional person" with certain characteristic attributes:

1. He renders a service or services.
2. He takes sole responsibility for his services; he is not ancillary to nor yields that responsibility to any other professional person.

3. He adheres to a code of ethics.
4. He possesses at least minimum standards of competence based upon specific attainments in the areas of knowledge, skills, and values.
5. He has a firm sense of identity as a member of his profession.
6. He receives sanctions and rewards from society for the services he renders, and those services in return meet important needs of society.
7. He is an emerging, growing person in the pursuit of his professional functions.
8. His work is open to the scrutiny of his peers.
9. He is committed to the advancement of the basic scientific substrate of his profession.
10. He is concerned with training—with the professional preparation of the younger members of the calling who will succeed him.
11. He is concerned with and participates in the organizations which order the existence of his profession.

LASCP's statement represented the militant stance of a group of clinicians who were issuing a "declaration of independence," insisting on their rights as autonomous professionals. They were prepared to battle, within psychology, for recognition of clinical psychology as a profession deserving first-class status. At the same time, they were also declaring their identity as unique professionals, no longer content to be ancillary to psychiatry, as had been the case for the previous 20 years.

RELATIONS WITH PSYCHIATRY—THE ISSUE OF INDEPENDENT PRIVATE PRACTICE

Prior to World War II, there was little common training or work experiences for clinical psychologists and psychiatrists. The former were trained in an academic atmosphere that was basically intellectual and theoretical and stressed research and scholarship. The latter received their training in medical school, supplemented by internship and residency training, which stressed the acquisition of skills and the performance of pragmatic, problem-solving, clinical services. The clinical psychologist was apt to work in university-related activities such as teaching, testing, and educational or vocational counseling. The psychiatrist's work situation was in a mental hospital or clinic or, to a lesser extent, in private practice.

During World War II, psychologists were assigned responsibilities previously reserved for persons with psychiatric training. Psychiatrists and clinical psychologists soon discovered that they were carrying out similar functions, despite wide differences in background and preparation. In the post-war years, particularly as psychologists received clinical training at the university and at internship stations in hospitals or clinics, both professions increasingly overlapped in their training and the clinical services they offered. Inevitably, misunderstandings, rivalries, and jurisdictional disputes resulted, particularly as psychologists moved into the independent private practice of psychotherapy.

Both the American Psychological Association and the American Psychiatric Association agreed immediately after the war to establish a joint committee to deal with the strain developing between the two professions. Early reports of the committee tended to offer somewhat "bland principles [Hildreth, 1967]": endorsement of the American Board of Examiners in Professional Psychology, encouragement of research on better selection of candidates for training in both psychiatry and psychology, agreement on the team approach between disciplines, the need for extending scientific knowledge through research. The basic contention over whether to recognize (and how to regulate) the psychologist in the private practice of psychotherapy was politely avoided.

In 1949, the American Psychological Association declared itself opposed to the practice of psychotherapy by clinical psychologists that did not involve collaboration with physicians. The American Medical Association (1954) went even further, declaring psychotherapy to be a form of medical treatment that did not form the basis for the separate profession of clinical psychology. When the American Psychiatric Association adopted the AMA report as its official policy in 1958 and went on record as rescinding any earlier approval of legal certification for psychologists, the battle lines were drawn. Aroused by the official psychiatric view that all psychotherapy was solely within the domain of medically trained persons, the American Psychological Association (1958) moved to protect its members' rights to pursue their own profession by declaring its intention to attempt to defeat amendments to any basic science or medical practice acts that would restrict the role and practice of psychology. In addition, APA expressed its willingness to join in the legal defense (including its costs) of any member engaged in professional practice who was charged with the practice of medicine for engaging in psychotherapy.

Beginning in the early 1960s relations between the two professional groups grew somewhat more amicable. A joint committee representing both APAs (the American Psychological Association and the American Psychiatric Association) has continued to meet and has attempted to draw up statements agreeable to both professions. In the meantime, opposition by medical and psychiatric organizations to legislation licensing or certifying psychologists has been tempered for the most part. The private practice of psychotherapy by psychologists is by now a fait accompli in many parts of the country, although some medical groups continue to insist that such practice be under the direct supervision or at least in genuine collaboration with physicians. Many psychologists in practice tend to ignore the emphasis on medical direction, insisting that theirs is an autonomous profession.

Today, the professions coexist. Individual psychologists and psychiatrists continue to have satisfactory and cooperative working relationships. Particularly within medical settings such as hospitals, clinics, or medical schools, there tends to be minimal interprofessional conflict since roles and responsibilities in a team approach are more easily defined. The major conflict remaining between the professions continues to be over independent private practice, an area of increasing activity for clinical psychologists.

Psychiatrists continue to criticize the adequacy or competence of psychologists to engage in independent professional practice. Psychiatrists, being physicians, are said to be better prepared through training and experience to assume clinical responsibility for their patients. Both their internship and residency include 24-hour responsibilities in contrast to the eight-hour working day of the psychology trainee. Psychologists in training usually are younger than psychiatrists, less experienced in being responsible for their decisions, and have more academic, but less practical orientation toward their patients (Sternbach, Abroms, & Rice, 1969). Psychiatrists are thus allegedly better prepared to meet clinical emergencies. In addition, it is sometimes argued that the psychiatrist's medical background makes him better able to recognize physical disease in his patient and to differentiate physical from psychogenic etiology. Finally, psychiatrists are legally permitted to dispense drugs, use shock treatment, hospitalize patients, and sign commitment papers, which nonmedical therapists cannot do.

On the other hand, Szasz (1959) and Mariner (1967), both psychiatrists, take exception to the view that psychotherapy is a medical specialty, the exclusive province of psychiatry. Szasz argues that the subject matter and methods of medicine and psychotherapy differ in fundamental ways—the former views the body as a physiochemical machine, the latter views man as a social being; the former's methods are physical and chemical, the latter's interpersonal communication. He points out further that psychotherapy can hardly be considered a medical specialty when so many medically untrained people contribute to its theory and practice. Among the best-known psychotherapists in the world, many—such as Erich Fromm, Carl Rogers, Rollo May, Anna Freud, Melanie Klein, Erik Erikson, Theodore Reik, Otto Rank, and numerous others—are not physicians.

Mariner (1967) tackles the issue of clinical responsibility by pointing out that, operationally, one assumes responsibility when one agrees to perform a particular function, and that responsibility is defined and limited by one's professional field: should an ophthalmologist hospitalize a patient for eye surgery, he is likely to ask a general physician or internist to do the routine physical examination; if his patient develops post-operative pneumonia, he will not diagnose and treat the new condition, but again would call in the appropriate colleague. The psychiatrist, likewise, would not be expected to examine, diagnose, or treat his patient for physical diseases. He has assumed responsibility only for his patient's mental health—a nonmedical task equally appropriate to clinical psychologists. In reality, psychotherapy patients are not subjected to periodic physical examinations by either medical or nonmedical therapists. If the patient required medical attention, both would recommend outside medical consultation.

Mariner questions further whether the traditional medical view of taking responsibility for the patient is not actually detrimental to efforts to get the patient to take the responsibility for his own existence. Many so-called medical emergencies, such as suicide threats, are important and serious, but are not necessarily medical. Mariner suggests that they might more appropriately be called an "existential or humanistic emergency."

Mariner argues further that despite their medical training, psychiatrists in practice for a number of years tend not to trust their own abilities as physical diagnosticians except in the most obvious situations. While psychiatrists sometimes use psychotropic drugs (tranquilizers, antidepressants, sedatives, and stimulants), Mariner believes the long medical education is wasteful and inappropriate for the practice of psychotherapy. He reasons further that medical training is not in any way operationally necessary for the performance of administrative functions such as the signing of commitment papers, testifying to legal sanity, and so on; psychologists are generally restricted from doing so, not because they lack knowledge or judgment but because institutional regulations do not permit them to do so.

It is clear that neither profession has a monopoly on omniscience or virtue. Both require considerable training that many practitioners deem irrelevant to their work. Existing conflicts are largely over status, territory, and—to some extent—financial competition. Psychologists, particularly those in private practice, are not likely to settle for anything but first-class citizenship. Increasingly, such a view is supported by APA.

STATE LEGISLATION—THE REGULATION OF PSYCHOLOGICAL PRACTICE

Some form of regulation over professional psychological practice is necessary in order to insure that practitioners have met high professional standards and that the public is protected by knowing which psychologists have met these standards. Since sovereignty over such regulatory functions belongs to the states, efforts to obtain the necessary legislation have been carried on for the most part by state psychological associations, with APA attempting to provide guidelines developed in conjunction with the American Psychiatric Association.

Psychologists have sought two legal means to regulate and certify professional competence before permitting professional practice: licensing and certification. A *licensure law,* the more restrictive of the two, defines the practice of psychology by specifying which services the psychologist is qualified to offer the public. Such a law denies the person without a license the right to engage in such activities. A *certification law,* on the other hand, simply certifies the use of the title "psychologist," denying to all who are not certified the right to refer to themselves by that title. Such a law does not restrict practice or define permissible activities, but simply guarantees that the title "psychologist" (or "certified psychologist") will be used only by people who meet the standards established in the law.

The first legislation certifying psychologists was approved by the Connecticut Legislature in 1945. Since then, efforts have continued, on a state-by-state basis, with more or less opposition depending on the particular state's situation, until the present. In general, certification has been easier to obtain than licensure, since it has aroused less opposition from other professions (education, law, the ministry) whose use of psychological procedures might be curtailed by a licensing law that restricted those procedures to psychologists. Moreover, organized medical groups have tended to oppose licensure laws for psychologists as being in direct conflict with state medical-practices acts over the practice of psychotherapy. Their stand on certification laws has varied from time to time and from state to state, but generally has been more accepting of certification. Officially, the American Psychiatric Association stands opposed to any form of legislative sanction for the independent practice of clinical psychology, but such opposition has not been, nor is it likely to be, implemented by any efforts to obtain legislative restrictions on psychologists.

As an alternative to legislation creating certifying or licensing laws, some states have established *nonstatutory certifying boards* under the aegis of psychological associations in states without statutory controls. Although such associations lack legal powers, they may insist on certain standards being met before issuing a nonstatutory certificate, with efforts made to inform the public in that state regarding the meaning of such a certificate. Such a move is generally a stopgap, self-regulatory measure, as efforts are carried out to obtain the proper legislation. Once obtained, the nonstatutory boards are dissolved.

By 1971, psychologists were in the home stretch of obtaining statutory regulation of psychological practice in every state and in all Canadian provinces. As of 1971, 43 states, the District of Columbia, and six Canadian provinces had some form of licensing or certification. In addition, seven states and one province had nonstatutory certification programs.

The following states had enacted licensing laws by 1971:

Alabama	Kentucky	Tennessee
Alaska	Maine	Texas
Arkansas	Montana	Virginia
California	Nebraska	West Virginia
Colorado	New Jersey	Wisconsin
Florida	North Carolina	District of Columbia
Georgia	Oklahoma	
Idaho	South Carolina	

The following states and provinces had certification laws:

Arizona	Minnesota	Washington
Connecticut	Mississippi	Wyoming
Delaware	Nevada	Alberta
Hawaii	New Hampshire	Manitoba
Illinois	New Mexico	New Brunswick
Indiana	New York	Ontario
Kansas	North Dakota	Quebec
Louisiana	Oregon	Saskatchewan
Maryland	Rhode Island	
Michigan	Utah	

Nonstatutory programs, administered by state or provincial psychological associations, still existed in:

Iowa	Ohio	Vermont
Massachusetts	Pennsylvania	British Columbia
Missouri	South Dakota	

There is a considerable uniformity in standards from state to state. Most state laws contain a clause guaranteeing reciprocity, essentially an endorsement of the certificate or license granted in another state or province with at least equal standards, without the necessity of being reexamined in the new state in which the psychologist wishes to practice. With few exceptions, a doctorate from a recognized university is required, generally supplemented by two or more years of experience. Some states (Colorado, Minnesota, for example) require that such experience be postdoctoral. Almost all states require an examination, after initially admitting those experienced practitioners who are in practice at the time of legislation but who do not meet the law's formal educational requirements. (This is called "grandfathering.") In 1961, an American Association of State Psychology Boards was created to facilitate communication among state examining boards and to help maintain uniform standards (Henderson & Hildreth, 1965).

ETHICAL STANDARDS OF PSYCHOLOGISTS

As a profession grows, particularly as it moves away from its familiar, clearly defined academic base, it must develop an ethical code that will govern its expanded roles, responsibilities, and activities and protect the public against unethical behavior by its practitioners. In the late 1940s several APA committees were formed to look into the ethical issues and practices involved in various types of professional and scientific activities in which psychologists were engaged. Rather than formulate a set of ethical principles on an a priori basis, these committees called upon all APA members to submit descriptions of actual instances in their work experiences where ethical issues had arisen. In thus deriving a set of ethical principles on an empirical basis, the committee listed examples of good, poor, and undetermined ethical conduct to help guide their colleagues' judgment and behavior. The complete list of principles, together with illustrative examples from various work areas (practice, teaching, research, writing for publication, interprofessional relationships) were then published and distributed to all APA members in a booklet entitled *Ethical Standards of Psychologists* (APA, 1953). Of particular interest to clinicians were the ethical standards recommended in psychologist–client relationships. These included: (1) an honest representation of professional qualifications and the maintenance of a high standard of service; (2) standards to insure safeguarding the welfare of the client; (3) guarding confidential information; (4) reporting the results of clinical work in a manner most likely to serve the best interest of clients; (5) standards for establishing fees for clinical services; (6) standards for making referrals; (7) standards for handling medical problems of psychotherapy clients; and (8) standards for advertising or making public announcements of the availability of psychological services.

The present version of the APA code of ethics was adopted in 1963. It emphasizes the psychologist's belief in the dignity and worth of the individual, his commitment to increasing man's understanding of himself and others, and his ethical concern with protecting the welfare of clients or subjects, human or animal. Nineteen principles are enumerated, establishing specific standards of responsibility, competence, client welfare, representations to the public, use of psychological tests and their interpretations, research precautions and publication credits, as well as interprofessional relations, remunerations, and promotional activities.

APA's code of ethics is under continuing reassessment as new issues arise or old issues appear in new situations. For example, an ad hoc Committee on Ethical Standards in Psychological Research has recently been established (APA, 1968). Its purpose is to study the special ethical problems and procedure involved in psychological research on human subjects, an issue under increased public discussion and recent review by the Surgeon General. As with the first APA ethics committees, an empirical study is underway: psychologists are invited to submit specific examples of ethical decisions in research where conflicts may arise between the needs of science and the rights of individual subjects. As before, this procedure has two purposes: (1) to insure that the principles finally arrived at are actually relevant to the real problems of contemporary research and (2) to become more sensitive in identifying the actual ethical issues involved and moving toward consensus on good research practice. Ultimately, the committee will publish a set of principles underlying the actual decisions that responsible psychologists make when they follow what they regard as good ethical practice in research with human subjects.

AMERICAN BOARD OF PROFESSIONAL PSYCHOLOGY

In addition to legislation and the establishment of a code of ethics, another form of professional self-regulation consists of granting diplomas to certify the competence of specialists in certain applied fields of psychology. Not only does this provide an incentive for psychologists to achieve superior competence for which recognition and prestige will be forthcoming, but it offers the public greater confidence in the practitioners so certified. To this end, the American Board of Examiners in Professional Psychology was incorporated in 1947 as an independent corporation authorized to grant diplomas to specialists in three applied areas of professional psychology: clinical, counseling, and industrial psychology. Made up of a board of trustees from APA, ABEPP nevertheless was deliberately conceived as a separate corporate body with freedom to formulate its own independent policies and standards and be responsible for its own actions (Kelley, Sanford, & Clark, 1961).

By the fall of 1969, the board had awarded more than 1000 diplomas in clinical psychology on the basis of examination, and another 1647 under the initial "grandfather" clause. A fourth applied specialty, school psychology, has been added and the specialty of industrial psychology has been broadened and renamed industrial and organizational psychology. Of the four specialities, clinical psychology contributes almost 90 percent of all diplomates (Ross, 1970b).

The word "examiners" was dropped from the title in 1968, symbolizing the efforts of ABPP's board to be more than an examining committee, one that is also concerned with policy planning, validity research, and review of the professional field as a whole. In order to qualify for admission to the ABPP examination, now under the direction of regional directors in various parts of the country, a candidate must: (1) hold membership in APA or the Canadian Psychological Association; (2) have a Ph.D. degree in psychology from a university having APA approval for doctoral training in the applicant's specialty; and (3) show evidence of five years of acceptable qualifying professional experience. Written examinations, long part of the proceedings, have now been abolished, and oral examinations have been restructured to reflect the changing nature of professional practice and the diversity of roles, theoretical viewpoints, and techniques now prevalent.

The clinical psychology applicant is required to submit copies of one or more samples of his work. These samples may be verbatim or summarized accounts of his interactions with a client. In addition, the candidate is likely to be observed by the examiners in a session with a client with whom he has had no previous contact. The oral examination covers four areas: (1) appraisal, assessment, evaluation, diagnosis; (2) change, modification, treatment, consultation; (3) ethics and professional attitudes; and (4) utilization of research and theory in practice.

The meaning of the ABPP diploma has been debated since its initial issuance. Some practitioners have been critical, arguing that it suggests the imitation of medical specialty boards. Some have protested the investment of time, money, and the anticipated anxiety in being tested after having been away from such academic rituals for some years. However, being a Diplomate of the American Board of Professional Psychology appears increasingly to bring benefits. Federal civil service standards now explicitly state that ABPP should be considered in selecting psychologists for government service. Several governmental agencies grant a higher grade-level or a raise for ABPP diplomates. Thirty states now waive the state licensing or certification examinations for those who have earned the ABPP diploma by examination (Zimet, 1969). Within the profession, ABPP diplomate status carries prestige and warrants APA approval for engaging in independent private practice.

While the 1970s find the profession of clinical psychology firmly established, many urgent and critical problems nevertheless remain. Clinical psychology, much like other professions, is undergoing considerable internal strife and dissonance as it seeks new directions relevant to its awakening social responsibilities. At the same time, as the academic community reappraises its programs and purposes, many psychology departments are finding it urgent to reexamine a 25-year-old training model's current relevance and future applicability. The scientist–professional model has not produced the Renaissance psychologist. In practice, graduates of programs stressing such a model have rarely been scientific enough to suit the scientists (such as experimental psychologists) and rarely professional enough to suit the professionals (such as psychiatrists). The conflict within the profession is perhaps best illustrated by the irony of Albee's (1970) predicting the demise of clinical psychology almost on the same day as the first autonomous professional school of psychology opened its doors in California.

The profession is gripped by many problems and contradictions that it will have to resolve. For example, it has become commonplace for many clinical psychologists to reject the medical model at the same time that they demand full recognition (and reimbursement) under health insurance programs as health practitioners. The role of psychologists in any of the national health programs expected soon will need to be clarified. So will the issue of whether clinical psychology continues as a single level (that is, doctoral) profession, or becomes a multilevel profession with different kinds of work and responsibility commensurate with different levels of training. Clearly, adoption of the multilevel view, consistent with the needs for an expanded manpower source, will have many implications for academic training programs, professional work activities, and revisions in existing state laws regulating the practice of psychology.

New work situations, new forms of professional practice, new roles, conflicting demands, and multiple loyalties are likely to produce numerous problems for future clinical psychologists. Updated ethical guidelines are likely to become necessary as psychologists move into such unchartered areas as sensitivity training, weekend marathon group therapy, innovative techniques in individual psychotherapy, use of nonprofessional therapists, and research with human subjects. ABPP examination standards for establishing clinical competence, already undergoing change, will be strained even further as psychologists move beyond their traditional roles as diagnosticians, therapists, and researchers.

Clinical psychology is moving toward making its knowledge and skills more accessible and more responsive to the public. A variety of clinical services are available in a variety of community settings. Perhaps one hallmark of this trend is the recently announced new clinical training program at Harvard University. Basing its program on an interdepartmental structure, faculty are drawn from social relations, medicine, education, and the divinity school. Significantly, the intent of the program is reflected in its title *Clinical Psychology and Public Practice* (Hersch, 1969).

PART II Contemporary Clinical Psychology—Practice and Research

CHAPTER 4 *Clinical Judgment in Diagnosis and Assessment*

Every clinical judgment is partly based on diagnostic impressions of the client. Whether the clinician intuitively senses the internal conflicts producing his client's overt behavior or whether he deduces the meaning of such behavior rationally, by weighing all obtained data, he is engaged in a diagnostic process. The more experienced the clinician, the more sensitive he may become to subtle cues, the more his integration of data may take place at a subliminal level. He is often unable to reconstruct the step-by-step procedure he followed or to spell out a set of rules for it, particularly if his judgments were based on an intuitive process. However, the clinician may have followed certain procedures, even though he might not have been aware of their precise nature at any given moment. Actually, all clinical judgments or insights reflect the clinician's implicit value system as well as certain of his theoretical assumptions. These, together with his experience, determine how he perceives and organizes all incoming data about the client and how he draws clinical inferences and reaches certain diagnostic conclusions.

THE NATURE OF PSYCHIATRIC DIAGNOSIS

While some clinicians reject the formal diagnostic process as sheer ritual unrelated to future treatment or as a mere vestige of medical practice, others find the process useful to help predict the patient's behavior at a higher level of accuracy than could otherwise be obtained (Levy, 1963). In clinical medicine, accurate diagnosis is essential for supplying information regarding etiology, pathogenesis (the development of the disease), the stage of the illness, as well as the indicated treatment and probable prognosis. While the etiology for the majority of psychiatric disorders is not yet known, diagnostic labeling may nevertheless be useful in providing: (1) a description of the client's behavior or symptoms; (2) some implications for treatment; and (3) a prediction of the course of his disorder (prognosis). Levy suggests that psychologists should stop distinguishing between diagnosis and prognosis; since diagnosis serves only to justify the prognosis, the two are inextricably related.

THE PSYCHIATRIC CLASSIFICATION SYSTEM

Psychiatry has tended to follow the medical model to classify diseases. Particularly noteworthy were German psychiatrist Emil Kraepelin's efforts: in the late nineteenth century, he systematized and classified the various manifestations of mental disorders then known. Kraepelin's position was that mental illnesses were similar to physical illnesses; therefore they could be grouped into classes in terms of symptoms, etiology, and the course of the disease. Kraepelin's comprehensive presentation resulted in widespread acceptance of a standard set of nosological categories for mental disorders. Kraepelin's system makes a fundamental distinction between neuroses and psychoses; it classifies all disorders as either organic (those in which some physical pathology can be shown to account for the affliction) or functional (those in which no physical pathology can be discovered). Both dichotomies have persisted in modern psychiatric thinking and have remained basic to all subsequent classification systems, including current systems.

Eugen Bleuler (1857–1939), a Swiss psychiatrist contemporary with both Kraepelin and Freud, reformulated some of Kraepelin's nosological categories in keeping with the then emerging psychological explanations of behavior disorders. Most significantly, Bleuler named and described the precise nature of schizophrenia and its various subcategories. Bleuler disagreed with Kraepelin's view (see pp. 48–49) that dementia praecox was an incurable disease that invariably resulted in progressive dementia. Instead, he proposed that good or poor prognosis depended largely on the specific manifestation of the disorder. According to Bleuler, the term *dementia praecox* should be replaced by the term *schizophrenia*, suggesting a splitting apart of various psychic functions such as thinking and feeling. The term *schizophrenia* is now in current psychiatric use.

Until World War II, Kraepelin's classification system, with some modifications such as those provided by Bleuler, was the basis for diagnosing all mental disorders. During the war, Army psychiatrists and psychologists found they needed some way to classify relatively minor personality disturbances found in soldiers. Since people with such disturbances had rarely appeared in public mental hospitals prior to the war, there had been no provision for classifying them in the Kraepelinian system. A tentative classification scheme was developed under the direction of William Menninger of the Army's Surgeon General's Office and was later used in Veterans Administration hospitals and clinics with ex-servicemen. Finally, the American Psychiatric Association (1952) published an updated diagnostic manual for classifying what came to be called abnormal reaction patterns. Considered to be the official psychiatric classification system in this country for many years, it too was recently revised (American Psychiatric Association, 1968). The new *Diagnostic and Statistical Manual of Mental Disorders* (usually referred to as DSM-II) differs from the 1952 version (DSM-I) in modifying the names of certain disorders (that is, using "mental retardation" instead of "mental deficiency"), adding new diagnostic labels (like drug dependence), broadening the entire system into 10 categories instead of the previous three, and encouraging the use of multiple diagnoses, difficult under the DSM-I system. Of particular significance in developing DSM-II has been the desire to facilitate communication across national boundaries by devising a diagnostic system compatible with the International Classification of Diseases developed by the World Health Organization in Geneva, Switzerland (Spitzer & Wilson, 1969). Table 2 presents an outline of the 1968 DSM-II diagnostic classification system.

PROS AND CONS OF DIAGNOSTIC CLASSIFICATION

Clinicians disagree over the philosophy, value, and even the procedures of psychiatric diagnosis. Critics see modern efforts at classification, such as DSM-II, as a throwback to Kraepelin's descriptive approach of delineating separate clinical categories (Jackson, 1969). While the taxonomic approach in any science is initially descriptive, relying primarily on phenotypical categorization, such superficial resemblances are discarded as

Table 2. Abbreviated list of 1968 American Psychiatric Association Classification of Mental Disorders*

MAJOR CATEGORY	TYPES	SPECIFICATION
I. Mental retardation	Borderline Mild Moderate Severe Profound Unspecified	Each type follows or is associated with: Infection or intoxication Trauma or physical agent Disorders of metabolism, growth or nutrition Gross brain disease (postnatal) Unknown prenatal influence Chromosomal abnormality Prematurity Major psychiatric disorder Psychosocial (environmental) deprivation Other condition
II. Organic brain syndromes (OBS)	Psychoses associated with OBS	Senile dementia Alcoholic psychosis Psychosis associated with intracranial infection
	Nonpsychotic OBS	Mental disorders not specified as psychotic but associated with physical conditions: Intracranial infection Brain trauma Epilepsy
III. Psychoses not attributed to physical conditions listed previously	Schizophrenia	Simple Hebephrenic Catatonic Catatonic type, excited Catatonic type, withdrawn Paranoid Acute schizophrenic episode Latent Residual Schizo-affective Schizo-affective, excited Schizo-affective, depressed Childhood Chronic undifferentiated Other schizophrenia

* After American Psychiatric Association (1968).

Table 2. (continued)

MAJOR CATEGORY	TYPES	SPECIFICATION
III. Psychoses not attributed to physical conditions listed previously (continued)	Major affective disorders	Involutional melancholia Manic-depressive illness, manic Manic-depressive illness, depressed Manic-depressive illness, circular Manic-depressive, circular, manic Manic-depressive, circular, depressed Other major affective disorder
	Paranoid states	Paranoia Involutional paranoid state Other paranoid state
	Other psychoses	Psychotic depressive reaction
IV. Neuroses	Anxiety Hysterical Hysterical, conversion type Hysterical, dissociative type Phobic Obsessive compulsive Depressive Neurasthenic Depersonalization Hypochondriacal Other neurosis	
V. Personality disorders and certain other nonpsychotic mental disorders	Personality disorders	Paranoid Cyclothymic Schizoid Explosive Obsessive compulsive Hysterical Asthenic Antisocial Passive–aggressive Inadequate Other specified types

Table 2. (continued)

MAJOR CATEGORY	TYPES	SPECIFICATION
V. Personality disorders and certain other nonpsychotic mental disorders (continued)	Sexual deviation	Homosexuality Fetishism Pedophilia Transvestitism Exhibitionism Voyeurism Sadism Masochism Other sexual deviation
	Alcoholism	Episodic excessive drinking Habitual excessive drinking Alcohol addiction Other alcoholism
	Drug dependence	Opium, opium alkaloids, and their derivatives Synthetic analgesics with morphine-like effects Barbiturates Other hypnotics and sedatives or tranquilizers Cocaine Cannabis sativa (hashish, marijuana) Other psychostimulants Hallucinogens Other drug dependence
VI. Psychophysiologic disorders	Skin Musculoskeletal Respiratory Cardiovascular Hemic and lymphatic Gastrointestinal Genitourinary Endocrine Organ of special sense (eye, ear) Other type	

Table 2. (continued)

MAJOR CATEGORY	TYPES	SPECIFICATION
VII. Special symptoms	Transient disorders of any severity, including psychotic proportions, that occur without any apparent underlying mental disorder and that represent an acute reaction to overwhelming environmental stress	Tics Enuresis Disturbances of speech, learning, sleep
VIII. Transient situational disturbances	Adjustment reaction of infancy Adjustment reaction of childhood Adjustment reaction of adolescence Adjustment reaction of adult life Adjustment reaction of late life	
IX. Behavioral disorders of childhood and adolescence	Disorders occurring in children or adolescents, more stable, internalized, and resistant to treatment than those in "VII. Special symptoms," but less severe than the psychotic, neurotic, or personality disorders	
X. Conditions without manifest psychiatric disorders and nonspecific conditions	Psychiatrically normal individuals who nevertheless have problems severe enough to warrant psychiatric examination	Marital, social, or occupational maladjustment

knowledge increases. Classification then proceeds according to geno-typical categories, such as grouping by common etiological factors (Hunt, Wittson, & Hunt, 1953). The 1968 American Psychiatric Association classi-fication system remains for the most part at the phenotypic level, with mental disorders grouped by symptoms rather than etiology. This implies that separate and distinct disease entities exist. Actually, different indi-viduals may develop the same symptoms for different reasons, and, con-versely, different symptoms may develop in different individuals based on the same etiology. Moreover, a person may exhibit features from several different syndromes simultaneously. As a result, psychiatric diagnosis tends to be unreliable (see pp. 121–126), to change over time for the same patient, and to differ markedly depending on the subjective impressions of the diagnostician. So-called textbook cases are rare.

A major criticism of the present psychiatric diagnostic categories is that they are inconsistent with one another. For example, while some categories are based strictly on known etiology (organic brain syndromes, for example), others are based on overt behavioral symptoms (disturbances of speech, tics), and still others on prognosis (transient situational dis-turbances). Some diagnostic categories are subjectively descriptive (anti-social personality), some a combination of descriptive and presumed etiological factors (adjustment reaction of adolescence), others predomi-nantly etiological (psychophysiologic disorders). While it is recognized that ideally and for the sake of consistency, psychiatric disorders should all be classified by etiology, the present state of psychiatry lacks knowl-edge of the causes of most mental disorders (Eysenck, 1961).

From a humanistic viewpoint, Bugental (1963) has argued that the accumulation of diagnostic information about patients contributes little to actual therapeutic work, particularly when that therapeutic work is of an outpatient, interview type. Bugental acknowledges that diagnostic data is useful for administrative purposes or perhaps for research, but not for therapeutic purposes once grosser psychiatric disturbances have been ruled out. Moreover, he is concerned that diagnostic procedures treat the patient as an object or thing to be studied, manipulated, and labeled rather than as a unique individual. Here Bugental is joined by Rogers (1942) and many other practicing clinicians who have given up any attempt to make diagnoses, assuming the etiology of all functional mental disorders to be more or less the same and requiring more or less the same kinds of therapeutic intervention.

In defense of psychiatric diagnostic procedures, it has been argued that classification is a fundamental method of science since science is concerned not with individuals but with groupings or classes. Classification is fundamental to achieving order, permitting quantification of data on which rational, objective therapeutic and research decisions can be reached. Pasamanick (1963) condemns the neglect of diagnosis as misguided on the part of humanistically oriented clinicians. He considers it naive to believe clinicians ever approach new patients as unique individuals without, consciously or not, making some comparisons with previous patients or with the relevant literature. Should they strive to do so, they would be depriving their patients of knowledge derived from accumulated experiences concerning human behavior. Comparison and categorization is seen by Pasamanick as an inevitable as well as desirable part of the clinical process. He believes that different diagnoses of the same patient by different clinicians are not due to any inherent unreliability of the diagnostic process or categories but rather to the neglect into which diagnosis has fallen among many clinicians.

Perhaps the best argument for diagnostic classification is that it aids communication. A language with a parsimonious use of words or symbols helps place complex phenomena into categories whose meaning can be conveyed simply and briefly. Classification implies that certain characteristics of the class or category will apply to the individual so classified. For example, the label *paranoid schizophrenia* provides a shorthand way to communicate that the individual is seriously disturbed, perhaps incapacitated in dealing with reality, that he is likely to suffer from delusions and hallucinations, that psychotherapy is likely to be lengthy and difficult, that hospitalization may be required, that his persecutory ideas may make him dangerous to others as well as himself, and so forth.

In the same way, a common language makes psychiatric and psychological observations comparable. The international terminology of DSM-II should help facilitate communication among clinicians throughout the world. All scientific endeavors leading to testing hypotheses regarding etiology, treatment, or prevention rest on an agreed-upon classification of disorders. As Pasamanick (1963) illustrates, research studying the hypothesis that manic-depressive psychosis is associated with specific childhood experiences could hardly proceed if the research investigator were confronted with groups of patients called manic-depressive by one clinician, schizophrenic by another, and neurotic by a third.

In summary, while diagnosis lacks the excitement and dramatic appeal of other clinical activities such as psychotherapy or community consultation, it nevertheless may provide a useful, if not always essential, clinical function. That usefulness is increased when the diagnosis provides some insight into the etiology of the disorder, aids in prognosis, helps select the appropriate treatment, and generally suggests the most efficacious disposition of the patient. Despite the inevitable limitations of fitting individuals into any typology, particularly as they change over time and as the result of new experiences, the clinical diagnostic process is likely to continue. However, to be most effective, classification must be broadened to include the wide range of problems with which clinicians deal daily and must provide information designed to further clinical action and decision making, rather than having it become an end in itself.

THE CLASSIFICATION OF CHILDHOOD DISORDERS

A long-standing deficiency in most psychiatric classification systems has been its neglect of childhood disorders. DSM-I, for example, made no provision for learning problems, speech or reading difficulties, delinquent behavior, or school phobias, all of which child psychiatrists and psychologists commonly treat. DSM-II made some efforts to correct the situation (for example, it added "IX. Behavior disorders of childhood and adolescence"), but it provides an inadequate range of disorders. Various proposals have been made to classify psychiatric disorders in children (Ackerman, 1953), but most have proven unsatisfactory, particularly when they have imposed the conventions of adult psychiatric classification onto children. One noteworthy exception has been the psychiatric system of classification proposed by the Group for the Advancement of Psychiatry[1] (1966). Drawing heavily upon psychoanalytic theory, the GAP Report provides an expanded list of personality disorders in children (for example, overly dependent personality, oppositional personality, mistrustful personality) that better pinpoints specific syndromes.

Diagnosing psychiatric disorders in children presents certain problems

---

[1] This small group of psychiatrists, organized into committees, studies and reports on various current issues in psychiatry. Collaboration with experts from other disciplines is sought before their action-directed reports are produced. This group represents a progressive movement within psychiatry.

not found with adults, problems inherent in the nature of childhood itself. The child's personality is still forming and as a consequence is more vulnerable to inner tensions and environmental pressures. The child characteristically has little insight into his behavior or motivation. The symptoms he may display as a result of stress (thumbsucking, phobias, negativism) are likely to be age-related and lack the stability and consistency of adult symptoms. Diagnosis thus tends to be more difficult, particularly since the manifestations of any disorder are apt to be less clearly differentiated than in adults, and the clinical picture more apt to change with age or a shift in environment. The younger the child, the less fully developed the personality, the more difficult for the clinician to distinguish between normal reactions to stress and pathological responses. Particularly in the younger child, diagnostic interviewing or psychodiagnostic testing may have limited value in personality assessment. History taking, usually dependent on adult informants in the family, may result in a biased picture of the child or his problems.

Acknowledging the special problems inherent in classifying childhood disorders, many clinicians have resorted to diagnosing them as an adjustment reaction of childhood (see Table 2, a subitem of "VIII. Transient situational disturbances"), a catch-all category which avoids specificity. In an extensive study of 1200 psychiatric clinics in the United States, Rosen, Barn, and Cramer (1964) found that 32 percent of the children interviewed received no diagnosis, while another 30 percent received a diagnosis of adjustment reaction of childhood. Dreger (1964), in another sample, found 40 percent of the children so diagnosed. As he points out, the irony is that after elaborate diagnostic procedures are completed, the child is placed in a diagnostic category that says exactly what was known about him in the first place—that he has a problem!

Some attempts have been made to improve the inadequacy of current practices. Beller (1962) studied the content of clinical records in a psychiatric clinic for children and their families in New York City. In particular, he was interested in determining how the systematic and uniform collection and recording of clinical data could help the clinical researcher. Frequently, the research clinician would like to extract information from clinic files, only to find unevenly recorded data or information unusable in its recorded form. Diagnoses are sometimes carelessly made or not recorded at all. The same holds true for the treatment process, which, if carefully recorded, could provide the therapist with better means of evaluating the validity of his diagnoses and the effectiveness of his treatment techniques. Beller suggests that clinicians use a common frame of reference in arriving at a diagnosis. He urges that careful classification be a basic step in treatment planning and prognosis rather than an afterthought or a concession to administrative demands. From his study of clinic files, Beller also made a more complete classification of childhood disorders (see Table 3).

Despite Beller's efforts to provide broader categories more related to existing childhood syndromes, certain shortcomings remain. His diagnostic system follows the traditional Kraepelinian approach, with its primary distinction between functional and organic disorders. The system is essentially descriptive rather than dynamic, developmental, or etiological —all of which would be highly desirable, particularly in a classification system of childhood personality disorders. By emphasizing clusters of symptoms, it reveals little of the individual child's personality characteristics or modes of social adaptation. The approach, as in most diagnostic efforts, tends to be negative, searching for pathology without integrating such disturbed emotional or behavioral manifestations with other adequately functioning aspects of the whole person. Adaptation depends on more than the nature of the child's conflicts and symptoms; his total resources and integrative capacities ought to be considered.

Besides these diagnostic difficulties, some researchers feel that diagnosis evaluating the individual, alone, is inadequate. Ackerman (1958) suggests that the mental health of any individual, particularly a child, cannot be understood in the confines of individual experience or intrapsychic conflict; he has proposed a system of family diagnosis, a broader approach that embraces the dynamics of the family group and perhaps even the wider community. The dynamic balance between the individual and his family influences the precipitation of his disorder, the course of its development, the possibility of recovery, and the risk of relapse. Existing classification systems fail to acknowledge this intimate interrelationship.[2] According to Ackerman, the conceptual tendency to isolate the individual from his family makes individual diagnosis and particularly prognosis virtually impossible. Ackerman's view, gaining wider acceptance among clinicians,

---

[2] Family diagnosis has many implications for treatment and prevention of those disorders stemming from such an interplay of forces within the family unit. See Chapter 10 for a fuller discussion.

Table 3. Classification of childhood personality disorders*

MAJOR CATEGORY	TYPES	SPECIFICATIONS
I. Functional behavior disorders	Habit disturbances	Feeding and training difficulties Auto-erotic manifestations Excessive crying, thumb-sucking, masturbation, scratching, rocking
	Conduct disturbances	Defiance Negativism Destructiveness Hyperaggression Cruelty Restlessness or overactivity Tantrums
	Preneurotic disturbances	Inhibition of curiosity, of anger, of aggression Sleep disturbances Night terrors Fear of darkness, of animals, of thunder
	Neurotic disturbances	Anxiety states Depressions Phobias Conversions Obsessions Compulsions
	Psychosomatic disturbances	Migraine Colitis Ulcers Bronchial asthma Eczema Hives
	Character disturbances (in early childhood)	Multiplicity and pervasiveness of disturbances which are not structured around phase-specific conflicts, and which are present on almost every level of development

* Reprinted with permission of The Macmillan Company from *Clinical Process* by E. K. Beller.
© 1962 by the Free Press of Glencoe, Inc.

Table 3.   (continued)

MAJOR CATEGORY	TYPES	SPECIFICATIONS
I. Functional behavior disorders (continued)	Character disturbances (in early childhood, continued)	Over- or underintensity and rigidity of reaction from earliest infancy in the expression of physical needs, emotions, and moods, and in reaction to physical and social stimuli
	Borderline disturbances	Low tolerance of frustration— that is, responds to slight frustration with uncontrollable impulsivity or withdrawal into fantasy Severe tantrums with loss of contact Extreme mood swings, very tenuous relationships to people and events (Also same characteristics as listed under "Character disturbances")

	Psychotic disturbances	Withdrawal from reality
		Delusions
		Inability to identify self and other people
		Unintelligible and uncommunicative use of language
		Primary process thinking
		Major syndromes:
		  Infantile autism
		  Symbiotic psychosis

II. Mental subnormality	Idiocy Imbecility Moronity Borderline	
III. Behavior disorders with an organic base (secondary behavior disorders)	Etiology	Hereditary Congenital Traumatic Due to infection, nutritional deficiencies, toxicity

Table 3. (continued)

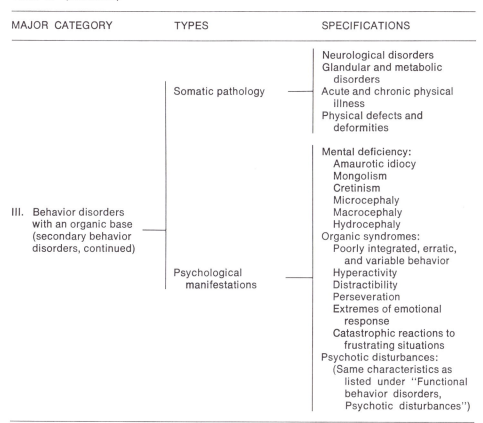

MAJOR CATEGORY	TYPES	SPECIFICATIONS
III. Behavior disorders with an organic base (secondary behavior disorders, continued)	Somatic pathology	Neurological disorders Glandular and metabolic disorders Acute and chronic physical illness Physical defects and deformities

	Psychological manifestations	Mental deficiency:
		  Amaurotic idiocy
		  Mongolism
		  Cretinism
		  Microcephaly
		  Macrocephaly
		  Hydrocephaly
		Organic syndromes:
		  Poorly integrated, erratic, and variable behavior
		  Hyperactivity
		  Distractibility
		  Perseveration
		  Extremes of emotional response
		  Catastrophic reactions to frustrating situations
		Psychotic disturbances:
		  (Same characteristics as listed under "Functional behavior disorders, Psychotic disturbances")

opens the way for testing new hypotheses as well as new diagnostic, treatment, and prevention methods extending beyond the isolated individual into his natural social environment.

THE RELIABILITY AND VALIDITY OF PSYCHIATRIC DIAGNOSIS

Diagnosis and classification fulfill several important functions: (1) administrative, including statistical record-keeping; (2) clinical, as an aid in indicating etiology, choice of treatment, and prognosis; and (3) research, particularly in those studies where psychiatric diagnosis defines membership in an experimental or control group or where diagnosis in general is used as the dependent or independent variable. In order to be useful for these purposes, however, the diagnosis must be reliable and valid. That is, there should be a high degree of consistency and accuracy between clinicians in applying the same diagnostic label to the same individual (called high interjudge or rater reliability). In addition, a diagnosis should provide an accurate prediction of subsequent behavior for individuals with a particular diagnosis.

Considerable research, with somewhat contradictory results, has examined the reliability of psychiatric diagnosis. Two major methods have been used. The first has studied the relative frequency with which different psychiatrists assign different diagnoses to apparently similar patients. The second method has investigated the degree of agreement on diagnosis by two or more psychiatrists seeing the same patient simultaneously or within a short time interval.

Many psychiatric hospitals or clinics commonly find certain diagnostic labels occurring with great frequency while others are relatively neglected. Since the reverse situation may occur at a neighboring psychiatric unit, this does not seem to be due simply to the greater occurrence of one disorder over another. Such differences may even exist between psychiatrists in the same hospital. Mehlman (1952) studied the diagnoses assigned to 4000 patients in a large state hospital to see if the relative frequencies of patients assigned to different diagnostic categories would differ among psychiatrists in a situation where patients are assigned to them at random. Presumably, each psychiatrist should have a similar proportion of each type of diagnosis, yet Mehlman's results showed considerable differences in the frequency of organic versus psychogenic diagnoses, as well as manic-depressive versus schizophrenic diagnoses. A similar study by Pasamanick, Dinitz, and Lefton (1959) investigated the relative frequency with which six different diagnostic categories were used to classify female patients in three separate psychiatric hospital wards. They report frequent instances of one psychiatrist diagnosing nearly all his patients as schizophrenic and an equally competent psychiatrist diagnosing a comparable group of patients as psychoneurotic. Similar variations in diagnostic judgments made by clinical psychologists are reported by Goldfarb (1959).

With one major exception (Wilson & Meyer, 1962), most research findings report enough variation in the frequency of diagnoses assigned to similar patients by different psychiatrists to raise serious doubts concerning the reliability of psychiatric diagnoses. Thus, despite clinicians' protests that their point of reference is always the individual patient, this research suggests that clinicians may in fact be so committed to a theoretical position that the patient's diagnosis (and later treatment) is largely determined by a psychiatrist's preconceived mental set and selective perception and emphasis.

The second method for studying reliability has been to compare the diagnoses made by two or more psychiatrists evaluating the same patient.[3] An early study by Ash (1949) investigated the extent of agreement among two or three psychiatrists who interviewed patients jointly but arrived at a diagnosis independently. Diagnoses were made both by major category (mental deficiency, psychosis, neurosis, psychopathic personality, and normal range) and specific diagnostic subcategory. Fifty-two males were interviewed, always by at least two psychiatrists and, in 35 of the 52 cases, by all three psychiatrists. The results were discouraging, suggesting that the diagnosis depended as much upon the psychiatrist who made it as it did upon the patient being diagnosed. There was agreement on the major diagnostic category of 51 percent of the patients by two psychiatrists, and 46 percent by three psychiatrists. With the more specific categories, agreement on diagnosis between two psychiatrists occurred in 49 percent of the cases, and in a mere 20 percent of the cases for all three psychiatrists. Critics have objected to the small number of subjects used and the limitations of the joint interview method. Moreover, 75 percent of the subjects in the study were diagnosed as being in the normal range, a population that is not representative of patients with whom psychiatrists generally work. Nevertheless, the low degree of agreement casts considerable doubt on the reliability of the diagnostic process.

As methodological flaws in earlier studies have been corrected, the subsequent results have been somewhat more encouraging. For example, another study (Beck, Ward, Mendelson, Mock, & Erbaugh, 1962) used a larger sample of 153 outpatients and made certain the diagnoses were made by a number of equally experienced senior psychiatrists. In addi-

---

[3] The student who has had the same essay examination or oral interview graded, with strikingly different results, by two separate professors will appreciate what is involved in such interjudge reliability studies. Different professors may be looking for different answers or may have different implicit standards of what constitutes a good answer, so the student might get a high grade from one and a failing grade from another.

tion, prior to interviewing, the psychiatrists conferred with each other and agreed on a set of guidelines for establishing diagnostic criteria. Such guidelines went beyond the established ones set up by the American Psychiatric Association classification system. Another methodological advance involved a self-rating: following the interview, each psychiatrist indicated whether he was certain or uncertain that his diagnosis was correct. Interviews were conducted separately, within five minutes of each other, following each patient's interview. The results indicated an improved degree of agreement for subcategories, although considerable disagreement remained. When both psychiatrists were certain, they agreed in 81 percent of the cases; when both were uncertain, they agreed in 25 percent of the cases. With one certain and the other uncertain, about 50 percent agreement resulted. Finally, an agreement rate of 70 percent was found for the three major categories (psychosis, neurosis, character disorder), and 54 percent for specific diagnostic subcategories. As in previous studies, the more specific the diagnosis and the greater the number of diagnostic categories, the more seldom agreement was achieved.

These studies suggest that there is generally more agreement than what we can expect on the basis of chance, particularly for major categories like psychosis. Psychiatric diagnosis for subcategories (perhaps excluding schizophrenia) or for milder forms of mental disorders tends to be unreliable. The results of the diagnostic process appear to be especially poor for those types of clinical decisions that may hinge on proper diagnosis (that is, length of hospital stay, ward placement, type of treatment).

Several factors seem to be operating simultaneously, reducing the degree of agreement among psychiatrists. The inadequacy of the psychiatric classification system makes fine distinctions between categories very difficult. That symptoms overlap into other categories coupled with the fact that individuals with the same diagnosis (schizophrenia, for example) do not necessarily exhibit identical symptoms or always resemble each other behaviorally, together make accurate diagnosis hazardous, particularly in pinpointing a specific subcategory. In this regard, Zigler and Phillips (1961) examined the case histories of 793 patients admitted to Worcester State Hospital over a 12-year period and eventually diagnosed as having a functional disorder. Comparing patients in four major diagnostic groups—manic–depressive, schizophrenic, psychoneurotic, and character disorder—35 major discrete symptoms were reported in their case records. One striking finding was that of the 35 symptoms, 30 appeared in one or more patients diagnosed as manic-depressive, 34 in character disorders, and all 35 in some patients diagnosed as psychoneurotic or schizophrenic! Thus, Zigler and Phillips conclude that while some relationship may exist between symptom manifestation and diagnosis, the magnitude of the relationship is generally so small that membership in a particular diagnostic group conveys only minimal information about the patient's symptomatology.

Another source of error in reducing interjudge reliability, as Pasamanick et al. (1959) point out, is the theoretical bias of the clinician which may lead him to emphasize certain symptoms in reaching a diagnosis while overlooking other patient characteristics considered equally crucial by clinicians with a different bias. Other sources of error have been investigated by Ward, Beck, Mendelson, Mock, and Erbaugh (1962) in a study done in conjunction with Beck et al. (1962), cited above. In attempting to determine what accounted for the disagreement in diagnosis among the experienced psychiatrists in Beck's study, Ward et al. found three sources of error: (1) inadequacies of the diagnostic system's categories, accounting for 62.5 percent of the primary reasons for disagreement; (2) inconsistency from one diagnostician to another (different interview techniques, different weight assigned to different symptoms, different interpretations of the same data), accounting for 32.5 percent of the disagreements; and (3) inconsistency in patient behavior in the separate interviews, accounting for only 5 percent of the disagreement.

Reliability and validity are two sides of the same coin; we've just looked at studies investigating diagnosis in terms of its reliability. Other studies have evaluated diagnosis from the validity side, which is a more important factor for clinical decision-making.

One group of studies, looking into the long-term stability of diagnosis, indicates that a patient's diagnosis frequently needs to be changed during a single hospital stay or upon readmission, with little evidence that his clinical picture has changed. Masserman and Carmichael (1938) reported that as many as 40 percent of psychiatric diagnoses were changed during a single hospitalization period. Barbigan, Gardner, Miles, and Romano (1965), reporting on 1215 patients, found that 16 percent of the diagnoses were different on second admission, 28 percent on third admission, 51 percent on fourth admission, and 55 percent on fifth or subsequent admission. Cooper (1967) reports that only 20 percent of a group of 293 patients kept the same diagnosis over four hospital admissions in a two-year period. His data indicate that all but a small proportion exhibited a similar clinical picture for each admission.

The prognostic validity of psychiatric diagnosis has also been challenged. Frank (1969), in an extensive survey of research on psychiatric diagnosis, found little heuristic value in this mode of classifying behavior. His conclusions are distressing from several viewpoints. Various treatment plans in hospitals, clinics, or community mental health centers depend largely on diagnosis. Moreover, psychiatric diagnosis is a frequently used criterion in research into psychopathology. Psychiatric diagnosis is often the independent variable as two groups—one "normal" and used as a baseline, one "abnormal"—are compared, or when two groups with different diagnoses are compared. Yet, Frank's survey found little or no consistency in the dependent variable—social behavior or test performance —when the independent variable, the criterion for group selection, was psychiatric diagnosis. Numerous research studies (such as validation of new psychological test instruments) have used psychiatric diagnosis as the criterion for accurate test prediction—obviously a questionable research tactic, given the aforementioned evidence.

Frank (1969) concludes that the current diagnostic classification system lacks the reliability and validity that would make its use in clinical work or research advisable. Whereas the current classification system is not totally invalid and therefore useless for prognostic purposes, it needs to be improved to higher levels of validity. Several authors are beginning to use advances in statistical techniques (such as complex factorial designs), computer technology, as well as in new recording devices (telemetry, tape recorders, videotapes) to study behavior syndromes with much greater sophistication than was previously possible. What is likely to emerge ultimately is a regrouping of syndromes within a new diagnostic system of classification. Whether such a statistical system or any other proposed system proves more valid than the present clinical–descriptive system will depend in the long run on whether the resulting groupings turn out to have reliably different, discoverable etiologies (Maher, 1970).

THE PROCESS OF CLINICAL JUDGMENT

Psychiatric diagnosis is only an end product of the complex cognitive process of clinical judgment. Many of the problems of reaching a reliable, valid diagnosis are common in other clinical assessment procedures such as testing, interviewing, behavior sampling, or psychophysiological measurement. In each procedure, various kinds of information about an individual are systematically collected, organized, and interpreted in an effort to obtain as dependable and accurate an understanding of him as possible. The purpose of such an evaluation or appraisal is to form a clinical picture of the individual and his life situation prior to further clinical intervention.

How accurate are such judgments? What parts do intuition and experience play in arriving at valid conclusions? What differences exist between the cognitive process of more gifted and less gifted clinical practitioners? How might clinical judgment be improved? For many years it was believed that these questions were unanswerable, that clinical wisdom was an art not subject to experimental analysis. More recently, however, the judgment process has begun to be studied by psychologists of various specialties. Social psychologists, for example, have become interested in how people ordinarily form impressions of others, looking for general psychological principles people conform to without being aware of it. Research on the operation of systematic biases in forming social judgments has been carried out by Sherif and Hovland (1961). In the clinical area, a long series of pioneering studies by Hunt (1959) has attempted to demonstrate that clinical judgment follows the same laws and principles developed in the field of psychophysics, where laboratory studies of judgment have long been carried out in the area of sensation, perception, and aesthetics. According to Hunt, clinical judgments differ only in quantity, and not in kind, from psychophysical judgments. As such, they can be improved —that is, interjudge agreements raised—as judges are trained and scales created for rating relevant dimensions. Hunt views clinical intuition as following an orderly process of rational judgment, even if the clinician is not aware of the experimental basis for such judgments. Such a view is in sharp contrast to the popular depiction of intuition as some sudden, inspirational revelation.

THE RELIABILITY AND VALIDITY OF CLINICAL JUDGMENTS

Much like their psychiatric counterparts, clinical psychologists base their techniques of intervention on certain subjective decisions regarding their clients. Such decisions, for psychologists, have usually been based on interpretations of data from objective tests, projective techniques, interviews, or similar sources. Studies of the accuracy of these kinds of judgments have yielded disappointing results, just as they have in the area of psychiatric diagnosis.

One landmark study with rather sobering results regarding the accuracy of clinical prediction was undertaken at the University of Michigan (Kelly & Fiske, 1951). The purpose of this study was to evaluate a variety of procedures as predictors of students' later performance in graduate school or as professional clinical psychologists. Several hundred college graduates seeking admission to VA training programs in 40 universities around the United States immediately after World War II were evaluated by interviews and various objective, projective, and situational tests. From this large mass of data, numerous judgments, interpretations, and predictions were made. These were then compared to the criterion variables of the students' academic records or subsequent ratings of success in clinical work. Only a small portion of the objective tests were found to correlate with these criterion measures. Curiously, the Miller Analogies Test and the Strong Vocational Interest Blank—both simple, academic procedures—proved more useful as predictors than did those procedures utilizing extensive clinical observations or diagnostic clinical tests. The results with projective techniques, then enjoying great popularity among clinical psychologists, were especially discouraging. Predictions of success based on judgments derived from any one projective technique tended to produce very low correlations with the established criteria.

Results from the Michigan study, despite the services of highly competent clinicians as judges and the use of the best clinical procedures then available, were sufficiently poor that the study proved to be a setback for the optimism beginning to develop regarding the accuracy of clinical judgment. Equally distressing have been the findings that neither the amount of professional training and experience of the judge (Oskamp, 1962) nor the amount of information he has available (Giedt, 1955) appear to relate to his judgmental accuracy. Oskamp (1965) has shown that not only does increased information not increase accuracy, but it may have the detrimental effect of increasing the judge's confidence in his understanding of an individual, sometimes to a degree unwarranted by the facts. Oskamp, knowing the correct answers about an individual, found the average judge to be slightly overconfident when he had one-fourth of the total amount of information available and extremely overconfident when he had seen all the data. The danger, as Oskamp points out, is in the clinician becoming certain about decisions out of proportion to the actual correctness of those decisions.

Clinical psychologists have tended to place great reliance on personality tests to present a description of an individual's present and predicted future behavior. Little and Shneidman (1959) set out to investigate the agreements, or congruencies, of personality descriptions made by clinicians when such descriptions were based on different test instruments. Selecting cases from their files for which considerable test data and case history material were available, they studied the degree of interjudge agreement for: (1) various kinds of subjects—the psychotic, neurotic, psychosomatically disordered, and psychiatrically normal; (2) various tests —Rorschach, TAT, MMPI, and Make-A-Picture Story Test (MAPS); and (3) several kinds of interpretive tasks—Q sorting, ratings, or assigning diagnostic labels. Forty-eight clinical psychologists, each rated as expert on one of the four tests, served as test judges. Tests were obtained from 12 subjects. In addition, 23 psychiatrists and one psychologist evaluated the anamnestic (case history) materials and wrote a personality description based on these data alone. Each test judge analyzed and interpreted the test protocol in his area of expertise for four subjects, one from each category listed above, knowing a minimum amount of information about him. (This procedure is usually called *blind analysis.*) The results were very disappointing to those practicing clinicians who had relied on the reliability and validity of these tests. Judges who were experts on particular tests could do only slightly better than chance in their blind analysis. The reliabilities of the interpretations varied considerably, cutting across tests used and types of subject. In general, these were so low that Little and Shneidman concluded that efforts to establish the validity of these popular test instruments were premature until adequate interpreter reliability could be established. Although the study has been criticized (use of psychiatrist ratings as validation criteria for test interpretations is questionable, considering the disappointing results of studies on the reliability and validity of psychiatric diagnosis; blind analysis is not what practicing clinicians do, since they generally obtain other information from case history material and interview data), the results nevertheless offer a major challenge to the value of clinical judgments based on the usual psychodiagnostic test protocols.

CLINICAL AND STATISTICAL PREDICTION

Since it has been consistently shown that most clinical judgments tend to be: (1) of questionable reliability and validity; (2) relatively unaffected by the amount of information the judge has available; (3) seemingly unrelated to professional training and experience; (4) only minimally related to the confidence in which the judge holds his understanding to be; and (5) costly and time-consuming, considering the yield, it is not surprising that many clinicians have looked for statistical or actuarial prediction systems to replace the more fallible human judgments.

The 1954 appearance of Paul Meehl's influential book, *Clinical versus Statistical Prediction* helped focus attention on this significant issue in clinical judgment and gave new impetus to the view that statistical (or actuarial) techniques were superior in many cases to clinical (or intuitive) techniques. Meehl reviewed 16 to 20 studies that pertained to the comparative validity of these contrasting approaches to prediction (prediction of academic grades, occupational success, outcome of therapy) and found that clinical judgments rarely reached the levels of reliability and validity of the best objective measurement methods. While careful to reaffirm his faith in clinical judgments under certain circumstances, Meehl concluded that clinicians spend a great deal of time in tasks which could more efficiently be carried out by clerks using statistical methods, actuarial tables, or multiple regression equations. The increased availability of computers since Meehl's 1954 publication lends even stronger force to his argument.

The issue remains one on which clinical practitioners are sharply divided. Nor is the dispute limited to prediction in a clinical setting. The college admissions officer, attempting to forecast success in college for various applicants, may rely on interviews, letters of recommendations, or more objective data such as high school grades and college entrance examination scores. The personnel officer in industry may need to forecast what quality of work can be expected from a job applicant. Kelly (1967) has suggested that the issue is more accurately one involving personal versus impersonal methods of assessment. Proponents of the former are likely to consider their approach dynamic, global, meaningful, holistic, sensitive, and true to life. On the other hand, proponents of the latter see their approach as operational, verifiable, public, testable, hardheaded, empirical, and more scientifically precise (Meehl, 1954).

Since his earlier publication, Meehl has periodically surveyed other comparative studies reported in the research literature, each time concluding that none show the clinician predicting better than the statistician. A decade after his book, Meehl (1965a) reported 50 such studies: in two-thirds of these studies, statistical prediction was superior, while in one-third the two methods were substantially equal. Sawyer (1966), in a survey permitting 75 comparisons in 45 different clinical and nonclinical studies, supported Meehl's conclusions. He found the mechanical (that is, statistical) method always equal or superior to the clinical, whether the data was collected clinically or mechanically. Goldberg's (1968) review of the literature led him to conclude that over a large array of clinical judgment tasks, simple actuarial formulae can be constructed to perform at a level of validity no lower than that of the clinical expert.

Despite such evidence, many clinicians continue to rely on their individual clinical wisdom, unimpressed by any generalizations that might be drawn from studies that happen to have been published. Just as their personal experience has told them that psychotherapy is effective (in spite of Eysenck's (1952) challenge, described on pp. 215–218), similar personal experience with assessment procedures makes them confident of their own clinical judgment, despite disappointing results of numerous studies showing the low reliability and validity of most clinical judgments. The issue centers around how the clinician can best understand data about an individual so that he might make more accurate predictions about that individual's future behavior. Meehl (1956) has described the situation as follows:

> Here we sit, with our Rorschach and Multiphasic results spread out before us. From this mass of data we have to emerge with a characterization of the person from whose behavior these profiles are a highly abstracted, much-reduced distillation. How to proceed?
>
> Some of you are no doubt wondering, "What is the fellow talking about? You look at the profiles, you call to mind what the various test dimensions mean for dynamics, you reflect on other patients you have seen with similar patterns, you think of the research literature; then you combine these considerations to make inferences. Where's the problem?" *The problem is whether or not this is the most efficient way to do it* [Meehl, 1956, p. 264].

Meehl has characterized this time-honored procedure for generating personality descriptions from tests as the rule-of-thumb method. In its place, he has argued for the cookbook method, in which any given configuration of psychometric data associated with any configuration of a personality description is assigned a number. The transition from an individual's psychometric test pattern to a description of his personality pattern then becomes an automatic, mechanical, clerical task, proceeding by the use of explicit rules set forth in the cookbook. Efficiency is increased, and the clinician is freed to engage in other clinical activities, such as psychotherapy or research, which are more appropriate for his skills and advanced training.

Arguing in favor of clinical prediction, on the other hand, the following points have been made by clinicians:

1. Instead of ruling out clinical judgment and prediction, it would be better to train clinicians to look more closely at their criteria for making judgments to try to make them better judges. Hunt and Jones (1962), in their research on clinical judgment, have suggested how to make such judgments more objective and precise, thus making the data from subjective clinical appraisals more amenable to actuarial treatment.

2. The actuarial approach is applicable only when adequately developed tests permit their use. Meehl (1956) has bolstered his advocacy of the actuarial approach by referring to the configurational interpretations from the MMPI, without recognizing that it took several decades to develop actuarial tables for this one test alone. Moreover, the nature of the test itself (yes–no items) lends itself to actuarial analysis. Tests like the Rorschach, TAT, or Draw-A-Person would present a monumental, if not impossible, task.

3. Although statistical methods of prediction seem to have surpassed clinical ones in accuracy, neither has done very well. Particularly in pinpointing specific personality descriptions or predicting events that have a low probability of occurrence (but that nevertheless interest the clinician), neither method can boast a high percentage of success (Gough, 1962).

4. New discoveries, leading to new theories and greater understanding of human behavior, are not likely to spring from actuarial methods alone. New dimensions of behavior are most likely to be explored on the basis of clinical hunches, and those hunches derive from increased clinical sensitivity. Therefore, the clinician is essential to the process as a formulator of hypotheses (Kahn, 1960).

5. Judging man by machine or by rote statistical formula is distrusted by the public. Therefore, a clinician's judgment is preferred in most situations (Hunt & Jones, 1962).[4]

---

[4] Perhaps this, too, is changing. Witness the popularity of computer-dating devices for matching up men and women.

6. Actuarial predictions have proven superior because they unfairly compare the performance of the best tests with the performance of an unspecified group of clinicians. Assessment involves both statistical and clinical prediction, according to Holt (1958, 1969a), with clinical judgment taking place at many points along the way, not merely the final step. Holt distinguishes three types of predictive systems—naive clinical, pure actuarial, and sophisticated clinical. He points out that most published studies have pitted pure actuarial against naive clinical predictions (where qualitative data are processed intuitively by rule of thumb), resulting in the inevitable superiority of the former. In Holt's view, a third type of prediction—sophisticated clinical prediction—can combine the best of both. Such an approach, as Holt described it in a program to select men for training in psychiatry at the Menninger Foundation, used the refinements of experimental design (including job analyses, pilot studies, item analyses, and successive cross-validations) along with qualitative data and the clinician's intuitive and intellectual resources. The results were better than those achieved by naive clinical or statistical means based on test scores. Holt implies that Meehl and others have set up a straw man by describing the clinician as a casual, informal, imprecise, uncontrolled, intuitive hunch-player; this inaccurate picture may account for some of the discrepancy between clinical experience and the research data. Holt argues for a middle course between "the swamps of oversubjectivity and the deserts of overobjectivity." (However, while his call for sophisticated clinical prediction is appealing and may prove in the long run to be a more effective predictor than the actuarial method, the fact remains that typical clinical assessment procedures, as reported in the literature, compare poorly with typical actuarial procedures.)

7. Certain clinical decisions are so crucial (for example, is client A a suicidal risk, is client B homicidally dangerous, should client C be examined by a physician for a possible brain tumor?) that the clinician must follow his clinical hunch even if actuarial criteria indicate some predictions are improbable. Clinicians work with individuals, while statistical predictions are based on groups. Actuarial results may not apply to a single individual unless he fits the group on which actuarial tables have been established. Clearly, it is impossible to establish such tables to cover all events and people. Clinical experience with another individual is not replaceable by machine scores. Nor can actuarial data be available to predict new situations in which, by definition, such data has not as yet been accumulated.

The issue of clinical versus statistical prediction is far from settled, remaining an area of lively controversy in the clinical literature. The sensitive clinician, like the sensitive teacher or physician, must look beyond examination findings or test scores of various kinds to base his decisions on many factors, of which these so-called objective scores are just one set. The issue goes beyond pitting one method against the other or engaging in stunts like blind analysis. In practice, the clinician must weigh information accumulated from various sources—including first-hand knowledge of his client—and form hypotheses to be supported or rejected by additional evidence. At the same time, he needs to improve his assessment techniques, including a distinction of what function each technique measures best. He must make a sound choice of assessment procedures, using qualitative data (from interviews, life histories, projective techniques) as well as objective test scores (which may be machine scored and interpreted). The clinician, thus prepared, becomes a more reliable and valid data processor prepared to yield a set of predictions tailored to each case (Holt, 1958). Finally, the clinician's task is to relate whatever statistical probabilities are available to his intimate understanding of his client's specific life situation.

Thus, there is a place for both actuarial and clinical assessment procedures, so long as they are not asked to serve purposes for which they are not suited. Cronbach (1970) has suggested that the former is "compulsively cautious" and the latter "erratically overambitious":

> When clinical testers answer questions for which their methods and theory are badly suited, their answers are next to worthless and at best are costly beyond their value. When psychometric testers are faced with a clinical problem calling for understanding (that is, what lies behind a given child's anxious withdrawal?) they are unable to give any answer at all. Each in his own proper province will surpass the other and each outside his province is nearly impotent. Assessment methods have earned a bad name for themselves by trying to compete with measurement on its own ground [Cronbach, 1970, p. 692].

THE CLINICAL INFERENCE PROCESS

Considering the input from various tests, observations, and interviews, how does the clinician make refined clinical inferences about his client?

By what process does he extract meaning from or interpret his data? Sundberg and Tyler (1962) have outlined four stages in the assessment process: (1) the *preparation stage,* when the psychologist acquires pre-contact information about the client, determines the questions that need to be answered about him (for example, the reason for referral), and chooses tests or other techniques to answer the referral questions; (2) the *input stage,* when information is collected about the client and his living situation; (3) the *processing stage,* when the raw data are collected, scored, and interpreted, and the clinician formulates his inferences with the referral questions as a point of reference; and (4) the *output stage,* when the findings, conclusions, and recommendations are reported.

It is the third stage, that of processing the data and formulating clinical inferences, that interests us here. Sundberg and Tyler have distinguished three levels of inference: (1) Inference Level I, where there is a minimum amount of inference. Test scores, check lists, perhaps even a brief screening interview such as might be made by a psychiatrist at an Army Induction Center are used to rule out gross psychopathology. Inferences drawn from this level are almost entirely actuarial; (2) Inference Level II, where inferences, called descriptive generalizations, are based on a wider range of observations and other data than is available at the previous level. Statistical tables of norms are generally not available, however. Hypothetical constructs may be involved, with the clinician attempting to infer an inner etiology or causal state, perhaps physiological, to account for the observed behavior; and (3) Inference Level III, where the most inclusive interpretations are made, based on the widest integration of data. The clinician at this level attempts to form a consistent overall theory of the person–situation interaction. Explanatory speculations about the developmental, social, and physiological underpinnings of his behavior are likely, generally tied to a theoretical system of hypotheses and deductions.

The clinical inference process inevitably involves comparing the client with some previously established norms developed by the clinical psychologist. These norms may be an objective table of norms for test scores, for example, which simply require locating the client's raw score on the previously compiled distribution of scores for a normative sample. Such tables usually appear in the test manuals accompanying carefully standardized tests. Occasionally, a hospital unit where research has been conducted on a specific patient population will have its own local experience tables—perhaps signs of potential suicide risks. At the other extreme, the psychologist may rely on a more subjective set of norms, developing a clinical picture of his client based on other clients he has studied, who implicitly serve as a basis for making comparisons. Those who prefer to remain at low inference levels are likely to rely more heavily on statistical aids to interpretation, such as tables of norms, profile codes such as those used with the MMPI, and base-rate information or experience tables providing an actuarial baseline for comparisons. The higher the inference level, the more likely the clinician is to use his clinical hunches, insights, and intuition. The distinction reflects the perennial conflict, first pointed out by William James, between the tough-minded and the tender-minded scientist.[5]

CLINICAL INFERENCE THROUGH TAXONOMIC SORTING

Sarbin, Taft, and Bailey (1960) have taken the position that there is no special clinical intuitive process outside the realm of empirical analysis. All clinical inferences are simply special forms of statistical inference. (Inference is defined as a process in which a particular instance is assigned characteristics of a universal class on the basis of its being a member of that class.) These authors see the clinical inference process as fundamentally a process of syllogistic reasoning they term taxonomic sorting. Six stages in the process of clinical inference are differentiated:

1. The clinician begins with a *postulate system* based on his whole background of experience, including his beliefs, attitudes, assumptions, expectancies, and taxonomies (his personality theory or his theories regarding psychotherapy).

2. Under the requirements of his role as assessor and based on his postulate system, he constructs a *major premise* (for example, "client-centered therapy is frequently beneficial for persons who are bright and highly motivated but lack self-esteem").

3. From his tests, interviews, and observations, *minor premises* are made ("this new client is bright, highly motivated, and appears to lack self-esteem").

4. The process of *instantiation* (categorization or classification) takes

---

[5] Somewhat less charitably, Bertrand Russell is said to have characterized the groups as "simple-minded" and "muddle-headed" (Meehl, 1956).

place, in which the input is treated by the clinician as if it were an instance of a general class ("he is similar to other clients I have known who have benefitted from client-centered therapy").

5. The conclusion, or *inferential product,* is reached ("he has the characteristics associated with success in client-centered therapy").

6. The *prediction* is made ("I will recommend him for client-centered therapy, which I predict will be beneficial").

The process draws heavily on the syllogism of classical logic, but differs from syllogistic reasoning mainly because it is always probabilistic. Each step in the sequence assigns the client to categories and weighs the probabilities involved. Sarbin et al. (1960) have included their inference model of the clinician's conceptual activity within a general cognitive theory.

The clinician's diagnostic decisions invariably involve probability statements. The pediatrician, listening to a mother over the telephone as she describes her child's symptoms of mild fever, headache, and upset stomach, concludes that the child probably has the flu, particularly if other children he has examined within the last few days have been so diagnosed. His conclusions are based in part on the base rate of the disease's occurrence within the community at present. If the flu should approach epidemic proportions, the probability of his diagnosis being accurate increases substantially.[6]

A table of base rates is a frequently relied on aid to interpretation. Sarbin et al. (1960) have described the sequence of events in a hypothetical situation in which a clinician begins to interview a person in the diagnostic clinic of a mental hospital. The probability of being assigned any specific diagnostic label largely depends on the base rates developed at the clinic based on the previous clinic population. Thus, without regard to symptomatology, if he is viewed as a potential mental patient requiring hospitalization, the probability of categorizing him as schizophrenic is immediately six out of 10. (That is, for every 10 patients diagnosed in such a situation, hospital records show that six out of 10 have been schizophrenic.) The probability of being diagnosed as having an organic disorder is one out of 10, as is the probability of a manic-depressive

---

[6] Experienced auto mechanics or television repairmen develop similar base rates for diagnosing malfunctionings they are to repair. Each model is likely to have characteristic weaknesses to which the experienced repairman turns first. Should a particular model have a notable flaw, the probability of accurate diagnosis would increase substantially.

diagnosis. Nonpsychotic diagnoses occur two times out of 10. If the clinician calls the patient schizophrenic, there is a 50 percent chance that he will instantiate the patient as reactive schizophrenic (with eight out of 10 having a favorable prognosis) and a 50 percent chance that he will be categorized as a process schizophrenic (eight out of 10 having an unfavorable prognosis).[7] We find the probability of any patient entering the clinic being diagnosed as a reactive schizophrenic by multiplying the probabilities of .6 (proportion of patients diagnosed as schizophrenic) times .5 (proportion of schizophrenics diagnosed as reactive), which equals 30 out of 100. This probability is found without any additional knowledge of the patient. Base rates thus play a key role in diagnostic decisions which have important prognostic implications. Clinical decisions such as who should receive psychotherapy are essentially probability statements regarding success; they are likely to be based on formal clinic expectancy tables or, more likely, the clinician's estimate of clinic base rates for successful treatment.

While on the whole, extremely valuable and time-saving in making predictions about a new case, base-rate information may be misleading. Misdiagnosis in medicine may occur because a certain disease with symptoms similar to those presented by a new patient is prevalent in the community. In the same way, one may be incorrectly diagnosed as having a disease similar to one he had in the past. Patients in a mental hospital diagnostic clinic may be hospitalized because they were hospitalized before, despite the possibility that hospitalization is not called for, or perhaps was erroneously prescribed previously. Mendel and Rapport (1969) reviewed the bases for decisions regarding hospitalization made by 33 mental health professionals over an eight-day period for 269 persons being evaluated for admission to Los Angeles County General Hospital. Despite the fact that these clinicians (psychiatrists, clinical psychologists, psychiatric social workers) indicated on a follow-up questionnaire that the severity of the person's symptoms was instrumental in their decision to recommend hospitalization, the clinical records showed that those hospitalized and those not hospitalized were virtually indistinguishable in the

---

[7] A reactive schizophrenic is said to be characterized by a fairly normal prepsychotic adjustment, with schizophrenic symptoms appearing suddenly in response to stress. On the other hand, a process schizophrenic is said to be characterized by an inadequate prepsychotic adjustment; the schizophrenic condition develops gradually, with no identifiable precipitating stress, and the prognosis is correspondingly poorer.

Table 4. Relationship between decision to hospitalize, severity of symptoms, and history of previous psychiatric hospitalization*

	SEVERITY OF SYMPTOMS		HISTORY OF HOSPITALIZATION	
DECISION	MILD	SEVERE	PREVIOUS HOSPITALIZATION	NO PREVIOUS HOSPITALIZATION
Hospitalized	13%	87%	77%	23%
Not Hospitalized	11%	89%	34%	66%

* Adapted from Mendel and Rapport. *Archives of General Psychiatry*, 1969, **20**, 322–323. Copyright 1969, American Medical Association. Reprinted by permission.

severity of their symptoms (see Table 4). One the other hand, the clinicians did appear to be influenced by the person's previous hospitalization, without being aware of it. Further study ruled out the possibility that those previously hospitalized had more severe symptoms.

CLINICAL INFERENCE THROUGH INTUITION

To many clinicians, taxonomic sorting appears more logical than psychological. In the same way, despite the impressive array of data supporting the superiority of actuarial over intuitive methods in many areas of clinical judgments, some clinicians remain unconvinced that any statistical, mechanical approach can ever replace their intuitive understanding of another individual's life style. What the statistician or logician dismisses as mystical, subjective, and unverifiable, these clinicians see as empathic, insightful, sensitive, and deep. Based on clinical hunches and an understanding of human behavior, these psychologists are willing to operate at higher inference levels than other methods would permit. Rather than logically sort exact probabilities, the intuitive clinician often is prepared to make interpretations from limited and apparently unrelated inputs which suddenly make sense and produce insights. Probability figures based on group data may be inapplicable to a single individual, they reason. In its place, they prefer an idiographic method for studying an individual's unique personality, rather than seeing him as a member of a class or group.

One classic example of the use of intuition is reported by Reik (1948);

he describes a psychoanalytic session with a young woman who developed emotional problems following the breakup of a love affair with a physician.

> We had been discussing the problem for a few months and she still had not overcome her grief. At a certain point the analysis reached a deadlock. One session at this time took the following course. After a few sentences about the uneventful day, the patient fell into a long silence. She assured me that nothing was in her thoughts. Silence from me. After many minutes she complained about a toothache. She told me that she had been to the dentist yesterday. He had given her an injection and then had pulled a wisdom tooth. The spot was hurting again. New and longer silence. She pointed to my bookcase in the corner and said, "There's a book standing on its head."
>
> Without the slightest hesitation and in a reproachful voice I said, "But why did you not tell me that you had had an abortion?"

Reik, trusting his "third ear," had accomplished an important breakthrough in his treatment of the young woman with his sudden insight. Unlike most intuitive statements made by clinicians, Reik could verify its accuracy immediately:

> I had said it without an inkling of what I would say and why I would say it. It felt as if, not I, but something in me had said that. The patient jumped up and looked at me as if I were a ghost. Nobody knew or could know that her lover, the physician, had performed an abortion on her. . . . To protect the man she still loved, she had decided to tell me all except this secret.
>
> When I look back on the psychological situation, I can, of course, realize what brought me to my surprising statement. I must have felt for some time that the patient was keeping something secret when she spoke of the physician. Then came the session with the long pauses. I can follow the subterranean thread between her few associations now. Toothache, the injection by the dentist, the pulling of the wisdom tooth, the book that stands on its head. If I had followed this train of associations logically, I might perhaps—perhaps—have come to the same conclusion. Here was a displacement from below to above, from the genital region

to the mouth . . . an operation . . . pain . . . the position of the book, and the embryo on its head. I did not, however, use my logical powers, and I can only warn my students against using them in such situations. Logical operation subjects the analyst to errors and mistakes he would not make if he trusted his psychological rather than his logical gifts. An understanding of the process and the insertion of the logical links in the chain can and sometimes should be attempted afterward but not during the process [Reik, 1948, pp. 263–264].[8]

Sarbin et al. (1960), commenting on Reik's report, refuse to concede that Reik's successful postdiction was the result of any mysterious intuitive leap. Instead they argue that, like all people, clinicians are subject to learning without awareness, to influence through subthreshold inputs, to influence by hints, to selective forgetting, and so forth. Thus, they point out that Reik could have been virtually bombarded with inputs during earlier therapeutic sessions which activated such modules as pregnancy, abortion, and the like. Therefore, rather than use the concept of intuition to account for sudden insights, they view intuition as a form of inference which is a response to cues inaccessible to examination and report. The clinician may not be able to specify or identify the inputs and/or inferential process used for a given instantiation, but such a process is taking place.

Nevertheless, the clinician who relies on the intuitive process is likely to listen to cues from his own unconscious processes. His own associations are triggered by cues and associations made by his patient. The clinician's theoretical framework, value system, and prior experiences are all likely to influence what data he selects for assessment from the mass of data presented him. Once selected, he is likely to classify the bit of behavior into some general category which he considers important and relevant to the individual case. He is then likely to weigh the significance of the new data and, finally, interpret their meaning. While he may not be aware of such a step-by-step procedure, the clinician relying on intuition is probably following some similar more or less systematic inference process.

---

[8] Theodore Reik, *Listening with the Third Ear.* Copyright 1948, by Farrar, Straus & Company, Inc. Reprinted by permission of Farrar, Straus & Giroux, Inc.

CLINICAL JUDGMENT AS A DISCIPLINED INQUIRY

Although clinical judgments may be made in a number of ways, no one way—actuarial or clinical, taxonomic sorting or intuitive—provides all the answers. The cleverest and most experienced clinician is no match for statistical tables and computers, particularly when it comes to making most predictions about an individual only from test scores or other forms of quantitative data. No clinician has seen the wide sample of cases—nor has the memory to store and retrieve all he has learned about any particular individual—to perform such tasks more efficiently than a machine when such information is programmed into it. Intuition, long the hallmark of the clinician's clinician, may be arbitrary, unreliable, and prescientific. On the other hand, no machine can replace the clinician in sensing what another unique individual is experiencing, because such data derive only from interpersonal contact. No machine is inventive, asks open-ended questions, delves into previously unexplored areas, predicts single events, or has the insights and hunches of the clinician. By the same token, taxonomic sorting appears to be an oversimplified and somewhat artificial study of what a clinician does when he draws inferences and makes decisions and interpretations. Few new discoveries are likely to emerge from such an approach, nor are its resulting conceptualizations likely to produce very penetrating insights into human personality.

Several authors have urged that more research be carried out on the judgmental process so that clinical judgment becomes a more disciplined form of inquiry. Not content to consider intuition simply an art not open to experimental investigation, Hunt (1959) has shown that clinical judgments can be made more exact and objective by using scaling devices and other concepts derived from psychophysics. Thorne (1961), surveying types of errors made in clinical judgment, differentiates errors due to: (1) the clinician as a clinical instrument—problems due to personal bias, overconcern with professional status; (2) problems of case handling—inadequate screening methods, an incomplete sampling of behavior, inadequate follow-up studies, uncritical acceptance of client statements, poor communication of findings; (3) problems in the evidence-gathering process—failure to verify or evaluate complaints made by a patient; (4) problems in processing objective data—failure to recognize factors interfering with test performance, failure to reconcile test findings with other data, errors in handling test results; and (5) problems of relationships—improper timing of interpretations, poor judgment in establishing limits. Thorne's points are illustrated by many examples throughout his book, making it a practical guide for clinicians in making their judgments less subject to error.

Another promising approach has been the efforts to develop theoretical models of the clinical judgment process. The work of Sarbin et al. (1960) represents an effort to develop such a theoretical approach to clinical judgment within the broader context of cognitive theory. Osgood, Suci, and Tannenbaum (1957) have presented a similar view based on a two-stage process in judgment (decoding, or interpreting the stimuli; and encoding, or expressing an intention to respond in some way). By developing semantic differential scales, they have shown that the meaning of any concept can be specified on a limited number of derived scales. Kelly's (1955) theory of personality, dealing with the individual's personal constructs for cognizing and perceiving events, also involves a cognitive theory related to the nature of clinical judgment.

More recently, various mathematical models have been used to understand the judgment process better. One study (Bieri, Atkins, Briar, Leaman, Miller, & Tripodi, 1966) has applied the concepts and methods of information theory to analyses of clinical and social judgment. The judgment process, in this model, treats the stimuli as input, the response or judgment as output, and the mediating structure or judge as a communications channel.

Rather than dismiss or devalue intuition, these approaches aim to make it less arbitrary and vague. Holt (1961) points out that physicists, for example, use intuition a great deal—not as a supernatural revelation but rather as a creative process by which new theories and experimental ideas arise. The clinician's hunches are needed for hypothesis formation (knowing what to look for) and for any conclusions he draws (seeing the obtained data's relevance and meaning for his particular client). Cultivated intuition, buttressed by quantitative data, remains the best method for using the skills of the clinician as a clinical instrument.

CHAPTER 5 *Problems and Techniques of Psychological Assessment*

The purpose of the clinical judgment process is to arrive at a sufficiently clear picture of the client to make clinical decisions. For example, the clinician may need to decide whether the client is more likely to benefit from individual or family therapy, if the clinician's usual therapeutic techniques are appropriate for this client, whether hospitalization may become necessary, what the risks of suicide may be, or in general, whether he can work with the client or prefers to refer him to a professional colleague or social agency. Rather than a diagnosis, the clinician needs to make a psychological assessment of the person and his life situation in order to: (1) describe and understand him; and (2) make decisions based on predictions of the client's future behavior.

The assessment process was first described systematically by Henry Murray in 1938 in his publication *Explorations in Personality*. Murray studied 50 college men at the Harvard Psychological Clinic with a series of tests, observations, and interviews; the combined results gave a global picture of each individual. During World War II, Murray influenced the work of the Office of Strategic Services in selecting men for special assignments such as undercover agents or saboteurs. The OSS evaluation techniques, described after the war in a book entitled *Assessment of Men* (Murray, 1948), emphasized assessment over diagnosis. That is, using a variety of techniques patterned after the Harvard studies, the OSS staff was interested in appraising a candidate's strengths—courage, ingenuity under stress, leadership skills—rather than, more negatively, searching for his pathology.

The term *assessment* has come into increasing use since Murray's work was first reported. In 1949, the Institute of Personality Assessment and Research was established at the University of California; it was devoted to studying individuals through a variety of assessment procedures. The Clinical Psychology Assessment Project carried out by the University of Michigan (Kelly & Fiske, 1951) followed the then developing procedure of using a variety of tests, observations, questionnaires, and interviews in assessing a candidate's strengths and predicting future performance. Various projects have carried out assessment studies—some largely intuitive, others more actuarial—based on data from observations, interviews, rating scales, questionnaires, personal documents, psychometric tests, and other projective techniques.

Psychological assessment is a process in which a variety of techniques may be systematically used to describe, understand, and evaluate the attributes or characteristics of an individual or group. Assessment procedures are carried out daily by school psychologists, vocational and educational counselors, industrial and personnel psychologists, and clinical psychologists. Clinical psychologists may use data from any of the sources listed in the previous paragraph. This chapter will concentrate on one such form of assessment—psychological testing—since it represents a clinical procedure most closely identified with the clinical psychologist, and one in which he, alone, among all the mental health professionals, has the training and skill to make a significant contribution to the clinical decision-making process.

PSYCHODIAGNOSTIC TESTING

Now more than 75 years old, the psychological testing movement in this country has undergone many changes. While once the clinical psychologist's exclusive function was thought to be testing, few psychologists today consider it even a large part of their work (Kelly, 1961a). Correspondingly, the nature of tests used has changed considerably. Whereas the 10 most widely used tests in the 1930s and 1940s were exclusively measures of intelligence—such as the Stanford–Binet, Wechsler–Bellevue, and Porteus Maze (Louttit & Browne, 1947)—by 1960, certain projective tests for measuring personality—such as the Rorschach, Draw-A-Person and Thematic Apperception Test (TAT)—had taken over in popularity among clinical psychologists (Sundberg, 1961). More recently, as research has shown these tests to have questionable validity, and as the efficiency of the clinical interpretive process has been challenged, there has been some shift in the direction of objective, machine-scored tests for personality assessment (Fowler, 1969).

Clinical testing reached the zenith of its popularity after World War II. Rapaport and his colleagues at the Menninger Clinic produced a two-volume report, *Diagnostic Psychological Testing* (Rapaport, 1946), which for a decade or more remained the primary reference to which clinicians turned in their psychodiagnostic deliberations. Rapaport was heavily committed to psychoanalytic theory and attempted to use the results of testing to present a clinical picture of the structure of an individual's personality (that is, defenses, drives, styles of adaptation). He used seven psychological tests: Wechsler–Bellevue Intelligence Scale, Babcock Story Recall Test, the Goldstein–Scheerer Sorting Test, Hanfmann–Kasanin Concept Formation Test, Word Association, Rorschach, and TAT. The data for his research came from the test results of 217 patients with a variety of diagnoses at the Menninger Clinic and Hospital. A group of 54 randomly chosen members of the Kansas Highway Patrol served as a control group, and the scores of the two groups were compared. In addition, differences between individuals with different diagnostic labels were compared for each test.

Despite its enthusiastic acceptance by most clinicians, the study had some obvious flaws from a research-design standpoint. The control group may not themselves have been free of psychological problems. In any event, they were likely to differ sharply in socioeconomic status, cultural background, and perhaps intelligence from the majority of patients who were hospitalized at an expensive private clinic and sanitarium. The experimental group itself, while differentiated diagnostically, were not differentiated further by other factors (age, sex, education, ethnic background) which might influence test findings. Overall, the search for signs that would point to a diagnosis, followed by efforts to establish which personality characteristics produced these signs, was methodologically roundabout and highly inferential.

Despite its shortcomings, the two volumes represent a landmark in clinical testing. Due largely to Rapaport's influence, clinicians began to use test batteries, or several tests used together, so that differences in performance on different kinds of tests (structured and unstructured) could give important clues about the personality characteristics of the testee.

Different tests were also thought to tap different levels of consciousness, so that in combination they provided a more global picture of the client. For example, signs of severe psychopathology or organic brain damage may be absent on one test but present on another that called for a different kind of performance, thus aiding the clinician in his psychodiagnosis. Due also to Rapaport's influence, clinical psychologists began to view diagnosis as more than taxonomy, as a broader category that includes not only a diagnostic label but also a detailed, individualized personality description.

Within the last decade, much of the enthusiasm about psychodiagnostic testing has waned. Tests once considered panaceas for solving difficult diagnostic questions are now questioned regarding their worth and usefulness. The use of extensive test batteries to help the psychiatrist arrive at a diagnosis appears to be held in relatively low esteem among an increasing number of clinical psychologists. Carson (1958) has confirmed that in many psychiatric hospitals, staff psychologists are apt to regard such testing as a necessary but tedious responsibility that they turn over to graduate-student interns. (This, of course, reinforces the notion that testing is a second-rate, low-level skill that interns will not have to perform once they achieve staff status!) Many complain that testing is time-consuming, that psychological reports are largely ignored by the hospital staff, and that the whole process has little bearing on treatment planning.[1]

University psychology departments, too, have tended to deemphasize training in clinical testing. Graduate students in clinical psychology today are likely to be less concerned than the student of 10 (and particularly 20) years ago with problems of diagnosis, probably reflecting the disenchantment of their professors with commonly used diagnostic testing procedures, as well as the general dissatisfaction among mental health professionals with diagnostic classification. In a recent survey, Shemberg and Keeley (1970) found university training in clinical testing shifting from its former emphasis on projective techniques to its present emphasis on objective approaches. They found this shift to be especially marked in newer clinical programs.

Several explanations have been offered for the change in status of

---

[1] One notable exception is the work done at certain state institutions, particularly those for the mentally retarded, where an appraisal of intelligence can best be made through psychological testing, and where, correspondingly, the psychologist's report may be instrumental in planning a treatment program.

diagnostic tests from almost universal, uncritical acceptance 20 years ago to the present skepticism. As noted in the previous chapter, Meehl's (1954) conclusions regarding the comparative inefficiency of clinical analysis compared to statistical analysis were a blow to many who respected clinicians' intuitive judgments. The failure of expert diagnosticians to predict the later success of beginning clinical psychology students in the Michigan Clinical Psychology Assessment Project (Kelly & Fiske, 1951) added to the disillusionment. Studies on the poor reliability and validity of clinical judgments based on psychological test data (such as Little & Shneidman, 1959) raised further doubts.

Beyond these obvious reasons, however, a number of other hypotheses may account for the decline of psychodiagnostic testing. Such a decline may have been inevitable, since testing is no longer clinical psychologists' only activity; as other activities such as psychotherapy, consultation, and administration assumed more importance, the amount of time devoted to any one function was bound to decline (Holt, 1967). Furthermore, psychodiagnostic testing may have been oversold initially, thus inevitably resulting in the too-great pendulum swing toward the present disillusionment. Schafer (1954) has pointed out that, as practiced in many clinical settings, testing is frustrating, particularly when it represents a service for a psychiatrist, a member of a profession with which psychology competes for status, autonomy, and power. The psychologist's report has no direct, immediate benefit for the patient tested; rather, its potential value rests with the psychiatrist, who is likely to be a psychiatric resident, himself incompletely trained and relatively inexperienced professionally. Schafer has noted that when only difficult cases are referred for testing, the psychologist is in the unenviable position of being considered a final authority in the very situation in which it is hardest to do a good job.

Holt (1967) has pointed out that the psychodiagnostic role never allows the psychologist a simple, direct, and human responsiveness to the patient: "Behind his poker face he must be passing judgments which it would be destructive, at times, to reveal to his subject, and thus he has to consider a suffering human being as if he were a specimen only to be analyzed and described. Moreover, the tester must demand without ever giving [Holt, 1967, p. 451]." Such a stance is likely to cause considerable discomfort for a psychologist, from which he may wish to escape by avoiding the whole testing relationship. As a result, many humanistically oriented clinicians, in particular, are apt to see clinical testing as a hindrance to psychotherapy, since the testing relationship implies the therapist will take an authoritarian role, ask direct questions of the client, and then later use this knowledge to manipulate the latter's behavior.

Perhaps the disenchantment with psychodiagnostic testing is partly a reflection of the mounting public concern regarding test use. Many critics, including Congressmen, have charged that testing, particularly with personality tests, constitutes an invasion of privacy. They have been especially concerned that test results have not been kept confidential, with adequate safeguards against abuse. While such criticism has come mainly from the press, parent groups, some civil rights organizations, and several popular books (Gross, 1962), many psychologists, too, have begun to question whether psychological testing has not become dissociated from the mainstream of behavioral science. Anastasi (1968) has noted that the technical aspects of test construction have tended to outstrip the psychological sophistication with which test results are interpreted. She notes that test developers frequently lose contact with other psychologists working in the areas of learning, child development, and individual differences.

In defense of psychological testing in general, and psychodiagnostic testing in particular, it can be argued that the measurement function in any science is necessary and cannot be discarded lightly. Furthermore, there is continued active psychiatric demand for psychological assessment, reflecting confidence in tests, and greater acceptance of the psychologist as a diagnostician than was the case 15 or 20 years ago (Tallent, 1965). Diagnostic testing continues to be useful for such diverse purposes as: (1) obtaining a more complete perspective of a client and his psychological processes early in his psychotherapy; (2) evaluating the effects of psychotherapy through before-and-after testing; (3) identifying individuals requiring psychiatric hospitalization as well as estimating their prognosis; (4) helping in difficult differential diagnostic decisions, where the clinical problem may be unusually complex or the interview and observational data inconsistent or inconclusive; (5) obtaining an independent appraisal to help make clinical decisions based on other data be more certain; (6) revealing deeper psychological disturbances than may have been revealed in a structured interview; (7) discovering the extent of psychological deficit due to organic brain dysfunction; (8) assessing possible mental retardation in children with slow speech and motor development or school difficulties; (9) discovering gifted children likely to benefit from enriched school programs; (10) appraising the level of intellectual and emotional development in very young children; (11) gauging the basis for special disabilities such as dyslexia (impaired reading ability); and (12) aiding in the selection procedures for job training or other special programs.

Rather than discard psychodiagnostic testing, the field needs to face the challenges of new research findings, new psychotherapy techniques, and a greater awareness of the social implications of testing. Older tests must have their norms updated and must show greater evidence of reliability and validity. This last point is a frequent source of criticism, particularly regarding personality tests, and new ways may need to be found to evaluate the usefulness of a psychodiagnostic test. Cronbach and Gleser (1965) have pointed out that the value of assessment procedures is in making decisions. Therefore, tests must be evaluated in terms of success with this aim, keeping in mind the level of accuracy required, the cost of obtaining the information, and so on. A test useful in making one type of selective decision (that is, should this person be hospitalized?) may not be useful in a classification decision (what is his diagnosis; how should treatment proceed?). At times, then, a brief test providing a rough answer may be preferable to a precise test answering one or two questions.

TYPES OF TEST VALIDITY

A test's validity tells to what extent the test does the job for which it was designed. Thus, the validity of a personality test is the extent to which it yields an accurate description of an individual's personality characteristics. Borrowing from information theory developed in the study of electronic communication systems, Cronbach and Gleser (1965) attempted to apply the *bandwidth–fidelity* concepts to the validity of psychological test instruments. Bandwidth refers to the degree of complexity of information communicated in a given space or time. Fidelity refers to the exactness with which a specific message is reproduced and communicated. The classic ideal for a psychometric test is high fidelity and low bandwidth; for example, a college aptitude test tries to answer just one question (should this candidate be admitted to this college?) with great accuracy by concentrating its content on a narrow range of items and using correlated items to increase the test's reliability. Beyond this one question, the test score offers little information for choosing majors or diagnosing academic weaknesses. On the other hand, most clinical tests, particularly projective techniques, have almost unlimited bandwidth, since they attempt to answer so many questions about a client in a short testing period. Inevitably validity suffers; increases in the complexity of information are obtained only by sacrificing fidelity.[2]

A test's use depends on more than a simple answer to the general question "Is this a valid test?" Cronbach (1970) has suggested that the question to ask is "How valid is this test for the decision I wish to make?" or "How valid is the interpretation I propose for the test?" The validity of any test depends on how well the test measures whatever it is designed to measure; no test can be said to have high or low validity in the abstract. In the latest *Standards for Educational and Psychological Tests and Manuals* recommended by APA (1966), procedures for investigating the relationship between test performance and other independently observable facts about the behavior characteristics being studied are classified under three principal headings: content validity, criterion-related validity, and construct validity.

Content validity refers to whether the test covers a representative sample of the behavior being measured. While an important consideration in all tests, it is especially important in achievement tests. There, the psychologist might want to measure how well an individual has mastered a specific skill or course of study as the result of education or training. Determining content validity means judging whether each item is relevant to what is being measured—a decision for the potential test user rather than the test author. Such an approach is difficult to apply successfully to personality tests, where the same item may evoke different psychological processes in different clients, thus measuring different functions in different individuals. In such a case, an inspection of the content gives little if any clue as to what the test is measuring in any individual case. Sometimes clinicians have confused content validity with *face validity,* which is what the test seems to measure, but may not really be measuring at all.

Criterion-related validity is a test's effectiveness in predicting an individual's behavior in specified situations. Test performance is compared to some independent criterion measuring what the test is designed to predict. For example, conclusions from a psychodiagnostic test may be compared

---

[2] The hi-fi buff will recognize the problem immediately. The fidelity of a disk recording depends on the width of the groove; grooves crowded together provide more music but at the expense of fidelity. With tape recordings, the slower the tape speed, the more information but the poorer the fidelity. All communication systems thus must compromise between bandwidth and fidelity.

to a psychiatrist's independent diagnostic judgment. If both are obtained at more or less the same time, *concurrent validity* is the criterion; if not, *predictive validity*—how well the test predicts future performance—is the criterion. Concurrent validity is more important for tests diagnosing an existing condition, while predictive validity is useful to determine prognosis. Sometimes the designer of a new test will correlate its results with an established test, the latter serving as a criterion measure for the validity of the former. This procedure, based on concurrent validity, is commonly used in constructing intelligence tests and comparing their scores with the individual's score on an established test such as the Stanford–Binet Intelligence Scale.

Construct validity is the extent to which a test measures a particular psychological concept or construct, such as anxiety, neurosis, or intelligence. Many tests bear the name of a construct (ego strength) but actually may not be measuring the concept at all or may be doing so incompletely. Construct validity reflects how well the test is measuring the construct or trait presumed to underlie performance on the test. The clinician is particularly interested in explaining what personality characteristics might account for a particular test score or test pattern. To do so, he must test specific hypotheses or theoretical formulations that account for what each scale is measuring. The MMPI scales, for example, have been assigned meanings on the basis of numerous studies, from which a psychological hypothesis about the meaning of each scale's score has gradually emerged. As with all tests, increased knowledge leads to more complete understanding of the relative strength of various influences producing the test score. More than other measures of test validation, construct validity focuses attention on the role of psychological theory in test construction.

MEASURES OF RELIABILITY

Reliability refers to the consistency of a measure, and is particularly important because of its bearing on validity. A test cannot measure anything well without measuring it consistently; therefore, a test must have reliability if it is to have validity. A test's reliability coefficient tells us how much faith to put in the scores obtained from the test. Measures of a test's reliability let us estimate how much of the results are a true measure of the characteristic being studied and how much are attributable to chance errors. In order to obtain such a measure of reliability, more than one measurement of the characteristic for the same individual is necessary so that the consistency of scores can be studied.

Measures of reliability are commonly expressed as correlation coefficients; when they are high, the clinician can be confident about the stability of scores he obtains. While high reliability does not insure validity, it is a necessary aspect of a test before validity can be considered. In choosing a test, the clinician must decide whether the test's reliability is sufficiently high for the use to which he will put the results and the degree of precision with which he needs to make his predictions and interpretations. An inaccurate, undependable test has no value. The clinician must keep the test's reliability in mind in interpreting changes in test scores between sets of measurements, such as before and after psychotherapy. Otherwise, he is liable to attribute changes in test scores to changes within the individual rather than those to be expected from a fallible test instrument.

There are three major measures of reliability. The simplest is *test-retest reliability*. The same test is administered to the same individuals on two separate occasions, and the two sets of scores are correlated. In this way, the stability of scores over time is measured. However, since practice may affect the retest scores differently in different individuals and memory may be a factor if the time interval between tests is too short, the resulting correlations may be spuriously low or high. To avoid that difficulty, sometimes alternate forms of the same test are used. In such a situation, an individual is tested with one form on the first occasion and an equivalent form on the second. The correlation between the scores provides a measure of *alternate-form reliability*. One difficulty, however, is that truly parallel forms of a test are very difficult, expensive, and time-consuming to construct because they must contain items with the same format, range, and level of difficulty and content. Despite such efforts, practice effect may nevertheless lower error variance. Sometimes one test is split into two comparable halves, and the *split-half reliability* becomes a measure of how closely scores on the two halves agree. This is called *internal-consistency reliability*. Its main drawback lies in the difficulty of obtaining comparable halves of a test.

Personality tests, particularly projective techniques, present special problems in measuring test reliability. Retesting, particularly over a long interval, may be an invalid measure of the test's reliability since personality changes are likely to have occurred. Retesting over a short interval may be influenced by memory. Alternate forms of the Rorschach or TAT, for example, are difficult to obtain. In the same way, there is no logical way to split the cards into two comparable halves. One solution, particularly applicable when tests are not scored objectively and inadequate normative data exist, is to depend on *scorer reliability* (although, technically, this is not a form of reliability of the test itself). The reliability of projective tests is enhanced when different clinicians attribute the same personality characteristics to the client on the basis of their interpretation of the identical test protocol. One inevitable stumbling block, however, is the unknown contribution of the interpreter's skill, particularly noteworthy on projective techniques (Anastasi, 1968).

THE ASSESSMENT OF INTELLIGENCE

While the determination of a client's intelligence level is no longer the principal function of most clinical psychologists, intelligence tests still form an integral part of their diagnostic tools. Either separately or as part of a test battery, intelligence tests provide a structured situation with emotion-arousing tasks kept to a minimum, in which the client is asked to produce organized responses. Thus, test responses not only provide an estimate of intelligence but also a global appraisal of adaptive functions, grasp on reality, reasoning processes, memory, alertness, typical approach to intellectual situations, and so on. Tests of general intelligence and special-purpose intelligence tests relevant to clinical assessment will be considered next.

THE MEASUREMENT OF GENERAL INTELLIGENCE

The clinical psychologist is interested in making a general appraisal of a child's intelligence level when the child is having academic difficulties, particularly when mental retardation is suspected. More than obtaining an IQ score alone, he is interested in comparing the client's current level of functioning with any estimates of his potential intellectual capacity as they might be revealed in the test or in past test performance. Occasionally, the clinician is asked to help make a differential diagnosis between mental retardation and emotional disturbance, since both may produce similar behavior patterns that call for different treatment procedures. Adoption agencies frequently insist on some intellectual assessment of any child before allowing him to be placed for adoption. Perhaps the clinician is asked to appraise the intellectual capacities of various candidates for a special training program (like the Peace Corps), because previous findings have suggested a relationship between intelligence and job performance. Or perhaps the clinician must assess a potential psychotherapy candidate, including some evaluation of his intellectual abilities, in order to predict which psychotherapy technique might best suit him.

For most clinical purposes of individual intelligence testing, either the Stanford–Binet or Wechsler scales is likely to be used.[3] The 1960 Revision of the Stanford–Binet Intelligence Scale (Terman & Merrill, 1960) represents the latest up-dating of the Stanford revision of the original Binet Scales. The rationale for this test follows Binet's original conception of intelligence as a steadily growing power, to be measured for any individual on the basis of how far he can proceed in answering progressively more difficult items. Items range from those appropriate to age two to superior adult. The client is tested over a range of age levels suited to an estimate of his intellectual level, beginning slightly below his expected mental age and continuing to that level at which all items are failed. The highest level where all items are passed constitutes the basal age; the level at which all items are failed the ceiling age. Typically, successfully passed subtests are spread over several year levels between these extremes. The client's intelligence quotient (IQ) represents the relation between his test score and his age:

$$IQ = \frac{MA}{CA} \times 100$$

where

MA = mental age (basal age plus credit for subtests passed beyond that level)

CA = chronological age

(The ratio is multiplied by 100 to achieve a whole number.)

[3] Schools, the civil service, or the military may also use group testing. Group tests alert the clinician to individuals with extreme scores, either high or low, along any dimension. The clinical psychologist may wish to follow-up with individual tests chosen on the basis of this initial screening information.

This latest revision of the Stanford–Binet has met with a favorable reception (Himelstein, 1966). Data on the reliability and validity of the test are encouraging. Most of the reported reliability coefficients for the various age and IQ levels are over .90 (Terman & Merrill, 1960). Content validity, based on the tasks to be performed at various age levels, is high despite the preponderance of verbal items at the upper levels. Data indicate that criterion-related validity, based on academic achievement, is high, particularly when correlated with courses such as English, which stress verbal content. Data on construct validity suggest it, too, is quite satisfactory (Anastasi, 1968).

Many clinicians use the Stanford–Binet not only as a standardized test but also as a clinical interview. The variety of tasks, particularly with children, provides an opportunity for numerous tester–client interactions, which may be rich sources of personality data for the experienced clinician. The client's approach to various kinds of problems—including his reactions to frustration, challenge, success, and failure—can be observed and evaluated.

The Stanford–Binet is better suited to measure intelligence for children than adults. Standardized on subjects from ages two to 18, norms for adults must be statistically extrapolated; interpretations based on these norms therefore lack the precision of the empirically determined norms for children. In addition, the content of most of the items is frequently uninteresting to adults, making rapport difficult and further making the obtained scores questionable. Finally, the concept of mental age as an index of development is inapplicable to adults. Mental age does not continue to increase much beyond adolescence, certainly not at the rate of increase in childhood. For these reasons, and because he was interested in developing an intelligence test for adults that had clinical diagnostic value, Wechsler published the Wechsler–Bellevue Scale in 1939. Becoming available at a propitious time—the start of World War II, when military clinical psychologists needed a test to evaluate emotional disturbance or the presence of brain damage in addition to measuring intelligence—the Wechsler–Bellevue quickly became the standard instrument of military clinical testing. The test retained its prominence for use with adults for a decade after the war. In 1949, a downward extension of the Wechsler–Bellevue appeared, the Wechsler Intelligence Scale for Children (WISC) for ages seven to 16. In 1955, Wechsler replaced his original adult scale with a more carefully standardized Wechsler Adult Intelligence Scale

(WAIS). Finally, the Wechsler Preschool and Primary Scale of Intelligence (WPPSI) was introduced in 1967, designed for four to six-and-one-half year-olds.

All three Wechsler scales follow the same general pattern. Items similar in content are grouped into subtests and arranged by increasing order of difficulty. The major division is between verbal tests (with five or six subtests, depending on the particular Wechsler scale) and performance tests (five subtests). In this way, a verbal IQ, a performance IQ, and a full-scale IQ are obtained, in addition to scaled scores on each of the subtests. Table 5 indicates which subtests are included under the verbal

Table 5. A comparison of Wechsler subtests for various ages*

ADULTS (WAIS)	CHILDREN (WISC)	PRESCHOOL- PRIMARY (WPPSI)
	VERBAL SCALES	
Information	Information	Information
Comprehension	Comprehension	Comprehension
Arithmetic	Arithmetic	Arithmetic
Similarities	Similarities	Similarities
Vocabulary	Vocabulary	Vocabulary
Digit span	(Digit span)	(Sentences)
	PERFORMANCE SCALES	
Block design	Block design	Block design
Picture completion	Picture completion	Picture completion
Picture arrangement	Picture arrangement	Animal house
Object assembly	Object assembly	Mazes
Digit symbol	Coding	Geometric design
	(Mazes)	

* Subtests in parentheses represent alternates, to be used if one regular subtest is spoiled during administration or if the examiner has a special reason for including an additional subtest.

and performance scales and shows the similar subtests used for different age levels on the Wechsler Scales.

Wechsler (1958) views general intelligence as an aspect of "the total personality structure." Operationally defined, it is "the aggregate or global capacity of the individual to act purposefully, to think rationally, and to deal effectively with his environment [Wechsler, 1958, p. 7]." Rather than a mere sum of a number of abilities, intelligent behavior involves the combination of many abilities, coupled with drive and incentive toward achieving some goal. The best way to evaluate intelligence, however, according to Wechsler, is to measure its various aspects, as he proposes to do through the various subtest scores. Moreover, after developing his original scale out of his experience as a clinical psychologist at Bellevue Hospital in New York City, Wechsler was interested in using the test patterns for clinical diagnosis. That is, he believed that certain intellectual patterns were characteristically impaired in different nosological groupings. (Pattern analysis will be discussed presently.)

Reliability coefficients are reported to be very high for each of the subtests and the various age groupings. All three IQ scores on the WAIS have reliability coefficients above .90 (Wechsler, 1958); thus they are also highly reliable in terms of consistency with one another. Wechsler has also provided an extensive discussion of the content validity of the various tests, arguing that the psychological functions tapped by the various subtests fit his definition of intelligence and that the tests have proven their validity on the basis of clinical experience. Concurrent validity, based on correlations with the Stanford–Binet for adolescents and adults, is high, around .80. Construct validity brings into question the construct of intelligence, as defined by Wechsler. Intercorrelations of subtests and verbal and performance IQs, as well as factorial analyses of the scales, have produced sufficiently satisfactory results to suggest the verbal and performance scales have much in common, although the allocation of subtests to one or the other scale may be somewhat arbitrary (Anastasi, 1968).

Clinically, the Wechsler Scales have provided information about a client far beyond the intellectual aspects of his functioning. Unusual responses, the types of items failed, reaction times to various subtests, as well as the qualitative analysis of his responses, may provide useful clinical clues. Perseveration in repeating digits may lead the clinician to search for possible organic brain damage; failure to answer an easy item but success in answering a more difficult one may suggest pseudo-retardation. Similarly, difficulties in attention and concentration, slow adaptability to a new learning situation, test anxiety on particular types of items, personal preoccupations, rigidity of thinking, and many more clues are familiar to the experienced clinician.

Wechsler originally intended to develop an intelligence test for adults that would aid in psychiatric diagnosis. Twenty years later, Wechsler remained interested in studying the configurational pattern of subtest scores (called *pattern analysis*) in order "to find a way or formula for identifying diagnostically different groups, and eventually the individuals composing them, on the basis of their differential performance on a number of tests administered as a battery [Wechsler, 1958, p. 165]." Rapaport (1946), Schafer (1948), and Wechsler were instrumental in identifying diagnostic signs by linking personality characteristics to test profiles. Rapaport provided an extensive rationale for what psychological characteristics of the client were called for on each subtest of the Wechsler–Bellevue, in order to interpret the significance of test scatter (the extent of variations of an individual's subtest scores).[4] Wechsler (1958) provided typical scatter patterns for individuals with various disorders: organic brain disorders, schizophrenia, anxiety states, juvenile delinquency, and mental deficiency. For example, Wechsler suggested the following pattern for schizophrenia:

> Verbal IQ higher than Performance IQ
>
> Sum of Picture Arrangement plus Comprehension less than Information and Block Design
>
> Object Assembly much below Block Design
>
> Very low Similarities with high Vocabulary and Information, definitely pathognomonic.

The analysis of score patterns proved popular among many clinical psychologists as an aid in clinical interpretation of test findings. However, subsequent research has suggested that pattern analysis has little validity (Cronbach, 1970). Errors in measurement in subtest scores could account for a considerable amount of scatter. No normative baseline of variation was presented, making it difficult to evaluate the scatter in pathological groups. Finally, patients in different diagnostic categories did not necessarily show different patterns, nor did those in the same category necessarily show similar ones. Few clinical psychologists now are likely to rely on the analysis of scatter alone, although some (like Pope & Scott, 1967;

---

[4] Scatter actually is the average deviation of the subtest scores around the individual's verbal or performance mean, depending on which type of subtest is involved. The assumption is that a wider scatter of scores is more characteristic of pathological individuals.

Allison, Blatt, & Zimet, 1968) believe that clinical evidence shows that at least an informal study of subtest profiles is useful in providing additional clinical clues.

SPECIAL PURPOSE INTELLIGENCE TESTING

Since there are literally hundreds of intelligence tests in print (Buros, 1961), many of which interest clinical psychologists, this section cannot provide comprehensive coverage. Instead, special areas in which a clinician may be asked to make an intellectual appraisal are described, along with representative tests for those areas. First, however, it should be pointed out that no test of intelligence can sample all cognitive functions, despite our view of intelligence as a global capacity. Most tests of children's intelligence, in particular, measure those intellectual skills prerequisite to classroom learning and school achievement. Usually they present items most familiar to white, middle-class children, thereby possibly gauging a minority child's intellectual capacity inaccurately. These tests mainly call for conventional answers that stress conformity but do not credit creativity.[5] With these cautions in mind in interpreting the results of any intelligence test, the following special areas are of interest to clinicians:

Infant intelligence testing. Tests for discovering neurological or sensory disorders that might limit normal mental and emotional development present the clinician with an interesting challenge in test administration, scoring, and interpretation. He must exercise considerable patience to get a representative sample of behavior regulated by intellect. Moreover, he must decide what constitutes intelligent behavior in infants and how it can be measured. He cannot rely on the infant following standardized test instructions, nor can he call for verbal responses. Factors such as fatigue, distractability, the infant's poor internal state, and lack of motiva-

---

[5] Guilford (1967), after many years of factorial research, has concluded that many factors exist in what he terms the "structure of intellect." That is, a large number and variety of skills make up what we call intelligence. Guilford has drawn the useful distinction between: (1) *convergent production* operations, used in most intelligence tests, where from a number of alternatives there is convergence to one correct answer; and (2) *divergent production* operations, neglected on most intelligence tests, where from one question there is divergence to a number of possible answers. The latter type is more likely to measure creativity.

tion may affect test performance. Good rapport is essential. Scoring to a large extent depends on whether the clinician observed some fleeting bit of behavior that indicates the infant can perform the task but that may never again show up during the testing session. The experienced clinician must depend largely on general observations of the infant's reactions to simple tasks such as those requiring imitation, following a bright object with the eyes, or simple eye–hand coordination. The reliability of infant intelligence tests is usually relatively low because of these difficulties in administration and scoring. Validity, measured by predicting the infant's intellectual level in future years (as might be requested for a potential adoptee) is rarely entirely satisfactory since these tests are of little value in predicting future ability levels or school performance. Their main clinical purpose is to provide a rough picture of the infant's developmental level and to rule out gross motor or sensory disturbances.

Most clinicians experienced in working with young children prefer to use either the Gesell Developmental Schedules or the Cattell Infant Intelligence Scale (Stott & Ball, 1965; Escalona, 1968). The Gesell Developmental Schedules (Gesell & Amatruda, 1947) are essentially standardized observational procedures for assessing the infant's level of behavioral development in four areas: motor, adaptive, language, and personal–social. The clinician bases his conclusions primarily on his observations of the infant's responses to various stimulus objects—ball, cup, rattle—and secondarily on information supplied by the mother. Responses are scored according to the detailed description of behavior expected at different developmental levels (norms), as determined after many years of research by Gesell and his associates. The Cattell Infant Intelligence Scale (Cattell, 1947) is a downward extension of the 1937 Stanford–Binet, appropriate for ages three to 30 months. Test items are grouped into age levels, all items passed are tallied and a mental age and IQ computed, all in the Binet tradition. The Cattell materials duplicate many used by Gesell as well as those from the lower levels of the Stanford–Binet, plus it adds some original test items. Beginning largely with perceptual items (following a person with the eyes or looking for a spoon), the test adds motor items (transferring objects from hand to hand) and finally, at higher ages, verbal items (pointing to objects named by the examiner). Both the Gesell and Cattell scales and the recently revised and restandardized Bayley Infant Scale of Development (Bayley, 1965), while lacking the reliability and validity of tests for older children and adults, nevertheless are diagnostically useful to supplement a pediatrician or neurologist's examination by measuring the nature and extent of organic deficits that may hamper normal development.

Intelligence testing of the physically handicapped. Whatever a child's physical handicap—visual, auditory, orthopedic, neurological—his intellectual development has been affected. The handicap itself, subsequent changes in school and social experiences, special treatment received from family members, deprivation of stimulation—all affect test performance. Norms on the level of growth expected at different ages may be misleading. The psychologist, perhaps assessing a handicapped child to help reach a decision regarding educational placement, must be aware of more than the present level of functioning; he must take into account the child's background, the nature and extent of his disability, his physical limitations, and his opportunities for maximizing what potential is available. To compound the problem, there is growing evidence that multiple handicaps (deaf–blind; physically handicapped with subnormal intelligence) are the rule rather than the exception (Mittler, 1970). Most such children suffer from some form of learning disorder.

With children having extensive multiple handicaps, standardized testing may provide less valuable information than careful observational methods. Not only does the child's intellectual level need to be gauged; the effects of the total handicap must be assessed so the child can make the most efficient use of what intellectual assets remain available. With less severely impaired children, testing may be used more, but needs to be administered, scored, and interpreted carefully. Deaf children, for example, are likely to be handicapped on verbal tests because of their limited linguistic development. The Hiskey–Nebraska Test of Learning Aptitude (Hiskey, 1966), developed and standardized on deaf and hard-of-hearing children, is suitable for ages three to 16. Norms for both the deaf and partially hearing are available. Instructions may be given in pantomime so the test is entirely nonverbal. Correlation with established intelligence tests for children with normal hearing is reasonably good. The blind child can respond to an oral presentation by the examiner, but cannot handle test items requiring visual–motor coordination or space perception. Whenever possible, the tests of general intelligence are used, modified to accommodate the special problems of the blind. The verbal tests of the Wechsler scales have been used, omitting the performance tests. The Hayes–Binet Scale

(Hayes, 1942), a highly verbal test using material from the 1937 Stanford–Binet, is sometimes used. Neither is entirely satisfactory, since words may have different meanings for blind children than for the nonblind. In general, verbal sections of established tests should be used with caution unless they have been standardized on blind children.

Neurological handicaps, particularly when minimal brain damage is suspected, have been increasingly studied by psychologists. While there is considerable controversy over attributing such difficulties to brain damage, most clinicians agree that learning disorders are common and may arise from a lack of basic perceptual abilities. Disturbances in visual perception are especially common, resulting in poor eye–hand coordination, poor recognition of words, "mirror writing," and so on. A useful, reliable diagnostic test designed to measure perceptual development in children aged three to eight is the Frostig Developmental Test of Visual Perception (Frostig, 1964). The test measures five perceptual skills (eye–motor coordination, figure–ground discrimination, constancy of shape, position in space, and spatial relations) relevant to school performance. Carefully standardized, with high reliability and validity based on classroom adjustment, the test is useful for planning a specialized remedial educational program based on the individual child's perceptual difficulties.

Intelligence testing of the verbally handicapped. Beginning with some of the early methods for diagnosing mental retardation in children, this kind of testing has interested psychologists for almost a century. During World War I, the Army Beta, a group-administered nonlanguage test was used to measure the intelligence level of foreign-speaking or illiterate soldiers. In addition, so-called culture fair tests such as the Leiter International Performance Scale, the Progressive Matrices, and the Porteus Mazes have been available for many years. Each stresses performance tasks and attempts to circumvent the necessity of any knowledge or language of a given culture. Particularly within the last decade in the United States, many psychologists have increasingly insisted that most intelligence tests penalize culturally disadvantaged persons because they are heavily weighted with items requiring language skills, which may be a poor indicator of general intelligence or intellectual capacity. In this regard, Hewett and Massey (1969), both school psychologists, have provided useful information in testing black and Spanish-speaking children. They cite significant aspects of black ghetto culture—modes of communication and life styles as well as differences in motivation—and the language and work tempo of the Spanish-speaking child, which are likely to affect performance on tests such as the WISC.

Perhaps the best tests of intelligence level of the verbally handicapped are the Peabody Picture Vocabulary Test or the Illinois Test of Psycholinguistic Abilities. The Peabody Picture Vocabulary Test (PPVT) (Dunn, 1965), found useful in testing nonreaders, stutterers, expressive aphasics, and withdrawn children, is a rapid screening device in which the child is presented with a series of 150 cards, one at a time, and asked to point to one of the four figures on the card that matches the examiner's orally presented stimulus word ("put your finger on banana"). The test, with alternate forms, was standardized on over 400 subjects between the ages of two and one-half and 18. It has the advantage of not requiring language but only a pointing response; its disadvantage lies in only measuring vocabulary, just one segment of intelligence. Shaw, Matthews, and Klove (1966) have reported only small correlations between the PPVT and the WISC. The Illinois Test of Psycholinguistic Abilities (ITPA) (Kirk, McCarthy, & Kirk, 1968) is a promising new approach for delineating and measuring special cognitive abilities and disabilities in children as well as testing intelligence. Based on a theoretical communication model, it measures the processes involved in understanding and speaking a language. Various functions are tapped: (1) the comprehension of visual and auditory symbols (decoding); (2) the organizing process of relating and manipulating these symbols in a meaningful way (association); and (3) the expressive process in which meaning is transmitted through words and gestures (encoding). Twelve subtests are included, designed to isolate specific psycholinguistic abilities and disabilities. While still relatively new, the ITPA, standardized on children aged two years and four months to 10 years and three months, seems particularly useful for diagnoses leading to specific remedial programs.

THE ASSESSMENT OF ORGANIC BRAIN DYSFUNCTION

Determining the existence, nature, and extent of organic brain damage in an individual is frequently of great interest to various professionals. Lawyers are anxious to have such an evaluation of any head injuries their clients may have sustained in an accident. Pediatricians may wish to determine the bases for their patient's slow speech or motor development. Physicians working in the field of geriatrics may want to evaluate a patient's intellectual impairment or evaluate his ability to be self-sufficient. Neurologists and psychiatrists need to make a differential diagnosis between functional and organic disorders, each of which calls for different treatment procedures. Educators are interested in devising special classroom programs for the brain-injured child.

Such evaluations are generally carried out by neurologists, who follow an established clinical procedure in their diagnostic examinations of individuals suspected of brain injury or disease. Recent memory, remote memory, abstract thinking, knowledge of time and place, judgment, language usage, and other characteristics are appraised in adults. In children, hyperactivity, distractability, low frustration tolerance, irritability, aggressiveness, and certain perceptual difficulties are noted as diagnostic signs. The contribution of the clinical psychologist has been to develop specialized tests to measure these deficiencies in various areas of functioning. Such tests must not only differentiate brain-damaged individuals from the general population; they must also reliably differentiate signs due to functional bases from signs that result from demonstrable brain dysfunction.

In constructing tests for assessing brain damage, it is important to note that organicity—that is, dysfunction due to structural changes in the central nervous system—is not a unitary concept. Brain injury may lead to a wide variety of behavior patterns, even producing opposite patterns in individuals with similar injuries; it may produce different effects in adults, children, and infants. The age at which the injury is sustained may affect subsequent behavior, based partly on intellectual development prior to the damage. Any time that has elapsed between injury and testing may obscure the extent of the damage, since compensatory readjustments may have begun. While a person with even mild or moderate brain damage will suffer some loss of capacity, considerable compensation for such a loss may occur in a strongly motivated individual determined to recapture his former achievement level. (The aphasic person who relearns speech is an example of this last point.) Rather than viewing the brain as damaged or undamaged, the locus and extent of the particular injury must be evaluated for a particular individual. As Yates (1966) has pointed out, brain damage in any given individual will produce: (1) a general deterioration in all aspects of functioning; (2) a differential effect, depending on the location and extent of damage; and (3) a highly specific effect if damage occurs in highly specified areas of the brain, such as speech areas. All three effects must be considered in evaluating the deficit in functioning brought about by the brain injury or disease.

Once psychometric instruments are selected for measuring loss of specific functions, the clinical psychologist must cope with several other problems particularly unique to neuropsychological testing. One such problem is the lack of a baseline, or the brain-damaged individual's pre-traumatic level of performance, which is needed in order to measure any loss. For many years, clinicians followed Wechsler's Deterioration Indices (Wechsler, 1958) by comparing those functions said to hold (that is, be retained) despite brain damage with those that don't hold (that is, deteriorate) with damage. The former were thought to include, on the Wechsler scales, those functions called for in Information, Vocabulary, Object Assembly, and Picture Completion; the latter include those functions necessary in Digit Span, Similarities, Digit Symbol, and Block Design. Following Wechsler's formula, a deterioration quotient was obtained; the lower the "don't hold" subtest scaled scores, the higher the probability of brain impairment. However, there has been considerable recent criticism of this approach (see Rabin, 1965). The reliability of subtest scores is not high enough to permit confidence in such an interpretation except for very large differences. Moreover, the indices frequently fail to differentiate organic from functional disorders. The difficulty, as noted earlier, is in thinking of organicity as a single category and thereby assuming all brain-damaged individuals will react alike, without regard to differences in acuteness, chronicity, localization, or premorbid personality.

Clearly, no single psychological test can be considered an adequate measure of brain damage. Moreover, psychological tests are not particularly effective in identifying which part of the brain is damaged (Talland, 1963), since any impairment in performance observed on such tests may result from a wide variety of organic dysfunctions. Instead, when brain injury is known to exist, tests may serve a useful diagnostic function in determining the pattern and measuring the degree of deficit. Smith and Philippus (1969) have compiled a comprehensive list and research bibliography for some 65 psychometric instruments measuring loss of various functions due to brain damage. The remainder of this section will deal with assessment techniques designed to measure impairment due to organic brain dysfunction in the following areas: perceptual–motor, memory, and concept formation.

Individuals with diffuse brain damage frequently have difficulty with spatial perception. More specifically, those with temporal lobe lesions commonly have trouble copying geometric figures from memory. Perhaps the best known and most popular psychodiagnostic test for measuring difficulties in perceptual–motor coordination is the Bender Visual Motor Gestalt Test (Lubin, Wallis, & Paine, 1971). The Bender–Gestalt consists of nine simple geometric designs composed of dots, lines, angles, and curves arranged in a variety of relationships. The cards are presented one at a time, and the client is instructed to copy each design while looking at the sample in front of him (see Figure 4). As originally introduced by Bender (1938), the designs came from Max Wertheimer, a

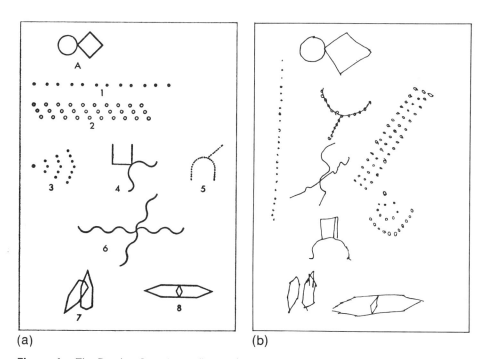

(a)   (b)

Figure 4. The Bender–Gestalt test figures (a) are to be copied by the subject as they are presented to him one by one. The drawings of a man in his late sixties with a history of alcoholism and excessive use of barbiturates are shown in (b). Note especially the poor planning, the rotation of some figures, the distortion of some figures, and the inadequate motor control. (Courtesy of James L. Way, Ph.D.)

founder of Gestalt psychology, who used them to study visual perception. Bender, a psychiatrist, was interested in applying the designs to a clinical situation in order to help diagnose organic brain disturbances correlated with trauma or toxic agents. For many years the test was analyzed by an intuitive procedure such as the inspection technique described by Hutt (1953). Objective scoring systems have now been developed for adults (Pascal & Suttell, 1951) and for children (Koppitz, 1964), although many clinicians continue to prefer either a subjective analysis or some combination of subjective and objective procedures. Interestingly, the Bender–Gestalt technique has been used to uncover personality dynamics as well as to differentiate perceptual–motor difficulties due to brain damage, mental retardation, or emotional disturbance. When evaluated with objective scores or by some systematic inspection procedure—particularly in the hands of a clinician skilled in using this test—considerable diagnostic value may result (Billingslea, 1963). However, in general, the validity of the test remains unproved, especially in the diagnosis of organicity in young children.

Memory loss, particularly the impaired capacity to retain recently learned material, can frequently be assessed through simple tests of general intelligence (such as repeating a series of digits). However, no entirely satisfactory clinical test of memory is available. The Wechsler Memory Scale (Wechsler, 1945) has been widely used for many years. The scale, with equivalent forms for retesting, is useful in examining adults with such defects as senility, amnesia, and aphasia. It provides a rapid screening device for measuring such functions as immediate recall, memory span, orientation to time and place, and similar characteristics frequently found impaired with brain damage. However, the norms are not adequate, nor does the test manual provide data on reliability and validity.

The Benton Visual Retention Test (Benton, 1963), another test of recent memory, consists of 10 cards with fairly simple designs which are exposed one at a time for 10 seconds. The client is instructed to draw the design from memory immediately after the card is removed. Thus, in addition to immediate recall, spatial perception and perceptual–motor coordination are tested. The client's drawings are scored and the errors classified (size errors, rotations, perseverations—that is, persistence in drawing a figure in a way that was appropriate for the previous stimulus but is inappropriate for this one). Norms are available for various ages (8 through adult) and intellectual levels. Three equivalent series of 10 designs are available for use with alternate presentations. Similar to the Benton, the Graham–Kendall Memory-for-Designs Test (Graham & Kendall, 1960) also provides age and intelligence level standardization. Brilliant and Gynther (1963) compared the predictive diagnostic accuracy of the Bender–Gestalt, the Benton Visual Retention, and the Graham–Kendall Memory-for-Designs by testing 120 patients without knowledge of their psychiatric diagnosis. They found that performance on all three commonly used tests of organicity did predict clinical diagnosis at a very high level of significance. The best single measure was the Bender–Gestalt, which correctly identified 82 percent of all patients.

Tests of concept formation are particularly useful in gauging the methods a client uses to solve problems requiring abstract thinking. Kurt Goldstein, a neuropsychiatrist, from his experience with brain-damaged soldiers in World War I, concluded that the major effect of such damage was the loss of abstract thinking. By this he meant that such individuals have difficulty shifting from one aspect of a situation to another, or conceptualizing a common characteristic in a variety of seemingly disparate items or objects.

After many years of research, Goldstein and Scheerer (1941) published a monograph in which five tests were described for measuring an individual's ability to engage in abstract thinking. The Goldstein–Scheerer Tests of Abstract and Concrete Thinking, a series of tasks calling for copying designs, sorting colors and objects, and reproducing patterns from memory, has been used by clinicians for many years. Yet, the tests suffered from inadequate norms, the lack of a standardized scoring system, and no data on reliability. Because of this, plus evidence that abstract reasoning loss is not limited to brain damage but may occur also in schizophrenia (Bolles & Goldstein, 1939), the tests have limited diagnostic usefulness. However, since they offer a good opportunity for clinical observations of the thinking processes of clients engaged in a variety of tasks, they continue to be used. The same may be said of the Hanfmann–Kasanin Concept Formation Test (Hanfmann & Kasanin, 1942) in which the examinee is required to sort blocks of various color, shape, height, and surface size into categories and then to state the principle of his classification. Thought disturbances due to brain damage as well as schizophrenia may be detected in this manner.

PROJECTIVE TECHNIQUES IN PERSONALITY ASSESSMENT

Personality assessment is part of all clinical testing since personality characteristics invariably influence performance on all tests. However, those tests whose specific purpose is to appraise personality may be divided into two categories: (1) projective tests, where the stimulus is deliberately ambiguous and thus open to a variety of interpretations by the client, generally evaluated by qualitative means; and (2) psychometric tests, or so-called objective personality tests, including inventories, questionnaires, and rating scales, generally evaluated by more quantitative measurements.

The advent of both psychoanalysis, with its emphasis on the importance of unconscious motivation, and phenomenology, with its emphasis on understanding an individual through the perception of his subjectively experienced world, was instrumental in leading clinical psychologists to seek methods that go beyond a person's defenses to reveal his impulses, drives, conflicts, and anxieties. Frank (1939) is generally credited with introducing the term *projective methods* in the assessment of personality. By this he meant those test instruments that reveal how an individual organizes his experiences and in the process disclose his private world of meanings, patterns, and feelings without the individual necessarily being aware of it. According to Frank, the projection of the individual's personality into the stimulus material was analogous to an externalization (perhaps as a movie projector projects an image on the screen); subsequent clinicians have tended to tie the concept to the Freudian defense mechanism of projection.

Projective techniques have certain distinguishing characteristics: (1) they present relatively unstructured stimuli, permitting a large, sometimes unlimited, variety of possible responses; (2) they use indirect, disguised methods so that the client is not aware of what constitutes a "good" or "bad" response or how that response will be interpreted; (3) they encourage considerable freedom of response, producing more personalized responses than would a typical yes–no personality questionnaire; (4) they are sensitive to unconscious or latent aspects of personality; (5) they produce a global, composite picture of the whole personality rather than measuring separate traits; and (6) they are open to a wide variety of interpretations, frequently involving much subjective clinical judgment.

Lindzey (1961) has classified projective techniques on the basis of the types of responses they elicit from the subject, reasoning that such a system comes closest to differentiating the underlying psychological processes tapped by the various tests. He has distinguished five general types of response: (1) association; (2) construction; (3) completion; (4) choice or ordering; and (5) expression.

ASSOCIATION TECHNIQUES

Association techniques require the examinee to respond to the stimulus material with the first associations (words, images, or ideas) that occur to him, without hesitating or stopping to organize his thoughts. Similar to Freud's free association method, this technique is thought to provide a bridge to unconscious processes. Two tests that fall within this category are the Word Association Test and the Rorschach. The Word Association Test, with a long experimental psychology history dating back to Galton and Wundt, was used for clinical purposes by Kraepelin around the turn of the century. Carl Jung, the eminent psychiatrist and early co-worker of Freud, used the method as a diagnostic device early in this century, although his work did not appear in English translation until 1918. In this country at about the same time, Kent and Rosanoff (1910), two psychiatrists, constructed a similar test for clinical purposes. Both the Jung and Kent–Rosanoff tests consisted of 100 words, presented orally, to which the examinee was to respond with the first word that came into his consciousness. Interpretations were based on an analysis of reaction times, idiosyncratic content, and, in the case of Kent–Rosanoff, comparisons of responses with frequency tables of expected responses (norms). While these lists included essentially neutral words only, Rapaport (1946) added many highly charged sexual and emotional words in his psychodiagnostic studies. However, the test has proved to be of limited clinical usefulness because of inadequate norms, a poorly developed theoretical basis, and its general inappropriateness to individuals with limited language skills.

By contrast, the Rorschach Inkblot Test is among the most widely used projective techniques for both clinical assessment and personality research (see Figure 5). Developed in 1921 by Swiss psychiatrist Hermann Rorschach (1921) as a useful device for psychiatric classification (patients in different diagnostic categories responding differently to the blots), the test received little attention for the next decade. However, beginning with Beck's (1930) doctoral dissertation about the test, followed by German-born

Figure 5. This inkblot is similar to those used in the Rorschach Test. It is deliberately made ambiguous and is therefore subject to various interpretations; the subject's responses of what he "sees" may reveal ordinarily hidden aspects of his unique personality.

psychologist Bruno Klopfer's immigration to the United States, and the establishment of the Rorschach Institute and Rorschach Research Exchange in 1936, the test slowly gained preeminence over all other projective methods. Today, the Rorschach's usefulness goes beyond diagnosis alone to provide a broad, multidimensional view of personality structure.

The test uses a standard set of 10 cards, each showing a bilaterally symmetrical inkblot, such as might be produced by folding a sheet of paper over drops of ink. Half of the cards are in shades of gray and black on a white background, while the remainder involve colors in varying hues and intensities on a white background. The cards are presented to the examinee one at a time in a standardized order, and he is told to state what the blots look like or suggest. Following the first phase of administration, wherein the examiner keeps a verbatim record of the responses, the examinee is asked to reexamine the cards and report what characteristics of the blot contributed to his associations. This last procedure is essential for scoring purposes.

Unlike many other projective techniques where interpretation of the test performance is primarily subjective and intuitive, the Rorschach relies on a formal scoring system supplemented by intuitive clinical analysis. Most clinical psychologists today subscribe to the scoring systems of either Beck (1944) or Klopfer (see Klopfer, Ainsworth, Klopfer, & Holt, 1954). With minor technical differences, both score all test responses for location (which area of the blot was used), determinants (use of form, color, shading, movement), content of responses, and whether the response qualifies as popular (that is, common) or original. The scoring information is typically summarized in a psychogram. Interpretations of the data are likely to begin with a formal analysis of the psychogram and the various ratios between determinants. An analysis of content and a sequence analysis (that is, analysis of the order of responses or associations) is likely to follow. Since the Rorschach yields hypotheses on such a wide variety of intellectual and emotional aspects of the individual, interpretation depends to a great extent on the clinician's skills and experiences in integrating quantitative and qualitative data in presenting a global picture of the individual's personality. It can be used with both adults and children; with children, the Rorschach is said to provide a measure of the child's developmental level (Halpern, 1960).

Despite the abundance of research studies using the Rorschach—now believed to number in the thousands—considerable controversy remains over the test's usefulness. Like many projective techniques, the Rorschach has been criticized for trying to deal with interrelated aspects of personality too complex for analysis, showing poor reliability and validity, and having inadequately developed norms. In an effort to establish norms for groups that particularly lack them, Ames and her colleagues at the Gesell Institute of Child Development at Yale have published Rorschach norms for children aged two through 10, adolescents 10 through 16, and those older than 70 (Ames, Leonard, Métraux, & Walker, 1952, 1954, 1959). Practicing clinicians are likely to follow a more subjective set of norms based upon their personal clinical experiences.

Whether the Rorschach is reliable and valid is a difficult issue to resolve. Some clinicians argue that the Rorschach is not a test at all, but a technique for eliciting information about personality; consequently it cannot, nor should it try, to satisfy the usual psychometric criteria for reliability. However, despite the difficulties of applying the usual reliability measures to the Rorschach test, Zubin, Eron, and Schumer (1965) have surveyed such attempts and found their results disappointing. They concluded that "although a high degree of scorer reliability can be obtained when there is pretraining and supervised practice with respect to a specific system, most other estimates of reliability have yielded unsatisfactory results [Zubin, Eron, & Schumer, 1965, p. 238]." Many practicing clinicians continue to have faith in their own analyses from Rorschach data although mounting evidence questions its validity. Studies of validity —through: (1) "blind analysis"; (2) the use of clinical signs (of organic brain damage, for example); (3) matching Rorschach experts' findings with case histories or psychiatric interviews; and (4) investigating the underlying assumptions of Rorschach determinants (color, movement)— have produced generally unfavorable results. Results obtained through an analysis of content, valid if the Rorschach were considered a clinical interview, have been somewhat more promising.

The recently developed Holtzman Inkblot Test (Holtzman et al., 1961), modeled after the Rorschach, has attempted to correct some of the latter's technical deficiencies. Alternate forms with 45 cards each are provided, administration and scoring are standardized, and norms are available for children and adults. Group methods of administration and computer scoring make this test useful for rapid, large-scale screening as well as individual diagnosis and assessment. Reliability is easier to measure because of the parallel forms (test-retest reliability) and large number of cards (split-half reliability). These, along with scorer reliability, are reported as quite satisfactory; validity also appears promising (Holtzman, 1968). Despite this, it is not likely that clinicians trained in the Rorschach will easily replace that test with the Holtzman Inkblot Test until more convincing data are available concerning the latter's ultimate superiority. In the meantime, the Rorschach is likely to retain its preeminence among projective techniques.

CONSTRUCTION TECHNIQUES

Construction techniques make somewhat more complex cognitive demands on the examinee than do association techniques. He is required to construct or create a product, typically a story, rather than simply respond with spontaneous associations. The Thematic Apperception Test and its variations are examples of such an approach.

The Thematic Apperception Test (TAT), first developed by Murray and his co-workers (Morgan & Murray, 1935), is frequently used by clinicians to investigate a client's personality dynamics. The TAT was originally intended to be a useful tool for studying fantasy in normal subjects, but it soon began to prove useful for clinical purposes as well. Like the Rorschach, the TAT has generated voluminous research literature, and the test has found wide acceptance among clinicians and nonclinicians alike; among the latter group, for example, social psychologists and anthropologists have used TAT cards to study and compare various cultures and subcultures.

The TAT consists of a series of drawings and reproductions of paintings depicting scenes of varying content and degree of ambiguity designed to stimulate the imagination. Thirty cards are included, one of which is blank. The examinee is handed the cards one by one, and is asked to interpret each picture by creating a separate story, being sure to include what is happening, what events led up to the present scene, and what will be the outcome. In practice, the clinician is not likely to use the entire set of cards, but rather to choose those that are calculated to evoke the particular conflicts, wishes, moods, and experiences of the client he is interested in exploring. The examiner records the stories as nearly verbatim as possible without intruding on the examinee's fantasies. Typically, the initial card used depicts a boy seated at a table with a violin in front of him; the last card is blank, encouraging the examinee to create any story he wishes.

The TAT can be considered a wideband instrument providing a variety of interrelated information about the client's needs, conflicts, drives, and defenses as the client reveals them by reacting to the partially structured situations depicted on the cards. The clinician's task is to interpret the relationships in the stories, not accept them at face value. He should use the data to infer what relationships may be wished for, feared, and so on. In a sense, TAT fantasies are similar to dreams and other fantasies produced in psychoanalysis in that they facilitate reaching the client's latent, unconscious conflicts and motivations.

TAT protocols may be interpreted using various systems of test analysis. Shneidman (1951) has classified all such methods under five categories: (1) normative—typically tabular and statistical in nature, based on norms developed through personality research; (2) hero-oriented—emphasizing the story hero's wishes, strivings, and conflicts as though these were projections of similar characteristics in the storyteller; (3) intuitive—most inferential, likely to be based on psychoanalytic theory, and calling for the clinician's insights and unconscious resonance to the storyteller's unconscious; (4) interpersonal—stressing the relationships and exchanged feelings between the characters in the story; and (5) perceptual—with an emphasis on the formal (as opposed to content) aspects of the cards (that is, distortions of scenes on cards, idiosyncratic use of language, loose or queer twists within stories).

Unlike the Rorschach, which depends on either the Beck or Klopfer system of interpretation, the TAT has numerous systems, with no one system especially prominent. Murray's initial system, still popular, was essentially hero-oriented; each story was analyzed in terms of the hero's needs and the environmental forces that affect him. Since then, many other scoring systems have been reported (see Shneidman, 1951, for a comparison of 15 TAT experts with different systems analyzing the same TAT protocol). As Harrison notes, "the same schisms that cut across many regions of psychology—the experimental versus the clinical, the nomothetic versus the idiographic, the atomistic versus the holistic—plague thematic apperceptive endeavors [Harrison, 1965, p. 572]." For example, one school of thought favors making the scoring system more objective, statistical, and psychometric, while another insists on maintaining the clinician's impressionistic approach that is global and stresses the uniqueness of the individual. In practice, the clinician is apt to find the more detailed scoring methods cumbersome and time-consuming, considering their yield. The clinical researcher, on the other hand, is likely to find the emphasis on quantification to be sound and highly desirable.

Norms have begun to be accumulated regarding the length of stories, speed of response, typical plots resulting from the stimulus quality of each card, and so on (Eron, 1950; Atkinson, 1958), although many practicing clinicians still rely heavily on their personal subjective norms, accumulated from their own experience with the TAT. The ideal situation of norms specific for males and females, different age groups, or different social class and ethnic background is still far from being realized (Zubin et al., 1965). Scorer reliability is reasonably good, particularly when there is pretraining with a common scoring system that follows systematic rules. Scorers using different scoring systems are far less likely to show such interjudge agreement. Some of the other conventional methods for studying reliability are inapplicable to the TAT. The test cannot be split in half because each picture is designed to elicit a different aspect of personality. Equivalent forms are not available, and it is unlikely that they could be constructed. Test-retest reliability is difficult; too long an interval may produce changes in the themes that reflect personality changes rather than casting doubt on the test's reliability. However, particularly under the conditions stated above, scorer reliability gives satisfactory results. In regard to validity, Eron (1950) has shown that the TAT is diagnostically not useful in the sense of yielding signs or patterns thought to be characteristic of different psychiatric groupings. However, the TAT has proven successful in predicting such specific behavior as school and college grades and in discriminating between overachievers and underachievers (Harrison, 1965). The successful work of Atkinson (1958) in using a TAT-type set of cards to elicit attitudes regarding achievement suggests the test may have construct validity when used for such a focused purpose.

Various modifications of the TAT picture have been made to make the test suitable for specific groups (such as the elderly, blacks) and specific situations (schools, adult–child relationships, the Navy). In addition, the Children's Apperception Test (CAT), a series of cards with animal characters in human-like relationships, has enjoyed considerable use with children aged three to 10 (Bellak, 1954). Based on the assumption that children identify more readily with animal than with human figures, the test presents scenes intended to elicit common conflicts in early development as predicted by psychoanalytic theory (conflicts over orality, Oedipus complex, toilet training). The Blacky Test (Blum, 1949), a series of 12 cartoons involving a dog, is designed to elicit responses bearing on variables derived from the psychoanalytic theory of psychosexual development (oral eroticism, oral sadism, castration anxiety). Both tests suffer from inadequate norms, the lack of an objective scoring system, and the questionable assumption that young children do identify more readily with animal figures. In addition, the clinician not committed to psychoanalytic theory is not likely to find these tests useful. On the other hand, those who are so committed are likely to find such theory-based assessment devices particularly suitable for clinical practice as well as research. The Make-A-Picture Story (MAPS) Test (Shneidman, 1952) suitable for children and adults, presents 22 background scenes (living room, street, cave) along with 67 appropriately scaled cut-out figures (adults, children, animals, legendary figures). The examinee is shown one background scene at a time, with all the figures visible, and is asked to populate the scene with one or more figures and then to tell a story in TAT-like fashion. As a result, the MAPS enables the clinician to go beyond the usual story interpretation to a qualitative analysis of the choices and placements of the figures. However, normative data for the most part are absent and would be extremely difficult to obtain because of the limitless possible combinations of figures, backgrounds, and stories. Correspondingly, reliability and validity evidence for the MAPS have been slow in forthcoming (Zubin et al., 1965).

COMPLETION TECHNIQUES

Completion techniques present the examinee with an unfinished product which he is expected to complete in any manner he wishes. His responses are likely to be more complex and thus less immediate than those called for by associative techniques. The most commonly used example of such a technique is sentence completion testing.

Sentence completion tests typically consist of a number of sentence stems—"I was most happy when . . . ," "My greatest fear is . . ."—that the examinee is instructed to finish in writing as rapidly as possible in order to make a complete sentence. Speed is emphasized to prevent the individual from censoring or otherwise faking the remainder of the sentence. The test comes in many forms, may be given to children and adults, individually or in a group. The number of items may vary from 40 to as many as 100 for adults.

Combining characteristics of the Word Association Test and the TAT, sentence completion tests are used to assess an individual's attitudes, conflicts, and motives, or at least those he is able and willing to reveal under the test conditions. Several such tests are currently in use; the Rotter Incomplete Sentence Blank (Rotter & Rafferty, 1950) and the Forer Structured Sentence Completion Test (Forer, 1950) are among the more popular. The former, containing 40 incomplete sentences, provides a single score or index of personal stability by cumulating the scores on each sentence on a +3 to −3 degree of conflict scale, according to a scoring manual. The latter, a 100-item inventory with separate forms for men, women, adolescent boys, and adolescent girls also cumulates scores in key areas such as aggression, anxieties, wishes, and so on. Many other sentence completion forms are in use, each likely to contain custom items for evoking responses from the special patient populations for which it was designed.

One consequence of the ease with which sentence completion tests

can be constructed is the proliferation of such tests, usually poorly standardized, with inadequate or absent norms, and containing many items
with little more than face validity. In addition, the purpose behind the test
is often transparent to the examinee, who may falsify his responses to
the sentence stems. Finally, the analysis of test responses is generally
more intuitive than objective, thus likely to reduce scorer reliability. Rohde
(1957) has attempted a large-scale standardization of her sentence completion test. Providing a scoring system based on Murray's system of
needs and the press of the environment, she has reported high interjudge
agreement, which holds promise for the future. But once again, clinicians
in practice are not likely to use long, time-consuming quantitative scoring
procedures, although clinicians in training may benefit by using check-list
systems (see Rohde, 1957; Forer, 1950) as aids to test interpretation.
Goldberg's (1965) review of published validity data on the sentence completion methods suggests that the test compares favorably with other
standard instruments in the assessment of personality. However, such
relatively high validity coefficients may point to little more than that the
consciously controlled verbal productions on the test are likely to be
highly correlated with similarly controlled verbalizations revealed in psychiatric interviews, the usual validity criterion. By remaining at relatively
conscious levels, then, the test reveals aspects of the examinee's personality that are consistent with his overt behavior.

CHOICE OR ORDERING TECHNIQUES

Choice or ordering techniques call for a relatively limited, simple response from the examinee. Typically he is required to choose, from a
number of alternatives, a particular response that fits a specified criterion
—correct, relevant, attractive, and so on. He has a fixed number of possible choices, and little if any spontaneity is required, in contrast to some
previously mentioned techniques. He must simply select the most appropriate of several hypothetical responses.

Perhaps the best known test in this category is the Szondi Test, named
after the Hungarian psychiatrist who created it. Introduced in this country
by Deri (1949), a student of Szondi's, the test captured the imagination
of some clinicians for a decade or so, but interest in the test has waned
in recent years as research has challenged its validity and questioned
its rationale. Basically, the test contains 48 portrait photographs of Euro-

pean mental patients from eight diagnostic categories. They are divided into six sets of eight pictures each, with each of the diagnostic categories represented in each set. The pictures are presented in a standard order, in sets of eight, and the examinee is asked to choose the two he likes best and the two he likes least. When all the six sets have been presented (and a total of 12 most liked and 12 most disliked pictures chosen) the examinee is then instructed to choose the four most liked from the "liked" pile, and the four least liked from the other pile. The results are recorded on a profile record form. Each testing rarely takes more than 15 minutes, although Deri (1949) reports the test should be readministered for from six to 10 days in succession to take into account the day-to-day changes in the dynamic relationships of various drives.

The test is an outgrowth of Szondi's genetic theories regarding the impact of recessive genes on personality and behavior. His notion that choices reflect the examinee's reactions to the genetic characteristics of the pictured mental patients is questionable and has received no experimental validation. Despite its somewhat enthusiastic reception and use in the early 1950s—the period of highest enthusiasm for projective techniques in this country—the test's theoretical rationale found few advocates among American psychologists. In addition, no normative data were provided. Nevertheless, David (1954) provided a bibliography of over 300 titles discussing the test between 1939 and 1953, reflecting a flurry of activity among European and American clinicians, alike, to investigate the test's genetic assumptions, provide case studies, and use the test for diagnostic purposes with various clinical groups. By 1961, Sundberg reported the Szondi Test to be less popular, although still used enough to rank thirty-fifth among all psychological tests used in clinical services in the United States. By 1971, Lubin, Wallis, and Paine's report on a national survey of psychological test use did not include the Szondi Test among the 72 tests used by 10 percent or more of the respondents to their survey. The test has little more than historical value now, but perhaps serves to remind us of naive, overenthusiastic acceptance and the resulting expenditure of many clinical man-hours without sufficient care in examining Szondi's theory or the validity of the test's clinical assumptions.

EXPRESSIVE TECHNIQUES

Expressive techniques require the examinee to combine or incorporate stimuli into some novel, creative production. However, unlike the constructive techniques, the emphasis here is as much on his manner, process, and style as on his ultimate product. The various drawing techniques are the best examples of this category.

The Draw-A-Person Test (DAP) (Machover, 1948) derives from Florence Goodenough's early work in using human figure drawings to estimate intelligence levels in children. Such drawings were incorporated into a number of intelligence scales such as the Stanford–Binet and began to be used by clinicians as projective devices, particularly in assessing the examinee's self-image in relation to the environment (see Figure 6). For many years, the DAP has been one of the most widely used test instruments (Sundberg, 1961; Lubin et al., 1971). Quick, easy to administer, and requiring no materials beyond a pencil and paper, many clinicians have found the test to be a simple, useful opening to an extensive test battery. The test may be used for children and adults alike, requires no verbal skills or artistic abilities, and may be administered individually or to a group. The examinee is simply given a blank sheet of paper and told to draw a person. Beyond being encouraged to draw a whole person, the examinee receives no other instructions at this time. After the first figure is drawn, he is asked to draw a person of the other sex. Sometimes an inquiry period follows in which he is instructed to make up a story involving the characters and to answer questions (age, education, occupation, and so on) about the characters he has created. Throughout the test, the clinician notes the examinee's comments, whether he drew a man or woman first, which body parts are emphasized and which minimized, any blocking on body parts, the sequence of drawing the body parts, the relative size of the drawings, placement on the page, erasures, full-face versus profile drawings, and many other performance characteristics. For children, a popular variation of the DAP is the Draw-A-Family or Draw-Your-Family Test.

Test analysis is essentially intuitive and based on the hypothesis that an individual will project his own body image into the drawings, investing them with his own needs, anxieties, and conflicts. More specifically, it is assumed that each body part drawn has symbolic, unconscious meaning for the individual, based on his experiences with and fantasies about his own body. Machover's (1948) work, based upon her clinical experiences but offering no normative data, is a catalog of personality characteristics symbolically represented by various body parts, facial expressions, posture, clothing, and background scenes. Thus, the head, for example, as well as the facial features, are considered by Machover to be expressive

Figure 6. Pre-therapy (upper) and post-therapy (lower) drawings of a 10-year-old school-phobic boy. Client was seen for brief, intensive individual psychotherapy culminating in return to school after several weeks. Note that the bottom figures are steadier in stance, full face (suggesting less evasiveness), less grotesque looking, and more age appropriate. The reduction in head size suggests reduced anxiety over intellectual performance. (Courtesy of Irene Goldenberg, Ed.D.)

of social needs and responsiveness; an enlarged or elaborated head might point to the individual's emphasis on intellectual aspirations and strong need for rational control of impulses and fantasies. Arms and hands are considered contact organs: if long and powerful, they represent ambition and aggressiveness; if hidden, possibly masturbation conflict and guilt. In the same way, Machover considers the figure's stance to represent his sense of security and his clothing to represent the social image he would like to project. Background elaborations, more characteristic of the drawings of children than adults, are thought to be closely tied to the individual's fantasy life. Machover believes comparison of the male and female figures reveals the examinee's attitudes toward the opposite sex, toward his own sex role, and possibly toward parental figures insofar as they represent the basis for his sexual identifications. In addition to Machover's pioneering efforts, an extensive discussion of drawings as projective techniques is available (Hammer, 1958).

The major criticism of Machover's system of interpretation reflects a criticism concerning many projective techniques—that is, the lack of normative data and the paucity of objective, reliable methods of interpretation. Despite the routine use of the DAP by many clinical psychologists, Swensen's (1957) thorough review of available studies concerning Machover's hypotheses indicates little empirical support for them. Nevertheless, Swensen concedes that figure drawings may have value as one type of data in a diagnostic test battery or as a quick, rough screening device, but cautions against their use alone for diagnostic purposes. Clinicians remain divided on the issue of the test's usefulness. Hammer (1968) recently challenged some of Swensen's conclusions. He feels there is frequently a "compelling congruence between the dynamics of patients and their figure drawings [Hammer, 1968, p. 385]," thus encouraging their continued use as part of a test battery. On the other hand, Eron and Chertkoff (1966) see little virtue in the DAP beyond its simplicity of administration or value as an icebreaker before a more extensive battery of tests or a clinical interview. They note that it is often ignored in the analyses of test results or is used only when it corroborates or amplifies impressions gained either from other techniques or the case history.

One other drawing technique, the House-Tree-Person Test (H-T-P) (Buck, 1948), deserves mention and remains a popular test among clinicians (Lubin et al., 1971). In this test, the examinee is asked to draw a house, a tree, and finally a person on separate sheets of paper, while the examiner observes the same aspects of the process as for the DAP. Following the drawings, an interview is conducted, including a set of standardized questions. Suitable for children as well as adults, the H-T-P is analyzed quantitatively as well as qualitatively. Buck's (1948) rationale for including these three items is that they are universally familiar and that each symbolically represents part of the examinee's personality: that is, the house is thought to arouse associations regarding the individual's home life and family relationships; the tree arouses associations regarding his unconscious feelings about himself and his place in the environment; the person arouses associations concerning a more conscious view of his self-image and his relationships with others. A drawback of the test is its length, which may lose the attention of the examinee, particularly an adult. In addition, scoring is elaborate and somewhat unwieldy. Beyond that, it appears to have the virtues as well as the deficits of the DAP.

OBJECTIVE METHODS IN PERSONALITY ASSESSMENT

The difference between objective and projective personality tests has been put this way: "When the subject is asked to guess what the examiner is thinking, we call it an objective test; when the examiner tries to guess what the subject is thinking, we call it a projective device [Kelly, 1958, p. 332]." We have seen that projective techniques inherently risk the clinician's misreading the examinee's thoughts and distorting the clinical meaning of a particular response or response pattern. Objective measures of personality try to circumvent that risk by keeping the administration, scoring, and test interpretation as free from examiner bias as possible. They usually provide: (1) group norms, against which an individual's responses may be compared; (2) quantitatively scorable test responses, so any examiner who follows the rules will get the same set of scores; (3) relatively easy test administration and scoring, both requiring less specialized training than is the case for projective techniques; (4) the possibility of group testing and machine scoring, both aids to efficiency; and (5) test interpretation that keeps inferences, hunches, and intuition to a minimum.

In practice, the dichotomy between "projective" and "objective" does not always exist. We have seen that many projective tests, such as the

Rorschach, do rely on formal scoring systems along with a more subjective, impressionistic analysis. In the same way, some objective tests call for a certain amount of subjectivity in scoring and some clinical judgment in evaluating the results for any specific individual. Nevertheless, despite some overlap, projective techniques are more apt to rely on subjective clinical judgment and are open to criticism for their lack of normative data and questionable reliability and validity. Objective tests of personality, while perhaps sacrificing some of the depth claimed through the use of projective devices, attempt to provide a more carefully determined, more scientifically defensible clinical picture of the individual.

Although personality questionnaires were used in the 1880s for Galton's work with individual differences in mental imagery, only during World War I did such tests find clinical use. At that time, the U. S. Army needed a self-report device that would contain an inventory of questions usually asked in a psychiatric interview and that could be readily adapted for mass testing. As a consequence, the Woodworth Personal Data Sheet was constructed, listing psychiatric symptoms and behavior deviations as items to be checked by Army recruits as part of their induction procedures. Those who reported having numerous symptoms were examined further. This procedure's main purpose was to detect, through a rough screening device, those who were likely to break down during combat. The Woodworth Personal Data Sheet, essentially a standardized psychiatric interview, became the prototype of numerous adjustment inventories that were popular in schools and industry for the next two decades. The Bell Adjustment Inventory and the Bernreuter Personality Inventory were commonly used. Such tests usually yielded scores on several dimensions (neurotic tendency, dominance, self-sufficiency). Inevitably, clinicians became interested in developing personality inventories to aid psychiatric diagnosis.

The Minnesota Multiphasic Personality Inventory (MMPI), the most widely used test of its type today, was originally constructed by a team of psychologists and psychiatrists as an objective means of arriving at a psychiatric diagnosis. A pool of over 500 items, many borrowed from older inventories, and many included because they seemed to have face validity in differentiating diagnostic groupings, was administered to clinically diagnosed adult neuropsychiatric patients at the University of Minnesota Hospital. A control group of normals, relatives who were visiting the hospitalized patients, was also tested. Scoring keys were empirically developed for various clinical scales (schizophrenia, hypochondria, para-

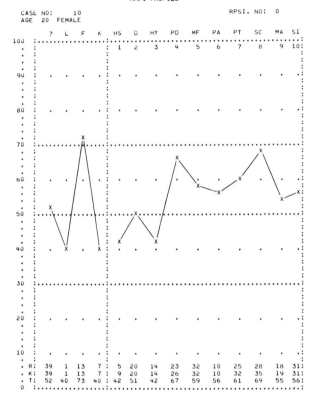

MMPI PROFILE

CASE NO: 10   RPSI. NO: 0
AGE 20 FEMALE

```
            ?   L   F   K   HS   D   HY  PD  MF  PA  PT  SC  MA  SI
        . R:  39   1  13   7 :  5  20  14  23  32  10  25  28  18  31:
        . K:  39   1  13   7 :  9  20  14  26  32  10  32  35  19  31:
        . T:  52  40  73  40 : 42  51  42  67  59  56  61  69  55  56:
```

CRITICAL ITEMS

THESE TEST ITEMS, WHICH WERE ANSWERED IN THE DIR-
ECTION INDICATED, MAY REQUIRE FURTHER INVESTIGATION BY THE
CLINICIAN. THE CLINICIAN IS CAUTIONED, HOWEVER, AGAINST
OVERINTERPRETATION OF ISOLATED RESPONSES.

27 EVIL SPIRITS POSSESS ME AT TIMES. (TRUE)
48 WHEN I AM WITH PEOPLE I AM BOTHERED BY HEARING VERY QUEER
    THINGS. (TRUE)

170 I AM WORRIED ABOUT SEX MATTERS. (TRUE)

200 I BELIEVE MY SINS ARE UNPARDONABLE. (TRUE)

44 MUCH OF THE TIME MY HEAD SEEMS TO HURT ALL OVER. (TRUE)
337 I FEEL ANXIETY ABOUT SOMETHING OR SOMEONE ALMOST ALL THE TIME.
    (TRUE)
354 I AM AFRAID OF USING A KNIFE OR ANYTHING VERY SHARP OR POINTED.
    (TRUE)

Figure 7. Computer print-out of MMPI profile of a 20-year-old female.
(From Fowler and Miller, "Computer Interpretation of the MMPI," *Archives
of General Psychiatry,* 1969, **21**, 506. Copyright 1969, American
Medical Association. Reprinted by permission.)

noia) based on the placement of items in any scale when individuals with that diagnosis responded to the item statistically more often than normals did (Hathaway & McKinley, 1942). Over 200 scales (covering such areas as delinquency, treatment readiness, overt anxiety, impulse control) are now reported to be used by clinicians (Dahlstrom & Welsh, 1960).

The MMPI in its present form is a 566 true–false item personality inventory, individually or group administered, suitable for adolescents and adults. Items range from frank admission of psychotic symptoms ("I see things or animals or people around me that others do not see") to statements of milder symptoms ("I have a great deal of stomach trouble"), perceptions of others ("My family does not like the kind of friends I have"), and seemingly innocuous statements ("I enjoy detective or mystery stories"). The test is by far the most widely administered personality test of any kind and has been translated into more than 17 languages. It has been the subject of over 1000 research papers.

Each of the 566 test items appears in one or more of the 10 basic clinical scales or the four supplementary validity scales. Scores on these scales are plotted on an MMPI profile (see Figure 7). The scale scores, shown below the profile, are arranged into the following categories:

?	Number of Items Unanswered
L	Lying
F	Conformity
K	Personal Defensiveness
Hs	Hypochondriasis
D	Depression
Hy	Hysteria
Pd	Psychopathic Deviation
Mf	Masculinity–Femininity
Pa	Paranoia
Pt	Psychasthenia
Sc	Schizophrenia
Ma	Hypomania
Si	Social Introversion

The validity scales are the first four items; they are essentially correction keys that tell the clinician to what extent he should take the scores on the clinical scales at face value. Significant scores on any of the four validity scales indicate the test might be invalid because of carelessness, lack of understanding, malingering, or unwillingness to expose problem areas.

The MMPI profile is a visual representation of the relationship among scores; in particular, it reveals any possible deviation. Scores over 70 are thought to be especially significant. In general, the greater the number of elevated scores, the greater the personality disturbance. Research on the MMPI proceeded during the 1940s, and Hathaway and Meehl (1951) eventually prepared a useful atlas of MMPI profiles, in which coded profiles and brief case histories were arranged according to the similarity of profile patterns for almost 1000 patients. Coding, an empirical system for designating any particular pattern of scores, proved especially worthwhile; the clinician could code an MMPI profile and then look in the atlas for case histories of others with the same code numbers. The similar personality characteristics of individuals with the same coded profile suggested that a new client might also have these characteristics. To help establish the construct validity of each code, continuing research has accumulated empirical data about persons who show a given profile pattern or code. By 1960, Dahlstrom and Welsh compiled an MMPI Handbook, which contains further aids for delineating profile patterns and analyzing various test pattern configurations. More recently, computers have been used to automate test scoring as well as test interpretation. Figure 8 shows the computer print-out automated report of the MMPI profile shown in Figure 7.

The computer processing of personality test data is particularly suited for a true–false inventory such as the MMPI.[6] Moreover, Meehl's interest in the MMPI has led to the application of many of his suggestions (see Chapter 4, pp. 129–132) regarding the use of actuarial methods for deriving personality descriptions from the MMPI. In particular, the efforts of Marks and Seeman (1963) have been noteworthy in providing an extensive set of personality descriptions, empirically derived, of 16 MMPI coded profiles of adult psychiatric patients.

Although the MMPI was originally used to aid in psychiatric diagnosis, its major use today is to provide a clinical picture of the examinee's personality characteristics. Several programs of automated interpretation are

[6] Work on computerizing scoring and interpretations of the Rorschach (Piotrowski, 1964) and the Holtzman Inkblot Test (Gorham, 1967) are also underway, but such systems do not begin to rival the considerable progress made with the MMPI.

ROCHE PSYCHIATRIC SERVICE INSTITUTE

MMPI REPORT

CASE NO.   10   RPSI NO.   0
AGE 20   FEMALE   JANUARY 14, 1969

THE PATIENT'S RESPONSES TO THE TEST SUGGEST THAT SHE UNDERSTOOD THE
ITEMS AND FOLLOWED THE INSTRUCTIONS ADEQUATELY. IT APPEARS, HOWEVER,
THAT SHE MAY HAVE BEEN OVERLY SELF CRITICAL. THE VALIDITY OF THE
TEST MAY HAVE BEEN AFFECTED BY HER TENDENCY TO ADMIT TO SYMPTOMS EVEN
WHEN THEY ARE MINIMAL. THIS MAY REPRESENT AN EFFORT TO CALL ATTENTION
TO HER DIFFICULTIES TO ASSURE OBTAINING HELP. THIS SUGGESTS THAT SHE
FEELS VULNERABLE AND DEFENSELESS, WHICH MAY REFLECT A READINESS TO
ACCEPT PROFESSIONAL ASSISTANCE.

THIS PATIENT HAS A TEST PATTERN WHICH IS OFTEN ASSOCIATED WITH SERIOUS
PERSONALITY DISORDERS. PSYCHIATRIC PATIENTS WITH THIS PATTERN FREQUENTLY
SHOW OBVIOUSLY DEVIANT BEHAVIOR. THEY ARE USUALLY DIAGNOSED AS HAVING A
PERSONALITY DISORDER OR PSYCHOTIC REACTION. USUAL MANIFESTATIONS ARE
POOR SOCIAL ADJUSTMENT, AND UNUSUAL OR BIZARRE THINKING AND BEHAVIOR,
FREQUENTLY IN THE SEXUAL AREA. MEDICAL PATIENTS WITH THIS PATTERN ARE
CHARACTERIZED BY VAGUE PHYSICAL COMPLAINTS AND CONSIDERABLE ANXIETY.
MANY APPEAR TO BE EARLY PSYCHOTIC REACTIONS, ALTHOUGH THEY RARELY SHOW
FRANKLY BIZARRE BEHAVIOR.

IN GENERAL, PEOPLE WITH THIS TEST PATTERN ARE SEEN AS ODD OR PECULIAR.
IT SHOULD BE EMPHASIZED THAT THE PRESENCE OF THIS PATTERN IS NOT CON-
CLUSIVE EVIDENCE OF A PERSONALITY DISORDER. HOWEVER, THE HIGH INCIDENCE
OF UNUSUAL BEHAVIOR AMONG PATIENTS WITH THIS PATTERN SUGGESTS THAT THE
PATIENT SHOULD BE CAREFULLY EVALUATED.

SHE IS A RIGID PERSON WHO MAY EXPRESS HER ANXIETY IN FEARS, COMPULSIVE
BEHAVIOR AND RUMINATION. SHE MAY BE CHRONICALLY WORRIED AND TENSE, WITH
MARKED RESISTANCE TO TREATMENT DESPITE OBVIOUS DISTRESS.

THIS PERSON FEELS UNABLE TO DEAL WITH THE ENVIRONMENTAL PRESSURES FACING
HER, OR TO UTILIZE HER SKILLS OR ABILITIES TO FULL ADVANTAGE. AT PRESENT
SHE FEELS UNABLE TO COPE WITH LIFE AS SHE SEES IT. SHE MAY RESPOND TO
HER FEELINGS OF INADEQUACY WITH INCREASINGLY RIGID BEHAVIOR OR WITHDRAWAL
DEPENDING UPON INDIVIDUAL FACTORS.

THE TEST RESULTS ON THIS PATIENT ARE STRONGLY SUGGESTIVE OF A MAJOR
EMOTIONAL DISORDER. APPROPRIATE PROFESSIONAL EVALUATION AND CONTINUED
OBSERVATION ARE SUGGESTED. PSYCHIATRIC CARE MAY BE REQUIRED.

NOTE: ALTHOUGH NOT A SUBSTITUTE FOR THE CLINICIAN'S PROFESSIONAL JUDGMENT
AND SKILL, THE MMPI CAN BE A USEFUL ADJUNCT IN THE EVALUATION AND MANAGE-
MENT OF EMOTIONAL DISORDERS. THE REPORT IS FOR PROFESSIONAL USE ONLY AND
SHOULD NOT BE SHOWN OR RELEASED TO THE PATIENT.

Figure 8. MMPI automated clinical report on a 20-year-old female.
(From Fowler and Miller, "Computer Interpretation of the MMPI," *Archives
of General Psychiatry*, 1969, **21**, 504. Copyright 1969, American
Medical Association. Reprinted by permission.)

now operating in the United States, providing print-outs based on scores
fitting carefully specified profile patterns; more such programs are expected (Butcher, 1969). An individual's computerized MMPI test results
consist of a three-page print-out containing: (1) an MMPI profile (Figure
7); (2) a narrative report which the computer has selected according to
its programmed instructions (Figure 8); and (3) raw scores (not illustrated)
on the usual scales plus scales of particular interest to the clinician (also
in Figure 7), in addition to a Critical Items category, which bears on serious symptoms indicated by the individual's answers to certain questions

(see Figure 8). Some have questioned the ethics of using machines for such personal decision making, the cost of establishing a computerized scoring program, and the danger of MMPI print-outs being used by professionals with little knowledge of the MMPI. Fowler and Miller provide educational material to professional users, enabling them to administer the test properly and use the report appropriately. Many advocates of such automated reports point to the fact that no clinician, with whatever experience, can match the memory function of computers, nor should he waste time hand-scoring on even a small portion of the more than 200 existing scales. There is no question of supplanting the clinician, since the computer's value depends on the hunches, experiences, and data provided by clinicians who write the programs for computer analysis. In the same way, the clinical decision process still depends on the clinician, who evaluates the computer interpretation and attempts to apply it to his individual client.

CHAPTER 6 *Parameters of Individual Psychotherapy and Psychoanalysis*

Psychotherapy is a process aimed at achieving constructive behavioral and personality changes in a client as a result of his experiences in a relationship with another individual trained to understand and facilitate such changes. When a formal assessment procedure has helped make a clinical decision about the client's[1] case, assessment and psychotherapy are integrated aspects of the same clinical judgment process. Assessment, the evaluative procedure that has its origins in the diagnostic conventions of medical practice, typically serves a screening function, guiding the therapist to select those individuals for psychotherapy whom he believes he is most likely to help. (Paradoxically, the most obviously disturbed individual is often the one who is least likely to be taken on as a client outside a mental hospital.) In those situations where a formal assessment procedure is less likely to occur, as in the private practice of psychotherapy, the clinician nevertheless may use the initial interviews to gauge at least some of the following factors to determine whether the client is a suitable candidate for psychotherapy: (1) the nature, severity, and extent of the client's emotional problems; (2) his readiness, motivation, and capacity for change; (3) his ability to grasp the objectives and procedures of psychotherapy and to form the necessary collaborative relationship with the therapist; (4) the degree of his discomfort or manifest anxiety; (5) how accessible his feelings are; (6) his capacity for self-examination and self-

---

[1] The terms *client* and *patient* will be used interchangeably for the remainder of this chapter. More and more clinical psychologists appear to favor the former, particularly since the latter connotes a medical type of doctor–patient relationship, not considered desirable in psychotherapy. However, the term *patient* continues to be used with sufficient regularity that its inclusion here appears justified.

disclosure; and (7) some picture of the client's reality situation. Most psychotherapists have a limited number of techniques at their disposal, prefer working with certain types of clients or problems, and have some awareness of their own limitations, all of which are additional factors in reaching decisions regarding a potential client's suitability for psychotherapy with them.

Over the last two decades, clinical psychologists have become increasingly committed to individual psychotherapy for a variety of reasons. The clinician doing psychotherapy is likely to enjoy the autonomy, status, power, glamour, economic reward, and perhaps most important, the feeling that he is productively engaged in the purposeful act of helping relieve another individual's suffering. For any combination of these reasons, or perhaps for other more personal ones, a recent survey of clinical psychologists' practices (Goldschmid et al., 1969) reveals that while a clinician's time is typically distributed among several activities, individual psychotherapy constitutes most of his daily work. Table 6 indicates that

Table 6. Percentages of time devoted to various clinical activities*

CLINICAL ACTIVITY	NONE	LESS THAN 30 PERCENT OF TIME	MORE THAN 30 PERCENT OF TIME
Individual psychotherapy	14%	53%	34%†
Diagnostic interviewing	35%	63%	2%
Objective tests	36%	64%	1%
Projective tests	34%	66%	1%
Consulting	23%	76%	3%
Teaching	20%	68%	11%
Research	25%	63%	12%
Supervising	27%	69%	4%
Administration	34%	61%	6%

* Data adapted from Goldschmid, Stein, Weissman, and Sorrells, *The Clinical Psychologist Newsletter,* 1969, **22**, 91.
† Percentages are in rounded numbers and should be read as totaling 100 percent for each row.

34 percent of the sample of members of Division 12 (Division of Clinical Psychology) of APA spend one-third or more of their time doing individual psychotherapy, with the next most time-consuming activity being research

(12 percent). Only one percent of the sample devote a comparable amount of time to objective or projective testing.

Despite this evidence of clinical psychologists' commitment to individual psychotherapy, much controversy remains over what constitutes psychotherapy, for what types of problems it is effective, whether it is effective at all, whether its procedures are grounded in a solid theoretical foundation, or whether its claimed successes are personal or artistic triumphs of the therapist rather than the result of a scientifically defensible set of clinical intervention techniques.

One reason for such controversy is that psychotherapy is a generic term for a wide variety of orientations, approaches, and clinical techniques, all of which have articulate adherents and claim successes. The various theories and techniques of psychotherapy have not grown out of systematic research, but instead have emerged from clinical practice. Consequently, dozens of systems of psychotherapy exist,[2] based partly on each theorist or technique innovator's clinical experiences, the client populations he has seen, and his assumptions regarding personality development. Since all so-called schools of psychotherapy get positive results with some clients, it is difficult to evaluate the ultimate value of any approach, its applicability to other groups, or even whether the results claimed are due to the reasons proposed by the supporters of the particular approach. For example, Freud's original formulations were based on his observations of primarily middle-European, mid-Victorian, middle-class neurotics, usually hysterics; by contrast, Rogers based his ideas mainly on articulate, reasonably self-sufficient college students, most of whom had temporary adjustment difficulties. In the same way, Jung's theories emerged from his work with successful, middle-aged intellectuals, while Sullivan worked largely with schizophrenics. With such divergent sources of observation, it is not surprising that different schools of psychotherapy should emerge, each with a different theory and technique, and each, conceivably, beneficial for specific types of clients or problems. It is the overenthusiastic extrapolation of the theory or technique to client populations for which it was not intended and for which there is little evidence to suggest its effectiveness that causes difficulties.

[2] Harper (1959) has delineated 36 systems, but undoubtedly many more exist. Since the practice of psychotherapy ultimately is fitted to the personality characteristics of the individual practitioner, there may even be as many systems of psychotherapy as there are psychotherapists.

THE COMMON CORE AND COURSE OF PSYCHOTHERAPY

Regardless of theoretical differences, the methods of experienced clinicians from different schools overlap considerably in their practice of individual psychotherapy. Each tries to facilitate the helping relationship by creating a therapeutic atmosphere (sometimes defined differently by different systems). Each encourages the expression of previously hidden thoughts and especially feelings. Each attempts to adopt a nonjudgmental attitude, particularly in the sense of not imposing the therapist's values on the client. Each assures confidentiality and attempts to build trust. In a frequently cited study, Fiedler (1950) compared the therapeutic relationships established by psychoanalysts (that is, Freud's followers), nondirective therapists (Rogers' followers), and Adlerians (followers of Alfred Adler, an early psychoanalyst who later developed his own system of psychotherapy). By having judges evaluate the recordings of therapy interviews made by novices and experts from each of these major schools of psychotherapy, Fiedler found that the therapeutic relationships established by experts from the different schools resembled each other more than did those of experts and novices of the same school. Similarly, Heine (1953) compared the reports of patients who had undergone psychotherapy by one of these three methods and found that they attributed changes within themselves as much to the quality of the therapeutic relationship as to the particular therapeutic technique.

Essentially, individual psychotherapy, especially with neurotic adults, would include these characteristics: (1) It is a dyadic interaction between a client who is emotionally distressed, and (2) a therapist, who is "a trained, socially sanctioned healer whose healing powers are accepted by the sufferers [Frank, 1963, p. 2]," (3) engaged in an ongoing, unobserved, collaborative transaction or encounter that is structured as to time, place, and overall purpose and that (4) is likely to rely heavily on verbal communication of the client's thoughts, feelings, attitudes, and behavior. (5) The client, confused, frightened, and baffled by his own inexplicable behavior, comes to believe in, and develop hope from, the therapeutic process, in part because (6) the therapist appears to have a system of theoretical constructs as well as intervention techniques for understanding, explaining, or reducing the client's previous incomprehensible and seemingly uncontrollable feelings and behavior. (7) In a permissive, supportive atmosphere with an empathic, caring, nonpunitive, nonpossessive therapist, (8) the client begins to vent his feelings, examine his actions, disclose and reevaluate his learned behavioral patterns, including his self-defeating behavior, and to understand and accept previously rejected aspects of himself. (9) In the process of engaging in a sustained experience of intimacy with another person without getting hurt and with an opportunity for growth, the client learns to take risks, be less defensive, and become more open and honest with all his feelings, (10) which he begins to apply to relationships outside of psychotherapy as he assumes responsibility for all his behavior, learns new methods of living with himself and others, gains new satisfactions from life, and (11) has less need for psychotherapy, which, usually by mutual consent with the therapist, he terminates.

In general, psychotherapy is a process in which a trained clinician helps a client resolve his emotional difficulties, develop more constructive attitudes, and alter his behavior in the direction of becoming a more independent, self-fulfilled, growth-directed individual. Underlying all systems of psychotherapy, consequently, is the proposition that man is capable of change, and furthermore that he is capable of bringing this change about himself, provided he is aided by a trained, concerned therapist as he seeks such change.

THE SPECIAL CHARACTERISTICS OF CHILD PSYCHOTHERAPY

Enough important differences exist between the problems and life situations of children and adults to make child psychotherapy differ significantly in methods and goals from adult psychotherapy. To begin with, the child is biologically as well as psychologically immature and dependent on adults. The very nature of that dependency makes him more vulnerable to, at the same time that he is less able to affect changes in, his current reality situation, such as a home with a great deal of conflict between parents. While an adult may seek changes in an unbearable situation through separation, divorce, change of job, and so on, the child is rarely permitted a similar privilege but must go along with decisions made for him. For this reason and others to be discussed below, child therapists usually insist that children be treated with one or both parents, either in separate psychotherapy or all together in a family therapy approach (see Chapter 10).

The child rarely has the knowledge or level of sophistication to seek psychotherapy for his problems. Therefore, he comes for therapy because someone else (a teacher, family doctor, or perhaps his parents) decides he requires professional help. He may lack understanding of his own behavior (and therefore lack motivation to change neurotic behavior) or he may be satisfied with the very behavior that concerns or upsets others, especially his parents; indeed, the problem may be more theirs than his. He may resist his parents' efforts to get him to a therapist, seeing it as punishment or collusion between adults. He is apt to be frightened and unresponsive. In addition, he may lack the ability to verbalize, introspect, and gain insight from a therapist's interpretations, an important requirement in much adult psychotherapy. Finally, his current symptoms (such as bedwetting or phobias) may be transitory—reflecting his extreme vulnerability to the presence of real but temporary stress—instead of a deeper, more chronic psychopathological condition requiring psychotherapy.

All child therapists at one time or another find themselves in a situation in which they must attempt to balance the sometimes conflicting needs of the child, his parents, and school or juvenile authorities. It is frequently difficult to win a child's trust and confidence and to assure him of the confidentiality of the relationship. Certain parent–child interactions inimical to the goals of therapy must be worked out with both the child and his parents, with both sides recognizing that each plays a part in the child's difficulties. Since continuation of therapy rests with the parents and not the child, many child therapists find themselves losing a client at the very moment a child exhibits behavioral and personality changes if they take a direction the parents do not like.

The reliance on verbal communication, such an essential part of adult psychotherapy, is frequently absent in child psychotherapy. Instead, play therapy is used, particularly with a child who is preverbal, mute for psychogenic reasons, excessively inhibited, or perhaps overly fantasy-ridden or withdrawn (Hammer & Kaplan, 1967). A special playroom—where the child is encouraged to choose among and play with dolls, clay, blocks, guns, paint, and other materials—gives the child an opportunity to discharge actively some of his pent-up emotions and impulses in a safe environment. Proponents of play therapy point out that play is a more natural mode of communication for a child than verbalization. The child therapist can therefore participate more easily in the child's world through play, learning how he structures that world and masters its problems. It is important to point out, however, that the therapeutic benefits of play are intended to be more than simply cathartic. The child can learn to express ordinarily withheld feelings such as anger in the presence of an adult who can accept them, communicate such acceptance, and perhaps then offer alternative ways for the child to react to whoever the child thinks is responsible for arousing these feelings. Play, alone, is not sufficient to bring about change; rather, its use as a tool to help the child understand, accept, and integrate all his feelings can produce therapeutic change (Hammer & Kaplan, 1967).

Play therapy is used in different ways, depending on the therapist's theoretical orientation. For example, Klein (1932), a pioneer in children's psychoanalysis used play as a substitute for the free association process adults use in psychoanalysis in order to get at the child's underlying conflicts and unconscious processes. Erikson (1963), a leading current figure in psychoanalysis, sees play as the best situation for studying the child's unconscious conflicts as well as providing him with a means for expressing and seeking mastery over early traumatic experiences. Axline (1947), operating from within a client-centered framework developed by Rogers (see Chapter 7) bases her use of play techniques on the principle that the child has the capacity for growth and self-help; therefore, Axline suggests, the child's use of play is not determined by the therapist but depends instead on the child and how he chooses to express himself. While no limits are set on the child's verbal expression of feelings, Axline does suggest that the therapist establish "those limitations that are necessary to anchor the therapy to the world of reality and to make the child aware of his responsibility in the relationship [Axline, 1947, pp. 75–76]." Axline feels it is not essential to work with parents while the child is in therapy. (Axline has published a particularly illuminating report of an actual therapeutic encounter with a client, Dibs, using client-centered play therapy—Axline, 1966.)

Play therapy is by no means the only technique of child psychotherapy. Particularly with older children or those who possess sufficient verbal and intellectual capacities to deal with their problems verbally, various techniques, patterned after those developed for adults, are used. In addition to psychoanalytic and client-centered procedures, existential child therapy (Moustakas, 1966) is frequently used; it emphasizes helping the child become aware of his unique self and his real feelings as he asserts his individuality through his decisions and actions. In addition, certain techniques of behavior modification have been successful, particularly in eliminating phobic behavior, a common neurotic problem of children (Rachman

& Costello, 1962), and in building social behavior in autistic (that is, psychotic) children (Lovaas et al., 1965).

DIMENSIONS FOR CATEGORIZING SYSTEMS OF PSYCHOTHERAPY

A set of hypotheses, propositions, or principles concerning human behavior is crucial for the practicing psychotherapist. He is frequently confronted by individuals with a complicated and varied set of behavior patterns which are of vital concern to them, but with which he personally may have had little experience, or perhaps about which little may be known. Psychotherapists frequently find themselves proceeding beyond the boundaries of verified knowledge in dealing with some clients. In such cases, as Ford and Urban (1963) have noted, the therapist has the ethical obligation to proceed carefully and systematically, lest his efforts make the client worse. If the therapist has not treated such a condition before or if he lacks verified knowledge, they suggest he rely on a theory, from which may emerge the hypotheses needed to understand the unfamiliar behavior or psychotherapeutic problem. While some clinicians see psychotherapy as a totally artistic, individualistic process which relies exclusively on intuition, Ford and Urban have urged a more scientific, systematic effort to make clinical observations of a client's behavior more orderly and more related to other aspects of his behavior.

Most therapists are systematic to some degree in that they follow relatively consistent ways of observing and are consistent in the phenomena they seek to observe. Thus, Freudians attach importance to sexual and aggressive material, Jungians to universal symbols, Adlerians to examples of power struggles, while followers of Sullivan are apt to focus on the interpersonal difficulties of the client. The value of a theoretical orientation is that it helps organize the mass of data provided by the client and helps provide a framework for giving meaning to that data. Consequently, the therapist's assumptions and procedures can be communicated more clearly to colleagues, be learned by students and, perhaps most important, be subjected to research investigation.

All systems of psychotherapy need a set of propositions concerning:

1. The nature of man. To illustrate, psychoanalysts: (see p. 219) see man as driven by instincts (sex, aggression) which are often antisocial in nature. One goal of psychoanalysis, then, is to help the client accept and express these impulses in a socially acceptable way. Humanistic psychotherapists (see Chapter 7), on the other hand, see man as filled with untapped talents, free will, and a potential for continuing personal growth. The goal of such psychotherapy, consequently, is to help the client become a more fully functioning, self-actualizing person.

2. A theory of normal personality development. Freudian psychoanalysts, for example, have conceptualized a comprehensive theory of personality structure (id, ego, superego), personality dynamics (instincts, defense mechanisms, and so on), and stages of personality development (such as infantile sexuality). Consequently, psychoanalytic treatment is aimed at uncovering early conflicts which resulted in fixations at early developmental levels. However, Rogers has emphasized the self as the major concept of his theory of personality development. Consequently, his therapeutic approach, client-centered therapy (see Chapter 7), focuses on the elaboration of the client's self-concept as he learns to actualize the self's natural values and gain self-fulfillment.

3. A theory of abnormal functioning, or psychopathology. To illustrate this point, Albert Ellis (1962), founder of rational–emotive psychotherapy, believes a neurotic indoctrinates and reindoctrinates himself with faulty, illogical, irrational ideas, such as the necessity of being loved or approved of by virtually everyone, or the necessity of being thoroughly competent in all possible respects in order to consider oneself worthwhile. Consequently, Ellis' technique of psychotherapy is to unmask his client's illogical thinking or self-defeating verbalizations, teaching him instead to reverbalize such sentences in a more logical, productive way. Joseph Wolpe (1969), a behavior modifier, bases his theory of neurotic development on physiological predispositions or the result of the previously learned inappropriate anxiety reactions becoming exacerbated by current stress (see Chapter 7). As a result, Wolpe's therapeutic efforts include systematic desensitization based on relaxation as the client gradually learns to become comfortable in a situation that previously evoked fear and anxiety.

4. The role of the therapist. To demonstrate this point, psychoanalysts are apt to see the therapist as a deliberately neutral, aloof, blank screen who stays out of the patient's sight to minimize any cues the patient may receive from the analyst; without such cues, the patient can project onto the blank screen of the analyst only what he chooses to see, thus providing useful information for further analysis. On the other hand, Rogers (1957) has emphasized being a real person—that is, genuine and without facade—in order to reach the client better and help facilitate his growth. As a further illustration of the relationship of the therapist's role to the therapy he practices, Whitaker and Malone (1953) view psychotherapy as an emotional exchange between two individuals in which the therapist's involvement accelerates his own growth as well as the client's. Sullivan (1954) urges that the therapist be a participant–observer.

5. **Time orientation.** While some therapists, notably psychoanalysts, stress uncovering and reconstructing the past, others—such as Gestalt therapists (Perls, 1970)—emphasize the here and now (see Chapter 7). Perls has been emphatic in maintaining that only the now exists at any one moment, and that talking about the past may actually be a way the client avoids facing the real problems of the present. Existentialists (May, Angel, & Ellenberger, 1958) believe the expectations of the future determine present behavior as much as the past does. Their focus is on helping the client gain a perspective on the choices open to him as he makes the decisions and commitments that determine his future existence.

6. **The influences of unconscious processes.** Freud, for example, saw most human behavior as influenced by unconscious forces within the individual over which he has no awareness or control. Jung (1928), an early follower of Freud, also stressed unconscious processes, seeing the unconscious as composed of several layers. Of these, Jung noted particularly the personal unconscious (where repressed ideas are stored) and the racial or collective unconscious (deeper than the personal unconscious and representing significant memories of the human race that are part of everyone's heritage). On the other hand, neither the behavioral nor phenomenologically oriented therapies see man as the victim of unconscious forces, but instead stress conscious choice, will, and learning to create new behavioral patterns.

7. **The role of insight versus action.** Insight therapies (Wolberg, 1967) stress the necessity of self-understanding in producing personality and behavior change. Thus, in psychoanalysis, the analyst is likely to make interpretations which give the analysand (the analytic patient) insight into the meaning of his behavior, as such behavior is rooted in early unresolved and now unconscious conflict. Insight therapists, therefore, look beyond the immediate problem to seek out the underlying conflict and bring it to

the patient's awareness. The assumption is that such self-knowledge of previously unrecognized motives will help the patient reduce his symptoms. Action therapists (London, 1964), largely behavioristic in orientation, are more directly interested in behavior change without necessarily providing understanding why the patient's present symptoms first appeared. Their focus is on helping the patient feel better, whether or not he gains awareness of the original causes for his feelings of distress and anxiety.

8. **The goals of psychotherapy.** All systems of psychotherapy have a common goal: helping the patient unlearn old, maladaptive responses and replace them with new, genuine, realistic, and more fulfilling response patterns. More specifically, the goal of any single psychotherapeutic system refers to the long-range, ultimate aims, purposes, directions, and outcomes that practitioners of that system seek (Mahrer, 1967). For example, Freud's ultimate goal for his patients was simply the ability to love and work. The client-centered therapist (Rogers, 1951) seeks to promote the client's growth, maturity, spontaneity, and creativity by helping him release his natural inner resources and potential. Sullivan's followers, who stress the importance of interpersonal relations in normal development, see as their goal each patient's ability to integrate all parts of his self-system (including parts previously rejected as the "bad me"), to reduce his loneliness, and to reach out and try to become closely related to others (Sullivan, 1954).

THE PROCESS OF INDIVIDUAL PSYCHOTHERAPY

A major deterrant to fully understanding the process of psychotherapy is that psychotherapy is not a unitary phenomenon. Therefore, its practice is influenced by a combination of at least the following factors: (1) the *therapist* (psychoanalyst, psychiatrist, clinical psychologist, social worker, marriage counselor, minister—each with different training, experience, and personal characteristics); (2) the *patient or client* (each of whom has different kinds of problems, life histories, personality characteristics, motivations, verbal abilities, intelligence levels, ages, levels of education); (3) the *setting* (hospital, outpatient clinic, prison, college counseling center, church, private practice office); (4) the *method of psychotherapy* (psychoanalysis, behavior modification, crisis intervention, family therapy, guidance, pastoral counseling, and others).

With so many factors appearing in different combinations, it is difficult to evaluate the meaning of any results of psychotherapy. Nevertheless, considerable research is aimed at discovering and isolating those elements of the psychotherapeutic process that produce constructive changes in the client. The impact of the therapist, the client, their interaction, and the methods of therapy used have all been studied.

THE IMPACT OF THE THERAPIST

Do some personality and behavioral characteristics of the therapist particularly facilitate constructive change in the client? Holt and Luborsky (1958) performed an extensive clinical assessment of the personality characteristics of psychiatric residents at the Menninger Foundation, a major training center in psychiatry in the United States. Studying the psychiatrists at various stages of their training, Holt and Luborsky were able to isolate three characteristics of those who received the higher ratings (from supervisors) as psychotherapists. These psychotherapists were: (1) genuine (as opposed to artificial); (2) socially adjusted to co-workers; and (3) free from status concerns. In addition, the authors found that the best therapists possessed more insight, tended to make a mature heterosexual adjustment, and possessed adequate emotional controls. One interesting observation was that many therapists, in first becoming open to the emotional states in their clients, often experienced considerable anxiety themselves; those psychiatrists who eventually became the best therapists tended to go through such a phase before learning how not to overidentify with the client and his problems. On the other hand, those who received poorer ratings as psychiatrists tended from the beginning to be unaffected by emotional disturbances in others, and consequently were likely to be too closed off from their own feelings to develop much empathy.

Perhaps there is no "ideal therapist personality" for all types of patients or settings. Certain therapist personality characteristics might enhance therapeutic techniques with some patients but prove a hindrance to others (Goldstein et al., 1966). In this regard, Whitehorn and Betz (1954, 1960) have been able to differentiate psychotherapists who were highly successful with hospitalized schizophrenic patients (designated type A therapists) from other therapists (type B) who showed less success with such patients. Subsequently it was possible to develop an A-B scale based on responses to 23 items on the Strong Vocational Interest Blank that differentiated the two types of therapists. However, McNair, Callahan, and Lorr (1962) were interested in seeing if such a distinction in therapeutic skills applied to neurotic outpatients as well. They selected 20 therapists with the highest scores on the A-B scale and 20 with the lowest from among 55 therapists working in seven Veterans Administration outpatient clinics. These therapists appeared to be matched in regard to experience, theoretical orientation, and rating of competence by other clinical psychologists. Working with matched groups of outpatients, the results indicated that neurotic patients treated by B therapists actually improved significantly more than patients of A therapists—the opposite results of those obtained by Whitehorn and Betz on schizophrenic patients. No theoretical explanation has yet been offered to account for these empirically observed differences. Perhaps greater therapeutic success in each case may reflect therapist–patient similarities of some sort or perhaps A and B therapists react differently to different types of disturbances. The meaning of the A-B scale or its relationship to psychotherapy is still unclear, although it holds promise for exploring the impact of the therapist on both the process and outcome of psychotherapy (Carson, 1967).

However, the therapist's personality, values, interests, and experience level are undoubtedly significant, although they may not be the major factors in determining therapeutic outcome (Strupp, 1971). Frank (1963) has suggested that much of the therapist's influence may be due to the distressed patient's perception of him as a source of help as well as his faith in the therapist's desire and ability to help him. Part of the therapeutic mystique arises from the therapist's sociocultural role and image as healer and part from those personal qualities—intelligence, sense of responsibility, sincerity, good judgment, confidence, warmth—that he reveals and that inspire confidence. Carkhuff and Berenson (1967) have attempted to isolate those "dimensions of human nourishment" that have a facilitating or retarding effect on all human relationships—therapist–client, parent–child, teacher–student. Those core dimensions in the therapist that make for growth in the client are described as: (1) empathic understanding; (2) respect or positive regard; (3) genuineness; and (4) personally relevant concreteness (that is, the ability to help the client discuss specific feelings and experiences fluently and directly).

Theorists of different psychotherapy systems agree that empathy, acceptance, nonpossessive warmth, therapist genuineness, therapist sensitivity, and accuracy in understanding the client's inner experiences are important characteristics in bringing about favorable therapeutic outcomes. In addition, empathy seems related to the therapist's age, suggesting that his personal and professional life experiences are one basis for empathic ability (Truax & Carkhuff, 1964). In the same way, personal psychotherapy for the therapist is usually considered desirable in increasing his therapeutic effectiveness, removing blind spots, and teaching him what it feels like to be a psychotherapy client. Candidates wishing to become psychoanalysts are required to undergo psychoanalysis themselves. However, research has not yet established that therapists or analysts who have undergone personal psychotherapy or psychoanalysis necessarily are more successful with their patients than those who have not. One difficulty in such research is that those having undergone psychotherapy are generally older and more experienced; these additional variables confound any results attributable to personal psychotherapy alone.

Recently the term *the fifth profession* has been introduced (Henry, Sims, & Spray, 1971) to describe psychotherapists. The term underlines the fact that psychotherapists from four distinct professions—psychoanalysis, psychiatry, clinical psychology, and psychiatric social work—are sufficiently similar in cultural, social, and religious background as well as current political affiliations and ideologies to warrant classification as a homogeneous group. Despite differences in their professional training, practicing psychotherapists resemble psychotherapists from other disciplines in values, attitudes, work characteristics, and professional identity more than they do members of their own discipline not engaged in psychotherapy. The psychologist who is a therapist is likely to do little research; the psychiatrist practices no physical medicine; the social-worker therapist does not use his knowledge of public welfare or community organization.

Basing their study on a sample of 4300 psychotherapists in three major metropolitan areas—New York, Chicago, and Los Angeles—Henry et al. (1971) found marked similarities in early experiences, family relationships, and related factors, all influencing occupational choice as psychotherapists. Typically, the psychotherapist was raised in a large metropolitan area, comes from a middle- or lower-class background, and aims at considerable upward social mobility. Therapists with Jewish backgrounds are more common than Jews' proportion in the general population would suggest, and the vast number of these psychotherapists have Eastern European ethnic ties. Psychotherapists in this sample tended to reject their parents' political belief systems, particularly if conservative; despite the high socioeconomic status of most psychotherapists and their involvement with a middle- and upper-middle-class clientele—which suggest a conservative outlook—they tended to be liberal politically. In terms of their therapeutic activities, the differences between therapists did not distinguish one professional group from another.

THE IMPACT OF THE PATIENT OR CLIENT

Medical practice is based on accurately diagnosing and carrying out specific treatment procedures for specific patient conditions; pneumonia calls for one set of treatment procedures, a broken arm another, a heart attack still another. Psychotherapy, on the other hand, rarely matches a therapeutic technique to a specific patient problem. Most therapists seem unbothered by this, satisfied that their techniques have wide applicability and that the process of psychotherapy is more or less the same regardless of the patient's problems. However, Strupp and Bergin (1969) have attempted to redirect therapists to search for specific therapeutic procedures for specific conditions. According to them, the most significant question in psychotherapy research is: "Which patient characteristics and problems are most amenable to which techniques conducted by which type of therapist in what type of setting [Strupp & Bergin, 1969, p. 46]?"

Research designed to answer this question should help produce specific therapies directed at particular kinds of patients or problems, but little systematic research has yet been directed to this question. At present, Strupp and Bergin point out that there is no evidence that different types of patients or symptoms are differentially responsive to different forms of psychotherapy. One encouraging exception is the efforts of behaviorally oriented therapists to reduce phobic conditions in patients through desensitization procedures (see Chapter 7).

The patient's likability appears to affect the course and outcome of psychotherapy by influencing the therapist's personal reactions to him as an individual. High intelligence, verbal skills, and the capacity for self-understanding are particularly appealing for therapists such as psychoanalysts who stress self-exploration and the verbalization of feelings. Gibson, Cohen, and Cohen (1959) reported that 60 percent of the patients in psychoanalysis were college graduates, compared to 6 percent of the general population in that category at the time of their report. Frank

(1963) has suggested that patients who seek out and remain in psychotherapy are particularly likely to have the characteristics of influencibility, emotional reactivity, and accessibility to others, in addition to feeling dissatisfied and emotionally distressed.

Schofield (1964) has coined the term *YAVIS Syndrome* (youthful, attractive, verbal, intelligent, successful) to denote the combination of patient characteristics therapists find appealing and often use as criteria, perhaps unconsciously, in selecting patients. In a study of psychiatrists, clinical psychologists, and social workers all primarily engaged in individual psychotherapy, Schofield asked, among other things, what their "ideal patient" was like—that is, what is "the kind of patient with whom you feel you are efficient and effective in your therapy [Schofield, 1964, p. 130]?" Table 7 shows their answers.

Table 7. The ideal psychotherapy patient as viewed by three professions*

	PSYCHIATRIST	CLINICAL PSYCHOLOGIST	SOCIAL WORKER
Sex	Female	Female	Female
Age	20–40	20–40	20–40
Marital status	Married	Married–single†	Married
Education	Some college or degree	Some college or degree	High school plus
Occupation	Professional–managerial	Professional–managerial	No clear preference

* Adapted from Schofield, 1964, *Psychotherapy: The Purchase of Friendship.*
† Equally occurring preference.

Patients with the following characteristics are likely to be considered poor risks for individual verbal psychotherapy, particularly as it is traditionally practiced: (1) too old (over age 60) or too young (under 15); (2) limited education; (3) low intelligence level; (4) poor verbal skills or introspective ability; (5) too poor and occupationally unsuccessful; (6) emotional disturbance too severe and chronic (alcoholism, drug addiction, schizophrenia) or too low a level of anxiety; (7) poorly motivated to participate actively in helping himself; (8) little history of personal achievement (in school or work) or persistence; (9) difficult reality situation to change; and (10) receives some secondary gain from being disturbed (extra attention, control of situations). All of these patient characteristics or situations mitigate against success for many therapists, who understandably prefer to work with individuals for whom the prognosis is brighter, thus assuring themselves greater success. However, many therapists are beginning to recognize that something must be done to reduce the alienation between lower socioeconomic groups and mental health professionals. Two national programs—the antipoverty program and the community mental health program—have spotlighted the multitude of people with unmet therapeutic needs who require and deserve attention, yet who are suspicious of such services from middle-class therapists. Efforts are underway (see Chapter 8) to develop concepts, methods, programs, and services that are appropriate, effective, and related to the needs and life-styles of the poor (Reiff, 1966).

THE IMPACT OF THERAPEUTIC INTERACTION

Considerable research has been directed toward what takes place during psychotherapy that brings about any given result. Snyder (1961) has proposed that the relationship between therapist and client be systematically explored, since the nature of that relationship provides the essential core of all psychotherapy. Since all therapists, regardless of theoretical position, experience success with some clients, the active change agent in therapy may be found in the nature of the interaction between these two individuals. Bordin (1959) has suggested that the various theories about psychotherapy are nothing more than efforts to explain what attributes of the therapist–client relationship account for the client's behavior changes during psychotherapy.

One difficulty in applying Bordin's notion is that the therapist does not always know what he did that brought about a change in his client. In this regard, Frieda Fromm-Reichmann, a highly gifted psychoanalyst with schizophrenics, is reported to have had the following experience:

One day a young schizophrenic girl annoyed her as she was leaving the office in the evening. Dr. Fromm–Reichmann became quite angry and scolded her. After she came home during the night she felt rather badly. After all, one should not treat a schizophrenic girl in that manner. She is a sick girl and should be treated with more consideration. She was very surprised when she found a letter from this girl the next morning in her mailbox. The girl expressed her deepest gratitude and thanks. "It was the first time in a long time that somebody treated me like a normal human being [Dreikurs, 1961, p. 85]."

A great deal is communicated between therapist and client beyond a verbal exchange. Values, attitudes, judgments, and feelings are all expressed, if not verbally then through gestures, posture, or facial expressions, despite all efforts by many therapists to keep such communications hidden. The client is likely to react to the therapist's warmth, attractiveness, interest, trust, credibility, likability, or openness (Goldstein et al., 1966). Many clinicians believe that these factors, often unwittingly communicated by the therapist, are the intangible but nevertheless highly significant keys to understanding the benefits derived from psychotherapy.

Because so much and at so many levels is communicated in a single therapeutic session, it has been difficult to ascertain which aspects of the process are potent change agents and which are inert. Nevertheless, researchers such as Strupp (1971) have urged that the so-called process studies of the therapeutic exchange be continued by focusing on the naturally occurring events in psychotherapy. Frequently this has been done by having clinicians rate in-therapy behavior after listening to tape-recorded psychotherapy sessions. For example, Butler, Rice, and Wagstaff (1962) used such tapes to develop a system for classifying such psychotherapy process variables as therapist and client voice qualities, word usage, and tendency to focus on feelings, all of which were found to be related to successful outcomes of new therapy cases (Rice & Wagstaff, 1967).

Another technique for studying the therapeutic process, developed by Strupp (1960), is to show movies of psychotherapy sessions to therapists, stopping the film at selected points and asking how each would respond if he were the therapist in the film. In this way, Strupp has been able to determine more accurately what therapists from different schools—with different professional training and different levels of experience—actually do, rather than what they say they do according to their theoretical position. Some researchers have taken physiological measures (heart rate, skin resistance) of the client during psychotherapy in order to correlate emotional and somatic concomitants of change to what is taking place in the therapeutic process. While such process measures have the advantage of being objective and reliable, they have not been used extensively, partly because their complicated electrical multichannel hook-ups tend to interfere with, and thus possibly change, the therapeutic situation. Meltzoff and Kornreich (1970), in reviewing such studies, acknowledge that general emotional disturbances are reflected by physiological changes, but find present experimental techniques still in the exploratory stage. They question the results of such studies unless they clarify what specific aspects of the therapeutic situations the client perceives as cues for his physiological reactions and whether specific physiological changes have the same meaning for each client.

One promising approach to research on the process of psychotherapy has been the content analysis of therapeutic interviews. With the advent of audio tape-recording equipment, and more recently videotape techniques for psychotherapy training (Berger, 1970), it is now possible to analyze the data of therapeutic interviews that were previously accessible only to the therapist involved. Consequently, there has been considerable interest in studying the communications of therapists and clients alike in an objective, systematic, and quantitative way. Several hundred such studies have been reported over the last 20 years (see Marsden, 1970). Typically, content analysis involves procedures for dividing the verbal content of interviews into small units and assigning those units into broader categories in order to conceptualize the trend of what is taking place as therapy proceeds. An early application of this technique by Dollard and Mowrer (1947) involved the *discomfort–relief quotient* (DRQ). By classifying each sentence or thought unit as representing discomfort (tension, pain, suffering) or relief (comfort, pleasure, enjoyment) or neither, the DRQ was obtained by dividing the number of discomfort words by the total number of discomfort and relief words. Although it was a crude way of measuring change as therapy progressed, it nevertheless pointed the way for developing measures of verbal behavior and attempting to relate them to corresponding internal changes taking place in the client.

A more sophisticated technique of content analysis has been developed by Matarazzo, Saslow, and Matarazzo (1956). This technique studies observable human interactions as measured and recorded over units of time. For example, such formal aspects of the verbal exchange as the duration of silences or the duration of therapist's and client's units of speech are tabulated during an interview. Matarazzo and his associates have been able to show significant changes in client behavior within the same interview, corresponding to deliberately planned changes in the behavior of the interviewer. In this way, the therapist's planned strategies can be applied to future therapy situations to increase the probability of therapeutic success.

THE IMPACT OF VARIOUS THERAPEUTIC APPROACHES: PSYCHOTHERAPY ANALOGUE STUDIES

Since research on the natural, ongoing phenomenon of psychotherapy is fraught with practical as well as ethical problems and must deal with complex human behavior difficult to predict, control, or understand, many psychologists have turned to the experimental laboratory to set up experimental situations analogous to psychotherapy. The major advantage of such analogue research studies over in-therapy studies is the greater experimental control of relevant variables. The researcher is able to design his experimental situation with greater precision and sophistication, manipulate certain technique variables experimentally while eliminating extraneous variables, specify and measure outcome criteria with greater exactness, and so on. The major difficulty, of course, is that the experimental situation thus established will no longer resemble the psychotherapy situation, making any conclusions and generalizations from such experiments inapplicable to what actually takes place in psychotherapy. For example, Martin (1971) has pointed out that research on behavior modification (see Chapter 7) has shown the technique to be effective in reducing conditioned fears of animals, such as mice, snakes, and spiders. However, such learned fears may not be true phobias, which are displaced anxiety-reducing fears. Therefore, Martin has argued that the demonstration of an experimental technique for reducing fears of animals may not necessarily demonstrate that technique's effectiveness in treating such neurotic problems as phobias.

The impetus for a great deal of analogue research has come from researchers who have favored behavior modification as a form of therapy. An early study by Greenspoon (1955) on verbal conditioning suggested that if the interviewer said "mmm-hmm" every time a subject used the plural form of a noun, the subject significantly increased the number of plural responses he made thereafter without being aware of doing so. The Greenspoon effect of verbal conditioning in psychotherapy has been reported many times; smiles, head-nodding, or words of approval can be used to reinforce certain words; these results presume that changes in the client's verbal behavior during therapy sessions will be accompanied by changes in other aspects of living. However, it remains controversial whether verbal conditioning can actually play a significant role in effecting long-term, major personality and behavioral changes in clients.

In a carefully designed study, Paul (1966) compared the effectiveness of various therapeutic approaches (particularly insight therapy versus a modified systematic desensitization technique of behavior modification) for reducing anxiety among students in a public speaking class. A battery of personality and anxiety scales was administered to 710 college public speaking class students. Of those expressing a desire for treatment for anxiety (approximately half), 96 were identified as most debilitated by anxiety as a result of a pretreatment test speech. Following a screening interview, 74 subjects were divided among groups I through IV (see below), and the remaining 22 (Group V) were not contacted further. Each subject was assigned to one group only; all groups were equated on observable anxiety. The groups were:

I. Insight-oriented psychotherapy ($N = 15$). Therapists attempted to reduce anxiety by helping the client gain insight into the bases and interrelationships of his problem.

II. Modified systematic desensitization ($N = 15$). Therapists attempted to teach relaxation techniques along with gradual, systematic desensitization to those situations in which anxiety had been associated with giving a speech.

III. Attention-placebo ($N = 15$). Therapists attempted to provide a warm, interested, and helpful attitude. Used to determine the extent of improvement from nonspecific treatment effects such as suggestion, attention, expectation of relief, and so on. The drug used was a placebo pill, but subjects were told the drug prevented the occurrence of anxiety.

IV. No-treatment classroom control group ($N = 29$). These subjects continued in their respective speech classes but received no treatment.

V. No-contact, nonclassroom control group ($N = 22$). Subjects met selection criteria, but were never contacted to participate in study. This group is included to assess any possible improvement resulting from individual attention and speech practice obtained by the no-treatment control group.

Each subject in groups I through III received five hours of therapy over a period of six weeks. To control for the possible influence of differences between therapists, Paul had all five experienced therapists engaged in all forms of therapy. On termination of the experiment, a post-treatment test speech was given to all the participants except the no-contact nonclassroom control group. Results (see Figure 9) showed the modified systematic desensitization method to be consistently superior to other methods in reducing observable measures of anxiety related to public speaking. No significant differences were found between the effects of insight therapy

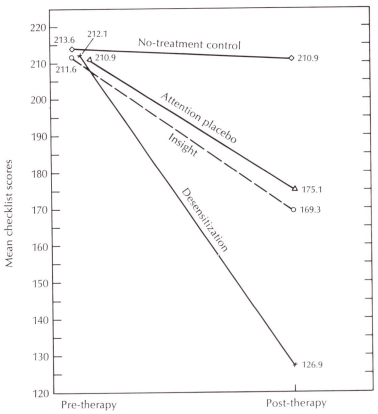

Figure 9. Changes in mean scores of observable manifestations of anxiety based on measures obtained at the beginning and at the end of psychotherapy. (From *Psychotherapy and the Modification of Abnormal Behavior*, by Strupp. Copyright 1971 by McGraw-Hill Book Company. Used with permission of McGraw-Hill Book Company.)

or attention-placebo treatment, although both were superior to the no-treatment control groups. From these results, Paul concluded that treatment based on a learning model (desensitization) is more effective in alleviating anxieties such as are aroused during public speaking than is treatment based on a disease model (insight therapy).

Strupp (1971) has challenged the implications of Paul's conclusions, particularly whether such an analogue study is sufficiently similar to psychotherapy to have its results generalizable. For example, Strupp has questioned whether the subjects in the experiment had anything in common with typical psychotherapy patients, since all presumably were adequately functioning adults who had not applied for psychotherapy. They were more likely to resemble typical subjects in a psychological experiment than patients seeking help for neurotic problems. Moreover, insight therapy may be a misnomer for what can be accomplished in five sessions; insufficient time was allotted for gaining understanding, and the focus of any understanding gained was not specifically directed at reducing the symptom of public-speaking anxiety. Such criticisms make it difficult to generalize Paul's conclusions to actual psychotherapy or to the superiority of one form of therapy over another.

Despite such problems inherent in analogue studies, many psychologists insist that controlled experimentation is ultimately superior for research purposes to in-therapy studies which must deal with so many uncontrolled (and uncontrollable) variables and events. If psychotherapy can be conceptualized as a learning process, then the same principles of learning and research strategies appropriate to other areas of learning are applicable to psychotherapy. Analogue studies provide one way of using experimentation to help make the process and conditions conducive to therapeutic learning more explicit.

THE EFFECTIVENESS OF PSYCHOTHERAPY

Ultimately all issues in psychotherapy hinge on the answer to one simple question: "Does it work?" If the efficacy of psychotherapy cannot be established, then all the extensive research on the therapeutic process is superfluous. Therefore many clinicians have urged that outcome research, despite its complexities, take precedence over process research; only after it can be demonstrated that a particular behavior change can be produced consistently as a result of a particular therapeutic manipulation should efforts be made to study the process involved in the manipulation (Goldstein et al., 1966).

Outcome research involves more than an investigation of the effectiveness of psychotherapy. To be meaningful, such research must focus on identifying those elements (such as therapist personality characteristics, therapist techniques) that produce constructive changes in the client. The task is made extremely difficult, as previously noted, because such a bewildering number of variables (differences between therapists, clients, settings, techniques) affects the various possible combinations. Thus Meehl (1965b) has reminded us that some individuals are more suitable patients than others, and also that some therapists are more skilled than others. Therefore, supposing that one-fourth of the patients currently in therapy are suitable cases, and that approximately the same proportion of therapists are good at their job, "then the joint probability of a suitable patient getting to a suitable therapist is around .06 (.25 × .25), a very small tail to wag the statistical dog in outcome studies [Meehl, 1965b, p. 157]." Small wonder that outcome studies frequently produce such discouraging overall results.

A further complication in outcome studies is that the data from various forms of psychotherapy are often pooled, even when they bear scant resemblance to one another. Consider answering the question "Is psychotherapy effective?" with data from all of the following sources: (1) a 15-minute, once-a-month suggestion-giving session between an inexperienced prison psychologist and an inmate with a third-grade education; (2) a 50-minute hour, four times a week, extending over four years, involving an experienced psychoanalyst and a highly educated, verbal, successful business executive; (3) four hypnosis sessions, once a week, administered by a general physician to a male patient with problems of impotency; and (4) verbal conditioning by a ward nurse with a chronic hospitalized schizophrenic. If all these sources are classified as psychotherapy and their results are averaged, the resulting report of the overall effectiveness of psychotherapy loses precise meaning.

One last point, before looking at the results of research on the effectiveness of psychotherapy, concerns the issue of what represent acceptable criteria for evidence of a desirable outcome. Strupp (1971) draws an analogy to education in attempting to assess whether a college education is effective. The criterion—specifically, whatever is meant by "effective" —can be met by the graduate becoming a better or happier person than he otherwise would be, by being able to get a better job, and so on. Different educators may use different criteria. In the same way, if different schools of therapy have different goals (symptom removal for behavior modifiers, self-actualization for humanistic psychotherapists, ego integration for psychoanalysts), then meaningful comparisons between the proportion of claimed successes between these schools cannot be made.

The positive value of psychotherapy, taken for granted by most clinicians for 50 years, was first challenged by Hans Eysenck, a British psychologist, in 1952. Using as his data the results of studies of psychoanalytic and eclectic forms of therapy published between 1920 and 1950—a total of 24 reports covering over 8000 hospitalized patients and outpatients, all of whom were diagnosed as neurotic (see Table 8)—Eysenck concluded that these data failed to support the hypothesis that psychotherapy facilitates recovery from neurotic disorders. In order to provide a baseline for comparative purposes, Eysenck included as control groups those individuals diagnosed as neurotic and discharged annually, having received no psychotherapy, from New York State hospitals between 1917 and 1934, and a group of 500 patients who received disability insurance benefits for neurotic disorders, for which they received treatment (but not psychotherapy) by general practitioners. Pooling these results, no form of psychotherapy claimed as high a success rate as occurred spontaneously (that is, without psychotherapy), leading Eysenck to conclude that it had not been demonstrated that psychotherapy is effective. A later survey of published studies by Eysenck (1965), on the outcome of psychotherapy with military and civilian neurotics and adults and children, led Eysenck to conclude further that the therapeutic effects of psychotherapy are small or nonexistent. According to Eysenck's interpretation of the data, more than two-thirds of severe neurotics (72 percent) are reported to show spontaneous recovery or considerable improvement without psychotherapy within two years of onset: few therapists claim as high a success rate. Moreover, Eysenck believes that successes therapists claim may simply reflect the natural, spontaneous improvement of neurotics after a period of time. A survey of the results of psychotherapy with children (Levitt, 1957) reported roughly the same percentages as Eysenck's, lending further support to his conclusions.

Eysenck's original 1952 report aroused considerable controversy among psychologists. Many practicing therapists were particularly alarmed because they interpreted Eysenck's findings to mean he had disproved the effectiveness of psychotherapy, which Eysenck had not claimed. (He did

Table 8. Response of neurotic patients to psychotherapy and no psychotherapy conditions*

FORM OF TREATMENT	NUMBER OF CASES	PERCENT CURED OR IMPROVED
PSYCHOTHERAPY		
Psychoanalysis	760	44%
Eclectic approaches	7293	64%
NO PSYCHOTHERAPY		
Hospitalization (New York State)	119	72% †
Treatment by general physicians (insurance claimants)	500	72% ‡

* Adapted from data presented by Eysenck (1952).

† Within one year after hospital admission. Figure represents percentage recovered or improved according to records of New York State hospitals, 1917–1934.

‡ Within two years after onset of neurotic condition. Insurance company records for neurotic disabilities showed that 45 percent of the patients recovered after one year, 72 percent after two years, 90 percent after five years.

not exclude the possibility that some clients who didn't seem to be helped by therapy might actually have been worse off without it.) In general, the following arguments have been mustered against Eysenck's viewpoint and conclusions:

1. The pooling of data from varying patient populations inevitably must have resulted in considerable variation in the accuracy of the neurotic diagnosis, as well in the meaning of "improvement." Comparing different kinds of patients with different histories of disorders receiving different forms of psychotherapy (subsumed under eclectic, but also differences within psychoanalysis) by different therapists with different criteria of success makes general statements regarding the effectiveness of psychotherapy meaningless.

2. The control groups were not comparable to the groups undergoing psychotherapy. The 72 percent spontaneous recovery rate (see Table 8) may be inflated. In addition, there is no way of knowing whether the hospital dischargees with no therapy or the insurance claimants were as seriously emotionally disturbed as the patients receiving psychotherapy. In the case of the former, neurotics are not usually admitted to state hospitals; those admitted may be discharged rapidly. Also, they are not likely to be comparable to psychoanalytic patients in terms of education or socio-

economic status, making comparisons all the more dubious. In the case of those individuals receiving insurance benefits for neurotic disabilities, there may have been some pressure on insurance company physicians to judge them cured and ready to resume work, thus easing the insurance company's responsibility.

3. Those control group members said by Eysenck to have received no formal psychotherapy may actually have received a great deal of attention, empathy, advice, and encouragement by hospital staff members, insurance physicians, friends, clergymen, bartenders, beauticians, and others. It is naive to assume that an emotionally distressed individual will not take his troubles somewhere if he cannot go to a recognized psychotherapist. It is questionable whether true "spontaneous recovery" of emotional problems exists. Rather, to call the remission of symptoms spontaneous is actually to admit we do not know how else to account for their reduction or disappearance. However, despite our lack of knowledge and the temptation to attribute the changes to "natural" causes, something did bring about the changes.

4. Some therapists may be producing positive effects, but others may be causing deterioration in their patients. Lumping together all data may result in these contrary phenomena cancelling each other out to some extent, with the overall result poorer than what occurs "spontaneously" in a control group. Eysenck's data showed that in one sample of adults, 39 percent improved, and in another 77 percent improved. Averaging such results along with others may therefore have produced the result that psychotherapy, on the average, appears to be ineffective.[3]

Eysenck acknowledged certain shortcomings in his study, particularly the necessity of relying on questionable actuarial comparisons because no controlled experiments on the effects of psychotherapy were available to him in 1952. In addition, he was aware that the control-group baseline data could be criticized as being too high. Due to Eysenck's challenge, however, considerable research based on more rigorously designed experiments has taken place in the last two decades. Meltzoff and Kornreich (1970) have recently provided an exhaustive study and evaluation of some 866

---

[3] The so-called *deterioration effect* (Bergin, 1970) is beginning to be considered with increasing seriousness as therapists face up to the fact that psychotherapy can do harm as well as good. While most studies follow the custom of reporting their results as percentages improved or unimproved, it would be helpful, although understandably personally difficult, if the proportion harmed by psychotherapy were included.

published reports on psychotherapy. While they find that Eysenck's 1952 conclusions may have been justifiable, they point out that his 1965 paper was based on a small, unrepresentative sample of the available data, and his conclusions, therefore, were not justified. According to these authors, carefully controlled research, necessarily including a matched no-therapy control group, has demonstrated the effectiveness of psychotherapy.

Believing that clinical practice should be influenced by research findings and that it is possible to do rigorous research on psychotherapy, Meltzoff and Kornreich's survey has helped place many of those therapeutic variables once considered unresearchable within the scientific realm. In their survey of published results of psychotherapy, the authors distinguish those studies which are based on adequate research designs from those whose designs are questionable. An adequate study must meet the following criteria:

1. Freedom from major design flaws that might invalidate the conclusions;
2. Use of an appropriate control group and adequate sampling;
3. Relative freedom from bias;
4. Employment of reasonably objective, reliable, and valid criteria measures; and
5. Presentation of suitably analyzed and interpreted data [Meltzoff & Kornreich, 1970, p. 76].

When the assessment of the literature is limited to those 55 studies which adequately test the effectiveness of psychotherapy, 84 percent (or 48) of the adequate studies were found to show that therapy had positive effects. Interestingly, they found that the better the quality of research, the more likely were the results to be positive. Finally, Meltzoff and Kornreich found the ratio of adequate to questionable studies to be steadily increasing. They suggested that earlier surveys which found that psychotherapy has, on the average, no demonstrable effect, were based on: (1) an incomplete survey of the existing research, and (2) an insufficiently stringent appraisal of the data. Their own conclusion is that adequately controlled research has demonstrated the effectiveness of psychotherapy.

PSYCHOANALYSIS

Since modern psychotherapy may be considered to have begun with the discoveries of Sigmund Freud (1856–1939) 75 years ago, and since those discoveries continue to affect how psychotherapy is practiced today, it seems fitting to begin a more detailed study of psychotherapy by investigating Freud's system, called psychoanalysis.[4] Throughout the remainder of this section the term psychoanalysis should be understood to represent both: (1) an empirically derived theory concerning normal personality development as well as the development of psychopathology, particularly neuroses; and (2) a system of psychotherapy for treating abnormal behavior. While many original followers of Freud (Adler, Jung, Rank, Reich) later defected from Freud's camp and developed new theories and techniques of psychotherapy, the term *psychoanalysis* properly belongs to the system developed by Freud.

Without question, Freud remains even today, 30 years after his death, the towering figure in psychotherapy. Even opponents of his views acknowledge the importance of his basic discoveries, including the influence of unconscious processes on everyday behavior, defense mechanisms, the deterministic view that all behavior has psychological meaning and cause, the use of cathartic methods whereby the patient is urged to report to the therapist all his thoughts, feelings, and associations. This so-called talking cure remains the common denominator of all modern psychotherapy.

Freud,[5] a physician and neurologist in Vienna in the 1880s, had received a thorough grounding in research methodology; his published studies in histology, physiology, and neurology are evidence of his carefully documented empirical observations. Freud's medical interests, especially in neurology, inevitably extended to neuropsychiatry, which at that time was completely organic in its viewpoint regarding the origin of psychopathological conditions and their treatment. At first Freud used the then current medical procedures: baths, sedation, electrical stimulation, rest cures.

[4] For simplicity's sake, the classical psychoanalytical model will be presented. However, the reader should be aware that many derivatives of this classical position exist and are practiced today by those who still consider themselves to be working within the psychoanalytic framework.

[5] The definitive biography of Freud is the three-volume set *The Life and Work of Sigmund Freud,* written by Ernest Jones (1953, 1955, 1957), himself the dean of British psychoanalysts until his recent death.

However, he quickly became dissatisfied with these methods and turned to hypnosis after observing dramatic demonstrations by Charcot, the French neuropsychiatrist, of hypnotic suggestion removing such symptoms of hysteria as functional (that is, nonorganic) blindness, paralysis, amnesia, and so on. As Freud began to use hypnotic techniques with his own patients, he was able to remove certain symptoms only to find them frequently replaced by others; he remembered another Viennese physician, Josef Breuer, telling him of his hypnotic experiences with Anna O., a patient with a variety of hysterical symptoms. Included in Breuer's daily treatment procedure was a period when the patient would talk freely and he would listen. Anna O. recognized the value of the talking cure—or "chimney sweeping," as she also described it—and slowly began to recall and relive earlier emotional experiences in her life; in time, her current symptoms disappeared. Through spontaneously induced hypnotic states supplemented by hypnotic states induced by Breuer, the patient also received considerable relief.[6]

Although Breuer never applied the technique to other patients, Freud was intrigued, particularly because the method provided a way to get at forgotten memories which seemed to be causally related to current symptoms (Breuer & Freud, 1895). Rather than being forgotten, these memories seemed to persist below the level of consciousness and to seek expression through the manifestation of symptoms. Breuer had called the process by which the patient expressed the affect associated with the symptom *abreaction*. Freud adopted the method, trying to get his patients to recall the supposedly traumatic event that they had banished from memory, in the belief that such recall should make the symptoms disappear. Slowly, Freud abandoned the use of hypnosis, having found it impossible to hypnotize every patient. Instead, he adopted a technique of encouraging catharsis without hypnotic suggestion as a way to help discharge the pent-up emotions while simultaneously recalling the forgotten memories that were the basis for the hysterical symptoms. By 1896, Freud had his patients lie on a couch (a carryover from the hypnotic method) and follow the so-called basic rule of psychoanalysis, namely, that they report everything that came to mind without censorship or predetermined choice of subject matter, no matter how seemingly insignificant or unrelated to previous thoughts.

[6] At times Freud termed Breuer the founder of psychoanalysis (Jones, 1953), although the essentials of psychoanalysis—the method and the later discoveries and theory—belong to Freud and were made long after the two men were no longer collaborators.

Sitting behind the patient and out of his line of sight to avoid distracting him, Freud listened to the patient's free associations (that is, his stream of consciousness monologue) as they led to uncovering repressed ideas and unconscious conflicts. While continuing to recognize the importance of abreaction in helping the patient release pent-up emotions, Freud's emphasis had now shifted to removing amnesia, recovering repressed memories, and making the unconscious conscious (Greenson, 1967). While he continued to refine and modify his theories throughout his life, the basic technique of psychoanalysis was thus fairly well established by the first decade of the twentieth century.

THE BASIC POSTULATES OF PSYCHOANALYSIS

1. Psychic determinism. Freud's first assumption about neurotic symptoms was that they were caused by some antecedent events or conditions. Previous explanations of neurotic behavior had ignored what was to become the cornerstone of the dynamic point of view—namely, that all behavior is lawful, is motivated, and serves some psychological purpose. Assuming that all behavior is caused, Freud tried to understand what purposes a particular symptom served in a patient's life. In addition, he sought to discover from the history of the initial appearance of the symptoms what their underlying causes were. Just as neurotic symptoms did not occur by chance, so Freud reasoned that seemingly accidental everyday behavior—slips of the tongue (which have come to be known as Freudian slips), accidental writing, momentary forgetting of names or where objects were mislaid—also had unconscious meaning and cause. Freud believed these ostensibly unmotivated bits of behavior, called *parapraxes,* expressed unconscious motives and conflicts. Freud (1901) referred to such phenomena as the *psychopathology of everyday life,* emphasizing that no aspect of human behavior is ever completely accidental, but is always an expression of some unconscious psychic conflict.

2. Levels of consciousness. The assumption that unconscious psychological processes exist and continue to influence conscious thoughts and behavior did not originate with Freud, but was a much discussed idea when Freud was a student. Freud had seen Charcot use posthypnotic suggestion to demonstrate that past experiences could survive in memory even though the patient was unable to recall them consciously until signalled to do so. In addition, Freud's own experiences with neurotic patients had shown him that they frequently could not recall crucial but traumatic events in their lives but could do so with great clarity under hypnosis, as though the memories were preserved somehow. He inferred that ideas, thoughts, and memories must exist outside of awareness, at some unconscious level.

Freud postulated three levels of consciousness—the conscious, preconscious, and unconscious levels. The *conscious* level consists of material in an individual's immediate awareness. The *preconscious* level consists of memories which can ordinarily be readily brought into consciousness. The *unconscious* level, on the other hand, contains both memories repressed from consciousness, as well as inherited ideas and wishes that have never been conscious. Infantile wishes, for example, may be forbidden expression, become repressed into the unconscious but continue to seek expression in an adult without the individual's awareness of what is taking place. Unconscious thoughts and memories lack the logical consistency of conscious thought. They tend to be illogical, irrational, and often primitive. However, they are frequently a powerful influence on conscious thought and behavior.

    3. **Topographical structure of personality.** Freud conceived of mental phenomena in a topographic fashion—that is, as regions of the mind. The three major regions he called id, ego, and super-ego. Rather than anatomic entities in the brain, these are merely hypothetical constructs invented by Freud to conceptualize the structure of personality. The *id* consists of the basic instinctual drives and is the source of psychic energy, called *libido*. Id strivings, entirely unconscious, are primitive and demand immediate gratification when tension is built up. This is said to be characteristic of the infant, all of whose behavior is pleasure-seeking. (The id is said to operate on the *pleasure principle*.) The *ego* develops from the id in the process of meeting reality. Freud characterized the ego as that hypothetical structure whose function is to mediate between the id impulses and the demands and restrictions of reality. (It is said to obey the *reality principle*.) The ego, therefore, has both conscious and unconscious components. It has the executive function of delaying gratification until such gratification can be expressed in socially approved ways. The ego's role, too, is to repress (push down into unconsciousness) socially unacceptable impulses. In contrast, the *super-ego* has a judicial function, corresponding to the popular notion of conscience. Its job is to provide a moral restraint on id

impulses (particularly of a sexual or aggressive nature) based on the rules of learned, proper social conduct. Infractions of those rules lead to guilt feelings, the work of the super-ego. The super-ego, representing as it does an internalized image of parental authority, is also partly conscious and partly unconscious. While these three structures of personality are ordinarily in harmonious balance in normal adults, this equilibrium is disturbed in neurotics, where a battle persists between instinctual forces (id) and rational (ego) and moral (super-ego) forces. The ego postpones the gratification the id wants immediately, while the super-ego, at war with both the id and ego, seeks to block gratification completely.

4. Stages of psychosexual development. Of all Freud's theories concerning mental phenomena and the development of neuroses, his theory of infantile sexuality most outraged Viennese Victorian society at the turn of the century. Freud's insistence on searching for psychological rather than physical causes led him to search the past life experiences of his adult patients to identify those early traumatic experiences and conflicts which he thought were the causative agents in their neuroses. Startled because nearly all his female patients reported they had been seduced as a child by their fathers or uncles, he ultimately realized he was dealing with their childhood sexual fantasies rather than descriptions of real events. From this he concluded that the sexual drive does not simply appear as mature genitality, but must exist long before puberty. What most shocked his professional colleagues and the public was his theory that the sexual drive is among the most important instincts, even among "decent" people, and furthermore that it manifested itself from infancy on.

Freud's emphasis on infantile sexuality underscored how decisive the first several years of life were in the formation of adult personality in general, as well as in forming neuroses and perversions in particular. In his famous *Three Essays on the Theory of Sexuality* (Freud, 1905) he postulated that libido (the energy of the sexual instinct) is centered in various parts of the body in the course of development. The oral phase (roughly from birth to one and one-half years) occurs first, followed by the anal phase (roughly one and one-half to three years) and the phallic phase (three to seven years). A latency period is said to occur between the ages of 7 and 12, followed by the reemergence of sexuality at puberty and the ultimate phase of genital primacy. If the child is traumatized at one or another stage of development, Freud believed he developed a fixation at that point and might, as an adult, regress to that point under stress. For example, it is common for an orally fixated person to overeat when frustrated or for an alcoholic to turn literally to a bottle when under pressure.

The first manifestations of sexuality in the infant center around mouth activities during the *oral phase*. During this oral erotic period, sucking and chewing are pleasurable beyond their nutritional yield, as demonstrated by the common behavior of thumbsucking and the pleasure from pacifiers in infants. The development of teeth provides the first opportunity for aggressive behavior in the infant. During the *anal phase*, sexual pleasure is said to be linked to activities involving the anus. During efforts to toilet train him, he undergoes his first formal experiences with discipline and control by his mother. However, since only he can control the expulsion or retention of his feces, he may react with compliance or defiance to this demand. Frequently a power struggle may develop between mother and child at this stage. Aggressive impulses may take the form of negativism and stubbornness (retention) or hostile, destructive, sadistic behavior (expulsion) during the anal period. The *phallic phase* is marked by pleasure deriving from the genital region. Touching, rubbing, and exhibiting the genitals are typical autoerotic activities.

During the phallic phase, Freud believed a boy developed sexual fantasies and wished for so-called incestuous relations with his mother while viewing his father as a rival (these fantasies seemed only vaguely related to the boy's later adult sexuality). Freud called this phenomenon the *Oedipus complex* because it seemed to him to parallel the Greek tragedy, *Oedipus Rex* by Sophocles, in which Oedipus killed his father and married his mother. However, the boy fears punishment from his father and also has some positive identification with him; as a result he was thought by Freud to develop castration anxiety, a fear that his father will cut off his penis in retaliation. Consequently, the sexual feelings are dissipated or displaced onto objects outside the family.[7] From seven until 12, Freud believed the child was in a *latency period*, where sexual and aggressive fantasies were repressed, and sexual impulses remained relatively dormant. At the onset of puberty, Freud thought that the phallic impulses were

[7] Freud's explanation of the Oedipus complex in girls is less satisfactorily described. Freud's notion was that the girl feels castrated because she has no male sex organs. As a result, she blames her mother, who also lacks these organs, and turns to her father for gratification. Therefore, the reverse sequence is said to occur in girls, with castration anxiety leading to an Electra complex, analogous to the Oedipus complex, in which girls unconsciously desire an incestuous relationship with their fathers.

revived and the libidinal energy attached to other objects than himself or his parents. His adult heterosexual interests represent the ultimate phase of *genital primacy*.

5. The psychodynamics of neurosis. Neurotic conflict, according to Freud, is an inevitable consequence of the frequent incompatibility of the individual's inner needs and the restrictions of society. As he seeks expression of his id impulses, the ego intervenes and attempts to prevent its direct discharge or access to consciousness. The super-ego makes the instinctual impulse seem forbidden to the ego, leading to conscious feelings of guilt. As a result, the individual must repress the impulse, which nevertheless continues to retain some of its psychic energy. Since repression is never completely successful, some of this energy is transformed into anxiety. Anxiety, the major symptom of neurotic conflict, signifies that the ego has not been able to control the instinctual drives totally. Since the ego must constantly expend its energies to attempt to control these drives from gaining access to consciousness, it becomes weakened and less able to use its varied defense mechanisms to hold back the discharge of anxiety-arousing instinctual impulses. These impulses are ultimately discharged in some disguised and distorted form and are manifested clinically as neurotic symptoms.

An adult neurosis always has its basis in childhood. If the child has not satisfactorily resolved the problems of a particular phase of psychosexual development, a certain portion of libido remains fixated at that stage, leaving less available for dealing with the demands of subsequent stages. Under stress as an adult, he may regress to that stage in his development where he is most strongly fixated.[8] For example, obsessive–compulsive neurotics are thought to be fixated at the anal phase. Obsessive thoughts (such as excessive worry and rumination) or compulsive rituals (excessive handwashing) are ways of avoiding objects or situations suggesting "dirt," as the ego attempts to ward off any anal drive. Typically, such neurotic individuals remain in conflict over aggressiveness or submissiveness, cruelty or gentleness, dirtiness or cleanliness, disorder or order (Fenichel,

---

[8] Freud sometimes used the analogy of an army invading a foreign country. If they experience difficulties at any point, they may leave an extra large garrison there, permitting fewer soldiers to continue the thrust forward. Should the soldiers who continued to move ahead experience difficulties, they are apt to retreat to the previous heavily guarded garrison. Psychoanalytically speaking, they might be considered as regressing to their fixation point.

1945). Conversion hysteria, on the other hand, represents a fixation at the phallic level; like all neuroses, it represents a compromise between an id impulse and ego attempts at control or modification. Specifically, the conversion hysteric's symptoms arise out of an unresolved Oedipal conflict. These symptoms, more common in Freud's day than the present, might take the form of hysterical blindness or hysterical paralysis without a physical basis. Each is considered an unconscious neurotic compromise between a sexual impulse and ego censorship, resulting in conversion of repressed sexual energy into a bodily disturbance. Thus, the hysterically blind person may unconsciously wish to avoid seeing something sexually unpleasant or unacceptable, while the hysterically paralyzed person may resolve his sexual conflict (perhaps over masturbation) by developing a paralyzed hand.

No adult is free of some neurotic conflict, since it is not possible to develop through the various stages of psychosexual development without experiencing some trauma. However, some individuals make more effective use of defense mechanisms (repression, sublimation, rationalization), which are unconscious, self-deceptive methods by which the ego protects the individual from experiencing anxiety. These individuals nevertheless show signs in their adult character of unresolved early problems, although the anxiety may be held relatively in check. Thus, so-called oral characters are likely to be passive, dependent, gullible ("he'll swallow anything") people; those fixated at the oral biting phase are likely to be bitter, cynical, and sarcastic ("biting remarks") in an attempt to express aggressive impulses. Anal characters, depending on whether retention or expulsion characterized their reaction to toilet training, are likely to be orderly, obstinate, parsimonious, and controlled or messy, wasteful, and irresponsible. Phallic characters are concerned with power, rivalry, and achievement.

THE TECHNIQUE OF PSYCHOANALYTIC TREATMENT

Psychoanalysis attempts to liberate the libido from infantile—that is, pregenital—fixations. As the ego is strengthened, it deals more effectively with both inner pressures (id, super-ego forces) and the external pressures of reality. Both sets of pressures, previous sources of anxiety dealt with by inadequate neurotic defenses, are now met by a more flexible, less constricted set of ego defenses. As id impulses are permitted access to consciousness, and as the super-ego becomes more reasonable and tolerant rather than punitive, there is greater harmony between ego, id, and super-ego forces. As unconscious conflicts are made more conscious and resolved, the individual develops more energy to gain a reasonable measure of happiness from the external world. Anxiety is reduced and growth is made more possible as the individual develops a sense of identity and learns to love, enjoy sex, find satisfactory work, and achieve a comfortable balance between his internal impulses and external demands and restrictions.

1. Free association. Free association is the major method for producing the clinical data on which psychoanalytic treatment is based. Perhaps one of Freud's most important discoveries was that the patient's free verbal expression of every thought, feeling, or impulse serves to: (1) reduce conscious control and inhibition over what is verbally expressed; (2) provide a link through a chain of associations from one statement to the next; and (3) establish an avenue for reaching unconscious material associated to conscious material and ultimately bringing it into consciousness.

The technique of free association is to have the patient lie on the couch, so that he cannot see the analyst who sits behind him, and to report all his thoughts without regard to logical connection or social convention, despite any feeling that they are unimportant, painful, or embarrassing. The couch is used to avoid being distracted by an awareness of the analyst's presence and his reactions. In addition, since reclining is associated with sleep, it is likely to stimulate fantasy and therefore help get closer to unconscious processes and away from the logic and reasoning of conscious mental processes of ordinary waking hours. Finally, the invisibility of the analyst is likely to stimulate fantasies about him, frequently reflecting deeply ingrained unconscious feelings of the patient toward significant figures in his earlier life (see discussion of transference below). Usually the analyst remains silent and neutral so long as the patient continues to associate freely. However, should the association come to a halt and the patient feel blocked, the analyst is then likely to intercede to help get the patient through his temporary resistance.

Freud sometimes explained the free association method as analogous to a traveler sitting next to a window inside a moving train and describing to someone next to him the changing view outside. Munroe (1955) has presented the following brief excerpt from the free associations of a psychoanalytic patient:

The patient begins with a brief report of the previous day—a sort of routine in his analytic sessions. Nothing special: he had a conference with his boss about a going project. He didn't quite like the boss's policy, but it was not too bad, and who was he in the hierarchy of his institution to contradict the boss? By now this was an old issue in the analysis: did he habitually give in too easily, or did he evaluate correctly the major contours of his job? In any event, the conference was just a conference like any other. He'd had a dream—something about an ironing board, but that was as far as he could go. Associations to ironing board? Well, we have one. "Matter of fact, my wife said our maid irons badly. She could iron my shirts better herself, but I don't think she could and I'm sure she wouldn't. Anyhow, my shirts look all right to me. I wish she wouldn't worry so much. I hope she doesn't fire that maid." The patient suddenly hums a bit of *Lohengrin* and has to hunt for the words on the request of the analyst. It is the passage where Lohengrin reveals his glorious origin. ("My father, Parsifal, wears his crown and I am his knight, Lohengrin.") Patient: "Now I think of that last report X [his boss] turned in. That was *my* work—only I can't say so. That ironing board—my mother was ironing. I jumped off the cupboard, wonderful jump, but I sort of used her behind as support—she was leaning over. She told father I had been disrespectful and he gave me a licking. I was awfully hurt. I hadn't even thought about her old behind—it was just a wonderful jump. Father would never let me explain. My sister says he was proud of me. He never acted that way. He was awfully strict. I wish he hadn't died when I was so young—we might have worked things out [p. 39]."[9]

In this illustration, the patient's present feelings of being treated unfairly by his boss are associated with some repressed feelings from childhood regarding mistreatment by his parents. He identifies with the maid, whom he feels his wife is mistreating. The reference to *Lohengrin* is most likely a self-reassuring defensive maneuver.

2. Dream analysis. Many of Freud's early patients spontaneously reported dreams and then proceeded to give free associations to them. Freud soon realized that during sleep the conscious mind was relatively inactive and that the unconscious forces were given more free play because of the relaxation of the usual ego controls. He began to study the properties of dreams and to develop a theory for explaining their origins

[9] Munroe, *Schools of Psychoanalytic Thought.* Reprinted by permission of the publisher, Holt, Rinehart and Winston, Inc.

and meaning. His 1900 publication of *The Interpretation of Dreams* is considered by many to be his masterpiece.

Freud considered dreams to be the "royal road to the unconscious." That is, dreams had psychological meaning and the free association method could be used to get to the unconscious conflict reflected in the dreams. Freud believed dreams were unconscious attempts at wish-fulfillment. Since the dreamer was not consciously aware of these wishes, they appeared only in a distorted form, through sensory images. Freud postulated a censorship function which kept the direct expression of these unconscious wishes from entering the dream in a direct and undisguised manner. During sleep, certain persistent thoughts, called residues of the previous day, perhaps insignificant and consciously overlooked at the time of their occurrence, remain in the preconscious and become attached to unconscious infantile wishes. (For example, the ironing board in the dream reported on p. 228.) The residues provide the content, and these wishes provide the force, which together produce the dream. However, distortions take place through what Freud called the dream work. Dramatizations, condensations in time and space, displacements onto incidental items of unconscious wishes, and especially symbolization are examples of the mechanisms of dream work. Symbols are unique for each individual, although certain universal symbols (such as church steeples forming phallic symbols) exist.

Freud distinguished the manifest content of dreams (what is remembered and reported) from the latent content (the unconscious wishes concealed behind the manifest content). It was the latter which provided a key to unlocking the unconscious conflict represented in the dream.

3. Transference. The core of psychoanalytic treatment revolves around the development of transference, another important discovery of Freud's. Transference is the experiencing of feelings, drives, attitudes, fantasies, and defenses toward a person in the present, which is a repetition or displacement of past reactions to significant individuals from the patient's early childhood (Greenson, 1967). The patient repeats his earlier reactions rather than remembering them. That is, by reenacting the past, he is directly able to relive now, with the analyst, his earlier unresolved conflicts and to come to understand and master these early conflicts through psychoanalysis. Wolberg (1967) believes psychoanalysis is transference analysis, with the analyst using various techniques for facilitating transference reactions. By remaining neutral, anonymous, silent, out of the patient's sight while seeing the patient several times a week over several years, the analyst remains a fairly mysterious person about whom the patient knows little or nothing, but about whom he develops strong feelings and on whom he projects characteristics he unconsciously believes are there.

Freud thought transference reactions developed especially in neurotic patients. In particular, the patient's feelings toward important people during his Oedipal period were thought to be reenacted via transference behavior in his expressions of love, sexual longings, rivalry, or fear of castration regarding his relations with his analyst. Since Freud believed the libidinal development of psychotics had never reached the Oedipal level but remained dominated by an earlier primary narcissism (self-love), he thought psychotics could not form the attachments to people necessary to develop transference reactions. Consequently, Freud and his followers considered psychoanalysis to be unsuited for various forms of psychosis, including schizophrenia and manic–depressive psychoses.

Transference reactions may be positive or negative or more likely, both. Transference neurosis refers to the peak of transference feelings, when most of the patient's unconscious conflicts become centered around the analyst and are relived during the analytic situation. Equally involved in such an intense relationship, the analyst may develop strong irrational and unconsciously motivated attachments to the patient, called counter-transference (Menninger, 1958), which he must recognize and work through.

4. Interpretation and working through. The analyst acts as a catalyst by listening to the free associations, making inferences about the unconscious conflicts involved in dreams, and helping interpret the transference reactions. He uses his own unconscious processes, his empathy, his intuition, and his understanding of personality structure to enable the patient to gain insight into the roots of the unconscious conflicts within him and to help him resolve them.

Along the way, various resistances occur; they are defenses of the patient operating against the efforts of the analyst (forgetting appointments, blocks in free associations, silences). Resistances are the work of the unconscious ego against the awareness of anxiety or other painful affect due to some instinctual impulse seeking expression. The analysis proceeds step by step as resistances are worked through. The analyst makes interpretations to identify resistances and help the patient overcome them so the patient can return to his efforts of gaining insight and increased ego control.

The working through process involves the sustained effort, usually protracted over several years, to overcome resistances and resolve neurotic patterns. As the transference neurosis is resolved and the libido becomes detached from the analyst, it no longer returns to its former objects, but is now at the disposal of the ego. Psychoanalysis is thought to be ready for termination when the patient has faced, understood, and emotionally resolved his neurotic conflicts and is able to obtain gratification from his instinctual drives in society rather than being helplessly driven by them.

EVALUATION OF PSYCHOANALYSIS

ARGUMENTS FOR PSYCHOANALYSIS

1. The theory and method of investigation of psychoanalysis have had a powerful influence on all aspects of life. Boring (1950), in his monumental history of psychology, considers Darwin and Freud to have produced the greatest revolution in our thinking, with Freud's contribution still too recent to be fully evaluated. In any event, Freud's impact clearly goes beyond psychology to the humanities, social theory, religion, education, and many other fields. Whether Freud's specific theories of instinct, libido, fixed energy systems, or topographic structure of personality survive is less important than the fact that he pointed the way to examining human nature in a tenacious, daring, and insightful manner.

Freud's influence has been felt by scientist and layman alike. His *Totem and Taboo* (Freud, 1913), in which he hypothesized that primordial human society consisted of hordes of brothers led by a powerful father, inevitably resulting in Oedipal conflicts, provided an important stimulus to studies in anthropology, particularly the origins of society and the relationship between culture and personality. At the other extreme, books such as those by Spock on child care reflect psychoanalytic ideas regarding child-rearing practices such as the proper timing and methods of weaning or toilet training.

In general, Freud's ideas have permeated science and everyday life to a greater extent than most of us realize. Unconscious motivation, the influence of childhood experiences on adult personality formation, conflict, anxiety, guilt, dream symbolism, the Oedipus conflict—all are part of our vocabulary and our way of looking at the human condition.

2. Psychoanalysis provides the most comprehensive and detailed system of personality yet formulated. It gives some sense of order and continuity to the course of personality development. It takes into account both biological and experiential factors. It emphasizes that behavior develops genetically, so that in a sense the child is father to the man. It explodes the myth that sexuality does not exist in young children, leading in general to a more open awareness of the role of sexuality in our lives.

At the same time, Freud's efforts represent the most ambitious undertaking to date in understanding the basis for neurotic conflicts and the meaning of neurotic symptoms. By differentiating real anxiety (a fearful reaction to environmental danger) from neurotic anxiety (a fearful reaction to being punished for allowing id impulses to get out of control), Freud was able to show both similarities and differences between normal and neurotic reaction patterns.

3. Psychoanalysis is the most thorough psychotherapeutic system for achieving a deep-seated modification of the neurotic personality. Wolberg (1967) has differentiated: (1) *supportive therapy* (aimed at bringing the patient to an emotional equilibrium as rapidly as possible, with the amelioration of symptoms and the strengthening of existing defenses) as in drug therapy or in a hospital therapeutic community (see pp. 336–337) where it is practiced through guidance, persuasion, and the environmental manipulation possible there; (2) *reeducative therapy* (aimed at modifying behavior through conditioning techniques and/or interpersonal relationships) as in behavior therapy or the phenomenological therapies (see Chapter 7); and (3) *reconstructive therapy* (aimed at achieving extensive personality growth and the development of new adaptive potentialities by giving the patient insight into his underlying unconscious conflicts) as in psychoanalysis.[10] Wolberg considers reconstructive therapy to produce the most stable growth and maturation, leading not only to the resolution of disabling symptoms and disturbed interpersonal relationships, but also to a sense of greater self-esteem and direction of instinctual drives in the interest of the patient's gratification.

4. Psychoanalysis gives a rightful place to the role of unconscious processes in influencing behavior. By going beyond the outward manifestations of behavior, Freud made it apparent that more subtle and ordi-

---

[10] It has been suggested that another way psychoanalysis is different from other forms of psychotherapy is that it goes down deeper, stays down longer, and comes up dirtier.

narily less accessible thoughts and feelings continue to be important determinants of that outward behavior. By stressing psychic determinism, he showed that previously inexplicable behavior had meaning and cause, which frequently could be found by discovering the patient's underlying unconscious conflicts. The search for such hidden meanings and hidden connections has led to a deeper, more complete picture of human motives and conflicts.

5. Psychoanalysis has led the way in establishing high standards for training and practice. Psychoanalysis is a long, arduous, intensive experience for the analyst as well as his patient. In addition to requiring extensive theoretical knowledge, only the bare outline of which is included in this book, psychoanalytic practice demands a therapist who is himself relatively mature and free from disabling neurotic conflicts. The various psychoanalytic institutes throughout the world have led the way in setting up training programs, usually taking several years to complete and including seminars in psychoanalytic theory, psychoanalysis of each analytic candidate, and analytic work—supervised by an experienced psychoanalyst—with a number of patients. Technically, a practitioner cannot be considered a qualified psychoanalyst until he completes such training. In general, psychoanalysts are members of local psychoanalytic institutes through which they continue their education during the course of their professional careers by attending regular meetings at which they report to one another their treatment of specific cases.

ARGUMENTS AGAINST PSYCHOANALYSIS

1. This theory of personality development, based on the resolution of sexual conflict, is too narrow and less appropriate to our times than it was to Freud's nineteenth- and early twentieth-century Vienna. While there is little question that sexual conflicts and guilt feelings continue to play a part in the etiology of many neurotic problems, few clinicians today believe such conflicts are the sole, or even the most significant, cause of such disorders. Freud deserves a great deal of credit for his courage and persistence in the face of criticism in making us aware of sexual drives in children as well as the neurotic problems that may result if such drives are not coped with successfully. However, Freud's theories regarding sexual repression seem more appropriate to a Victorian social climate where sex was almost unacknowledged than to present-day society where children's sexual curiosity and interest are dealt with in a more permissive fashion. As a consequence, symptoms of conversion hysteria, so common in Freud's time, are rarely seen today. Instead, clinicians today are far more likely to deal with their clients' feelings of despair, aimlessness, and alienation.

2. **Interest in psychoanalysis has waned in recent years because of the difficulty in verifying its concepts by research methods.** Freud's observations of his patients were made under uncontrolled conditions; he did not attempt to keep a verbatim account of what transpired during the analytic hour. His inferences, leading to his theories, were based on a line of reasoning rarely made explicit; other explanations of the same data are possible. There is the danger, always a possibility in looking for evidence to support a new theory, that new data are perceived in such a way as to lend support to the theory, which makes the theory a self-fulfilling prophecy. Freud may simply have found what he was looking for, confirming and reconfirming possible misperceptions. No scientist is likely to accept such a theory at face value without insisting on the kinds of research programs psychoanalysis thus far has failed to produce. In the same way, little research has examined what actually takes place in psychoanalytic treatment, what aspects of the process are therapeutic, and whether there is any evidence that psychoanalysis produces better, more stable results than do other psychotherapeutic methods.

But psychoanalysis is not merely untested to date; in its present form, it is not testable. Freudian theory is markedly deficient in providing a set of rational rules for predicting behavior, given certain current events. For example, what precisely is the relationship between traumatic experiences, guilt feelings, repression, and the appearance of the consequent unconscious conflicts as dream symbols? How intense must an experience be before it can be classified as traumatic? How weak must the ego be before id impulses overwhelm it? Because just such specification is absent, no laws that have any predictive meaning can be derived (Hall & Lindzey, 1957). The fact that psychoanalysts write in a language that is imprecise ("the ego, id, and super-ego are engaged in a struggle") only makes matters worse and scientific precision all but impossible.

Psychoanalytic theory shows up poorly in the light of modern psychological knowledge. The concept of a fixed amount of energy (repression permitting less energy to be available for further development) is a carry-over from nineteenth-century physics and is no longer defensible. The theory of man driven by instincts was abandoned by most psychologists several decades ago. In the same manner, libido, the topographical structure of personality, indeed, the "mind" itself, are questionable concepts in modern psychology.

3. Psychoanalytic treatment lacks widespread applicability or demonstrable effectiveness. Psychoanalysis is time-consuming (usually lasting several years), expensive (usually well over $10,000), and frequently emotionally painful. Because it aims at a permanent alteration of the patient's personality structure, there is no way of knowing at the start just how long treatment will take for any single individual. In addition, resistances at various stages slow the process. Realistically, as currently practiced, classical psychoanalysis is applicable only to affluent people with considerable free time, who are highly intelligent, capable of insight, well motivated, and with a great deal of intellectual curiosity about themselves and their early problems. While such people usually are the ones who benefit most from psychotherapies that rely heavily on verbal communication, there is no evidence that psychoanalysis is more effective than other forms of therapy for them.

Psychoanalysis remains applicable primarily to those neurotic disorders where anxiety is the outstanding characteristic. Psychotics and individuals with other personality disorders are not considered able to benefit from classical psychoanalysis (although analysts like Fromm–Reichmann have reported successes with modified psychoanalytic techniques).

Considering the amount of professional training necessary, few psychoanalysts begin their psychoanalytic practice before the age of 35. Since each patient is seen four to five times a week for several years, probably fewer than 100 patients are treated in a professional lifetime—very few, in view of the long training required. Considering that at least upper-middle-class membership is probably required for treatment, that an enormous proportion of people have the types of problems psychoanalysts do not treat, and that the results of psychoanalytic treatment are not especially outstanding, then the practice of psychoanalytic treatment becomes increasingly difficult to justify.

4. The relatively small circle of psychoanalytic practitioners today remains, for the most part, a closed guild unresponsive to the enormous growth in psychological knowledge accumulated over the past 50 years.

For many classical psychoanalysts, the theory and practice of psychoanalytic treatment remains today much the same as it was in Freud's time. The analyst remains an aloof, authoritarian blank screen who never engages the patient as a real person—this, despite the accumulation of research evidence (see pp. 202–204) that therapy is facilitated when the therapist is genuine, real, empathetic, and accepting. The psychoanalytic conceptions of neurosis are based on the medical model of disease—the sick patient who requires treatment for some underlying causes of which the neurotic symptoms are only the outward manifestation—which also has been rendered untenable by newer conceptualizations.

Psychoanalytic practice, especially in America, remains for the most part a medical specialty. While there are some training centers, particularly on the East Coast, which qualify psychologists to practice psychoanalysis, the overwhelming number of candidates for training in psychoanalysis are physicians. Interestingly, Freud himself was strongly opposed to limiting psychoanalysis to the medical profession. Nevertheless, psychoanalysts in the United States remain a more or less insular group with closer ties to medicine than psychology. One unfortunate consequence of such a situation is that the cross-fertilization of ideas between psychoanalysts and clinical psychologists, so necessary for the growth of both disciplines, is effectively prevented.

5. Deviations from Freudian psychoanalysis have resulted in theories and therapeutic methods which stress social, cultural, and interpersonal factors over instinctual, biological forces. So-called *neo-Freudians* such as Erich Fromm (1947) and Karen Horney (1937) have emphasized that personality is fashioned primarily by the culture rather than instinctual forces, as Freud had insisted. Their viewpoint challenged Freud's idea that neuroses necessarily developed from early childhood experiences or always had a biologically determined sexual basis. Anthropologists such as Mead (1939) have shown that the stages of psychosexual development outlined by Freud are not universal but depend to a large extent on the attitudes of a society toward sexual expression. In the same way, the Freudian view that women inevitably felt inferior to men and fantasized about possessing a penis (so-called penis envy) is now seen to be the result of cultural forces, when it exists at all, rather than any biological inferiority.

Finally, the so-called *ego psychologists*—such as Heinz Hartmann (1964), Erik Erikson (1963), and Anna Freud (1946), daughter of Sigmund

Freud—have argued for a greater emphasis on the role of the ego in the total personality and have pursued the study of man's adaptive functions as he learns to achieve mastery over reality and a sense of personal identity. Indeed, many practitioners of traditional classical psychoanalysis have begun to modify their techniques as they have responded to the impact of the contributions of both neo-Freudians and ego psychologists.

CHAPTER 7 *Behavior Modification and the Phenomenological Therapies*

Three major approaches to psychotherapy dominate contemporary clinical psychology: psychoanalysis, behavior modification, and the phenomenological therapies. Psychoanalysis historically has been the most prestigious, offering the most comprehensive theory of the development of psychopathology as well as the most clearly specified set of techniques for treatment. However, as some psychologists have become disenchanted with many aspects of psychoanalysis—its poor research possibilities, its relatively poor rate of success for the effort, time, and money involved, and the lack of empirical evidence for many of its assumptions—they have looked more and more to related fields for other theoretical bases for developing competing systems of psychotherapy. Behavior modification, based on learning principles, had its beginnings in the psychological laboratory rather than in the practice of neuropsychiatry, as was the case for psychoanalysis. Many of the phenomenological therapies derive their basic assumptions from existential philosophy.

BEHAVIOR MODIFICATION

Behavior modification is based on the following assumptions:

1. Psychology, as a behavioral science, is particularly interested in observable behavior. While not denying the importance of an individual's mental processes (his thoughts, emotions, conflicts, motives), behavioral psychologists believe they are being more scientific when they limit their

knowledge of psychological events to what they can observe (and perhaps measure) rather than what they can infer.

2. Based originally on the empirical investigation of animal behavior in the laboratory, behavior modification can be generalized to humans, both in terms of how abnormal behavior is learned and how it can be inhibited or extinguished.

3. Abnormal behavior and normal behavior are both learned in the same way. It is not necessary to presuppose that abnormal behavior is a consequence of some unseen motive or inferred underlying cause (London, 1964; Ullmann & Krasner, 1966).

4. Behavior modification—or behavior therapy, a direct application of conditioning principles and techniques—can be used to alter or remove specific undesirable, maladaptive, or abnormal behavior.

The behavior therapist is interested in designing a therapeutic program for changing overt maladaptive behavior. He makes no effort to uncover unconscious conflicts, diagnose the inner pathological conditions producing the behavior, or help the patient gain insight into the etiology of his condition. Instead, he sees neurotic symptoms, for example, as learned patterns of behavior that are unadaptive for the individual. According to Eysenck (1959), who is said to have coined the term "behavior therapy," there is no neurosis underlying the symptoms, but rather it is the symptom itself that we refer to as the neurosis. Therefore, extinguishing the symptom eliminates the neurosis. Like all other habits, neurotic symptoms are subject to extinction according to experimentally verifiable learning theory principles.

To illustrate the differences in theory and technique between psychoanalysts and behavior therapists, one study (Goldenberg & Goldenberg, 1970) has recently compared how each group views the etiology and treatment of school phobias in children. The school-phobic child manifests many physical and psychological symptoms of distress when he is forced to separate from familiar people (notably his mother) and familiar surroundings to go to school. Psychoanalysts are most likely to see school phobia as a symptom of separation anxiety, an unconscious communication of mutual dependence between mother and child, and of each one's dread of physically separating from one another. Consequently, the traditional psychoanalytic treatment involves helping the child gain insight into his feelings of maternal rejection, possibly due to her preference for other children, as well as understanding his excessive dependency on an over-protective mother. Behavior therapists, on the other hand, are more concerned with treatment than etiology, although they generally believe school phobia to be a learned maladaptive pattern of behavior. They may recommend a systematic desensitization, a reconditioning technique in which previously anxiety-arousing situations—in this case the school—gradually lose their power to elicit the phobic behavior. For example, the child might begin by sitting with the therapist in a car parked outside the school. Over several weeks, he would be encouraged, step by step, to approach the school building, go to the door, enter the building, approach the classroom, enter the empty classroom, be present with the teacher and later two classmates in the room, and finally be present with the entire class. A case reported by Garvey and Hegrenes (1966) followed such a procedure with a 10-year-old phobic child; the youngster was back in the classroom, voluntarily, by the twentieth day and manifested no subsequent signs of the school-phobic reaction in a two-year follow-up. No efforts throughout the treatment were directed toward investigating possible underlying psychological causes of his phobic condition.

A BRIEF HISTORY

The foundations for the behavioral model can be traced to the work of laboratory scientists rather than clinical practitioners. Russian physiologist Ivan Pavlov (1849–1936) and American psychologist Edward L. Thorndike (1874–1949) both made significant laboratory contributions to our understanding of how animal behavior is learned. From Pavlov's (1927) work with salivary responses in dogs emerged the concept of classical conditioning, a demonstration of how an animal could learn to respond (salivate) to a previously neutral stimulus (a bell) that had been presented immediately before a stimulus (food) that ordinarily produced the response. From Thorndike's (1911) laboratory studies on kittens, dogs, and chicks in puzzle boxes emerged carefully quantified observations of behavior and the principle of instrumental conditioning. This refers to those learning situations in which the subject's behavioral responses are instrumental in producing the desired reward or reinforcement. Thorndike's general principle of behavior, the Law of Effect, which he believed applied to many species and for many forms of behavior, emphasized that any organism will repeat behavior for which it is rewarded and avoid behavior for which it is punished or ignored. Virtually all methods of behavior modification are based on the principles of classical conditioning or instrumental conditioning (sometimes called operant conditioning), both derived from the laboratory studies of animal behavior.

Both Pavlov and Thorndike advanced the cause of studying behavior in general and animal behavior in particular. Following their example, those psychologists interested in objective observations of behavior began to study animal behavior; the impossibility of inquiring into animals' inner mental states and psychological processes was irrelevant (Wertheimer, 1970).

John B. Watson (1878–1958), in particular, is usually credited as the first to challenge introspective psychology and to substitute objective studies of behavior as the proper subject matter of psychology. Watson became disenchanted early in his career (around 1907) with the then prevalent practice of first observing and describing the behavior of an animal in a learning maze, and then inferring the nature of the animal's consciousness that resulted in the observed behavior. By 1913, Watson was ready to break with such introspectionism and to replace it with the more reliable data of overt behavior. Like some present-day behaviorists who were to follow him, he did not deny consciousness, but instead believed observed behavioral data required fewer inferences and was therefore more scientifically defensible.

Watson's first major statement outlining the behaviorist position appeared in 1913 ("Psychology as the Behaviorist Views It"), to be followed in succeeding years by several books (Watson, 1914, 1919, 1924) detailing a position that was scientific, objective, and based on the tangible evidence of experimentation. Although Watson's stance was formulated independent of Pavlov, he soon became aware of the latter's study of conditioned reflexes in animals, and applied the technique in studying learning in humans. For example, Watson attempted to demonstrate that the emotional responses in babies (such as fears) were simply conditioned reflexes. Habits were acquired, or learned, reflex patterns. Such was Watson's extreme environmentalist (that is, learning) viewpoint, that in one often-quoted passage, he insisted that if he were given "a dozen healthy infants, well-formed, and my own specific world to bring them up in, . . . I'll guarantee to take any one at random and train him to become any type of specialist I might select—doctor, lawyer, artist, merchant-chief, and yes, beggar-man and thief, regardless of his talents, tendencies, abilities, vocations, and the race of his ancestors [Watson, 1924, p. 104]." Thus was laid the groundwork for much of what later came to be called behavior therapy: the active manipulation by a psychologist teaching explicit behavioral patterns; the relatively simplistic "outside" view of man, whose actions define him as a person.

Two early clinical applications of Watson's views deserve mention, particularly since they represent a bridge between laboratory experiments on learning and clinical psychology. Watson and Rayner (1920), in a famous case, were able to produce a phobic reaction in little Albert, an eleven-month-old child. Having first ascertained that it was a neutral object, they presented Albert with a white rat to play with. However, whenever he reached for the animal, they made a loud noise behind him. After only five trials, Albert showed outward signs of fear in the presence of the rat; moreover, that fear was generalized to furry objects and other furry animals and persisted when tested four months later. Watson and Rayner, through a simple experimental procedure, were thus able to illustrate how a phobia can develop, even in an infant. This was the first laboratory demonstration of an experimental neurosis in a human. The impact on American clinical psychology was immediate, since it revealed that beyond simple motor patterns, certain "emotional tendencies" could be learned through conditioning and that this might explain the etiology of some phobias. Even more significant, by suggesting that the conditioning might be overcome through experimental extinction or various counterconditioning techniques, they were providing what Wolpe (1969), a leading exponent of the behavioral approach, considers the conceptual origins of behavior therapy.

Mary Cover Jones (1924), a student of Watson's, adopted some of his and Rayner's suggestions regarding reconditioning in attempting to reduce a phobia in a three-year-old boy, Peter. His initial fear of a white rat had generalized to other furry objects (a rabbit, a fur coat, a feather, cotton, wool). By slowly bringing a caged rabbit closer and closer every day as the child was enjoying his meal, a method of direct reconditioning was carried out. The feared object gradually became less frightening when associated with a stimulus (food) that aroused a pleasant reaction. Peter, whom Jones described as one of the most serious cases brought to her attention, recovered after such daily treatment extending over two months. Jones' work is classic[1] in the sense that it represents a prototype of the

---

[1] The similarity between the desensitization technique of Jones in 1924 and the tech-

behavioral model in clinical psychology: a strictly psychological approach, understood in learning-theory terms, based on conditioning techniques, with success measured in tangible behavioral change.

Beginning in the 1930s and continuing to the present, B. F. Skinner has emerged as the most influential contemporary behaviorist. Like Watson, Skinner has been concerned with the all-important influence of learning in shaping behavior. Skinner is more of a purist—his brand of behaviorism is more strict, descriptive, and empirical. For example, Skinner rejects any concept of implicit behavior, such as Watson's characterization of thinking as "subvocal speech" (Skinner, 1963). Instead, Skinner believes a science of behavior should limit itself to the discovery of relationships between measurable variables of observed behavior only.

Skinner's unique contribution to learning has been threefold: (1) his development of the concept of *operant conditioning;* (2) his emphasis on the role of *reinforcement* in learning; and (3) his discovery of *behavior shaping*. Skinner's research on operant conditioning, including the development of highly sophisticated equipment for electrically dispensing consequences and recording animal responses in a Skinner Box, represents a refinement of Thorndike's earlier work on instrumental conditioning. Unlike Pavlov's classical conditioning situation, in operant conditioning the subject first emits a response to a situation (such as pressing a lever in a Skinner Box), and only then does some event (the dropping of a food pellet) follow the emitted response. If the consequences of such operant behavior (that is, behavior in which the subject actively "operates" on his environment) are favorable (food), the emitted response is reinforced. The result of the reinforcement (or reward) of an operant is to increase the rate at which the operant response is emitted. A measure of the operant strength is thus obtained in simple behavioral terms, without inferring any particular mental activity on the part of the subject, animal or human. By *shaping*, Skinner means a method of modifying behavior by reinforcing successive approximations of the behavior desired by the experimenter. Any overt response that resembles the desired behavior or is a step in the desired sequence receives a reward, leading ultimately to shaping these partial behaviors into a complex sequence that the subject gradually learns. The clinical applicability of each of Skinner's contributions to learning will become clearer shortly.

nique previously described to desensitize a school-phobic child (Garvey & Hegrenes, 1966) should be apparent to the reader.

Skinner's position, with his insistence on explanations in strict behavioral terms, has profoundly influenced much of modern psychology, affecting many clinicians as well as nonclinicians. For example, Skinner (1953) has criticized the assumption that behavior disorders reflect some internal conflict. In his view, motivation does not reside within a person but comes from the reward or reinforcement of certain behavior. Consequently, such concepts as lifting the patient's repressions or providing him with insight are unnecessary to change his behavior. Instead, the problem becomes one of altering his environment to: (1) maintain adequate behavior; (2) extinguish inadequate behavior; and (3) learn effective new behavior. Token economy programs (see pp. 254–256) represent a recent development in the institutional treatment of long-term patients through the application of Skinnerian principles.

In the late 1940s and 1950s, Joseph Wolpe, trained in psychoanalysis, began to question Freudian theory regarding the development of neuroses. Turning to Pavlov's experimental work with the classical conditioning of animals, Wolpe began producing and treating experimental neuroses in animals. Inducing a neurotic reaction in a cat by electric shock, Wolpe was able to extinguish the reaction by feeding the animal in the presence of small and then increasingly larger doses of anxiety-evoking stimuli. Wolpe began by removing the animal and feeding him at a distance from the experimental apparatus where the shock was received. Gradually he moved the animal's feeding closer and closer to the original source of anxiety. Eventually the animal was able to eat in the place where he had previously exhibited the anxiety response. What was occurring, according to Wolpe, was a counterconditioning of the animal by providing a strong response (eating) that was incompatible with the neurotic response, leading to a weakening of the neurotic response. Wolpe (1958) termed the technique *reciprocal inhibition.*

Applying the same set of principles to humans, Wolpe reasoned that neurotic behavior is acquired in people in anxiety-producing situations in the same way it is learned by animals. Therefore, treatment should aim at the reciprocal inhibition of the neurotic response by introducing another response that is physiologically antagonistic to anxiety. If a response incompatible with anxiety can be made to occur in the presence of the anxiety-evoking stimuli, it should weaken the bond between these stimuli and the anxiety response. Wolpe described several techniques, the most prominent of which is *systematic desensitization.* Just as he had used eating as a strong response incompatible with anxiety in cats, so he used relaxation as a more appropriate counterresponse in humans. Training his patient to relax through hypnosis or other means, Wolpe led him to visualize, step by step, a series of situations ranging from those situations he had previously ranked as least anxiety-producing to those ranked as most anxiety-producing (called the *anxiety hierarchy*). Ultimately, as the patient continues to relax, previously anxiety-producing situations no longer lead to anxiety, the relaxation is supposed to generalize from the therapeutic situation to real life, and the original maladaptive response is overcome through systematic desensitization. (Systematic desensitization is described in greater detail on pp. 247–251.) This technique is particularly appropriate for treating phobic reactions. Wolpe claimed a 90 percent level of cures or marked improvements with his methods, considerably higher than the claims of any competing therapeutic systems.

Behavior modification techniques based on a variety of learning principles applied to a wide assortment of behavior problems (excessive smoking and drinking, eating problems, sexual disorders, problems of autistic children and chronic schizophrenic adults) now fill the clinical psychological literature. Particularly appealing to many clinical psychologists and an increasing number of medically trained psychiatrists, the techniques generally are brief and are based on established learning principles and experimental evidence. Today, in terms of research output as well as clinical activity, behavior modification represents one of the strongest trends in contemporary clinical psychology.

TECHNIQUES OF BEHAVIOR MODIFICATION

1. Assessment. The focus of attention for the behavior modifier is on overt behavior. Whether that behavior should be considered abnormal depends on three factors: the behavior itself, its social context, and an observer who is in a position of power. No specific behavior is in and of itself abnormal. Rather, being labeled abnormal is the result of the following sequence (Ullmann & Krasner, 1969): (1) An individual behaves in a certain way (hallucinates, stares into space, collects rolls of toilet paper) (2) under a particular set of circumstances (during a church service or in a classroom), (3) thereby upsetting, annoying, angering, or disturbing somebody (a teacher, a parent, or the individual himself) sufficiently (4) that some action results (a policeman is called, a psychiatrist is consulted, or commitment procedures are started). (5) Society's professional labelers (mental health professionals or court judges) come in contact with the individual and (6) determine which of the current set of diagnostic labels (schizophrenia) fits his behavior. (7) Efforts are then undertaken to change the emission of the offending behavior (through hospitalization, psycho-therapy, or medication).

Note that no behavior can be considered abnormal without some reference to the social situation in which it takes place and to the attitude of the observer who finds it objectionable or unpredictable. Thus, for example, singing at the top of one's voice in the shower in considered quite normal, but in the middle of a minister's sermon becomes unacceptable. The behavioral clinician, in the assessment procedure, is likely to address himself to three questions:

1. What behavior is maladaptive—that is, what subject behaviors should be increased or decreased?
2. What environmental contingencies currently support the subject's behavior (either to maintain his undesirable behavior or reduce the likelihood of his performing a more adaptive response)?
3. What environmental changes, usually reinforcing stimuli, may be manipulated to alter the subject's behavior [Ullmann & Krasner, 1966]?[2]

Assessment is a continuous part of any treatment program. The clinician must first answer the above questions, either through some brief history-taking interviews or by using certain psychological tests. Beyond that, assessment continues throughout treatment, measuring progress and ultimately evaluating success in some objective way. Thus, more than in any other approach, assessment and treatment are inseparable for the behavior modifier.

Wolpe and his followers are likely to conduct a history-taking interview. They emphasize determining what stimuli in the patient's present behavior evoke his maladaptive behavior with some probing into the early origins of his present difficulties. Once determined, counterconditioning procedures can then be instituted to change the maladaptive, learned habit. Other behavioral clinicians, adhering more to Skinnerian principles

---

[2] Leonard P. Ullmann and Leonard Krasner, *A Psychological Approach to Abnormal Behavior,* © 1969. By permission of Prentice-Hall, Inc., Englewood Cliffs, New Jersey.

of operant conditioning, are less concerned with any case history. They focus on current overt behavior and the current reinforcements for maladaptive behavior. They argue that investigating anything but the present is unnecessary, since current reinforcements need not be the same as the reinforcements that originally led to the development of the behavior. Their efforts are directed, instead, toward helping the subject acquire new behavior through schedules of reinforcement that shape new responses in the direction of increased socially appropriate behavior.

In the same manner, psychological tests are used by some behavioral clinicians who believe well-standardized tests provide a more uniform, objective, quantifiable situation than does the ordinary preliminary, diagnostic, or history-taking interview. Wolpe (1958) and Salter (1949) have reported certain objective personality inventories to be useful in treatment planning. Nevertheless, behaviorally oriented clinical psychologists urge caution in using projective techniques such as the Rorschach Inkblot Test or the Thematic Apperception Test. They are apt to challenge the validity of interpretations drawn from these tests, based as they are on the discovery of inner aspects of personality which have never been empirically demonstrated to exist (Lundin, 1969). In addition, experimental results with the validity and reliability of these instruments of clinical diagnosis have been disappointing (Little & Shneidman, 1959), and there are no norms in most cases. Moreover, results appear to be too dependent on the intuitive skills and experiences of the individual psychologist to suit the behavior modifier.

The behavioral clinician is more interested in answering "what" than "why"; he concerns himself with what behavior must be changed, rather than why the person behaves as he does. He is interested in extinguishing that maladaptive behavior, not treating any underlying disease, speculating on its historical antecedents, or formulating a picture of the person's personality dynamics. He makes no effort to diagnose and categorize the behavior problem. Instead, he determines what maladaptive behavior is to be changed and decides what behavior should be taught in its place.

2. Systematic desensitization. Perhaps the best known technique introduced by Wolpe is what he calls systematic desensitization based on relaxation (Wolpe, 1958). The technique involves: (1) constructing anxiety hierarchies, lists ranking the severity of anxiety in various anxiety-producing situations; (2) training the patient in deep muscle relaxation; and

(3) counterposing relaxation and the anxiety-evoking stimuli from the hierarchy list. Wolpe begins with a series of fairly extensive interviews to determine what behavior is to be modified. Let us assume the patient has a number of phobic reactions. In such a case, Wolpe attempts to determine what specific circumstances evoke intense anxiety and what circumstances produce milder anxiety. Together with the patient, he constructs an anxiety hierarchy—a graduated list ranging from the most disturbing situations to those which are least disturbing. The patient is then given systematic instruction in deep relaxation, sometimes through hypnosis. When relaxed, the patient is presented with each item on the anxiety hierarchy, beginning with the least disturbing item, and asked to visualize the situation. Step by step, he is asked to imagine items higher on the anxiety hierarchy, letting the therapist know whenever he becomes anxious. When he can imagine a situation that previously evoked the highest level of anxiety without anxiety, he is said to have become desensitized to the phobia. The relaxation is believed to generalize easily at that point from the therapeutic situation to real-life situations.

Wolpe has recently presented a case illustrating the elimination of a phobic reaction through systematic desensitization:

Miss C. was a 24-year-old art student who came for treatment because marked anxiety at examinations had resulted in repeated failures. Investigation revealed additional phobic areas. The hierarchies are given below. All of them involve people, and none belong to the classical phobias. (Freedom from anxiety to the highest items of each of these hierarchies was achieved in 17 desensitization sessions, with complete transfer to the corresponding situations in actuality. Four months later, she passed her examinations without anxiety.)

Anxiety Hierarchies

A. *Examination series*
   1. On the way to the university on the day of an examination.
   2. In the process of answering an examination paper.
   3. Before the unopened doors of the examination room.
   4. Awaiting the distribution of examination papers.
   5. The examination paper lies face down before her.
   6. The night before an examination.
   7. On the day before an examination.

      8. Two days before an examination.
      9. Three days before an examination.
    10. Four days before an examination.
    11. Five days before an examination.
    12. A week before an examination.
    13. Two weeks before an examination.
    14. A month before an examination.

B. *Scrutiny series*
    1. Being watched working (especially drawing) by ten people.
    2. Being watched working by six people.
    3. Being watched working by three people.
    4. Being watched working by one expert in the field. (Anxiety begins when the observer is 10 ft. away and increases as he draws closer.)
    5. Being watched working by a nonexpert. (Anxiety begins at a distance of 4 ft.)

C. *Devaluation series*
    1. An argument she raises in a discussion is ignored by the group.
    2. She is not recognized by a person she has briefly met three times.
    3. Her mother says she is selfish because she is not helping in the house (studying instead).
    4. She is not recognized by a person she has briefly met twice.
    5. Her mother calls her lazy.
    6. She is not recognized by a person she has briefly met once.

D. *Discord between other people*
    1. Her mother shouts at a servant.
    2. Her young sister whines to her mother.
    3. Her sister engages in a dispute with her father.
    4. Her mother shouts at her sister.
    5. She sees two strangers quarrel.

A typical hypnotic session with this patient, when she appeared well relaxed, ran as follows:

"I am now going to ask you to imagine a number of scenes. You will imagine them clearly and they will generally interfere little, if at all, with your state of relaxation. If, however, at any time you feel disturbed or worried and want to draw my attention, you will be able to do so by raising your left index finger. First I want you to imagine that you are standing at a familiar street corner on a pleasant morning watching the traffic go by. You see cars, motorcycles, trucks, bicycles, people, and traffic lights; and you can hear the sounds associated with all these things. (Pause of about 15 sec.) Now stop imagining that scene and give all your attention once again to relaxing. If the scene you imagine disturbed you even in the slightest degree I want you to raise your left index finger now. (Patient does not raise finger.) Now imagine that you are at home studying in the evening. It is the twentieth of May, exactly a month before your examination. (Pause of 5 sec.) Now stop imagining the scene. Go on relaxing. (Pause of 10 sec.) Now imagine the same scene once again—a month before your examination. (Pause of 5 sec.) Stop imagining the scene and just think of your muscles. Let go and enjoy your state of calm. (Pause of 15 sec.) Now again imagine that you are studying at home a month before your examination. (Pause of 5 sec.) Stop the scene, and now think of nothing but your own body. (Pause of 5 sec.) If you felt any disturbance whatsoever to the last scene, raise your left index finger now. (Patient raises finger.) If the amount of disturbance decreased from the first presentation to the third do nothing, otherwise again raise your finger. (Patient does not raise finger.) Just keep on relaxing. (Pause of 15 sec.) Imagine that you are sitting on a bench at a bus stop, and across the road are two strange men whose voices are raised in argument. (Pause of 10 sec.) Stop imagining the scene and just relax. (Pause of 10 sec.) Now again imagine the scene of these two men arguing across the road. (Pause of 10 sec.) Stop the scene and relax. Now I am going to count up to 5 and you will open your eyes, feeling very calm and refreshed."

She opened her eyes, looking, as is commonly the case, a little sleepy and smiling placidly. In reply to questions, she reported that she felt very calm and that the scenes were quite clear. She stated that in both the scene belonging to the examination series and that belonging to the quarrel series there had been moderate anxiety at the first presentation and less at subsequent presentations, but in neither instance had the decrease been down to zero.

It was noted that the responses of this patient were of the commonplace kind that do not presage any difficulties. Since visualization was clear and there was evidence of decrease of anxiety with each repetition of a scene, it was predicted that we would make our way through all the hierarchies without much trouble; and the course of events bore out this prediction [Wolpe, 1969, pp. 117–118, 126-127].[3]

Wolpe uses other techniques similar to systematic desensitization so

[3] Reprinted by permission from J. Wolpe, *The Practice of Behavior Therapy.* Copyright 1969, Pergamon Press, Inc.

the patient can learn responses that produce an inhibitory effect on anxiety response habits. For example, Wolpe teaches *assertive responses* to patients who are behaviorally inhibited and who suppress such responses ordinarily because of fear of the consequences of such expression. He coaches his patients to act deliberately assertive in as many social situations as possible. His rationale is that each assertive response to some extent reciprocally inhibits the concurrent anxiety, thereby weakening the anxiety response habit. The reduction of the anxiety drive, in turn, is the main reinforcing agent in the resulting habit change. In the same way, sexual responses, relaxation responses, and various other anxiety-relief responses can be learned and can inhibit or eliminate neurotic habits.

   3. Aversive counterconditioning. Counterconditioning techniques aim at replacing maladaptive responses by other responses that are antithetical to them. Certain behavioral problems (excessive smoking, eating, or drinking, and stuttering and deviant sexual behavior) have been treated by using punishment, leading ultimately to the replacement of the undesirable response by one that is more acceptable to the patient. If the undesirable behavior becomes a source of conditioned aversion, it is assumed that it will lose whatever attractiveness it once held for the person, permitting its replacement more easily by other behavior patterns. Perhaps the best known example of such an approach is in the treatment of chronic alcoholism. Sometimes the alcoholic patient is given a strong emetic in his drink. Upon drinking, he becomes acutely ill followed by vomiting. Eventually, the mere sight of a drink may make him ill, evoking the conditioned response of nausea (Franks, 1963). The technique has not been entirely successful due to individual differences in reactivity to the drug and the difficulty of monitoring the alcoholic's behavior outside the laboratory. The probability of relapse after the drug is removed is high. More recently, behaviorist clinicians have begun using electric shock instead of drugs as the aversive stimulus. Following a classical conditioning experimental design, they have administered electric shock when the client swallows alcohol, but no shock when he swallows nonalcoholic beverages. A preliminary study by Morosco and Baer (1970) found that alcohol ingestion can be made to acquire aversive properties through this procedure, with these results maintained in a 19-month follow-up report.
   In recent years, aversive counterconditioning has been used predominantly in treating sexual problems. A painful stimulus such as an electric shock is associated with an inappropriate sexual act or sexual object,

leading to a reduction of the inappropriate behavior. For example, Feldman and MacCulloch (1965) showed slides of nude and partially dressed males and females to male homosexuals. If the patient did not remove the male figure by depressing a switch in a brief period, he received a painful electric shock. Termination of the shock was followed by a female picture. In addition, the patient could avoid shock by requesting a female picture. After about 15 sessions of 20 minutes each, the experiment was terminated. Follow-up studies up to 14 months after treatment found homosexual behavior to have been eliminated in over half the patients.

4. Modeling. Modeling, a behavior modification technique used by Bandura (1969), involves the acquisition of new responses by imitating another's (the model's) behavior. A great deal of learning, particularly by children, takes place this way in real life. Bandura and his associates have demonstrated that children who observe adult models in aggressive acts are more apt to imitate their aggressive behavior than are children who did not observe such models. Learning through imitation, moreover, can take place by watching film sequences of the models. These findings suggest that modeling can help build new responses that later can be maintained through schedules of reinforcement.

An experimental demonstration of modeling, in this case in the treatment of snake phobia, has been offered by Bandura, Blanchard, and Ritter (1969). Subjects, young adults with severe snake phobias, were divided into four matched groups on the basis of their degree of fearfulness of snakes, and each group was presented with a different experimental condition. One group watched and then imitated a live model as he engaged in progressively more fearful activities with a snake. Gradually the subjects in this group were guided to touch the snake with a gloved hand, then a bare hand, and so on, until they could permit the snake to crawl over their bodies. (This procedure was termed *live modeling with participation.*) A second group, trained in relaxation, watched a film in which children and adult models appeared to enjoy handling a snake in progressively more fear-arousing circumstances (termed *symbolic modeling*). A third group received systematic desensitization, described above, in which deep relaxation was paired, successively, with imagined scenes of increasingly fear-arousing situations with snakes (termed *systematic desensitization*). A fourth group acted as a control and received no treatment. Figure 10 shows the number of snake approach responses made by

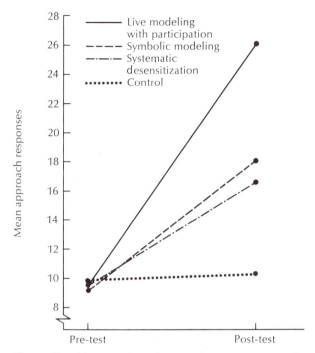

Figure 10. Mean number of approach responses to snakes by subjects before and after receiving their respective treatments. (Bandura, Blanchard, and Ritter, "The Relative Efficacy of Desensitization and Modeling Approaches . . . ," *Journal of Personality and Social Psychology,* 1969, **13**, 183. Copyright 1969 by the American Psychological Association and reproduced by permission.)

subjects in each group before and after treatment. Given an opportunity to approach and touch snakes voluntarily, the figure indicates that all treatment groups improved—that is, were more willing to touch the snakes —when compared to the control group, with the greatest gain made by the group receiving live modeling combined with guided participation. Almost all the subjects in this group successfully overcame their snake phobias.

5. Shaping. Shaping is an operant conditioning technique developed by Skinner in which the experimenter reinforces successive approximations of the subject's behavior as the latter moves closer and closer to the ultimate performance desired. The experimenter reinforces only those responses that are in the direction of the final goal, ignoring and therefore extinguishing all other responses. While the subject's initial response may bear little resemblance to the final desired behavior, he is gradually trained to engage in a complex sequence of behavioral responses.

Isaacs, Thomas, and Goldiamond (1960) have provided a dramatic demonstration of the use of shaping techniques to restore speech in chronic, mute schizophrenics. In one case, a male catatonic schizophrenic, mute and withdrawn for 19 years, was successfully brought to the point of speaking. He had been attending group therapy sessions without speaking or otherwise moving his body for prolonged periods of time. At one session, his eyes were noticed to follow a package of gum that had accidentally dropped from the therapist's pocket. Thereafter a therapist, who worked with him individually three times a week to shape his behavior toward speech, made use of this initial slight eye movement. For the first two weeks, a stick of gum was held before the patient's face; when his eyes moved towards it, that behavior was reinforced by giving him the gum. For the next two weeks, the gum was held before his face, but was not given to him until he made some lip movement. By the end of the fourth week he was making a croaking sound and moving his eyes toward the gum, which he then received. During the next two weeks, the gum was held up, but when the patient emitted the croaking sound the therapist said "Say 'gum, gum.'" That is, receiving the gum was made contingent on vocalizations increasingly approximating the word "gum." By the end of the sixth week, a total of 18 sessions, the patient said, "Gum, please." This response was accompanied by other words and answers to questions, but only to the therapist. Through a similar process, his verbal responses gradually generalized to other people.

6. Token economy programs. Token economy programs, increasingly used in psychiatric hospital wards, are systems based on the use of positive reinforcers to reward patients for socially constructive behavior. Subjects are reinforced with tokens, such as poker chips, which may be exchanged later for special privileges (private sleeping accommodations, movies, weekend passes) not available to other patients.

Token economy programs are especially applicable to regulated institutions such as psychiatric hospitals or hospitals for the mentally retarded which offer at once seemingly intractable therapeutic problems as well as opportunities for controlling and experimentally manipulating treatment conditions (London, 1964). In these situations, by giving token rewards to those patients who exhibit desirable behavior, dramatic behavioral changes have been reported. Ullmann and Krasner (1969) differentiate three aspects of a token economy program:

1. The designation by the institution's staff of certain specific patient behaviors as good, desirable, and reinforceable.

2. The establishment of a medium of exchange, objects that stand for something else. These frequently are in the form of poker chips, but may also be tokens or trading stamps.

3. The use of the tokens, back-up reinforcers themselves, to acquire valued items or privileges. These may range from food to being allowed to sit peacefully in a chair.

Such a program assumes that a patient knows how to emit behavioral responses that will lead to reinforcements in the hospital and to maintain a more socially responsible role when he leaves the institution. Such programs have been successfully used with chronic psychiatric patients (Ayllon & Azrin, 1968; Atthowe & Krasner, 1968) as well as with mental retardates (Girardeau & Spradlin, 1964) in an effort to develop social, educational, and vocational skills in individuals previously considered untreatable and relegated to back wards. By rewarding desirable or adaptive behavior and by failing to respond to undesirable behavior, thus extinguishing it, behavior may be shaped in the direction sought by the hospital staff. Ayllon and Azrin (1968) found that psychotic patients who had been unwilling to work for more than three years did learn to finish jobs (washing dishes, doing laundry, helping attendants) in return for the desired tokens. Atthowe and Krasner (1968) reported decreasing apathy among hospitalized patients, with a marked interest in their appearance, social interaction, and interest in trial visits outside the hospital. Spradlin and Girardeau (1966) reported an increase in the frequency of desirable behavior among hospitalized retarded adolescent girls (making beds, dressing, self-care activities, developing basic work skills) through such a program. This is in sharp contrast with the typical behavior of institutionalized mental retardates, who often require complete custodial care.

EVALUATION OF BEHAVIOR MODIFICATION

ARGUMENTS FOR BEHAVIOR MODIFICATION

1. Behavior modification is an approach that draws together clinical practitioners and experimental researchers. At a time when the so-called scientific and professional proponents within psychology are increasingly polarized, the behavioral model can include both. Communication is thus improved by using identical language and research outlook. Experimental psychologists become more interested in carrying out research on clinical phenomena as hospitals and other clinical facilities encourage their efforts and provide a setting for the experimental analysis of maladaptive behavior. Researchers are thus in a position to study larger, more significant units of behavior than they are likely to encounter in the laboratory. Clinical psychologists, too, are likely to function more effectively as they choose clinical techniques that have a sound experimental basis and do not rely too heavily on intuition, clinical "hunches," or the individual clinicians' necessarily limited experience.

The clinical model has blurred the clinical–experimental distinction and tends to merge the traditional subject areas in which each specialist works (Krasner & Ullmann, 1965). The behavioral clinician is essentially a researcher into clinical phenomena who defines his terms operationally, determines what variables he will manipulate, hypothesizes what outcome he expects, and how he will measure his results. As with any scientist, his assumptions may need to be reexamined in the light of his results, and new hypotheses may have to be tested. Treatment is less likely to fail because of subject resistance or the subject's lack of readiness.

2. Behavior modification translates theory into practice directly with a minimum of assumptions, inferences, or value judgments regarding behavior. No hypothetical constructs are needed to explain the subject's inner state or the presumed etiology of his condition (MacCorquodale & Meehl, 1948). Public or overt behavior and symptoms are what interest the behavioral clinician, not underlying pathology, unconscious conflicts, body language, or personality dynamics.

The model is a direct application of learning theory; it considers all behavior—including maladaptive behavior—to be learned. Designating certain behavior as pathological, as the medical model does, involves judgments influenced by the normative standards of the judges as well as considerations of the behavior's social context. For example, aggressiveness in children may be positively reinforced and regarded as a sign of masculinity and healthy social development by some parents, while other parents may view it as symptomatic of personality disorder.

The behavioral clinician makes little distinction between "good" and "bad" behavior except insofar as the subject's behavior causes such personally distressing or socially inappropriate results that the subject wishes to change it.

3. Behavior modification provides brief, systematic treatment with fixed goals, concrete ways of measuring progress, and wide applicability. Other forms of treatment, notably psychoanalysis, are often inefficient, costly, time-consuming, and of questionable effectiveness. They may be inappropriate to large segments of the population, particularly the poor and undereducated. Within the psychoanalytic framework, it is difficult to measure success beyond the feelings of the psychoanalyst and his client, who are hardly objective observers. Although analysis is theoretically terminated by mutual consent of analyst and client, either one may terminate it for reasons the other may consider arbitrary or unwise.

In contrast, behavior modification is of short duration, and both therapist and subject can gauge the progress of treatment by the extent to which the subject's symptoms persist or have been extinguished. Well-defined criteria determine when treatment is terminated. That decision can be reached by the subject as well as the therapist. Once the subject's symptoms disappear, he has achieved what he came to treatment for, and he is ready to terminate. Since he need not be highly verbal, have high abstract ability, or be especially insightful, subjects from all social classes with different degrees of sophistication and intellectual capacities may benefit from the behavioral approach. Even the most severely disabled, chronic hospitalized psychiatric patient, or mental retardate who is unreachable by more traditional means may benefit from such a therapeutic program.

4. Manpower needs are more likely to be met by an approach that is brief, practical, deals directly with real-life situations, and does not require extensive training. The behavioral clinician has learned to apply certain technical skills to bring about behavioral change. He does not need an elaborate grounding in philosophy, the humanities, and social sciences, or in medically related subjects. He need not speculate on the nature of inner man or to attempt to reconstruct his subject's formative years. His subject need not be considered a "sick" person suffering from some psychopathological condition that may necessitate hospitalization or other medical procedures.

Instead, the individual is considered to be someone who, perhaps simply through a chance association with an unhappy event, has learned some maladaptive behavior. This maladaptive behavior, once learned, can be unlearned in the same manner as any other behavior. Further, as Eysenck (1959) has noted, once the maladaptive behavior (or symptom) is removed, the removal of other symptoms is facilitated. As he emits more adaptive responses, the client's environment begins to change as others respond differently to him than they did in the past. Such feedback reinforces the adaptive behavior. Consequently, the adaptive behavior is likely to generalize to other situations.

The entire procedure is relatively brief, direct, and thoroughly practical. Since the goal of treatment is clear to both individuals, little time is wasted on tangential efforts or groping for direction. The behavior modifier systematically proceeds toward the goal of behavior change in a joint effort with his client. Unlike the psychoanalyst, he himself need not have been analyzed, have a healthier personality than his client, or even involve himself personally with the person he treats.

Training such a clinician is relatively less complicated than training the usual Ph.D. clinical psychologist or M.D. psychiatrist or psychoanalyst. Many such clinicians can function effectively without doctoral education. Albee (1968) draws a parallel with the field of education, where bachelor's level teachers carry on the daily professional work, supported by more highly trained research workers in several fields. In the same manner, the day-to-day administration of token economy programs in hospitals (Ayllon & Azrin, 1968) is likely to be carried out by nurses and attendants, freeing psychiatrists and clinical psychologists for research and other clinical services demanding their individual attention.

5. By challenging the widespread myths and shibboleths of traditional psychotherapy, behavior modification has helped force it to reexamine its theoretical assumptions as well as techniques. Before the impact of the behavioral approach, few attempts were made by psychotherapists to define their terms operationally, investigate their own hypotheses experimentally, or assess the outcome of their efforts. Certain assumptions, usually based on psychoanalytic formulations, prevailed and went unchallenged. If therapeutic failures occurred, it was the patient's resistance that was at fault, or he did not have real insight, or perhaps his lack of motivation or lack of readiness for treatment prevented success. In such a closed system, there was little need to question either the theory or the technique's applicability to a particular patient.

Among the many prevalent notions upset by the behavioral approach, at least two have had a profound effect on the current practice of psychotherapy. The first longstanding assumption is that insight leads to behavioral change. As one critic of this view puts it:

> One of the firmly rooted assumptions in psychotherapeutic practice is that the development of insight on the part of the client is both a major goal of the therapeutic endeavor, intrinsically worth promoting, and a primary means of achieving, step by step in the therapeutic process, the overall objective of more effective functioning. If a client can be helped to understand why he behaves as he does or to recognize and understand the origin of the neurotic tactics that continually defeat him, he will gradually abandon the inappropriate behavior and substitute therefore more rational tactics in the management of his life [Hobbs, 1962, p. 741].

Hobbs, although himself not a behavior modifier, feels that, contrary to theory, insight need not necessarily bring about changes in behavior. By the same token, in some situations (such as play therapy with children), behavior changes occur without such rational self-understanding developing at all. Hobbs concludes that insight may be the result of behavioral change or its by-product rather than its cause.

Insight has been the traditional trademark of most forms of psychotherapy. Emphasizing talk over action and hoping for personality change over mere behavior change, most therapists have used explanations and interpretations to produce insight. Beyond such intellectual insights were emotional insights that the patient discovered as he worked through his neurotic conflicts and ultimately changed his behavior. Among the significant contributions of behavioral clinicians is their insistence that the payoff in psychotherapy is action without the necessity of insight. Yet the notion of insight retains appeal, particularly among those who rely exclusively on rationality in problem solving.

Behavioral clinicians, on the other hand, believe all treatment must translate itself into action, not merely explanations. Rather than infer motives, they are interested in changing behavior. They are prepared to supply what their clients came seeking—relief from distressing symptoms of maladaptive and inappropriate social behavior. They do not offer, instead, interpretations or insights that may not relate to the behavior the client wishes to change, or that may not change his behavior even if they do relate to it.[4]

A second prevalent notion challenged by the behavioral clinicians involves the concept of *symptom substitution.* According to traditional psychoanalytic formulations, symptoms are merely outward manifestations of underlying conflict and psychopathology. Therefore, to treat and remove the symptom without resolving the underlying cause will simply result in replacement of the old symptom by a new one. Psychoanalysts argue that the underlying conflict must be treated; as understanding through insight increases, inner conflict is reduced and the symptom will disappear without being replaced later by another one.

Behavioral clinicians argue that research (Baker, 1969; Grossberg, 1964) has indicated little evidence for this widely held notion of symptom substitution. Despite that fact, they believe it remains a part of psychotherapeutic folklore; this notion has prevented the adoption of behavioral programs aimed at symptom relief, as in cases of enuresis, for example (Yates, 1958). Wright (1970) also finds the research literature to be persuasive in discounting the frequency of symptom substitution. In addition, he points out that certain symptoms themselves, such as school phobia, are capable of creating greater conflict in the individual and those around him than any underlying conflict that may have initially produced the symptom. His point is that some symptoms are more disruptive than others. These need to be eliminated whether other symptoms replace them or not. Removing the behaviorally disruptive symptom can be extremely beneficial not only to an individual but also to the family, classroom, and school that are disrupted by his symptoms.

---

[4] In addition to behavioral clinicians, many other therapists—those with a humanistic, existential, Gestalt, or experiential approach—also place little or no reliance on insight as a necessary producer of behavioral change. Many insist on supplying the client with a growth-producing, here-and-now experience through the therapeutic relationship rather than providing insight through an uncovering and reconstruction of the past. See pp. 265–292 for a discussion of these approaches.

ARGUMENTS AGAINST BEHAVIOR MODIFICATION

1. Behavior modification is a sterile, mechanical, dehumanizing orientation to human behavior. At best, the behavioral clinician is a technician schooled in manipulating behavior. At worst, he is an authoritarian, coercive person who uses his status and power to change behavior because he or society decides it is maladaptive or socially inappropriate.

In either case, the person beneath the symptoms may be obscured; he may simply be viewed as a defective object needing repair. Szasz (1967), for example, is critical of Eysenck for not being interested in the personal life of his patient, but instead seeing him in less human terms as merely the bearer of neurotic symptoms.

For such individuals as autistic children—who early in their lives withdraw from human contact, and in the process may begin to think of themselves as less than human—the operant conditioning procedures advocated by Lovaas (1964) may only further the dehumanization process. Eisenberg and Kanner (1956), two leading authorities on early childhood autism, have suggested a link between the early parent–child relationship and the etiology of this disorder. Specifically, they conclude that "emotional refrigeration has been the common lot of autistic children." Eisenberg (1957) goes even further, condemning that such children have been raised to be conforming, obedient, undemanding automatons in what he calls "a caricature of Watsonian behaviorism." If so, the behavioral approach—cold, detached, technique-oriented rather than relationship-oriented—may serve to further reinforce the very condition it attempts to alleviate.

2. Behavior modification's aim is rehabilitative rather than creative and growth-producing. The behavior modifier repairs and patches up but does not help the client expand beyond his previous condition before the onset of symptoms. In attitude, the outlook is essentially negative, undoing behavioral deficiencies and relieving symptoms. It fails to see the full range of human potential in the client or to explore with him how to expand his unique individuality. It offers no opportunity for creative self-fulfillment but instead settles for better adjustment. Moreover, by manipulating his outward behavior, it discourages him from examining his inner motives and conflicts; consequently, he is less likely to understand and take responsibility for his own actions.

The behavioral approach pays scant attention to the inner man and his past, his motives, his intimate feelings, his private thoughts, or indeed his consciousness. Unlike other clinical orientations, it makes no effort to be person-centered, value-oriented, or to help the client become more growth-oriented, spontaneous, and autonomous. It fails to help the client develop courage to increase his self-determination and find personal meaning. In Rogers' words, man must choose to become himself—"not a puppet, not a slave, not a machine, but his own unique individual self [1963, p. 89]." It is difficult to see how the behavior modifier can be of much help in this endeavor.

Furthermore, by emphasizing the similarities between human and animal learning and behavior, the behavioral clinician actually obscures much of the uniquely human repertoire—love, growth, humor, reason, hope, purpose, self-fulfillment, to name but a few special human qualities. Certainly an emotionally troubled person deserves more than reinforcement schedules or deconditioning gadgetry, despite the claim for their efficiency and practicality. Whereas behaviorism originated, quite properly, as a reaction against anthropomorphizing animal psychology, the pendulum may now have swung too far. According to Maslow (1965), behaviorism has "rodentomorphized" human psychology, studying the person as one would a white rat. As Maslow puts it, "It is indeed a mistake to attribute human motives to laboratory animals, but is it a mistake to attribute human motives to humans?"

3. **Behavior modification's effectiveness is limited to only certain cases.** Carkhuff and Berenson (1967) point out that behavior modification techniques are primarily well suited to: (1) experimental settings, such as a laboratory, where greater precision and control are possible than in the usual clinical setting; (2) situations in which the social and physical environment can be manipulated directly (a hospital); (3) situations with acute time pressure. They find behavior modification most effective in shaping behavior essential to basic living in the most severely disabled populations or in less severely disabled populations with relatively isolated anxiety reactions. However, their results indicate that clients who function at a higher level feel treatment has been inadequate. Thus, it is difficult to see how a successful business executive who seeks more meaning from life or a housewife frustrated and bored by her daily routine and seeking greater fulfillment is likely to benefit from the behavioral approach.

Wolpe's desensitization technique may indeed reduce phobic reactions, although that too has been challenged by other clinicians who claim only simple avoidance reactions and not true phobias are overcome by such a technique. Lovaas' (1964) methods may indeed reduce antisocial and self-destructive behavior in autistic children, although this effort, impressive as it is, is really designed to make them more amenable to a more personal psychotherapeutic relationship. Ayllon and Azrin (1968) may help increase motivation toward success in hospitalized patients through token economy programs. However, before any of these approaches can be judged successful, some inquiry must probe the internal feelings and motivation of the client, whether he experiences reduced conflict and an increased sense of worth and well-being. One reason behavioral clinicians claim such a high percentage of cures may be that they settle for less and thus attain success more easily than other clinical approaches do.

Janis, Mahl, Kagan, and Holt (1969) have questioned whether the behavioral model applies to various types of anguish that arise in stressful life circumstances—grief over loss of a loved one, shame over failure, guilt over ethical violations, vague feelings of self-discontent. The behavioral model inadequately explains personality changes following a stressful crisis and provides little basis for predicting whether any individual's reaction will be adaptive or maladaptive. Nor does it help to explain why some persons mobilize their resources under stress while others do not.

4. Behavior modification is simplistic, narrow, naive, and reductionistic. Despite the protests of the behaviorists, many clinicians find that mental activity cannot be so easily dismissed or ignored. For them, the data of consciousness, to say nothing of the expression of unconscious forces, is invaluable in understanding their client. In the same way, to dismiss the past and the individual's personal biography with it is naive and unnecessary. Clearly, 75 years of clinical discovery, beginning with Freud's early work, cannot be ignored or rejected.

Learning theories based on animal research are too narrow to provide techniques for dealing with complex human behavior. The assumption that making external behavior more adaptive will improve inner feelings and reduce inner conflicts is naive. Finally, the price clinicians are asked to pay to gain efficiency as well as certainty regarding their techniques is to focus only on that small, sometimes insignificant part of the whole person reflected in his outward behavior. To accept such a view, ignoring the person's essential humanity rather than nurturing it, itself represents an antipsychotherapeutic viewpoint.

5. Behavior modification's view of what constitutes science is too limiting. A true science of behavior, such as psychology claims to be, should study the richness and variety of human experiences and activities. It must not confine itself merely to external behavior because that is most accessible and requires fewest inferences. To do so is to overlook the whole man, whose essential humanity may not reveal itself externally in any simple, easily measurable form. The behaviorist should not make such a virtue of his limited view of human beings. Instead, he should work with other psychologists to contribute to a unified, empirically based, scientific concept of what truly constitutes a whole human being.

As Maslow (1965) notes, if science is identified exclusively as exactness with quantification, with precisely defined variables under careful control, then early work on any problem—when hunches, naturalistic observations, speculations, and theories reign supreme—must necessarily be repudiated as unscientific. Clinical psychologists, trained to be researchers and anxious to avoid anything unscientific, are likely to avoid those unexplored problem areas and focus only on what they can observe and measure behaviorally. In the process, they may ignore the forest for the trees. Maslow sees "the greatest single psychological discovery ever made" as the discovery of unconscious motivation. It has clearly added enormously to our understanding of man. Yet few research efforts have explored its implications further, nor would the behavioral clinician consider it a legitimate and worthy area for research.

Rogers (1963), too, has urged the scientific study of the private world of inner personal meaning disregarded by the behaviorist:

> Valuable as has been the contribution of behaviorism, I believe that time will indicate the unfortunate effects of the bounds it has tended to impose. To limit [ourselves] to consideration of externally observable behavior, to rule out consideration of the whole universe of inner meanings, of purposes, of the inner flow of experiencing, seems to me to be closing our eyes to great areas which confront us when we look at the human world. Furthermore, to hold to the beliefs, which seem to me to characterize many behaviorists, that science is impersonal, that knowledge is an entity, that science somehow carries itself forward without the subjective person of the scientist being involved, is, I think, completely illusory [Rogers, 1963, p. 80].

THE PHENOMENOLOGICAL THERAPIES

As the science of behavior, psychology continually seeks systematically to accumulate new data from observations of human behavior. Those data come from observations made by an outside observer; for the most part they provide a basis for predicting how people in general will behave.

For many clinical psychologists, this so-called objective, outside view of behavior is inadequate in attempting to understand an individual. They want to know his unique perception of the world because they assume his behavior is based primarily on that perception. They are interested in how he feels, what he experiences from moment to moment, and especially what personal meaning he gives those experiences. The observations these clinicians insist on making must be based on the client's behavior from his own point of view. They agree that behavior that appears irrational and confused to the outside observer appears reasonable and purposeful to the one who is experiencing the situation; at the time, his actions seem to him to be the best, most appropriate, most effective behavior he can muster under the circumstances. A legitimate and indeed necessary area for scientific investigation, therefore, is an individual's behavior as determined by his unique perception of the world, his personal frame of reference.

From the phenomenological point of view, all behavior stems from the individual's perception of a situation, rather than the physical or objective situation itself. Another way of putting it is to say all behavior is determined by, and pertinent to, an individual's phenomenal or perceptual field (Combs & Snygg, 1959). It is to that phenomenal field, changing from moment to moment, to which the individual responds at the instant of action. His behavior is always appropriate to the phenomenal self, that part of the total universe he experiences as "me" at any given instance. It is the phenomenal self that each individual seeks to maintain in all his behavior — *self-consistency?*

While not open to direct observation, the clinician nevertheless can appreciate the basis for his client's behavior by attempting to understand the client's phenomenal field. With this orientation, objective evaluations of another person's behavior, such as judging it pathological or the result of mental illness, are of little interest: all behavior makes sense; it is caused by the client's perception of reality, the only reality he can know. To him, his response is always justified, reasonable, and appropriate. The clinician's task is to empathize with the client's reality.

Many students in clinical psychology find such an outlook a refreshing change from the hard science approach of instrumentation and detached objectivity. They easily accept its premises, particularly since these premises provide a common-sense framework for understanding the relationship between the student's own perceptions and behavior. They find the phenomenological view familiar, since they have had numerous life experiences in attempting to gauge another individual's phenomenal field from his behavior. (It is not difficult to infer when, in the midst of a conversation, someone checks his watch several times at the same time that he impatiently shifts his weight from one foot to the other.) Perhaps most important of all, it provides the only frame of reference available for dealing with aspects of human experience—love, yearning, hurt, hope, hate, fear, despair—all too familiar in daily life and all but ignored by so-called scientific psychology.

Curiously, many scientists have ignored the personal, experiential, intuitive base from which their own hypotheses are generated. Insisting on being detached, impersonal, and tough-minded, many have adopted a so-called objective stance as though they themselves were value-free and not personally motivated in their scientific pursuits. As Polanyi (1958) notes, scientists as human beings inevitably see the world from a personal perspective. Bugental (1967) has argued that many psychological scientists present a most incomplete picture of people when they fail to use evidence from their own experience. He points out that all scientists—physical and social scientists alike—make basic assumptions about the inner workings of man whenever they observe or experiment on human behavior. Rogers (1963) has argued for a more inclusive science that acknowledges interpersonal or phenomenological ways of knowing. It would include not only data on behavior but also data from the perspective of the observer, including his inner world of experiencing, knowing, and feeling. Such an undertaking would also include the study of man's goals, values, intentionality, and purpose, using the data of self-perception and personal constructs.

The phenomenological viewpoint has sometimes been called the third force in psychology, because of its humanistic leanings. As past president of the American Association for Humanistic Psychology Floyd Matson notes, the "third force" arose as a protest against "the psychogenetic determinism of the orthodox Freudians, which made man a creature of instinct, . . . and . . . the environmental determinism of the behaviorists, which made man a creature of conditioning [Matson, 1969, p. 14]." The phenomenologically oriented clinician sees both views as providing a low estimate of the human condition. In one, man is pictured as an object with the characteristics of a machine; in the other, as a helpless victim driven by unconscious motives. Instead, phenomenologists urge seeing man as someone with choice, purpose, and self-determination rather than driven by forces over which he has no control. They see him as someone capable of maximizing his potential for love, growth, and joy.

Phenomenological clinicians set themselves the task of: (1) seeing the client in his real world—the unique, concrete world in which he alone lives and has his being or self; (2) helping him to become better aware of himself by experiencing all aspects of himself, including previously denied parts; (3) helping him to accept his unique self and responsibility for acting on any choices he decides to make; and (4) helping him maximize or actualize his self to fulfill his inherent potentialities.

At least four variations of such an approach are currently practiced by clinical psychologists. They are: (1) client-centered therapy; (2) humanistic psychology; (3) existentialism; and (4) Gestalt therapy.

CLIENT-CENTERED THERAPY

Carl Rogers' influence on psychologists, educators, social workers, as well as the general public has been enormous. Rogers, however, has always been first and foremost a psychotherapist, and it is here that he has made his greatest mark. His 1942 publication, *Counseling and Psychotherapy,* proposed a nondirective technique, a radical departure from the then current psychotherapeutic methods, particularly psychoanalysis. The book stressed technique over theory, however, and for a time Rogers was considered an antitheoretical practitioner (Maddi, 1968). That was corrected in *Client-Centered Therapy* (Rogers, 1951), a book deemphasizing technique in favor of providing a philosophy of counseling. The tentative formulations of a theory of personality and behavior presented there have been developed further in an article, *Psychology: A Study of Science* (Rogers, 1959) and in *On Becoming a Person* (Rogers, 1961a). An updated description of the distinguishing characteristics of client-centered therapy has also appeared (Rogers, 1966).

Rogers was one of the first psychologists to challenge the medically dominated views of psychotherapy. He became convinced early that diagnosis, a carryover from traditional medical practice, was incompatible with his views because: (1) it placed the therapist in an authoritarian position with a patient, a sick person, instead of in a peer relationship with a client, which has no connotation of illness; (2) it called for a detached, objective evaluation of another person instead of an attempt to see the world through the client's internal frame of reference; (3) unlike in medical practice, different diagnoses did not call for different therapeutic strategies, so that diagnosis was unnecessary; (4) it increased the client's dependent tendencies, causing him to feel that understanding and improving his situation was in the hands of an expert, rather than his own responsibility.

In the same manner, Rogers rejected the practice of interpretation to provide the client with insight or explanation from his past. To Rogers, this was too directive. It implied the therapist knew more about the client than the client did himself, and it encouraged dependency. For similar reasons, Rogers eschewed giving reassurance or advice. Instead, he urged his followers to: (1) establish a permissive atmosphere in the counseling relationship; (2) assume a nonjudgmental attitude; (3) reflect back the client's feelings; and (4) generally act as a catalyst to facilitate the client's self-growth and search for self-direction. He stressed a joint exploration of the client's immediate situation, his phenomenal field, rather than probing into and uncovering his past history. The subjective, phenomenological experiences of the client were to be emphasized at all times. Within him were the forces of growth, the potential to cure himself, the inherent tendency toward self-actualization.

The focus of client-centered therapy is the private world of the client, particularly his self-concept. According to Rogers, as changes occur in the client's self-perception and perception of reality during the therapeutic process, corresponding changes will occur in his behavior. Given the proper therapeutic climate, free of threat, the client can use his capacity to reorganize his perceptions and, as a result, alter his behavior.

Rogers' theory has been termed a self theory by Hall and Lindzey (1957) to emphasize the importance Rogers places on that differentiated portion of an individual's phenomenal field which includes the conscious perceptions and values of the "I" or "me." Rogers emphasizes self-reports revealing the client's self-concept and the self-in-relationship to others and to the environment. Where Rogers discusses the tendency toward self-actualization in any person, he means the pressure within that person to develop his inherent potentialities, consistent with his own self-concept, which defines how the self-actualizing tendency will be expressed. The self-concept develops from infancy on, when the individual first experiences the need for positive regard from others and the need for positive self-regard (Rogers, 1959). In the process of gaining approval and disapproval from significant people in his life, each individual slowly develops a conscious sense of who he is, a self. Any tendency toward self-actualization will take only the form of behavior consistent with his self-concept and his need for positive self-regard.

Since each individual has the potential for self-growth and self-direction, psychotherapy need provide only the proper conditions to facilitate the development of an already existing capacity. Rogers (1957) has outlined three attitudes in the therapist that constitute the necessary and sufficient conditions for therapeutic effectiveness: (1) the therapist's *congruence* or *genuineness* (that is, the therapist is his actual self, without facade, experiencing his own feelings and communicating them if appropriate in the encounter); (2) the therapist's *unconditional positive regard* for his client (that is, the therapist accepts the client in a warm, nonpossessive way without evaluating him, judging him, or placing conditions on such acceptance); (3) the therapist's accurate *empathic understanding* of his client's phenomenal world (that is, the therapist is sensitive to his client's personal meanings and private inner world as if it were his own, while never forgetting it is not, and is sensitive to the client's immediate situation, the so-called here and now). When these three attitudes exist in the therapist and are perceived and experienced by the client, a therapeutic climate is created in which constructive personality changes in the client can come about.

Roger's client-centered therapy has undergone continual development since its introduction. The emphasis on nondirective techniques and reflection of feeling has given way to an emphasis on the ongoing relationship between therapist and client with its focus on the immediate moment. Rogers is more concerned with the process of personality change than the search for historical causes of the person's present personality characteristics. He hopes the therapist can "use his whole person in the relationship [Rogers, 1961b, p. 188]." His theory has expanded to an overall consideration of the nature of man and his capacity to fulfill and actualize himself. Psychotherapy is just one specialized example of any constructive interpersonal relationship between two individuals—that is, a relationship that is safe and in which there is freedom to experience one's own feelings. Under such circumstances, "when man is truly free to become what he most deeply is, free to actualize his nature as an organism of awareness, then he clearly appears to move toward wholeness and integration [Rogers, 1966, p. 193]." Such a view serves as a philosophical basis for increasingly popular efforts at greater self-awareness through intensive group experiences—sensitivity groups, T groups, basic encounter groups. (See Chapter 10 for a more detailed discussion of group encounter experiences.)

HUMANISTIC PSYCHOLOGY

The recent revival of humanism in psychology has come about because a growing number of psychologists have become alarmed by the tendency of psychology generally to ignore man except as an inexhaustible source of data. Within clinical psychology, they are critical of the behavioral view that the client can best be understood as an object to be studied from the outside. In the same manner, they protest the psychoanalytic view that man is a victim of his past and inevitably responds to the present and future in terms of historical determinants. Instead, these clinicians propose that man be viewed as someone with free choice and the potential for continued growth.

The third force—humanistic psychology—is a phenomenologically oriented approach that uses the data of each individual's immediate experience to try to determine what it means for him to be alive as a unique human being. In this sense, it is similar to Rogers' client-centered therapy. Beyond that, the humanistic psychologist is interested in developing methods for enlarging and enriching human experiences, extending the possibilities of realizing man's special and extraordinary potential.

Humanistic psychologists are particularly critical of the nothing-but orientation in psychology, with its intent to show all human phenomena as nothing but a minimum number of learned response processes. They consider it misleading to describe human functioning and experience based wholly or in large part on studies of subhuman species. Instead, humanistic psychologists are most concerned with man's subjective experience and only secondarily concerned with his actions. Their interest is the individual—his exceptional and unpredictable aspects rather than his regular, universal, and conforming aspects (Bugental, 1967).

Gordon Allport was among the first to call for the study of the whole man. By this Allport meant those thoughts, attitudes, habits, values, and behaviors which together form the unique organization we call personality. From his earliest publications, he has urged psychologists to study the uniqueness of the person, his individuality. Allport has lamented that science has tended to regard the individual "as a mere bothersome accident [Allport, 1937, p. vii]." In later writings, Allport has continued to deplore the "arrogance, the superficiality, and the imperialistic character of modern behavioral science [Allport, 1955, p. 2]," with its mechanistic assumptions and brittle experimental methods. Joseph Wood Krutch also was an early critic of the methods for studying man that were originally devised mainly "for the study of machines or the study of rats, and [were] capable, therefore, of detecting and measuring only those characteristics which the three do have in common [Krutch, 1954, p. 32]."

First in Europe and later in the United States, Charlotte Buhler (1933, 1968) has written extensively on the human life cycle. She has emphasized the importance of studying the course of human life as a whole rather than studying isolated events and processes in their relation to specific phases and aspects of a person's life. Buhler recently has focused on the goal setting process and its significance throughout life as the individual strives for self-fulfillment.

Abraham Maslow (1954, 1962, 1964) and Erich Fromm (1947, 1955, 1956) have also been key figures in providing direct expression for the development of the humanistic orientation in psychology. Over the last 15 years, Maslow has provided many of the theoretical conceptualizations for (as well as leadership help in launching) the *Journal of Humanistic Psychology* and helped found the American Association for Humanistic Psychology. Fromm has written extensively on the necessity for man to fulfill his unique human nature and gain freedom, productivity, and individuality.

Maslow has been particularly concerned with psychological growth and development of the self-actualizing tendency. He believes neurosis results from deprivation of certain satisfactions early in life. Adult neurosis therefore involves ungratified wishes for these satisfactions—for safety, belongingness, identification, close love relationships, respect, and prestige. In contrast, nonneurotic people have sufficiently gratified these basic needs so that they are motivated primarily by trends toward self-actualization (Maslow, 1962). Thus, Maslow distinguishes between: (1) a *deficiency-motivated* person, dependent on outside sources to supply him with gratification and to repair his deficits; and (2) a *growth-motivated* person, seeking to enrich his life, enlarge his experiences, delight in being alive.

Self-actualizing people, limited in number to be sure, are without exception involved in a cause outside themselves. They have devoted their lives to the search for "being" (or "*B*") values—truth, beauty, goodness, self-sufficiency, simplicity, and so on (Maslow, 1964). They are spontaneous and natural. They express rather than cope. They do not feel consistently anxiety-ridden, insecure, isolated, unloved, or unworthy. They experience fully, vividly, selflessly, with full concentration and total absorption. At the moment of experiencing, the person is wholly and fully human. This is the self-actualization moment (Maslow, 1967), or a *peak experience*. All individuals experience such moments, but many do so only occasionally. Maslow (1967) believes peak experiences are most likely to happen to individuals who subject themselves to honest self-scrutiny and give up illusions and false notions about themselves.

While some of Maslow's specific ideas are not shared by all humanistically oriented psychologists, Maslow's view of man is probably acceptable to all. In this view, free choice is emphasized over determinism. Man is seen as capable of self-determination, able to work out his own solutions to problems of living, and able to establish for himself a personal set of rules for his own conduct. He is not a prisoner of the past but, given the proper therapeutic atmosphere, can direct his own future.

Such psychotherapy aims at far more than repairing what was previously dysfunctional in the individual or even returning him to some previous level of psychological functioning. Instead, it tries to surpass his previous developmental level and move toward ever-increasing use of his inner resources and increased satisfaction with life.

The process by which this is accomplished puts heavy stress on the relationship between therapist and client. The therapist is not a trainer or molder of another person or someone who can "cure" his client's "disease" or help him "adjust." Instead, his task is to help the client rediscover himself, unfold, gain awareness of what he is experiencing. Perhaps most important, the client must be helped to rely ultimately on himself to provide meaning for his experiences and to set meaningful goals and a uniquely suitable life style for himself (Tomlinson, 1968). He must help him become the best possible version of himself as a human being, defined by his own values, aspirations, and limitations (Temerin, 1963).

Humanistic psychotherapy is not based on any one technique, but is tailored to the individual client. Rossi (1967) distinguished between psychotherapies which stress the game dimension and those which stress the growth dimension. In the former, the therapist is concerned with his client's relation to the outside world and his ways of coping with reality. Repetitive patterns of maladaptive behavior are analyzed, and substitute adaptive patterns are sought in their place. In the latter, the emphasis is on the client's experience of his inner world. Efforts are directed toward seeking greater awareness of the self. According to Rossi, all forms of therapy that focus on outer behavior and/or interpersonal relationships—behavior therapy, psychoanalysis, Berne's (1961) transactional analysis, or Glasser's (1965) reality therapy—contain a strong game component. On the other hand, those therapeutic approaches that emphasize inner development over external relations—client-centered therapy, existentialism (May, 1958), humanistic psychotherapy—stress the growth component. Rossi contends that game therapies, with their prescribed roles and theories as guidelines, are easier and more comfortable for the therapist to practice. The growth therapies, calling on the therapist's awareness of his own phenomenological experiences and using that awareness in facilitating a similar growth process in another person, are more difficult. The growth therapist must deal with the new and creative, for which there is no authority or formal training. However, only growth therapy, through growth encounters with others,[5] enables both individuals to experience new awareness that in turn enhances growth in both.

Humanistic psychotherapy, then, attempts to deal with the whole man. It looks within the person for the capacity to be himself, grow, make choices, extend the range of his experiences, give personal meaning to those experiences, take risks, assume responsibilities, and continue the process of self-fulfillment and satisfaction throughout his life.

EXISTENTIALISM

Existential philosophy has been recently rediscovered in reaction to modern man's increasingly depersonalized and alienated feelings. Disillusioned with mechanical, objective, so-called scientific explanations of man's behavior, many European psychiatrists and psychologists turned to the philosophy of Heidigger and Kierkegaard to better understand the

[5] The development of so-called growth centers, such as Esalen in Big Sur, California, is based on just such encounters. See Chapter 10 for further discussion.

[handwritten margin note: is this the kind of extra-therapy situation that I've been thinking about? — the experience in the "real world" that brings "home" the impact & growth that's occurred in therapy?]

nature of man's being and the meaning of his existence to the individual. Heidigger in particular stressed the analysis of Dasein.[6] Kierkegaard also insisted that man is more than a subject (a thinking thing) or an object (to be analyzed and controlled): he is a real existing person who continues to define himself through his actions.

am I behaving consistently w/my beliefs? What brings about a change in a person's expectations of himself? Therapy? Introspection? Learning introspection in therapy? Realistic perspective of himself: his goals, limitations?

Ludwig Binswanger, the Swiss psychiatrist and colleague of Freud, is usually credited with integrating existential philosophy and the phenomenological method to develop Daseinsanalyse, existential analysis. Although psychoanalytic in training and outlook, Binswanger became increasingly concerned that orthodox psychoanalytic theory did not provide sufficient understanding of his patient's unique being. Used as an active verb rather than a noun, *being* means that an individual is constantly in the process of developing countless possibilities. Therefore, Binswanger argued that we can best understand another person by understanding what he is becoming and how he is developing his potential through his actions.

Characteristically, many existential therapists have remained psychoanalysts, suggesting that their approach is less a movement to establish a new school of psychotherapy than an effort to provide a new attitude, orientation, or perhaps a new dimension to more traditional views in psychiatry and psychology (van Kaam, 1967). Thus, little in the existential approach is dogmatic: there is no uniform technique, no effort to force preconceived theoretical conceptualizations on the patient or client, no systematic presentation of a new theoretical foundation for understanding human growth and development.

More than anyone else, psychologist Rollo May has been responsible for the current popularity of existential psychotherapy in this country. He brought the work of the European existential psychiatrists and psychologists to the attention of their American counterparts with his book, *Existence* (May et al., 1958). In it, May defined existentialism as an "endeavor to understand man by cutting below the cleavage between subject and object. . . [p. 11]." Man, the subject, cannot be separated from the object he observes. He exists in a world of which he is inevitably a part; the meaning of objective facts in that world depends on the subject's relation-

[6] Dasein literally means "to be (sein) there (da)." Its popular translation is simply "existence." It refers to the fact that man is a being who has a "there" in the sense that his existence occupies a particular point in time and space at any given moment (May et al., 1958; Boss, 1963).

ship to them. Efforts to depersonalize him and render him an object places essence before existence. By contrast, modern existential philosophers like Sartre have argued that existence must precede essence—what one does and how he lives define what he is.

American existentialists in particular are optimistic about man's potential to assert his individuality, his existence. They stress man as an existential being who has freedom and choice and therefore is responsible for the person he becomes.[7] The distinctive character of existential analysis is its concern with ontology, the science of being, and Dasein, "the existence of this particular being sitting opposite the psychotherapist [May et al., 1958, p. 37]."

According to the existentialists, the quality of existence is peculiar to man alone, and therefore it is precisely with those uniquely human characteristics of man that they concern themselves. In particular, they are interested in man's capacity for awareness of his own being, which makes choices and decisions possible. Being conscious of his existence, however, he is also responsible for it. Moreover, he knows that at some future time he will cease to be, or he may even make the choice of ceasing to exist at any instant. Thus, death (nonbeing) is an inseparable part of being, since grasping what it means to exist also involves grasping that he might not exist. The existentialists believe man must confront his nonbeing if his existence is to take on vitality, realness, and immediacy. In the same way, what other clinicians view as psychopathology in an individual is seen by the existentially oriented clinician as a manifestation of nonbeing. Such nonbeing stifles the person's freedom to experience fully and tends to make him inauthentic (Bugental, 1965).

One of the major contributions of existential psychiatrists and psychologists is their conviction that man lives in three worlds simultaneously: (1) the *Umwelt* (literally, the "world around"), which is the biological world, the world of drives and instincts, requiring no self-awareness and thus characteristic of all organisms; (2) the *Mitwelt* (the "with world"), the world of interrelationships with other human beings, involving mutual awareness; and (3) the *Eigenwelt* (the "own world"), the world of self-awareness, self-relatedness, self-consciousness, unique to human beings.

---

[7] The similarity of Rogers' and Maslow's viewpoint is clear here. Rogers occasionally uses the same terminology, as when he speaks of the individual moving "toward being [Rogers, 1961, p. 175]." Maslow also has described the individual as intrinsically motivated to sustain his being through peak experiences.

It is on the basis of the Eigenwelt, the world of personal meaning, that each individual experiences the world. Rather than being three separate worlds, the existentialists emphasize that the three represent modes of "being-in-the-world" experienced simultaneously by the individual. They point out that while Freud uncovered man's Umwelt and Sullivan's (1953) interpersonal theory dealt with the Mitwelt, the Eigenwelt has been unexplored. Yet it is precisely in this world of consciousness and self-awareness that man lives and has his being.

Existential therapists use a variety of techniques depending on the client, the phase of his treatment, and the theoretical bias of the clinician. In any case, technique is deemphasized to preclude seeing the human being as an object to be analyzed, which has the connotation of being treated from the outside. In contrast to the common therapeutic belief that understanding follows from technique, the existentialists believe technique follows understanding.

Therapy is an encounter in which both the client and therapist participate with minimum concern for formal conventional roles. By opening their worlds to each other in such a shared encounter, both can grow (Binswanger, 1963). The emphasis is on *presence*—the real, immediate relationship between the two persons. The therapist attempts to understand and experience the being of the other person as far as possible. Should he become anxious in such a confrontation, he must resist the temptation to give up what is existentially real between them—presence—and fall back on his expert status or on techniques for analyzing the other's behavior. The other person, to the existentialist, is not a subject to be studied but an existential partner.

The aim of therapy is to help the person experience his existence fully, including awareness of his potential and his ability to act on it. The therapist focuses on the client's most influential personal experiences, and the two of them together discover what the client's basic behavioral patterns are and what major decisions and choices he has made. Together, too, they look for his past attempts to achieve some purpose as well as present attempts to reach some goals. Like most phenomenological clinicians, however, the existentialists primarily attend to "now events"—the client's experiences as they are happening. The past is important only if it persists in present thoughts and memories. The therapist is likely to direct the client's attention to his sensations, feelings, dreams, and fantasies, most of which he has presumably pushed out of awareness or has never before discovered. The focus is to help the client regain his lost being, help him develop his capacity to know his own values better, and improve his capacity to make decisions according to them. With this change comes the existential crisis of transition as the person moves from limited being to a new fullness with its concurrent anxieties over relinquishing safe, familiar patterns and facing as yet untried ways of living. Existential anxiety, however, is a fact of being and is unavoidable. To make the leap into the unknown is "an act of faith in one's own being [Bugental, 1965, p. 173]"—what theologian Paul Tillich calls "the courage to be." Most existentialists create a unique approach to fit the individual under study, making generalizations difficult. However, Boss (1963) has provided a number of case studies of existential treatment of individuals with different diagnostic labels. Binswanger, in May et al. (1958), has also presented a lengthy and detailed existential analysis of a woman with multiple psychological problems.

Existential therapy helps the client develop an attitude of commitment. He learns to give up neurotic anxiety and confront existential anxiety, believed to be a necessary condition of growth and self-exploration. He learns to become aware, look to the future, give up the nonbeing of routine patterns and habits. The authentic person who emerges continues the development of becoming as he continues to recognize, experience, and give meaning to his unique existence in the world.

GESTALT THERAPY

The rapidly developing interest in Gestalt therapy in various parts of the United States, particularly in the last decade, is due largely to the work of Frederick (Fritz) Perls. Trained in medicine and psychoanalysis, Perls was also attracted to the ideas of Gestalt psychology and existential philosophy. Emigrating from his native Germany with the rise of Naziism, he settled in South Africa, where he established an institute of psychoanalysis. However, Perls was beginning to challenge the accepted tenets of psychoanalytic theory as well as the orthodox techniques of psychoanalytic therapy. His first book, *Ego, Hunger, and Aggression* (Perls, 1947), introduced the technique known as Gestalt therapy. While this work went relatively unnoticed in the United States, it was the forerunner of *Gestalt Therapy* (Perls, Hefferline, & Goodman, 1951), published after Perls had immigrated to the United States. Perls helped establish institutes for Gestalt therapy in New York, Cleveland, and Los Angeles before affiliating with the Esalen Institute at Big Sur, California. Ever restless and eager for the challenge of new experiences, at age 75 Perls moved to Vancouver, B. C., to organize a therapeutic community he called a kibbutz. He died in 1970, at 77. Before his death, he held numerous workshops, made tape recordings and films demonstrating his Gestalt techniques. *Gestalt Therapy Verbatim* (Perls, 1969a) is an edited version of his seminars at Esalen from 1966 through 1968. His uniquely Gestalt autobiography, *In and Out the Garbage Pail* (1969b), focuses on awareness and combines playfulness with theory and reflections on his life.

Basic to understanding Gestalt therapy are the views of perception developed by Koffka, Kohler, and Wertheimer in the years before World War I. They objected to the atomistic approaches in psychology that reduced mental processes to elements, such as images, feelings, and sensations. Instead, they proposed that the whole is always different from the sum of its parts and that the unity of the perceiver and the object being perceived must not be lost. The perceiver is an active participant in his perceptions. Those perceptions take place in the present. The perceiver attempts to organize his perceptual field by differentiating the figure from the background in order to draw his attention to one dominant aspect of his phenomenological field. What the Gestalt psychologists contributed to our understanding of figural perceptions, Gestalt therapists apply to organic perceptions—that is, perceptions of one's own feelings, emotions, and bodily sensations (Wallen, 1970).

According to Gestalt therapy theory, the organized whole of the person, his Gestalt, must be maintained, not fragmented. He must become aware of himself, including an awareness of how he defeats himself. To become aware, he must learn to express what he is feeling from moment to moment. He must experience the blocks to his awareness and learn new ways to express himself and relate to others within the wholeness of his social environment. His own life experiences and observations of others are assumed to have provided him with values of how he wants to live. Increased self-awareness will provide increased self-direction. The person's own existing inner resources are assumed to be adequate to cope with his problems successfully once these resources are brought into effective action.

The therapist's role in Gestalt therapy is to help the client become

bodily or body-awareness: is my body matching my feelings? is my body consistent w/my feelings? (that's stretching. no good.) -very inconsistent w/what I want to do!

aware of *how* he uses his resources ineffectively and *what* he does to block the achievement of what he wants, not to answer *why*. Answers to why—involving explanations and interpretations based on a recovery of past memories and a search for past behavior—are considered unimportant for overcoming the patterns he now wishes to change. The focus throughout is on awareness of the moment, the here and now.

Perls (1970) sees Gestalt therapy as a rapprochement between the behavioral orientation, with its emphasis on behavior in the now, and the phenomenological orientation, with its emphasis on awareness of what is being experienced. To Perls, *nothing exists except the now*. In his formulation, now = experience = awareness = reality. Therefore, all therapy must stay with experience as it is happening and as the individual becomes fully aware of it. Efforts to avoid such awareness must be counteracted as they occur. It is in the now that the person is or is not facilitating his growth, is or is not enhancing his ability to cope with life.

Neurosis consists of five layers, according to Perls. The first layer he calls the *phony* layer, where the neurotic plays games, lives roles, attempts to get away from himself, and in the process gives up being himself and tries to be something or someone else. As he becomes aware of his manipulations through Gestalt therapy, he begins to experience the fears that maintain them; the second is the *phobic* layer. Here new behavior is avoided, as are fantasies of what the consequences might be if the person were honest and genuine. The third layer is the *impasse*, where the familiar environmental supports are stripped away and the person is panicked because he does not believe his own resources are adequate to go forward alone.[8] The fourth layer is the *implosive*, involving fears, doubts, and despair as the person recognizes his self-imposed limitations and begins to give up his "deadness" and come alive. The *explosive* layer is the final stage in becoming authentic. Perls sees four types of explosions —into joy, into grief, into orgasm, into anger—as the person's unused energies are liberated in an impactful way.

The Gestalt therapist's technique is to focus on the most obvious behavioral pattern in his client. Upon meeting the client and thereafter, he continues to ask himself what is the most apparent aspect of the client's behavior or manner which he, the therapist, perceives. As the therapist

---

[8] This formulation parallels Bugental's existential crisis. See p. 277.

becomes aware of the client's gestures, facial expressions, posture, voice, and so on, he calls attention to them in order to help the client become aware of his own behavior patterns.

In the same manner, the client is taught to take the responsibility for ownership of his thoughts or feelings, not blaming them on someone else or disclaiming ownership of them; the therapist does not allow the client to disown them. Greenwald (1969) has reported the following dialogue between himself and a 26-year-old married engineer during their initial session. The client was referred by his family physician because of functional gastrointestinal symptoms, including a spastic colon.

Therapist: I notice that as you talk about these things, some of which seem to be upsetting, you smile almost continuously.

Patient (obviously embarrassed but smiling still): Yes, people have mentioned this to me. I've done it for years. . . . Habit, I guess.

Therapist: Do you really feel like smiling or laughing as if you had heard a funny joke?

Patient: Oh no! It just comes on. . . . It's embarrassing. . . . It often makes me feel uncomfortable.

Therapist: I notice you refer to your smile as "it." Would you repeat your last sentence using "I" instead of "it"?

Patient: . . . my smile just comes on. . . . I am embarrassed . . . by my smile. . . . I often make myself uncomfortable by smiling. . . .

Therapist: Did you experience any difference when you restated your comments in the first person?

Patient: Yes, I became more uncomfortable. . . . Like you were making me face something that I wanted to avoid. . . .

Therapist: Very well . . . then would you make up a case telling how you need your smile to be comfortable and how it serves a useful purpose for you? Just verbalize your thoughts about this as they come.

Patient: That's hard to do. . . . I am not very good at these things (smiles continuously). . . . O.K. . . . I need my smile to be uncomfortable. . . . I mean I would be even more uncomfortable not smiling. . . . Right now I'm trying not to smile but it won't go away. . . . Now I am not smiling (patient strains to keep a straight face). . . . I'm afraid you'll think I'm angry at you (smiles again).

Therapist: What's your objection to being angry at me?

Patient: I want you to like me. . . . If I get mad at you, you won't like me. . . . You'll be mad at me.

Therapist: And then? . . .

Patient: You won't help me.

Therapist: And then? . . .

Patient: Well, I came here to be helped. I want to be helped with my problems or I wouldn't be here.

Therapist: You're telling me that the only way I'll help you is if you are always nice and friendly and smiling and avoid being unpleasant or angry?

Patient: Yes, of course.

Therapist: Then you have to be this way with everyone if you want or need something from them?

Patient: Yes. I've always been told that the mature person controls his anger . . . that a smile is what people like and if I am unpleasant or angry they won't like me or want to have anything to do with me.

Therapist: So you swallow your anger instead and keep it inside you where it builds pressure. With this in mind can you fantasize what your colon might be saying by means of your so-called symptoms?

Patient: This is really embarrassing (patient blushing and smiling and seems delighted). . . . I see what you mean . . . (laughs explosively).

The remainder of the hour flowed easily from this awareness of the hiding of anger and resentments behind his smile and the patient began to see some of the meaning of his symptoms [Greenwald, 1969, pp. 4–5].

The Gestalt therapist does not assume responsibility for his client's life. The client is not asked to commit himself to a program of psychotherapy, but rather to evaluate for himself the on-going therapy experience. Each therapy hour is a unit in and of itself, an opportunity for the client to become aware of himself during the hour's experience. Since the focus is always on the present, there is no need for continuity from session to session.

Perls has made some use of psychoanalytic tenets, although he gives them a distinctly Gestalt translation. What Freud calls the unconscious, Perls refers to as a potential not available to the person. However, Gestaltists argue that it is incorrect to fragment man and talk about the unconscious and the preconscious as though they literally existed. Perls prefers to see these as backgrounds from which figures emerge.

Perls also used dreams, but unlike orthodox psychoanalytic methods, he had the client play all parts in the dream, including any objects represented. He sees dreams as a message from the person to himself, possibly the most spontaneous expression of the human being. As such, every aspect in the dream is a creation of and a part of the dreamer. Since some of these parts are disowned, Perls has his client take the part of persons or objects in the dream and become aware of what feelings they experience in doing so. Interpretations are avoided. A basic premise of Gestalt therapy is that nobody knows more about the person than he, himself, does.

According to Perls, individual therapy is becoming obsolete, giving way to group situations and workshops. Through these workshops, presented in various parts of the United States and Canada, Perls developed a following and became something of a folk hero to therapists and laymen who were interested in the immediate relevance of his here and now view of experiencing life.

AN OVERVIEW OF MAJOR APPROACHES TO PSYCHOTHERAPY

Before proceeding to an evaluation of the phenomenological therapies, let us look at Table 9, which compares psychoanalysis, behavior modification, and the phenomenological therapies along the dimensions for categorizing systems of psychotherapy developed in Chapter 6 (pp. 198–201).

Table 9. Summary of dimensions for categorizing psychoanalysis, behavior modification, and the phenomenological therapies

DIMENSION	PSYCHOANALYSIS	BEHAVIOR MODIFICATION	PHENOMENO-LOGICAL THERAPIES
1. The nature of man	Driven by instincts, especially sexual and aggressive, often putting him in conflict with society	A product of learning, conditioning	Has purpose, choice, free will, self-determination
2. Theory of normal personality development	Successful resolution and integration of biologically determined stages of psychosexual development	Normal behavior learned through system of reinforcement; imitation	Sense of self develops from infancy. Each individual is unique, has tendency for self-growth

Table 9. (continued)

DIMENSION	PSYCHOANALYSIS	BEHAVIOR MODIFICATION	PHENOMENO-LOGICAL THERAPIES
3. Theory of psycho-pathology	Psychopathology develops from inadequate resolution of particular phases of psychosexual development	Behavior disorders stem from faulty learning, maladaptive habits	Poor self-regard begins early in life, leads to adult dependence on outside sources to compensate for own lack of self-esteem
4. Role of therapist	Blank screen, neutral, sits behind couch and out of sight of analysand	Teacher or trainer, helping patient learn new behavior patterns; personal interaction with patient not essential	A real person engaged in face-to-face interaction with client; acts as facilitator of whatever potential for growth exists in client
5. Time orientation	Emphasis on uncovering and reconstructing unresolved, unconscious conflicts from the past	Present behavior studied and treated, with little or no concern with the past or etiology of the disorder	Here and now; uses data of immediate experience
6. Influence of unconscious processes	Man driven by unconscious forces over which he has little awareness or control	Unconcerned with possible unconscious conflicts because they are too inferential and usually are impossible to measure	Acknowledged by some but deemphasized; greater influence stems from free choice and self-determination
7. Role of insight versus action	Insight leads to understanding, conflict reduction, and ultimately to personality change	Action approach aimed at inhibiting or extinguishing overt maladaptive (abnormal) learning and replacing it with effective new learning	Self-awareness, experiencing aspects of self, takes precedence over (and precedes) action
8. Goals of psycho-therapy	Genital primacy; liberation of libido from pregenital fixations	Removal of maladaptive symptoms; behavior change	Maximization of awareness, growth, spontaneity, fulfillment of personal potential

EVALUATION OF THE PHENOMENOLOGICAL THERAPIES

ARGUMENTS FOR PHENOMENOLOGICAL THERAPIES

1. A comprehensive science of man must use the data of his inner experiences. All clinicians agree that it is desirable to obtain as many objective measures of behavior as are relevant and feasible in order to form a clinical impression of the client. However, an approach limited to external measures only would surely result in an incomplete and one-sided view of a person. Indeed, phenomenologically oriented clinicians insist not only on including the so-called subjective data of feelings and thoughts, but emphasize that those data provide an understanding of what it means to be a unique human.

Unlike lower animals, humans have awareness, consciousness. They think, feel, dream, fantasize, and experience. Each individual has a unique view of reality. Each has a separate self, a personality, a set of aspirations and future goals all based on his perceptions of his world—his phenomenal field—and the personal meaning he has given to his experiences. His perceptions, motives, and conflicts are the bases for his ultimate behavior. While they are admittedly less concrete, real, and quantifiable than external behavior, they are nevertheless the very qualities that are distinctively human and must be taken into account in any clinical appraisal.

A view of science that does not include data from the inner experiences of man is too narrow. The currently fashionable efforts to use only precise mathematical methods of measurement may be inapplicable to those internal activities of man that elude quantification but are very real for every human. Any science of human behavior, including psychology, that ignores uniquely human qualities, will fail to provide a comprehensive theory to account for the distinctive, specific characteristics of man.

2. Phenomenological therapies highlight the essential humanity of man. The phenomenological clinician objects to the mechanical view of man as an object, the victim of outside forces or inner drives and learned habits. He insists that being human involves more than carrying out certain conditioned responses based on past rewards or merely acting out genetically programmed instincts. Humans are more than advanced animals. Individual differences should delight the clinician even if they may represent annoying complications to an experimentalist. Man is more than a combination of instincts, reflexes, operant responses, or habit strengths.

Humans can grow, change, make choices. They can discover, invent, conceptualize. They live in the present but have past memories and future goals. They have the capacity to be aware and to become self-directed.

Clinically, the client must not be viewed merely as an object to be studied and explained. External evaluations or diagnostic formulations contribute little for precisely that reason. Far more important, the person who is the clinician should try to reach and maintain contact with the person who is the client. What is ultimately therapeutic is two human beings sharing their existences.

This inner view of man's unique humanity is overlooked or dismissed by the behavioral clinician. Consequently, his client does not experience the freedom to explore his perceptual field, to become more aware of himself as a person with values and choices about how he wants to live. Clients in any of the phenomenologically oriented therapies are urged to get in contact with their inner experiences and to become more authentic by making their inner feelings more congruent with their outer behavior.

As Murray has pointed out, "The main body of psychology started its career by putting the wrong foot forward, and it has been out of step with the march of science much of the time. Instead of beginning with studies of the whole person adjusting to a natural environment, it began with studies of a segment of a person responding to a physical stimulus in an unnatural laboratory environment [1948, p. 466]." It is the humanity of the whole person that concerns the phenomenological clinician.

3. Phenomenological therapies stress the self-determining, self-directed quality of human behavior. Followers of the empiricist Skinner and the therapist Freud, while differing in outlook and sources of data, view behavior as rule-bound and predetermined, not determined by free will. In Skinner's novel *Walden Two,* the hero observes that "men are made good or bad and wise or foolish by the environment in which they grow [1948, p. 273]." Skinner's deterministic view relies little on any inherent qualities in man to determine his own existence. Similarly, Freud sees man as driven by forces within him that are beyond his control, which he must suppress or sublimate. In contrast, most phenomenologically oriented clinicians see man as having the capacity to make choices and affect his destiny.

The ahistorical view of the phenomenologists differs sharply from the historical determinism of the psychoanalysts. Man is seen as continuously evolving, becoming, as he exercises his freedom and makes choices. Rogers was among the first to place greater stress on the immediate situation than on the client's past. For Perls, nothing exists except the now. Whereas Freud saw the past determining the present, the existentialists look to man's view of the future to comprehend his present behavior. Indeed, May (1958) points out that while the past should not be neglected, it can be understood only in light of the future. The past is more than a collection of isolated events or a static reservoir of memories. According to May, what an individual seeks to become determines what he remembers of his past. In this sense, the future determines the past.

4. The application of phenomenological therapies to psychotherapy makes the process relationship-centered rather than technique-centered.
Both the psychoanalytic and behavioristic approaches stress technique. In the former, the neutrality of a detached analyst encourages transference —the process by which the patient irrationally transfers to the analyst the feelings and responses he had toward significant people in the past, usually in childhood. The behavioral model also involves a detached, objective therapist who uses manipulative techniques to shape another person's behavior, eliminate his symptoms, and train him to cope better with previously difficult situations. In both treatments, the therapist's personality is neutralized or considered insignificant.

Phenomenologically oriented therapies involve the interaction of two people, each committed to experiencing and understanding himself in relation to the other. As a consequence, both have an opportunity to grow and develop. As the therapist gives up his neutrality and becomes real, it becomes less necessary for the client to attribute or transfer characteristics to him because he no longer is vague and unreal.

Perhaps a common reason why all therapeutic approaches claim some success is that they establish a satisfactory relationship between therapist and client. When Heine (1953) compared the reports of clients who had gone to psychoanalytic, client-centered, and Adlerian therapists, he found that they reported similar changes in themselves regardless of the type of therapy. They tended to agree that certain elements in the relationship (trust in the therapist, feeling understood by him) were most helpful while others (therapist remoteness, advice giving, or emphasis on past history) were least helpful. Fiedler (1950) compared beginning and expert therapists from different schools of therapy and found that patient–therapist relationships of experts with different orientations resembled each other more than the relationships of experts and beginners of the same school.

What makes for a growth-producing therapeutic encounter? Hobbs (1962) points out that the neurotic lacks a sense of identity and purpose and tends to get little fulfillment from his usual life situations. It is only in the therapeutic relationship that he has an opportunity for what Hobbs calls a sustained experience of intimacy in a relatively safe situation. In a similar way, the existentialists emphasize presence, a real relationship between two humans who for a time share the same world and are concerned with understanding and experiencing each other's existence.

5. Phenomenological therapies hold out the promise of increased joy, freedom, self-fulfillment, and hope. They view man as able to achieve more than a satisfactory sublimation of his antisocial instincts, more than rehabilitation through symptom removal. Man is considered to have considerable potential for enlarging his range of experiences and enriching the quality of his satisfactions; he has the capacity to make choices; he has a value system; and, most important, he can base his actions on these characteristics.

Shutz (1967) has described a number of nonverbal, nonintellectual ways of expanding awareness and experiencing joy, which he defines as the feeling that comes from fulfilling one's potential. It relies less on verbal communication and more on body awareness, physical contact, and acting out of life situations and fantasies. Shutz describes various methods for increasing honesty and openness, release and joy. Shutz' work is phenomenological in orientation, emphasizing the here and now and the individual's self-perceptions. Its aim is to help people experience themselves and others in a more sensitive, accepting, and loving way.

ARGUMENTS AGAINST THE PHENOMENOLOGICAL THERAPIES

1. Phenomenological therapies are anti-intellectual and anti-scientific. The phenomenologists tend to distrust reason as such and instead rely on the awareness of internal feelings to guide behavior. Such a viewpoint tends to be unclear and therefore scientifically suspect, since information comes only through introspection, a highly personal and probably biased source. The usual scientific methods, relying as they do on objective, quantitative measurements, cannot be applied. The science of man must be based on more than vague generalities, all but impossible to verify scientifically, or romanticized notions concerning man's strivings for self-actualization through transcendental experiences.

One consequence of the emphasis on subjective experiences and sensory awareness has been the tendency to regard the intellect as the enemy of all that is naturally human and pleasurable. Such an anti-intellectual view is dangerous. While the liberation of each individual's human potential is an incontestably admirable goal, it can be achieved only through understanding and insight that require the unity of the whole person, which includes his intellect as well as his senses.

2. Phenomenological therapies justify experimentation with group encounter experiences whose results may be dangerous and whose benefits may be more apparent than real. The current fad in discovering oneself through expanded awareness has resulted in various forms of "instant turn-on." Numerous growth centers have sprung up recently, all designed to help individuals contact their real selves, have peak experiences, or attain intimacy with others through encounter groups. Such experiences, particularly when pursued by naive, innocent, or lonely people are as likely to be personally destructive as personally fulfilling. Few follow-up studies have been reported, particularly of those who have voluntarily attended a single weekend marathon session.

Perhaps most serious from a scientific viewpoint, the phenomenological approach has encouraged the proliferation of techniques that claim to be therapeutic but that disclaim the need for a theoretical basis or for research or adequate training for its practitioners.

Experienced clinicians are skeptical of any pervasive, long-term personality changes that may result from such encounter groups, especially those whose clients are not previously screened and for whom there is no continuing series of sessions. Despite their noble intentions, encounter groups are unlikely to help produce major, critical shifts in a person's life. While he may learn to express his feelings, he is not likely to learn to understand them or to gain any mastery over them. Indeed, he may learn little more than how to play interesting, dramatic games that give the illusion of instant inner awareness or intimacy but do little to modify behavior permanently or provide sustained gratification.

3. It is never really possible to know the subjective, inner world of another individual. The phenomenological viewpoint lacks any rational certainty; consequently, it is based on conjecture and inference. While a person's awareness of his inner state is a kind of observation no different in principle from external observation, it is nevertheless limited as a useful source of knowledge because of its subjective nature.

The modern phenomenological viewpoint only slightly resembles the rigorously scientific efforts of Wundt and Titchner to study introspection by disciplined self-observation (see Chapter 2). While both used the data of experience, the introspectionists trained their subjects to break down such experiences into irreducible elements—sensations, feelings, and images. Unlike the phenomenologists today, there was no place for meaning, although this elusive world of personal meaning lies at the heart of phenomenology, particularly in its clinical application.

Philosophers for centuries have speculated whether we can ever fully understand what takes place in another person's consciousness. Our clinical attempts sometimes are contaminated by our own projections, over-identifications with, and fantasies about the other person. Rogers, among others, has underscored the importance of empathy in such understanding. However, it is never clear how such accurate empathic understanding of a client's phenomenal world can be developed. A phenomenology without empathy, without putting oneself in another person's shoes, is of no use to the clinician. But phenomenology that relies on empathy must become far more specific in reconstructing the world of another person than it is today.

4. The introduction of a new and not clearly defined vocabulary imposes an unnecessary complication to an already complex set of phenomena. In their dissatisfaction with the restrictions imposed by traditional terminology, and in their zeal for verbal shortcuts, many phenomenologically oriented clinical theoreticians have coined new terms for their ideas. Maslow talks of B-values, peak experiences, meta-needs, meta-pathologies, even meta-counselors "to help with the soul-sicknesses that grow from the unfulfilled meta-needs [1967, p. 281]." Bugental (1965) and other existentially oriented clinicians speak of transcendence, ontology, contingency authenticity, Dasein, the I-process, and so on. Perls does not clearly distinguish the implosive and explosive layers of neurosis. Rogers tends to use language more familiar to everyday human experiences (self, unconditional positive regard, genuineness), but these too tend to be vague and to lack precise definition.

It is ironic that a point of view that seeks to deal most intimately with the human condition should burden itself with a terminology that obscures meaning. Such a tendency can lead only to a proliferation of jargon that itself is a barrier to understanding.

5. The ahistorical emphasis of phenomenological therapies down-

grades the significance of the past.   Phenomenologically oriented clinicians insist on dealing with the client's immediate situation with little concern for what life experiences led him to the here and now. In this sense, they share with the behavioral clinician a preoccupation with the present and a neglect of the past. In their own defense, some Gestaltists have argued that they are aware that some explanations from the past account for man's present behavior; but they insist it is wasteful to attempt such explanations because they have no therapeutic value in the present.

However, at any point in time, a person is the result of where he has been, where he is, and where he is headed. It is naive and foolhardy to dismiss the past. Understanding of how past conflicts developed and were resolved can help understand current methods of conflict resolution and perhaps develop more mature, less regressed future methods. While insight alone will not produce behavioral change, many clinicians argue that it is a necessary step in such change.

The issue of the unconscious is dismissed by some who adhere to a phenomenological frame of reference. Yet, just as nobody is free from his own history, it has been demonstrated clinically and experimentally that nobody is free from unconscious forces and conflicts which continue to seek expression and resolution. Despite the stress on free will and on man as a self-evolving, self-actualizing being, it would be a mistake to adopt a totally anti-deterministic view of human behavior.

Clinically, a careful history-taking provides the therapist with a more complete and well-rounded picture of his client. The clinician is less likely to subject a client to the additional stress of group encounter experiences, for example, if his history reveals severe emotional disturbances under stress. Those clinicians who avoid all history-taking may expose their clients to such difficulties prematurely and find that the client's fragile defenses break down still further.

Clients expect some review of their history. They are likely to see such an effort as reassurance of the clinician's interest. They may also begin, on their own, to see characteristic patterns as they remember their childhood experiences. In any case, they are likely to feel less threatened and less defensive than if they are immediately confronted with the here and now. If the clinician has his own unresolved emotional problems, it is more beneficial to the client that he remain neutral than confront the client in a destructive way.

PART III *New Directions in Clinical Psychology*

CHAPTER 8 *Community Mental Health*

The community mental health movement, rapidly gaining support from all mental health professionals, represents an attempt to look beyond the individual, the traditional focus of study and treatment, in order to promote the mental health of the wider community. Its aim is to augment rather than replace individual psychotherapy by providing a clinical approach that greatly expands the concept of mental health, stresses the prevention of psychopathology in the community, as well as offers the usual treatment and rehabilitation programs for emotionally disturbed individuals. The long-standing imbalance in the delivery of mental health services, benefiting white middle- or upper-class neurotic adults almost exclusively, would be partially corrected by such an approach, which would provide inexpensive, easily available mental health services through clinics distributed throughout the community, particularly in large urban centers.

Many clinical psychologists are concerned that the rigid adherence to intensive individual psychotherapy as the major tool for treating psychological problems has many undesirable consequences:

1. Since they work exclusively with the individual, clinicians' theories concerning human behavior tend to be tied to intrapsychic factors—such as the id–ego–superego conflicts in psychoanalytic theory—rather than to the interaction of the individual and outside social forces.

2. These theories tend to have a strong middle-class bias and consequently are often inadequate in helping understand problems brought about by poverty, lack of education, job discrimination, and so on. In this regard, Gursslin, Hunt, and Roach (1964), in a content analysis of various mental health pamphlets, found them describing the middle-class prototype

and the mentally healthy prototype as equivalent in many respects. Values such as adjustment, conformity, work, problem solving, planning ahead, the control of emotions, striving, and community participation were considered desirable. Thus, even in the mental health movement, the middle-class ethic has been propagated despite its possible inappropriateness to the lower class.

3. Devoting 50-minute hours to individual patients for months or even years is a time-consuming and inefficient use of mental health manpower.

4. There is considerable skepticism about the effectiveness of individual psychotherapy even with relatively affluent and well educated people with less serious problems. In addition, psychotherapy has been shown to be for the most part inapplicable to many of the more serious emotional problems, such as schizophrenia.

5. The undemocratic, discriminatory nature of the delivery of most mental health services becomes less and less tolerable, particularly as the needs of the disadvantaged are becoming clearer. In this regard, Hollingshead and Redlich's (1958) monumental study of the relationship between social class and mental illness in New Haven, Connecticut, documented what most clinicians knew from experience—that the one variable determining the type of psychiatric treatment received was the socioeconomic status of the patient (see Figure 1, p. 16). These investigators found treatment to be unrelated to diagnosis, age, sex, or any other relevant variable aside from social class. While middle- and upper-class patients received some form of extended verbal psychotherapy, usually psychoanalysis, lower-class patients received brief, directive, mechanical treatment such as electroconvulsive shock therapy. This, despite an apparently higher incidence of psychiatric disorders in the lower classes.

MENTAL HEALTH'S THIRD REVOLUTION

As a result of a growing awareness of the limited nature of individual psychotherapy, a greater sense of public responsibility, and federal and local government involvement in mental health (see pp. 299–300), clinicians have begun to add community consultation to their usual individualized clinical services.[1] This transition in viewpoint and role has been termed

---

[1] This change in orientation has resulted in work with such diverse agencies as public health, welfare, rehabilitation, urban planning, police departments, schools, as well as mental health clinics, hospitals, and community centers. It has involved professionals

mental health's third revolution (Hobbs, 1964; Bellak, 1964). The first mental health revolution can be identified with Phillippe Pinel in France, William Tuke in England, and Benjamin Rush and Dorothea Dix in the United States (see pp. 48–52). It represented the then heretical view that insane people were human and should be treated with kindness and dignity. Sigmund Freud led the second revolution by directing attention to the intrapsychic life of man and emphasizing the influence of unconscious conflicts and their effect on personality development. The third revolution, while not identifiable with any one person, involves applying public health concepts and strategies to mental health services. All three revolutions have resulted in changing assumptions regarding mental health and mental disorders. Pinel's work led to the recognition that asylum inmates were ill, not possessed by the devil. Freud taught us that people are driven by forces over which they have no control, plagued as adults by the unresolved conflicts of childhood. The third revolution may show us that mental and emotional problems are not the private misery of an individual "but a social, ethical, and moral problem, a responsibility of the total community [Hobbs, 1964, p. 824]."

The new community mental health orientation reflects the influence of ideas from sociology, social welfare, mental hygiene, and public health. Its most noticeable feature is its shift in emphasis from an exclusive interest in individual psychopathology to a concern with improving the community's social well-being. Since communities are highly diverse and vary in their mental health resources as well as attitudes toward behavioral disorders, community mental health programs vary; treatment and preventive programs are tailored to the specific needs and problems of each community. For example, a program in a ghetto area might help individuals deal with feelings of bitterness, rage, and helplessness that result from overcrowding and poverty and that frequently end in criminal and other antisocial acts. A similar program in a suburb might attempt to help individuals cope with problems of restlessness, boredom, drug-use, or perhaps feelings of apathy or alienation. The community mental health approach, then, is an outlook and set of principles which are applied differently to different settings.

As a result of this new orientation, the clinical psychologist must adopt

and nonprofessionals alike. In addition to the psychiatrist, clinical psychologist, and social worker, consultation increasingly includes physicians, public health nurses, rehabilitation counselors, educators, neighborhood aides, and even parents (Bindman & Spiegel, 1969).

new roles and functions if he is to provide effective services to the community. Problems inevitably have arisen in regard to: (1) how and where the clinician is to receive training for these functions; (2) how he can learn to change from his customary emphasis on the individual; (3) how to understand social phenomena without resorting to explanations that are mere extrapolations from individual psychodynamics; (4) what is to be his relationship with other professionals and nonprofessionals in new situations where the customary roles and positions are inapplicable and the new ones largely undefined; and (5) what impact he can make on institutionalized patterns in the community (Cowen & Zax, 1967; Reiff, 1970).

Glidewell (1966) has distinguished between community mental health specialists and other specialists with overlapping functions. Social psychiatrists are more steeped in the medical tradition of the practitioner, apt to be more concerned about the health and welfare of the individual patient than the welfare of the community. The same may be said of the psychiatric social worker, clinically trained to know about community agencies, but only as they relate to helping the individual client. Glidewell believes the concerns of social welfare workers tend to be primarily economic and sometimes political rather than psychological and social, thus hampering their work as mental health consultants.

Glidewell (1966) and Rosenblum (1968) agree that clinical psychologists and public health nurses are the two mental health professional groups most interested and most successful in community consultation. While few in either group have received formal training in community mental health, both are deeply indoctrinated in the clinical tradition but have a broader exposure to psychology and the social sciences than psychiatrists do. Such a background permits an easy shift from the role of responsible practitioner to nondecision-making consultant. The public health nurse, while frequently lacking scientific knowledge about psychosocial phenomena, nevertheless has a long tradition of functioning in the community as a consultant rather than a practitioner who provides direct services.

HISTORICAL ANTECEDENTS OF COMMUNITY MENTAL HEALTH PRACTICES

The philosophies and many of the activities of the community mental health movement have been developing gradually since the late nineteenth century. The evolution of such a community-oriented outlook is typical of many of the ideals, if not always the practices, of American culture. The outlook is optimistic, humane, and socially conscious. In a sense, it reflects the cherished American belief, manifested recently by our achievements in landing men on the moon, that all problems are capable of solution if only we can discover the key through advanced scientific methodology, high purpose, dedication, and persistence. Ewalt and Ewalt (1969) report that an early paper, "The Prevention of Disease and Insanity" by Dr. Nathan Allen in 1878, urged the adoption of "correct views of the true way of living." Allen assumed a relationship between the environment and mental disease. Further, in keeping with what later was to be part of community mental health philosophy, he believed the environment could be modified by educating the public, fostering healthy habits of family life, and intervening in social institutions.

In the 1890s, psychopathic hospitals were introduced. Unlike remote asylums, these hospitals were located in the community they served. They were oriented toward early detection and treatment rather than custodial care. Patients' families were asked about the patient's life history. Students and physicians were trained to advance knowledge concerning mental illness. The interdisciplinary approach to mental health, so commonplace today, was first developed in these hospitals. Aftercare services to recently discharged asylum patients, initially the volunteer work of charitable lay-women, became professionalized in 1907, the year usually considered to mark the birth of the profession of psychiatric social work (Rossi, 1962).

The development of psychiatric and psychological clinics also represents an important landmark in the history of community mental health services. Psychiatric clinics initially operated in hospital facilities and provided only diagnostic services on an outpatient basis. By 1909, the New York State hospital system instituted a traveling clinic. In that same year, psychiatrist William Healy established the first community clinic for Chicago children. Marking the beginning of the child guidance movement, Healy's Juvenile Psychopathic Institute (later renamed the Institute for Juvenile Research) carried out diagnostic and treatment functions, while at the same time carrying out research on the etiology of mental disorders. Lightner Witmer's Psychological Clinic at the University of Pennsylvania also offered diagnostic and remedial services to children, particularly those with learning difficulties. Witmer urged his colleagues to leave the sheltered laboratory for the "larger laboratory . . . of the schoolroom, the juvenile courts, and the streets [Witmer, 1907, p. 7]." A forerunner of community mental health and clinical psychology, Witmer called for the then new profession of clinical psychology to draw closer to sociology, pedagogy, and medicine. Child guidance clinics developed rapidly, particularly in the 1920s. Lowrey and Smith (1933) have estimated that in 1921 seven such clinics existed, whereas by 1927 there were over 100. Typically, such clinics began to use a team approach, with psychiatrists, psychologists, and social workers each contributing their findings about each patient. Many of these early clinics were geared to the welfare of children and concerned themselves especially with problems of prevention, as in the case of juvenile delinquency.

These early clinics developed with the support and encouragement of citizen groups such as the National Committee for Mental Hygiene, established in 1908 (see pp. 51–52). The Committee helped establish clinics for children to deal with mental illness early. The Committee urged the development of preventive programs, as well as procedures for regularly inspecting mental institutions. During World War I, the efforts of the Committee were directed toward reducing the mental health problems of the armed forces, at the same time calling the public's attention to the value of mental health programs. These efforts represented the first attempts at bringing the mental hygiene movement into the broader context of public health. In the two decades between world wars, the emphasis of the Committee shifted to broad, community-oriented programs involving all mental health professionals and aimed at preventing mental illness and promoting mental health.

World War II and its aftermath caused a sudden rapid growth of the community mental health activities that had been developing slowly during the previous two decades. The records of the Selective Service System demonstrated the range and severity of mental disturbances in this country. After the war, the government remained involved in mental health services, particularly through the benefits of the Veterans Administration to ex-soldiers. As a result, today the Veterans Administration operates the largest network of psychiatric services provided in the United States (Stretch, 1967).

Mental health was gradually coming to be recognized as a major public health problem. Former Brigadier General William Menninger, head of war-time psychiatric services for the United States Armed Forces, after the war exhorted his colleagues to turn psychiatry toward tension resolution in the community (Menninger, 1948). The National Mental Health Act of 1946, passed partly because of the persistent lobbying of the National Committee for Mental Hygiene over several years, resulted in the creation of the National Institute of Mental Health (NIMH). A national base for research and training programs was thus created with federal financial support. The 1946 Act also provided federal monies to assist the states in establishing mental health services, lending further commitment to the state–federal partnership in mental health.

In 1955, Congress passed the National Mental Health Study Act establishing the Joint Commission on Mental Illness and Health. The creation of this commission to study and recommend a national mental health program, showed the highest government recognition that mental illness was the most pressing public health problem in the United States. Responding to their finding of a severe manpower shortage among mental health professionals, the commission recommended training nonprofessional mental health workers to be aides in community mental health programs. Another recommendation called for a greatly expanded community clinic program, setting as its objective one fully staffed, full-time mental health clinic available to each 50,000 people (Joint Commission on Mental Illness and Health, 1961). Thus was born the concept of community mental health centers.

On February 5, 1963, President Kennedy delivered to Congress his historic special message on mental illness and retardation. Basing his message in part on the recommendations of the Joint Commission, he called for a "bold new approach" to care for the mentally ill, offering early detection and treatment in their own community. He urged the strengthening of community resources to prevent mental disorders. He proposed that services try to minimize disruption of the normal living patterns of patients and their families as this would be far more beneficial than the traditional institutional care offered by large state hospitals.[2] In the same special message, the President proposed a similar program of prevention and treatment for the mentally retarded. Congress responded by passing the Community Mental Health Act of 1963.

The Community Mental Health Act of 1963 called for the cooperation of local, state, and federal agencies in attacking the nation's mental health

[2] The Joint Commission recommended ending construction of large mental hospitals and providing services to the mentally ill in local settings to maximize the individual's established social relations in his community.

problems. Substantial federal financing was to aid states in constructing and staffing community mental health centers. These centers, to operate according to state mental health plans, together were to form the core of a national mental health program. All 50 states responded by contributing a share of the cost and by drafting new programs to bolster and expand their existing mental health plans. In terms of finances alone, the extent of the commitment to mental health by the federal and state governments can be gauged by the following statistics: the total federal NIMH budget was $67 million in 1960, the year of the Joint Commission report; by 1968 it was $348 million. The states spent about $1 billion in 1960 and approximately $2.5 billion in 1968 (Ewalt & Ewalt, 1969). On the local level, numerous community clinics have been established with state and local fund sharing. The Mental Health Act in New York and the Short–Doyle Act in California were early examples of the establishment of statewide programs under such local administration.

COMMUNITY MENTAL HEALTH CENTERS

The National Institute of Mental Health has established guidelines and regulations that states must follow to be eligible for federal construction grants. Many community mental health centers have already been established, frequently by adding services, staff, and new programs to already existing psychiatric hospitals. Such centers have begun to play an increasingly important role in delivery of mental health services in the United States.

A major objective of this federally aided program is to establish a nationwide network of local mental health services. Each center, for example, is expected to provide comprehensive mental health services to geographically limited population groups of 75,000 to 200,000 persons. For each center, a specific geographic catchment area is defined in regard to patient eligibility for services, ensuring that clinical services will be available reasonably close to the patient's residential area. Since the principal determination of a catchment area's boundaries is population density rather than geographic size, it is not unusual for an inner-city slum area of several blocks to qualify as one area, while two adjacent sparsely populated states might together make up another catchment area. In addition to physical proximity, residents of a community are expected to develop a functional attachment to a local center, supporting the center's operations financially and otherwise.

TYPES OF CLINICAL SERVICES

In order to be eligible for federal funding, each center must provide a comprehensive and coordinated range of services. That is, the center is expected to play a variety of roles in the community, offering a wide range of services which can be individually tailored to the nature and stage of a person's emotional disorder, his age, socioeconomic circumstance, and so on. Five distinct sets of services have been designated by NIMH as essential to the operation of a community mental health center:

1. *Inpatient care* for those who need intensive treatment
2. *Outpatient care,* like that generally provided in an outpatient clinic
3. *Partial hospitalization,* providing at least day care and treatment for patients able to return home evenings and weekends, as well as night care for those able to work but lacking suitable home arrangements
4. *Emergency care* on a 24-hour basis
5. *Consultation and educational services* to community agencies and professional personnel.

In addition to these essential features, certain desirable services were specified to complete a comprehensive community mental health center program:

6. *Diagnostic services,* including evaluations and recommendations for appropriate care
7. *Rehabilitation* services, including social and vocational rehabilitation
8. *Precare and aftercare,* ranging from screening patients prior to possible hospital admission, to home visits and follow-up services in outpatient clinics, foster homes, or halfway houses after hospitalization
9. *Training* for all mental health personnel, professional as well as nonprofessional
10. *Research and evaluation programs,* investigating the effectiveness of the center's services and research into the problems and treatment of mental illness.

Community mental health center staffs typically include various mental health professionals (psychiatrists, clinical psychologists, psychiatric social workers, public health nurses) as well as nonprofessionals trained to perform clinical and nonclinical jobs. The manpower shortage, already critical, continues to be an even greater problem if such an extensive set of clinical services is to be maintained. It is difficult to see at this time how the 2000 new comprehensive mental health centers expected to be in operation by 1980 can be staffed (Albee, 1968).

Many clinical psychologists have also been concerned by the continued adherence to the medical model. With the exception of consultation and educational programs, the five essential services, in particular, reflect a traditional medical view of treating disease rather than improving community mental health. Many psychologists are concerned, too, that medical domination will place them in secondary, ancillary positions to psychiatrists, despite the recommendation of the Joint Commission that roles and responsibilities be based on individual competence rather than professional title. Perhaps to calm some of these fears, Stanley Yolles, then Director of the National Institute of Mental Health, reported to a conference of psychologists that they were considered co-professionals in the treatment aspect of the program. In addition, Yolles, himself a psychiatrist, suggested that while psychiatrists continue to be trained to treat the mentally ill, psychologists had an opportunity to make each center "a community agent of illness prevention and promotion of health [Yolles, 1966, p. 40]." Nevertheless, most centers remain under medical administration and direction. A position paper by the APA (Smith & Hobbs, 1966) has urged that a wide range of community representatives be actively involved in setting goals and determining policies if comprehensive community mental health centers are to become effective community agencies. Moreover, APA cautioned against simply applying traditional clinical approaches, albeit in a new setting.

THE ROLE OF THE CLINICAL PSYCHOLOGIST

Just as many of the roles and functions of the clinical psychologist after World War II were determined by the needs of Veterans Administration hospitals, so many new roles have emerged from the recent commitment to community mental health. The roles available to the clinical psychologist in a community mental health center have been categorized by Rosenblum (1968) as follows:

1. *Diagnostician* and *therapist*
2. *Community mental health consultant* to schools, police, and other

social agencies, helping community caregiving agents to make use of mental health principles in their work

3. *Teacher* in inservice education and training programs

4. *Supervisor* of mental health professionals and nonprofessionals

5. *Researcher* surveying community resources, needs, and attitudes, carrying out biometrical and epidemiological studies on the development and prevention of psychopathology or evaluating existing center programs

6. *Administrator* of one or more aspects of community mental health center programs, who is involved in planning, staffing, and financing the program

7. *Change agent* participating directly in anti-poverty or community social action programs in the community

8. *Innovator–conceptualizer* helping community leaders analyze local mental health problems in order to formulate new programs aimed at alleviating or reducing the problems

9. *Lobbyist* helping promote new legislation toward increased social well-being of community members.

The rapid expansion of roles for clinical psychologists in community-oriented mental health programs has highlighted the need for more appropriate university training programs. In 1965, a Conference on the Education of Psychologists for Community Mental Health was held in Boston under the sponsorship of Boston University and the South Shore Mental Health Center of Quincy, Massachusetts (Bennett, Anderson, Cooper, Hassol, Klein, & Rosenblum, 1966). It was soon clear to the participants from various universities, all of whom were involved with clinical training, that it was time for psychologists to define their unique roles in the field of mental health, and then develop new training programs commensurate with these new models. The broad field of community psychology was recognized, encompassing many of the activities and concerns of clinical psychologists, social psychologists, and others. In general, community psychology was defined as being "devoted to the study of general psychological processes that link social systems with individual behavior in complex interaction [Bennett et al., 1966, p. 7]." Social system analysis, psychological ecology, social action programs, normal human development in various social settings, conflict resolution, community organizations, and community mental health were all considered areas of interest or subspecialties of community psychology, with clinical psychology as a variant of community mental health. As a result of the conference, a number of new training programs in community psychology have been started in various parts of the United States (Iscoe & Spielberger, 1970). In addition, APA created Division 27, the Division of Community Psychology, attesting to considerable interest among clinicians and other psychologists in developing this latest specialty.

THE PRACTICE OF COMMUNITY MENTAL HEALTH

Community mental health programs are likely to include the following practices:

1. Contacting new, previously unreached populations (low-income groups)

2. Using new treatment methods that go beyond individual one-to-one relationships (family therapy, group therapy, crisis intervention, therapeutic communities in mental hospitals)

3. Using new kinds of treatment facilities (community mental health centers, day-and-night centers) that link the individual and his community

4. Training nonprofessionals to perform roles previously considered the exclusive province of highly trained mental health professionals

5. Focusing on prevention programs in the community, applying the public health orientation to mental health

6. Increasing interdisciplinary outlook so that roles and leadership become more determined by individual competence

7. Increasing collaboration with community agencies—particularly those offering mental health services—thus focusing on the community at large as a social system

8. Trying to provide comprehensive services to all age groups, diagnostic groups, and geographically distributed groups

9. Researching community needs, resources, populations, incidence of psychopathology, and the effectiveness of available mental health services

10. Studying the origins, geographic distribution, and the risk of mental illness in a given community and conditions in the host environment

11. Supporting rehabilitation programs (sheltered workshops, halfway houses, home visitations)

12. Offering consultation and educational programs to professionals, nonprofessionals, and the public at large.

COMMUNITY-WIDE PREVENTION PROGRAMS

Preventing behavioral disorders is one of the most innovative aspects of community mental health, although few programs with this purpose are operating. The concept of prevention is borrowed from public health medicine. Typically, the public health worker is concerned with how prevalent an illness is as well as the morbidity and disability it causes. When one or more of these is high, he attempts to organize a control program in the community. Such programs attack the problem in two ways, by promoting good health practices and by offering specific protection, if available, against the disease. Such efforts to reduce or eradicate the incidence of a disorder, ultimately preventing its occurrence, are called primary prevention. Secondary prevention attempts to identify and treat disorders as early as possible in order to reduce their length and severity. Tertiary prevention deals with a disorder that has already occurred, minimizing whatever long-term impairment that results. All three types of prevention have been incorporated into community mental health programs.

Three approaches to primary prevention in public health can be differentiated: community-wide, milestone, and high-risk, (Bloom, 1968). In the community-wide approach, virtually all residents of a community continuously receive the program; efforts against cholera and typhoid fever through water purification are examples. The milestone approach offers protection from the disease at some milestone; for example, vaccinating children against smallpox when they enter kindergarten. The third approach, which Bloom calls high-risk, aims to identify those groups particularly vulnerable to specific disease conditions. Once identified, programs are specially tailored to the group to reduce or prevent the disorder; for example, machinists using grinding equipment must wear eye shields and coal miners must use breathing filters.

One way to apply the concept of *primary prevention* to mental health might be to lower the rate of new cases of mental disorders in a population by counteracting harmful circumstances in the environment before they produce the disorder (Caplan, 1964). Milestone programs might include mental health education when one enters school, enters the work force, marries, becomes a parent, or retires. High-risk programs might aim at specific groups who are particularly vulnerable to emotional and behavioral disorders, such as the recently widowed or divorced, children from a broken home, the elderly, the recently immigrated, the chronically unemployed, those who have recently attempted suicide, or those who are experiencing a crisis (see Chapter 9).

The public health approach to prevention seeks to reduce the risk of mental illness for the entire community by attacking those factors believed to be responsible for the disorder in large segments of the population. Early diagnosis and treatment in medicine have never been sufficient to eradicate or control a disease, nor can mental illness prevention be expected to do better. Moreover, despite efforts to increase the number of mental health workers, there can never be enough therapists for everyone requiring psychotherapy. Instead, the public health approach is to intervene as early as possible in the community by introducing primary prevention programs. Prenatal clinics, family planning centers, and Project Head Start for preschool children are examples of early intervention programs to which principles of prevention of emotional disorders can be applied. Another approach is to provide services for individuals in maturational crises (such as kindergarten entry, menopause, retirement) or situational crises (divorce) as a means of preventing the development of emotional disorders.

Primary prevention programs are aimed at groups rather than specific individuals in an effort to remove those harmful agents that can potentially affect all members of the community. When a primary prevention program deals with an individual, he is seen as a representative of a group; his treatment is determined not only by his needs but also in relation to the community problem he represents. Information from his case forms a broader picture of the members of his group or class. Instead of neglecting the individual, such a community focus takes on a wider responsibility for the welfare of the population as a whole. Studying not only why one individual becomes disordered but also why others in similar circumstances remain healthy increases our knowledge about what determines human resistance to stress.

Despite the obvious appeal of the goal of primary prevention—to reduce the incidence of mental disorders—such programs are extremely difficult to implement in practice. Sometimes changes in the whole social system are necessary if the entire community is to benefit. Offering help to those who have not sought it and may distrust it presents an additional problem. There is, too, a lack of professional manpower to carry out such a monumental task. Finally, there is the question of whether clinical psychologists, or even the new breed of community psychologists, have the know-how, the training, or the power to bring about community change. Clinicians, trained to treat clients on a one-to-one basis, are frequently at a loss when confronted with the issues of institutional changes. Reiff (1966) has concluded that at present the prospect of any really effective primary prevention program in community mental health is minimal. Bower (1963), on the other hand, has suggested a number of possibilities for prevention programs (see Table 10).

Even if successful primary preventive programs can be mounted, they cannot hope to be very effective until a great deal more is known about the separate etiology of specific mental disorders. Today, public health workers use concepts of secondary and tertiary prevention, both applicable to the field of mental health. *Secondary prevention* is an effort to reduce the prevalence of mental disorders by shortening the duration, reducing the symptoms, limiting the consequences, and minimizing their effects on others. In this way, partial prevention is achieved through early diagnosis and effective treatment of individuals who exhibit signs of emotional disturbance. This concept underscores what clinicians typically do, except that it highlights the effort to identify disturbances early in an individual's life or early in the life of the disorder, whenever they occur. Through community-wide screening procedures (in the public schools or the armed forces), rapid referral, local emergency services (such as walk-in clinics) open around the clock, no waiting lists, and prompt treatment with attainable goals, the impact of developing emotional disturbances may be kept to a minimum (Eisenberg & Greenberg, 1961). For example, emergency counseling with college students temporarily disturbed by personal stresses and/or those due to academic pressures, is usually effective if begun promptly. Since so much of the efforts at prevention occur at the secondary level, producing increased pressure for more manpower, nonprofessionals trained to detect signs of emotional disturbance or early signs of psychopathology are particularly helpful at this stage.

Tertiary prevention aims at limiting the disability and promoting the rehabilitation of individuals with mental disorders. By returning such an individual to his productive capacity as quickly as possible, the social and

Table 10. Suggestions for possible primary prevention programs applicable to various institutions and agencies*

INSTITUTIONS AND AGENCIES	NORMAL EMOTIONAL HAZARD	POSSIBILITIES FOR PREVENTIVE ACTION
1. Family	Loss of father through death, divorce, or desertion	Reinforcement of child-care services for working mothers
	Loss of mother	Reinforcement of foster-home services
	Adolescence	Increase in staff and professionalization of high school counselors, deans, and vice-principals
	Birth of sibling	Pediatric or well-baby clinic counseling
	Death	Management of grief—religious or community agency worker
2. Public health	Phenylketonuria (a form of mental retardation)	Detection and diet
	Childhood illnesses	Vaccination, immunization
	Stress caused by children—economic, housing, etc.	Reinforcement of well-baby clinic through mental health consultation to staff
	Pregnancy	Adequate prenatal care for mothers of lower socioeconomic status
3. School	Birth of sibling	Recognition of event by school and appropriate intervention
	School entrance of child	Screening vulnerable children
	Intellectual retardation	Special classes and assistance
	Teacher concern and anxiety about a child's behavior	Consultation by mental health specialists
	School failure	Early identification and prevention through appropriate school program
4. Religion	Marriage	Counseling by clergy
5. Job or profession	Promotion or demotion	Opportunity to define role through services of a mental health counselor
6. Recreation	Appropriate and rewarding use of leisure time	Active community and city recreational programs
7. Housing	Lack of space, need for privacy	Working with architects and housing developers

* Eli M. Bower, "Primary Prevention of Mental and Emotional Disorders: A Conceptual Framework and Action Possibilities," *American Journal of Orthopsychiatry*, 1963, **33**, 844. Copyright ©, the American Orthopsychiatric Association, Inc. Reprinted by permission.

occupational life of the community is improved. In the case of the hospitalized patient, tertiary prevention is concerned with preventing or reversing the social chronicity that frequently results from long-term institutionalization. Thus, periods of hospitalization are kept to a minimum and leaves of absence from the hospital are encouraged when feasible. Contact between the patient and his family, friends, and co-workers is maintained to continue communication between hospital and community. Community-based agencies such as day treatment centers or halfway houses have begun replacing community-isolated total-care institutions, such as large state mental hospitals. They are likely to provide rehabilitation through aftercare services, home visits, or self-help groups in which the ex-patient might participate with other former mental patients. A model for such an approach to prevention is Alcoholics Anonymous. Some community mental health centers now house local chapters of A. A., tying alcoholism to emotional problems and emphasizing their common commitment to prevention, treatment, and rehabilitation.

MENTAL HEALTH CONSULTATION

In addition to providing direct clinical services such as diagnosis and psychotherapy to individuals in emotional distress, the clinician with a community mental health orientation also may offer indirect clinical services, such as mental health consultation, to other professionals without making direct contact with individual patients or clients. In particular, the growing concern with prevention has led many clinical psychologists to assist the caretaking agents in the community (physicians, teachers, ministers, policemen, vocational counselors) in applying mental health principles to the performance of their usual professional roles. In smaller communities these clinicians are sometimes the only available source of professional expertise for developing locally based human welfare services. For example, Libo (1966) has described such consultative activities in New Mexico, involving sustained state-wide contacts with agencies, organizations, and practitioners in public health, welfare, education, clergy, medicine, recreation, county and municipal government, probation, parole, police departments, courts, hospitals, home extension clubs, civic organizations, and others.

The clinical psychologist as a public mental health consultant generally functions as a resource person, helping the professional workers in a community to: (1) increase their understanding and sensitivity to their clients; (2) function more effectively with their co-workers; (3) learn to detect early signs of mental illness; (4) make referrals to other mental health personnel when appropriate; (5) develop a conceptual framework of the aims of their agency's programs in order to analyze and plan such programs more effectively; and (6) develop a research methodology for evaluating the effectiveness of all of the agency's programs. Such consultation is usually offered to key administrators and supervisors to maximize their agency's effectiveness and ultimately enhance their staff's knowledge of mental health principles; it is not designed to teach such clinical techniques as psychotherapy.

Perhaps the best known and most influential consultation model is provided by Caplan (1970). Caplan views mental health consultation as an interaction between two professionals—the consultant, who is a specialist, and the consultee, who asks for help with a work problem. Such work problems are likely to involve how the consultee should treat one or more clients or how to plan and implement a program for certain clients. Professional responsibility for the client and any action taken for the client's benefit remains with the consultee. The consultee is free to accept or reject the consultant's suggestions. The consultant is usually a member of another profession and is employed outside the agency rather than a supervisor or administrator within the agency whose judgments must be accepted. In Caplan's model, the consultant has no predetermined body of information that he intends to impart to a consultee. Instead, he responds to the consultee's specific work difficulty, helping him to resolve it and thus increase his capacity to master similar future problems.

Caplan sees mental health consultation as an opportunity for a relatively small number of consultants to affect a community far more than they could through direct services. He differentiates four fundamental types of mental health consultation:

Case consultation: client-centered. This is the most commonly practiced form of mental health consultation. The two professionals discuss a particular case or group of cases. The consultant may assess the nature of the client's problem and recommend how to help him. This model is similar to a medical specialist offering his expert opinion on diagnosis and treatment to a general practitioner whose patient's problems are sufficiently complicated that he does not feel competent to handle them satisfactorily by himself.

Case consultation: consultee-centered. This form of consultation aims to remedy shortcomings in a consultee's professional functioning that are responsible for his difficulties with the case about which he is seeking consultation. The consultee's difficulties may be due to lack of knowledge about the type of problem the client presents, lack of professional skill, lack of self-confidence so that he is uncertain how to use his knowledge or skill, or lack of objectivity because of too great an emotional involvement. The focus of the consultation is not on the client but on the consultee, with the primary goal of improving his future professional performance by helping him overcome his particular difficulty.

Administrative consultation: program-centered. Here the consultant is invited by the agency administrator to help plan and administer new programs, evaluate existing programs, or help with organizational policies, including personnel difficulties. If the consultant is an expert in mental health program development and administration, he may be asked to study the agency's problems, assess the significance of the various factors contributing to the problems, and then report his appraisal and recommendations for alleviating the problems. This model resembles a management consultant firm's services to a big business or government organization, except that the consultant must be an expert in both mental health and administration.

Administrative consultation: consultee-centered. In this form of consultation, the specialist is called in by the agency's administrator to help the staff develop an improved capacity to master problems in the planning and maintenance of community mental health programs. The consultant focuses on remedying difficulties among the consultees that interfere with the task of program development and organization. For example, he may want to examine staff turnover rates in various departments, absenteeism, or sickness rates. He probably will want to talk to as many staff members as possible to make his analysis. Leadership patterns, lines of communication, intragroup tensions, and the decision-making process are all likely to be studied. Consultant intervention may take place at an individual, group, or organization level.

USE OF NONPROFESSIONALS AS MENTAL HEALTH AIDES

Just as consultative services allow relatively few mental health professionals to affect a community beyond their number, so the training of nonprofessionals for mental health services provides another such opportunity. Numerous training programs in the last five years have produced more than 500,000 nonprofessionals in various public services (Grosser, Henry, & Kelly, 1969). So successful have most of these training programs been that some predict training and supervision of nonprofessionals will one day replace one-to-one contact with clients as the mental health professional's major service (Guerney, 1969).

Several factors have contributed to the increased reliance on the services of nonprofessionals. The Joint Commission's report urged the training and employment of nonprofessionals to help reduce the manpower shortage. President Kennedy's call for a program of positive mental health focused on using community resources. An increasing militancy among low-income groups demanded some role in extending such services into their own communities. Mental health professionals have become increasingly aware that current clinical services either did not reach the low-income populations where the need was most acute or were inappropriate to the problems presented by the poor and uneducated. Further, there was growing recognition that extensive academic training did not necessarily produce more effective clinicians.[3] Caught up in the sweep of social change in America, many mental health professionals recognized that their social responsibilities took precedence over protecting their personal status or professional guilds. The earlier hierarchy of roles between professions and an orderly assignment of duties and responsibilities based on such roles began to give way. Instead, new community-based mental health programs developed, using the collaborative services of nonprofessionals with complementary, if not identical, competencies.

Reiff and Riessman (1965) draw the useful distinction between ubiquitous nonprofessionals and indigenous nonprofessionals. The *ubiquitous nonprofessional* is likely to have the same social background, the same

---

[3] Carkhuff and Berenson (1967) report an actual deterioration in therapeutic effectiveness after graduate training. Ironically, their results suggest that professional therapists never again achieve the level of therapeutic functioning they had on entering graduate school. Moreover, their data reveal that those graduate students best able to help bring about constructive changes in their clients received the lowest grade in their training programs!

attitudes and values, and to some extent, the same educational background as professionals. Middle-class housewives, college students, parents, and teachers are included in this group. Their contribution, particularly as aides to professionals, has been documented in numerous reports (Guerney, 1969). *Indigenous nonprofessionals* are from the lower socioeconomic groups. More than simply meeting a manpower shortage, they may be more effective in a lower-class environment than professionals because they have a natural role in that environment and are likely to have experienced problems similar to those of their clients. Also, such employment frequently serves to inspire further self-help activities—perhaps continuing one's education—as well as result in an increased sense of self-worth from those participating in the helping role (Pearl & Riessman, 1965).

An important contribution of the indigenous nonprofessional stems from his ability to serve as a bridge between the middle-class professional and his clients from the lower socioeconomic groups. He is less likely to arouse suspicion or distrust than the professional, who is often suspect as an outsider who may have come to study, patronize, or exploit residents. His suggestions are more likely than the professional's to be realistic because of his knowledge of the neighborhood and its inhabitants—for example, he knows that the community is likely to embrace external rather than intrapsychic explanations of behavior. His practical, down-to-earth orientation balances the professional's more theoretical approach.

Nonprofessionals, then, are a mixed group. Some are partially trained while others have no formal training at all. Some may be resuming training in order to support families, as in the case of ex-housewives. Others may see potential jobs or new careers in the expanding mental health services.

In a recent survey of over 10,000 nonprofessionals working in 185 NIMH-sponsored projects across the United States (Sobey, 1970), it was found that their major function has not been to relieve professional staffs of tasks requiring less than professional expertise, as might have been expected. Instead, nonprofessionals are being trained for new service roles and functions, many of which were not part of previous mental health programs. Table 11 shows the variety of mental health roles played by nonprofessionals in the various projects surveyed. Nonprofessionals probably perform an even greater variety of tasks than could be categorized in the survey questionnaire on which Table 11 is based. Moreover, the potential of new nonprofessional roles and functions seems to have been

Table 11. Distribution of nonprofessional staff categories in 185 NIMH-sponsored projects*

STAFF CATEGORY	NUMBER OF NON-PROFESSIONALS	PERCENT
Tutor teacher aides	2,267	21.7
Recreation and groupwork aides	2,092	20.0
Nursing and ward personnel	1,758	16.9
Other staff categories (other than listed)	1,122	10.8
Home visitors–enablers	1,020	9.8
Case aides	666	6.4
Physical, occupational, vocational, rehabilitation aides	355	3.4
Neighborhood community organizers	293	2.8
Special skill instructors	279	2.7
Community mental health aides	268	2.6
Reach-out aides	185	1.8
Foster parents	60	0.6
Homemakers	52	0.5
Total staff	10,417	100.0%

* From Francine Sobey: *The Nonprofessional Revolution in Mental Health.* New York: Columbia University Press, 1970, page 76. Reprinted by permission of the publisher.

scarcely tapped. Nonprofessionals were found to be employed in psychiatric hospitals, clinics and rehabilitation centers, general hospitals, correction agencies, public assistance programs, settlement houses, public health facilities, and in neighborhood organizations involved in citizen mobilization and participation. They participated in programs at all levels of prevention, treatment, and rehabilitation. Considering all 185 projects together, Sobey found the overall manpower ratio to be six nonprofessionals for every professional participant. Nonprofessionals were performing direct therapeutic services such as individual, group, and milieu therapy; they screened clients in a way that went beyond a merely clerical method; they helped clients adjust to the community; they offered special skills such as tutoring; they promoted self-help by involving clients with others having similar problems. Overwhelmingly, the professional project directors approved of the services performed by nonprofessionals as more than justifying the cost, training, and supervision time involved.

However, potential pitfalls of nonprofessional services should be noted. Even this breakthrough cannot close the manpower gap. As the supply of mental health services increases because more manpower is available, the demand for these services will accelerate even faster, soon outstripping the supply. Riessman (1970) has suggested that, contrary to previously held notions, the poor do seek mental health services when clinics are available in their communities, establish a receptive image, and offer appropriate services. Early detection and treatment (secondary prevention) has multiplied caseloads in community mental health centers. When mental health services are kept relatively free of stigma, self-referrals among the poor have increased. The use of auxiliary manpower provided by nonprofessionals has helped meet some of the demand, but it has been argued that they cannot hope to keep up with the demand, and moreover, that they provide second-class service. Some critics have been concerned that the danger in using nonprofessionals is that the service they offer is apt to be determined more by what this less expensive manpower is able to provide than what the client requires. Despite these objections, nonprofessionals can and must be trained. More experience and research is still necessary to determine the range of mental health roles for which they can be prepared, the most effective way to recruit, train, and supervise nonprofessionals, the best ways to overcome the resistance still found among many professionals, and finally what changes in roles and functions among mental health professionals will come about as a result of what Sobey calls the "nonprofessional revolution in mental health."

RESEARCH IN COMMUNITY MENTAL HEALTH

The clinical psychologist has a key role in planning, executing, evaluating, and communicating the results of community mental health research. With such an abundance of new programs, the clinical psychologist has an urgent responsibility to use his research training to study and evaluate the effectiveness of such programs. In doing so, however, he must shift from the laboratory, where research conditions are easily controlled, to study the broader, more complex but less easily defined and controlled events and conditions in the community. He may have to abandon research using a captive population (college students, hospitalized patients, prisoners) in order to study whole populations in their natural habitats. Rather than focus on individual behavior, he needs to attend to the social structure in which that behavior occurs. He needs to study the effect of social organizations on the individual to discover, through research, what social conditions reduce stress and promote mental health. All these unique features of community mental health research call for new settings as well as new research methods. Four research methods in particular are applicable to studies of community mental health: (1) epidemiological methods; (2) survey methods; (3) ecological methods; and (4) program evaluation methods.

EPIDEMIOLOGICAL METHODS

Epidemiology is an established medical public health speciality. Its practitioners attempt to determine the risk of attack by specific disorders in a community and to uncover clues about their origin and how they spread. The distribution of the disease and the distinguishing characteristics of affected individuals or social groups are particularly relevant. Once known, the epidemiologist concerns himself with devising measures of disease prevention or control and assessing the efficacy of such efforts through research. So successful has this approach been that epidemiology is considered the basic science in preventive medicine (Reid, 1960).

Epidemiological studies of mental disorders are not new, although there has been a marked increase in such studies in the last decade. Thus, Faris and Dunham, in their classic 1939 study of mental disorders in Chicago, found schizophrenia to be concentrated in areas of extreme social disorganization. Hollingshead and Redlich (1958) have also demonstrated the higher incidence of schizophrenia among the lower social classes of an urban community. The well-known Midtown Manhattan Study (Srole et al., 1961; Langner & Michael, 1963) identified more than 80 percent of a sample of New York City residents as belonging in some category of mental disorder, with perhaps 25 percent seriously impaired. Socioeconomic status was found to be the principal demographic variable related to mental illness, confirming the previously published findings. Table 12 reveals psychiatrists' "mental health ratings" of the 1660 respondents in the Midtown Manhattan Study. According to these results, less than 20 percent of the area's residents can be considered to be well (that is, without psychiatric symptoms).

Epidemiology in medicine and public health has traditionally concerned itself with infections or communicable diseases, although non-infectious ailments, such as heart disease as well as emotional disorders

Table 12. Distribution of 1660 respondents in Midtown Manhattan Study according to mental health categories based on severity of symptoms and associated impairment*

MENTAL HEALTH CATEGORY	DESCRIPTION OF CATEGORY	PERCENT IN CATEGORY	
Well	No evidence of symptom formation (symptom-free)	18.5	
Mild symptoms	Mild symptom formation but functioning adequately	36.3	
Moderate symptoms	Moderate symptom formation with no apparent interference in life adjustment	21.8	
Impaired		23.4	
Marked symptoms	Moderate symptom formation with some interference in life adjustment		13.2
Severe symptoms	Serious symptom formation, yet functioning with great difficulty		7.5
Incapacitated	Seriously incapacitated, unable to function		2.7

* Langner & Michael, *Life Stress and Mental Health.* Copyright 1963, The Macmillan Company. Reprinted by permission of the publisher.

(suicide, alcoholism), have begun to be studied. Such an approach attempts to determine what factors contribute to the prevalence of the disorder as well as the incidence of new cases within a community, whether it is a large city neighborhood, a rural town, a housing project, a military unit, a college, or a factory. Psychiatric disorders in a community may be studied in terms of rates, specific high-risk populations, the distribution of disorders by age, sex, ethnic group, social class, the availability of clinical services, the use of services by various groups, and so on. As a result, preventive intervention programs aimed at reducing specific environmental stresses and strengthening individual coping capacities may be instituted. At this point, however, we usually lack the empirical research data to support such programs. One notable exception is Mednick and Schulsinger's data (1965), which suggest that children of schizophrenic mothers are more likely than children of normal mothers to themselves become schizophrenic (see pp. 18–19). This promising epidemiological approach to identifying high-risk groups is an example of what can be generically called vulnerability research (Garmezy, 1971). While Mednick and Schulsinger have stressed genetic predispositions in families, vulnerability research in general may look to any set of factors (genetic loadings, excessive family disorganization, faulty prenatal or neonatal care, the sociocultural environment) which identify those children in a community who have a high risk of later onset of severe psychopathology.

Results from epidemiological research are frequently reported in correlational form. That is, factors associated with high and low rates of the disease are distinguished. While such an approach works well when the disease is easily diagnosed (cholera and tuberculosis, for example), many problems arise when dealing with behavioral disorders. Depending on how behavioral disorders are defined, their prevalance may vary enormously. Some clinicians actually believe in a strict definition that includes 100 percent of the population as having certain mental problems. On the other hand, if criteria were less stringent, perhaps 10 to 20 percent might be included. As part of the procedure in the Midtown Manhattan Study, a sample of 1660 people from Manhattan's East Side (population 174,000) answered a long, detailed questionnaire collected by trained interviewers. These answers then were analyzed by psychiatrists and each participant was diagnosed and given a mental health rating based on degree of impairment (see Table 12). While the overall social psychiatry approach holds much promise, nevertheless numerous sources of unreliability are inherent in such a data-gathering technique. Some interviewers are better trained, more skilled, or sensitive than others. Some may have been biased in the direction of looking for illness. The psychiatrists, not having actually seen the subjects, may have had the same bias. Defining mental illness by the presence of any symptoms is likely to cause both interviewer and psychiatrist to look for these symptoms, which he then is almost certain to find. In research terms, it frequently is impossible to separate which crucial factors—genetic, social, or environmental—account for the presence of high rates of mental disorders, particularly since there is no untouched comparison group available.

Nevertheless, the results from epidemiological research, based on improved methods of collecting and interpreting data, can be extremely valuable in establishing prevention programs. It would be worthwhile to study those commonly occurring life events that are apt to lead to emotional crises so that more meaningful programs of prevention or intervention could be instituted. It would also be valuable to compare the incidence of a particular mental disorder in various subgroups, at the same time looking for any reasons why that disorder might be absent when the suspected cause is present. The National Institute of Mental Health has planned to establish field stations across the United States to collect just such information on psychiatric patients and services as well as on mental health problems in rural, urban, and semiurban areas (Yolles, 1968).

Epidemiological research is necessarily longitudinal. It requires extensive data collected over an extended time-period. Studying the incidence of a disorder requires that the rate of occurrence of new cases over a prolonged period be determined. While the incidence of the disorder may be relatively low, its duration in time is likely to be high, again necessitating a long time span for study. Moreover, the onset of the disorder usually occurs over a substantial period of years. Attempts at a retrospective analysis of the etiology of the disorder are likely to be filled with conjecture, distorting the conclusions. Instead, Klein (1968) suggests a longitudinal study of a group of individuals born in a given interval of time and followed by means of successive observations over a specific period of years. While many practical problems must be met, the masses of data from such a study would be invaluable.

SURVEY METHODS

Survey research methods use systematic efforts to analyze the characteristics of large samples of the population (demographic studies) or of the community (ecological studies) to accumulate knowledge about community phenomena related to mental health. By using interviews, questionnaires, and actuarial records, general mental health problems in the community can be identified. In addition, the attitudes and perceptions of individuals in the community can be surveyed. Community needs and available resources can then be compared. Such knowledge is essential in planning intervention programs aimed at both rehabilitation and prevention.

The basic data for such research come from demographic studies, which describe age, sex, race, religion, marital status, household composition, education, occupation, family income, housing characteristics, and so on. These data describe in quantitative terms the social, cultural, and ethnic milieu of the population to be served (Bahn, 1965). For example, useful information can be obtained on the number of elderly people living alone, the number of children living with one parent only, the number and characteristics of immigrants in the target area. Taken together, a survey of the life situations and coping styles can be obtained. Such population surveys, repeated periodically, help with the early identification of psychosocial problems in the community and with planning of community service programs.

Periodic surveillance research can provide useful information about community processes: marriages, divorces, suicides, the prevalence of nonhospitalized individuals with serious emotional disorders, wide-spread fears, rumors, attitudes, morale. Upon understanding the pattern of these phenomena in a community, certain social action programs can be begun. These programs may be specific goal-oriented mental health education programs tailored either to specific populations or to types of problems unique to a specific community. Biostatistics (the analysis of vital statistics) and biometrics (the statistical analysis of biological data), two well-established public health specialties, can be useful in evaluating the effectiveness of new programs of intervention.

National surveys have attempted to discover American attitudes toward mental health, why people go for psychiatric help and to whom they go for such help. One such survey (Gurin, Veroff, & Feld, 1960) interviewed 2460 people coast to coast. Of the 345 respondents reported to have gone somewhere with a personal problem (Table 13), the highest proportion (42 percent) sought resolution of their marital difficulties. A large portion (18 percent) sought help for general adjustment problems, feelings of un-

Table 13. Nature of personal problems for which people sought professional help ($N = 345$)*

PROBLEM AREA	PERCENT
Spouse; marriage	42%
Child; relationship with child	12%
Other family relationships–parents, in-laws	5%
Other relationship problems; type of relationship problem unspecified	4%
Job or school problems; vocational choice	6%
Nonjob adjustment problems in the self (general adjustment, specific symptoms)	18%
Situational problems involving other people (that is, death or illness of a loved one) causing extreme psychological reaction	6%
Nonpsychological situational problems	8%
Nothing specific; a lot of little things; can't remember	2%
Not ascertained	1%

* From *Americans View Their Mental Health* by G. Gurin, J. Veroff, and S. Feld. Copyright 1960 by Basic Books, Inc. Reprinted by permission. Total is more than 100 percent because some respondents gave more than one response.

happiness, and the presence of specific symptoms, usually psychogenic in origin. Once recognizing the personal problem to be beyond one's own ability to solve, a troubled person was found to choose further help from a number of alternative sources (Table 14). The most frequently consulted

Table 14. Source of help used by people who have sought professional help for a personal problem (N = 345)*

SOURCE OF HELP	PERCENT
Clergyman	42%
Physician	29%
Psychiatrist (or psychologist): private practitioner or not ascertained whether private or institutional	12%
Psychiatrist (or psychologist) in clinic, hospital, other agency; mental hospital	6%
Marriage counselor; marriage clinic	3%
Other private practitioners or social agencies for handling psychological problems	10%
Social service agencies for handling nonpsychological problems (such as financial problems)	3%
Lawyer	6%
Other	11%

* From *Americans View Their Mental Health* by G. Gurin, J. Veroff, and S. Feld. Copyright 1960 by Basic Books, Inc. Reprinted by permission. Total is more than 100 percent because some respondents gave more than one response.

person was the clergyman (42 percent), followed by a physician (29 percent). Thirty-one percent went to a practitioner or agency subsumed under the heading "mental health professional," including psychiatrists, psychologists, marriage counselors, and other private practitioners or institutions set up to handle psychiatric problems. Significantly, those who actively sought help for personal problems were least likely to choose mental health professionals and tended to be more satisfied with the help they received than did those who chose psychiatrists and psychologists.[4] This survey, part of the report of the Joint Commission on Mental Illness and Health, revealed that mental health services were generally not available to members of the lower socioeconomic classes. One major result

[4] This finding should be interpreted with caution. It may simply reflect the fact that more severely disturbed individuals tend to see psychiatrists and psychologists, and not surprisingly, are less likely to feel helped than do those who consult someone other than a health professional for less serious problems.

was to underscore the necessity to make such services more easily accessible.

Another survey research method involves establishing *psychiatric case registers,* permitting a cumulative, periodically updated statistical record on all patients in a geographic area. Increased computer use has helped develop register systems to which demographic, clinical, and dispositional data on patients is reported by any local mental health facilities which a patient contacts. Psychiatric case registers have been established in several states (notably Maryland) and in several Scandinavian countries. Analyzing such cumulative patient records yields patterns of admission and readmission to hospitals and outpatient facilities. One can obtain an immediate picture of patients treated at any one time, identify those entering psychiatric care for the first time, and observe the pattern of services used by patients as they move from one type of facility to another. Examining readmission rates can lead to follow-up studies and comprehensive studies of the natural histories of various psychiatric disorders. Record linkage systems between the hospital and outside social agencies may help provide more appropriate services after hospital discharge. In addition, case register data can be studied along with epidemiological data, such as that of the Midtown Manhattan Study, in order to determine, for example, if those persons who showed impairment during a home interview were more likely than others to receive psychiatric treatment or require hospitalization. Such interviews would be valuable if they provided some early warning of a higher risk of later hospitalization; early intervention in the community could then be inaugurated. The cross-validation studies of these two independent sources of information hold much future promise. One potential ethical problem to be resolved is the potential invasion of privacy.

ECOLOGICAL METHODS

The ecological approach to community mental health is based on the thesis that predictable patterns of individual behavior characterize any one social situation and that the expressive behavior of individuals changes in different social settings (Kelly, 1966). The effect of the social setting on the behavior of individuals has long interested psychologists like Roger Barker and his colleagues. Barker has maintained that data from both the laboratory and the clinic inevitably produce somewhat distorted pictures of human behavior because they are based on behavior in highly artificial situations. Instead, he has urged that human behavior be observed in its natural setting. In 1947, Barker and Wright established the Midwest Psychological Field Station to study the behavior and living conditions of children in the small community they called Midwest, Kansas (Barker & Wright, 1955). Barker and his students have continued to develop methods appropriate to studying children's behavior in naturalistic settings while at the same time attempting to describe the psychological impact of the community on its inhabitants. More scientific records are needed showing the real-life distribution and degree of occurrence of basic phenomena: punishment, hostility, friendliness, social pressure, reward, fear, frustration (Barker, 1968). It is impossible to recreate in the laboratory the frequency, duration, scope, complexity, and magnitude of most of the human conditions experienced daily.

Barker has led the way in showing that the environment is more than a relatively unstructured, passive arena in which man's behavior, alone, determines events. Instead, he has carefully documented the existence of various *behavior settings* which coerce behavior according to a dynamic patterning all its own. Many aspects of behavior can be more accurately predicted from knowledge of the behavior setting (school, church, home, ballgames) than from knowledge of the behavioral tendencies and inner motives of particular individuals. Significant and dramatic changes occur in the same individual's behavior as he moves from one behavior setting to another. Studying specific social environments, their range of activities, and their effect on members' behavior has many implications for community mental health. The psychiatric hospital, for example, with its numerous behavior settings, provides an opportunity to study the influence of that social milieu on patient behavior; perhaps some behavior settings particularly encourage "sick" behavior on the part of patients. In a community, there unquestionably are high-risk behavior settings (for example, poverty areas) which mental health professionals need to understand as influencing future behavior (perhaps including crime, drug use, mental illness) as much as one's individual personality and intrapsychic motivations. New community services directed toward preventive intervention may come from such studies of the natural environment and its impact on individual behavior.

Ecological research may lead to better ways of identifying, in their natural setting, those who are most vulnerable to stress and subsequent deviant behavior. Perhaps an ecological conception of behavior can help redefine mental illness. From such a viewpoint, behavior is never sick or healthy, but always the result of reciprocal interactions between specific social situations and the individual. This might help explain the paradoxical situation, frequently seen in psychiatric hospitals, of chronic schizophrenics suddenly behaving in an adaptive, functional, and realistic way during some stressful occurrence (such as a hospital fire) for a brief period, only to return to their customary "sick" behavior under more usual circumstances. Beyond the individual, ecological research may increase understanding of which environmental factors correlate with either adaptive or maladaptive behavior for the total population.

In this regard, Barker and Gump (1964), in their analysis of a Midwestern high school, have studied the reciprocal interaction between specific social structures and the individual's adaptation to them. Their studies have documented how group size significantly affects individual behavior. For example, large schools are apt to have more behavior settings, but they also have a greater population density per setting than do small schools. Small schools, in which the population density is low, tend to involve all students more, modifying rules and admitting many who might otherwise be excluded from such settings. The student in the smaller school is likely to experience a heightened sense of obligation and responsibility to the setting. His satisfactions are more likely to come from being wanted or needed. Students in smaller schools were found to be less sensitive (and less evaluative) of individual differences, showing greater tolerance of each other. They tended to see themselves as having greater functional importance in the school's settings. On the other hand, they tended to be under more pressure to participate in more difficult and varied activities and be in more jeopardy of feeling greater insecurity. Students in larger schools are more likely to enjoy being spectators rather than active participants. Through such studies, Barker and Gump have demonstrated how behavior of any individual is the result of the interaction between that individual and the specific social situation in which he must function and adapt.

In many ways, the school represents an ideal setting for ecological study, since the school child is available for longitudinal observation, psychological testing, and periodic teacher ratings over a long-term period. A preventive intervention program in the schools may benefit the future mental health of the child and his family. Kelly (1970) has studied how different students develop different coping styles in school and how these are correlated with effective performance in different school environments. Going beyond the work of Barker and his colleagues, Kelly has been interested in explicating the social process that mediates between such variables as the size or density of a setting and the individuals' behavior in that setting.

Kelly has used a variety of natural settings—hallways, cafeterias, the principal's office—to observe differences in behavior in fluid-environment high schools (that is, schools with a high turnover rate of students) versus constant-environment (low turnover rate) high schools. Fluid-environment schools were characterized by a greater variety of dress among both boys and girls, a higher noise level, greater informality about school rules, and greater interest in imparting information about school life (including information on what teachers to avoid) to incoming students. By contrast, the constant-environment schools were apt to have greater uniformity of dress, little contact between students in hallways, and little responsiveness to new students until the new person initiated contact (Kelly, 1967).

On the basis of these naturalistic observations, Kelly became interested in studying teenage preferences for ways of coping with their high school environment. Comparing fluid- and constant-environment high schools of equal size, two in a Detroit suburb and two in Detroit's inner city, Kelly hypothesized that students with a high preference for exploratory behavior would be more likely to emerge as adaptive members in a fluid environment, but would develop maladaptive roles in a constant environment; in contrast, low explorers would emerge as effective members in a constant environment but would assume maladaptive behavior if the environment were fluid. Exploratory behavior was measured by a carefully validated questionnaire. While the final results of the study are not yet reported, the study itself is a good example of using an ecological method which emphasizes the mutual relations between individuals and their environments and which is carried out in a natural setting, not a laboratory. In studying high school adaptation, Kelly's purpose is to learn more about how people in general learn effective and ineffective coping responses to their particular social settings. Kelly (1970) contends that without knowledge of the process of adaptation to varied environments, it will be impossible to develop effective programs of preventive intervention.

PROGRAM EVALUATION METHODS

The call for research and evaluation of community mental health programs in the Community Mental Health Act of 1963 has led to many innovative demonstration projects in various parts of the United States. While such projects technically do not qualify as research, they nevertheless frequently generate numerous hypotheses which can then be subjected to more scientific evaluation. Project Head Start, for example, began as a summer demonstration project for socially disadvantaged preschool children in 1965 and only later became a full-fledged year-round educational program. Since its inception, a number of research projects have evolved to evaluate the program's effectiveness in preparing disadvantaged children for later functioning in the elementary school. Similarly various demonstration projects—studying a more effective deployment of scarce manpower, the usefulness of a child-care center permitting mothers to work or attend school, the feasibility of establishing free medical and psychological services for addicts in neighborhood store-front clinics, the desirability of establishing mental health consultation services to a variety of community agencies, and many others—frequently have later led to permanent programs once the effectiveness of the demonstration project was established.

Administrators of community mental health programs are frequently asked by funding sources, professional mental health groups, recipients of the programs, or the general public to demonstrate the need their programs serve and their impact on social problems. Questions about a program's cost or efficiency are often raised. A funding agency may support several similar demonstration projects simultaneously in order to determine which program attains its objectives with the least investment of time, money, and mental health personnel.

Like research in psychotherapy, program evaluation research in community mental health may investigate the process or the outcome of the program. Different evaluative techniques may be required at different stages of a program's development. Three stages in any program can be differentiated: program initiation, program delivery, and program implementation (Tripoldi, Epstein, & MacMurray, 1970). *Program initiation* is planning a program, specifying its objectives, and gathering an appropriate staff and clientele. *Program delivery* includes the extent the planned program reaches the intended beneficiaries, what obstacles impede the program, and whether the program's services are relevant to the recipients' needs. *Program implementation* refers to the extent the program accomplishes its intended purposes. In order to evaluate a Head Start program, for example, evaluation questions can be directed to different stages of the program. At the program initiation stage, the evaluation might concern itself with whether the community has an available low-income population, whether they are willing to participate, to what extent staff should be recruited from the indigenous population, and so on. Program delivery evaluation might concern itself with whether the most strategic site has been chosen, whether transportation is available, why some potential beneficiaries do not participate. Program implementation evaluation usually requires that the program be fully operative. At this point, evaluation research might be directed at determining the increase in reading readiness skills and vocabulary for those preschool children who participated; the control would be a matched group of children who did not attend Head Start classes.

Program implementation research, a form of outcome research, attempts to assess the success with which a particular program accomplishes its predetermined objectives. Such a research approach inevitably produces many problems of measurement. Any mental health program rarely has a simple, single objective; short-term objectives often differ from long-term objectives. The appropriate criteria for judging success are often hard to define. As in psychotherapy research, before the effect of a program can be measured, some base line is needed to determine how a matched group of nonrecipients changed from before to after the program. Another difficulty is choosing an outside unbiased researcher who nevertheless is interested in the program to evaluate it. Further complications may develop because publicly stated objectives may differ from the private objectives of an agency. Finally, an agency may have its corporate program objectives while the staff may have certain other personal objectives (Bloom, 1968).

Many intervention programs have a nonspecific ameliorative or preventive intent, making it all but impossible to measure specific change. Every evaluation implies a judgment of what constitutes success, which may or may not be appropriate to the population being studied. For example, programs to "upgrade" the culturally disadvantaged imply that middle-class values are desirable by all, which smacks of paternalism and self-satisfaction. What tends to be overlooked is that other forms of knowledge (such as how to survive in a ghetto) are culturally advantageous despite their inapplicability to middle-class living. Values are relative and must be explicitly stated by the experimenter doing program evaluations.

Other problems plague outcome research in community mental health. Some specific goals are easy to measure (reducing new hospital admissions, increasing the discharge rate, decreasing the staff–patient ratio). Other broader goals (improving the community's mental health, improving job satisfaction and morale) are too vague to be measured with any precision. In addition, the goals of certain programs relate to the distant future (mental health education in the elementary schools to reduce the incidence of adult mental disorders), making their evaluation impossible until some future date. Even if the researcher settles for measuring the achievement of short-term goals, he can never be certain that a fulfilled short-term goal will necessarily lead to fulfilling a long-term goal. In this regard, Caplan (1968) describes a parent-education program which has the eventual goal of producing healthy personality development in children. He raises a number of issues regarding evaluation. For example, it is not feasible to wait for the children to grow up to assess their personality development—it would take too long, and there would be no way to evaluate how life experiences affect the program's results; that is, the program may be good, but traumatic life experiences might wipe out any gain, making the program appear ineffective. When should such a program be evaluated? Even if done at intermediate steps, it is difficult to document that changes in parental attitudes invariably lead to improved methods of child rearing or that these improved methods result in healthier personality development in their children.

Several other aspects of any evaluation question deserve mention. It is frequently difficult to prove that changes in the recipients of a program were produced by the program. Even if this could be proved, it is not always certain what in the program produced the change. An ideal situation would mean using a matched control group (or a matched community) from whom services of the program would be withheld. However, the ethical and practical questions involved here are difficult to resolve. It is also difficult to determine the success of a program, since something qualitative may be lost in converting stated program objectives into observable, measurable criteria. Finally, it is important to specify who is judging the success or failure of the program. Mental health professionals, no less than psychotherapists, may be biased in evaluating their own methods and achievements. Recipients of the program are in a favorable position to evaluate the program. However, such self-reports may or may not be valid. The recipient may be reporting what he believes program evaluators want to hear. Changes he reports may not coincide with behavioral changes, and may not be long-lasting. Outside professional researchers may be desirable, assuming they understand the program and can make reliable evaluations of its effectiveness.

Despite the multitude of problems, program evaluation research is necessary and possible if certain precautions are taken. First, the goals of the program must be stated as specifically as possible in terms of measurable objectives. Both the population to be studied and the services or activities to be provided must be described in detail. It may be necessary to use before-and-after studies of a program as well as cross-sectional and particularly longitudinal techniques using matched sample groups. The kinds of changes desired must also be hypothesized beforehand; the means used to bring about the change, and by whom, must be explicitly stated. Methods for assessing such changes must be reliable and valid. They must be made by researchers without a vested interest in the results. They should be made at some regular interval. As many controls as possible should be used in order to be as certain as possible that the measured changes are due only to specific aspects of the program. The researcher must be able to explain his results, including any that were unexpected.

In his presidential address to the American Psychological Association, Hobbs described a program called Project Re-ED, aimed at the reeducation of emotionally disturbed children through what he described as "psychological and ecological strategies [Hobbs, 1966, p. 1105]." Instead of long-term outpatient psychotherapy or hospitalization that typically has been the preferred treatment for emotionally disturbed children, Project Re-ED has offered an alternative public health approach based on social intervention in the children's lives on a 24-hour-a-day schedule by a team of professional and nonprofessional mental health workers. Originally organized under an NIMH demonstration grant to Peabody College, residential schools for disturbed children were established in Nashville, Tennessee, and Durham, North Carolina. The program at each school contained several groups of eight children each, ages 6 to 12, each led by a team of two carefully selected and specially trained teacher–counselors. These teacher–counselors were responsible for the children around the clock. College students and various special instructors assisted, while mental health professionals were available for consultation.

The Re-ED program has a preventive orientation and has concentrated on early case finding and early intervention. Its underlying concepts come from ecological considerations and consider the child's entire social system instead of just his personal intrapsychic conflicts. The child's ecological system (see Figure 11) is made up of himself, his family, his school, and his community and neighborhood. Occasionally a social agency becomes involved, as when a child is designated as emotionally disturbed, and other professionals—clergymen, physicians—sometimes are influential. Improvement in any point in that ecological system (father stops drinking, superb teacher becomes available) may result in improvement in the child. Therefore, the Re-ED school is introduced into the system for as brief a period as possible, withdrawing when the system's components begin to improve. Its purpose is to make the system function effectively with the least disruption of normal living patterns. Parents are viewed as responsible collaborators in making the system work rather than as sources of contagion. Consequently, they actively participate in the school's ongoing program. In the school program itself, intervention fol-

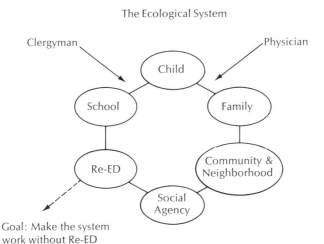

The Ecological System

Clergyman

Physician

Child

School

Family

Re-ED

Community & Neighborhood

Social Agency

Goal: Make the system work without Re-ED

Figure 11. Re-ED chart of the child's ecological system, the smallest unit in a systems approach to working with an emotionally disturbed child. (N. Hobbs, "Helping Disturbed Children: Psychological and Ecological Strategies," *American Psychologist,* Copyright 1966 by the American Psychological Association and reproduced by permission.)

lows a 24-hour schedule of planned behaviors and contingent rewards based on such fundamental concepts as: (1) life is to be lived now, not in the past or at some future date, through constructive encounters with other children and decent adults; (2) trust in adults can be developed, permitting the child to allow the adult to help him learn and overcome fears and guilt; (3) competence in school is possible, helps build self-esteem, and may be generalized to outside activities; (4) symptoms, particularly those that stand in the way of normal development, can and should be controlled; (5) group discussion can help each child learn to develop better control over events in his life; (6) expressing feelings is important; (7) community ties (YMCA, a museum, the library) are important, and many exist for the child's welfare; and (8) a child should know some joy each day.

The evaluation of the Re-ED project took several forms. In contrast to most residential treatment centers where disturbed children stay an average of two years, the Re-ED children stayed an average of six months. A comparison between observations at the time of enrollment and a six-month follow-up showed a success rate of approximately 80 percent for the 93 graduates. The improvement index was based on a composite of parents independently reporting a decrease in symptoms, an increase in social maturity on the basis of psychological testing, improved ratings by teachers on school adjustment, and less discrepancy between how the child is and what parents expect of him. The traditional hospital-based programs cost about $60 per day per child to operate, while the Re-ED schools cost between $20 to $25 per day for each child. Hobbs and his colleagues are in a process of obtaining comparison data from matched control groups to determine the extent to which Re-ED efforts are superior to naturally occurring changes during a similar time period.

EVALUATION OF THE COMMUNITY MENTAL HEALTH APPROACH

ARGUMENTS FOR THE COMMUNITY MENTAL HEALTH APPROACH

1. This approach has challenged the clinical psychologist to reexamine his customary assumptions regarding his role, his methods, his clientele, his goals, and the form of his clinical services. Direct clinical intervention in the community has also forced many clinicians to reexamine numerous previously held notions regarding mental health. As Hersch (1968) has noted, 15 years ago the profession took for granted relatively simple answers to these basic questions: Who is the patient? Who is the therapist? What is the process of treatment? What is the goal of treatment? What is the theory? What is the role of the mental health professional? Today, these questions have a variety of answers as traditional guidelines have become inadequate. The patient is no longer necessarily someone who voluntarily comes to a clinic for help, or is hospitalized as mentally ill. Now, we learn through survey research, many people in the community, especially in poor communities, do not come to the attention of mental health workers, but nevertheless show some degree of mental impairment. As such, they are appropriate recipients for programs of intervention. Similarly, the therapist is no longer the psychiatrist, clinical psychologist, or social worker who provides direct services to patients. Other professionals—nurses or community caretakers such as police or teachers—are apt to be front-line mental health change agents, as are the many nonprofessionals now being trained. The clinical process now involves not only more varied therapeutic techniques but also diverse indirect services aimed at intervention and prevention through education and consultation as much as through direct treatment. Promoting mental health rather than treating and curing mental illness has become the goal for community-oriented clinicians. Theories based on individual psychodynamic concepts are being increasingly challenged as too narrow for understanding an individual without understanding the social milieu in which his behavior developed and flourishes. Inevitably, the clinical psychologist's role as a mental health professional has changed. More than being a diagnostician, therapist, or researcher—all of which involve an intensive preoccupation with the individual—he has expanded his activities to include new roles (consultant, administrator, educator, supervisor, change agent) involving larger populations and newer methods of preventive intervention. Thus, mental health's third revolution has not only brought about a change in philosophy and clinical activities among mental health professionals, but a new public health dimension to the clinical psychologist's professional identity.

2. The preventive orientation of the community mental health approach has once again turned the attention of clinical psychologists to the problems of children as a way of influencing the mental health of future generations. The clinical study of the child, an early area of concern for clinical psychologists, is once again coming into focus. Pushed aside by the need for clinical services to veterans after World War II and the United States government's willingness to underwrite training programs and provide jobs that treated veterans, most clinical psychologists for the last two decades have worked with adults. With the new emphasis on prevention, a shift to studying the child is taking place. Section 1, Clinical Child Psychology, has recently been formed in Division 12, the Clinical Psychology division of APA. Several recent presidents of that division have been clinicians who work with children. Division 16 of APA, the School Psychology division, also includes many psychologists who work with children. Their direct, day-to-day contact over months or even years with children and parents makes the impact of a single psychotherapist appear meager indeed. Moreover, their services can be more prevention-oriented than treatment-oriented.

Some clinicians, like Ross (1970a), have noted that most university training programs in clinical psychology continue to be adult-centered. Usually students in such programs go through approved internships with little if any contact with children unless they make special arrangements for such training. Ross has argued for the reversal of this trend; that all clinical graduate students receive training working with children, with special provisions made for those wishing to work with hospitalized, psychotic adults. Hobbs (1964), too, has urged greater professional training emphasis on problems of children, on child disorders and early indications of later difficulties, and especially on normal patterns of development. To this end, he has suggested that the mental health professions invest approximately 25 percent of their resources to treat the mental health problems of the adult, devoting the major portion, 75 percent, to the mental health problems of children. According to Hobbs, this is the only way to make substantial changes in the mental health of the next adult generation and, perhaps, future generations.

Additional support for this viewpoint has come recently from the report of the Joint Commission on Mental Health of Children (1970), established by Congress in 1965. The Commission was to study and make recommendations regarding the resources, methods, and practices for diagnosing or preventing emotional illness in children as well as treating and rehabilitating children with emotional illnesses. The Commission's recent report documents the failure to provide proper psychological services to children of the poor, children who are delinquent, or those who are emotionally and educationally handicapped. Moreover, the report makes clear that all children are victimized by deteriorating public schools, readily available drugs, nonexistent jobs for adolescents, inadequate public health care facilities, poor adult models, and so on. Among its many recommendations, the Commission urged the establishment of a *national child advocacy system* to act as spokesman for children, as part of a national commitment guaranteeing children certain minimal rights. Such an advocacy system, once undertaken, can bring about positive changes in the extent of clinical services available to disturbed children, protect all children from failures of existing agencies to provide services, and in general provide a procedure at all levels of government for seeing to it that the rights and needs of all children (for an adequate education, physical care, social service benefits) are met.

3. Mental health manpower needs can begin to be met as clinicians consult with, supervise, and train professionals and nonprofessionals. Those receiving such training and supervision may take over many of the clinical services formerly reserved for mental health professionals. Experience has shown that they mainly perform such services very adequately, suggesting that the long, formal university and medical school programs may benefit from reexamination.

Increased manpower increases the availability of clinical services. People previously unreached are more likely to receive early treatment through community-supported agencies, thus aiding in prevention. Waiting lists in clinics are shortened, again encouraging those potential clients to apply for help when needed. The stigma of needing psychotherapy, for example, is reduced when the client is receiving counseling from a mental health aide who is likely to be his peer and who is likely to have had similar experiences and problems.

Increased manpower aids research in that the professional can take time from the pressing demands for clinical services. Nonprofessionals may contribute to research implementation through their first-hand knowledge of community problems and the increased likelihood that community inhabitants will cooperate with them. In addition, they may be trained as interviewers, for example, who help carry out a large-scale research endeavor.

4. The community mental health approach provides a broader context for understanding human behavior as an interaction between the individual

and his community. Sufficient data from research confirms the intimate relationship between the individual's behavior and the social context in which that behavior takes place. In particular, the relationship between mental health and socioeconomic status is clear. Only the most naive clinician would deal with his client's intrapsychic conflicts without considering the social and economic factors that may have contributed to his problems. As Marmor puts it, "poor housing, unemployment, malnutrition, illness, and all the other ego-crunching companions of poverty are now known to be as destructive to emotional well-being as a polluted water supply is to physical well-being [Marmor, 1970, p. 373]."

The clinician must understand social pathology to understand individual psychopathology. From this point of view, mental illness is not a condition but an expression of a social role in a particular social context. The community psychologist is in a particularly favorable situation to see forces detrimental to mental health in both the individual and the community.

From a more optimistic viewpoint, the community psychologist is also in a good position to observe what personal, familial, and societal factors make for positive mental health. Ironically, there is little definitive research on what makes a happy childhood, a happy marriage, or individual well-being in general. Answers to these basic questions, admittedly complex, can come only as we adopt a broader outlook of human behavior. Education in such individual child-rearing practices as breast-feeding, proper toilet training, or reduction of infantile trauma may all prove to be significant; perhaps, too, family planning, decent housing, and enriched early school programs will prove essential to mental health. The mental health consultant must be prepared not only to improve his client's welfare but also to find ways to help society nurture the greatest fulfillment in its members.

5. The community mental health approach provides an opportunity for the clinician to fulfill his social obligation as a professional and as a citizen. Generally speaking, the goal of most individual psychotherapy is the client's well-being. Mahrer (1967), in comparing the goals of various therapeutic approaches, found the following to be common: reducing psychopathology and suffering; increasing pleasure and experiencing; and enhancing self-acceptance and external relationships. But with the focus on curing individual pathology and repairing emotional breakdown, those broader social changes that might help promote mental health have usually been neglected. The community psychologist, with both a scientific and humanistic outlook, has an opportunity to promote constructive changes both in the individual and society.

The community mental health approach challenges the clinician to discover what social changes will increase the community's well-being. His primary prevention goals are identifying and eventually eliminating the hazards of living in a community (poverty, unemployment, racial conflict) or at least helping individuals cope better with them as long as they persist.

The clinician is obligated both as a professional and as a concerned citizen. These roles are not mutually exclusive. Helping strengthen an individual emotionally crippled by social forces—a task for the clinician— may go on simultaneously with helping alter those crippling social forces. Klein (1968) sees the mental health consultant's task as using his skills to enhance the community's effectiveness in providing security and physical safety for its inhabitants as well as providing them with support in times of stress.

Intervention in changing the nature of community life is analogous to British psychiatrist Maxwell Jones' (1953) pioneer efforts to change traditional mental hospitals into therapeutic communities. Jones has attracted many enthusiastic followers among hospital and community workers in this country and abroad. Basing his work on the principle that emotional disturbance is the result of an interaction between the individual and his social world, Jones proposed that changes in the patient's social milieu in the mental hospital ought to help in his treatment. Consequently, the entire hospital should be a *therapeutic community,* with all activities and relationships in the patient's life organized to be relevant and important to his treatment. The patient's role is to be a participating, responsible member of the hospital community along with other patients and staff. Responsibility for mutual care and decision making is shared by all. Treatment is not dispensed from doctors to sick, dependent patients, but comes from the interactions of the community life.

Communities outside hospitals also may be therapeutic in the sense that they contain self-restorative factors making for positive mental health. The clinician's role is to act as a catalyst in social action programs to stimulate the community's self-help role and improve community living. Since the federal, state, and local governments have made a commitment to mental health, the mental health professional has an opportunity and an obligation to advise government on what programs produce positive mental health results.

ARGUMENTS AGAINST THE COMMUNITY MENTAL HEALTH APPROACH

1. Far from signaling a mental health revolution, this approach merely perpetuates the medical model and its procedures. Methods for combating behavior disorders are based on the public health strategy of infectious disease control. Mental illness is seen as (1) a disease of acute onset, (2) which, if treated early, remains in remission unless triggered by some new stress (3) but, if untreated, deteriorates into irreversible chronicity; (4) hence, follow-up consists of maintaining arrest and avoiding relapse (Shatan, 1969). Thus, in reality, the community mental health approach merely accepts the medical model and touches it up somewhat with a few new strategies and goals and extends it to a greater proportion of the population.

Written into comprehensive community mental health center programs are such familiar medical approaches as inpatient and outpatient care, hospitalization, diagnostic services, precare, and aftercare. The recipient is seen as a sick person needing treatment and/or rehabilitation. The delivery of mental health services continues to follow the conventional pattern of delivery of health services, although sometimes provided through new agencies.

Mental health professionals and the public alike may become complacent, thinking they have significantly altered the mental health picture in this country. In fact, the community mental health approach has not produced any new conceptual framework for understanding the complex relationship between the individual and society. By extending clinical services throughout the community, for all its worthwhile intentions, it may actually have legitimized a two-class system of treatment—self-actualization through intensive individual psychotherapy for the well-to-do and rehabilitation for the poor (Reiff, 1966).

2. The community mental health approach is nothing more than the newest therapeutic bandwagon. Clinical psychology, particularly after World War II, entered the medical world of hospitals and clinics, patients and treatment, and emulated what clinical psychiatrists were doing. We have not yet extricated ourselves from that commitment. Now that there is a rush into community mental health, clinical psychologists should be careful that they do not stampede onto this new bandwagon.

One other temptation to jump aboard this bandwagon is that some clinicians have become disillusioned by those theories (psychoanalysis, for example) and methods (projective techniques) in which they have most heavily invested their efforts. But embracing community mental health may simply be trading an old enthusiasm for a new one without any more certainty of its ultimate usefulness.

Clinicians have no right to back any wholesale move in the direction of community mental health. Society has not given clinical psychology a mandate to tackle its social problems, nor is there much evidence that clinicians have the special knowledge, training, or competence to bring about social change if such a mandate were given. Dunham (1965) has questioned whether the mental health professional can participate in the structure of a community without changing his clinical skills into political ones. It has been argued that if the clinician wants to reorganize the community, he should run for public office like any other citizen.

3. The field of mental health needs to expand, not simply shift its attention. Mental health professionals should be wary of giving up what their training and experience best prepared them to do—provide direct services to emotionally disturbed individuals. Becoming a social-change agent in the community, while philosophically appealing, will only dilute the clinician's effectiveness, as he tries to be all things to all people. It is presumptuous to think the clinician knows what is best for the community or that he can develop treatment methods for the community as a whole. Efforts to develop prevention programs at this stage of our knowledge are premature, since we still do not understand causes of emotional disturbance to any satisfactory extent. Moreover, there is a considerable gap between such understanding and the implementation of programs producing community reorganization and social change. It is difficult enough to help change one individual, let alone a whole community.

Dunham (1965) feels that community mental health specialists may begin to resemble some university professors who consider themselves successful if they have hardly any contact with students, being too busy with larger undertakings such as research, consultations, and conferences. Dunham fears that the psychiatrist, for example, despite his training to work with individuals, may end up devoting his time to such nonservice matters as supervising nonprofessionals, consulting with community agencies, and educating the public on psychiatric principles and problems. Concern for the community must not preclude concern for the individual.

4. Using nonprofessionals as mental health aides will inevitably result in further manpower problems. Although training nonprofessionals, particularly indigenous nonprofessionals, increases the manpower pool and encourages the development of desirable new careers, it is likely to produce certain concomitant problems. As such individuals develop skills and pride in their accomplishments, they are also likely to develop a sense of frustration and discontent with their role and search for increased status and power in the mental health field. Bard (1969) has suggested that as the nonprofessional becomes professional, as indeed he must, he will become more exclusive and restrictive, limiting his numbers and once again providing a manpower problem.

One way to avoid that outcome, according to Bard, is to help existing public servants to derive increased satisfactions from their normal job functions without seeing themselves as emulating mental health professionals. Thus, Bard and Berkowitz (1967) have trained white and black policemen, biracially paired, to function as family crisis intervention specialists in West Harlem in New York City. These men, trained to respond to family disturbances, see themselves as policemen with no desire to be anything but policemen. Other policemen, as well as inhabitants of the community, have begun to use these men as family crisis consultants. They have not become mental health specialists, but they function with a more enlightened mental health attitude and with certain intervention techniques. Bard suggests that using existing organizational structures to produce social change may be more effective than creating new structures.

5. Despite its many merits, the community mental health approach contains many fallacies and roadblocks. Lawrence Kubie (1968), an outstanding psychoanalyst, has pointed to a number of fallacies inherent in the community mental health approach. For example, he challenges the notion that the best place to treat the mentally ill person is in his home community so that there is the least possible break with family, friends, job, or school. Kubie reminds us that the patient became ill in these surroundings, and experience has shown it to be essential to remove him from such stresses in order to begin the recovery process. To do otherwise, according to Kubie, would be analogous to treating a malarial patient in the very swamp where he contracted the illness.

Kubie also challenges the fallacy that the shorter the hospitalization the better. He notes that because bad hospitals are bad for patients doesn't mean that hospitalization per se is bad and that shortening the length of hospitalization is necessarily advantageous. By encouraging rapid turnover, resulting statistics may make new forms of treatment appear more effective than is justified. Shatan (1969), too, criticizes the community mental health movement adopting assembly-line techniques in the guise of mounting a total crusade against mental illness. His concern is that the clinical, humanistic emphasis on the unique value of each individual will be lost.

Kubie (1968) has questioned whether it is realistic to expect change in the social order without considerable opposition from those vested interests who benefit from maintaining the status quo. Decent housing, a noble ideal, depends on reducing real estate greed. Any efforts to effect social changes will inevitably confront many entrenched and tenacious community forces. These "psychonoxious" forces must be dealt with before a community can become therapeutic.

CHAPTER 9 *Crisis Intervention and Other Brief Psychotherapies*

As psychologists have begun to think in community mental health terms, it has become evident that changes must be made both in how clinical services are traditionally delivered and what populations are customarily served. If the focus is to be on prevention, early detection, and rapid intervention to help individuals maintain themselves in their communities, local programs must be established to provide inexpensive, easy-access, short-term treatment aimed directly at resolving immediate problems. The slow pace of traditional psychiatric clinics, with long waiting lists and involved intake procedures, is inappropriate for individuals who require immediate help. Yet, it is often taken for granted in most psychiatric clinics that there will be a long wait for psychotherapy and perhaps a wait even for an initial screening interview. One reason for such a situation is that many mental health workers are committed to long-term psychotherapy, which drastically reduces how many new clients they can see. Another reason, however, involves the inefficient, but time-honored sequence of a psychiatric diagnostic intake interview, an exhaustive case study by a psychiatric social worker, a battery of tests by a clinical psychologist, which are then considered in an intake conference, when it is decided whether the individual is a suitable psychotherapy prospect.

Obviously, such a slow procedure cannot benefit someone who is experiencing a crisis and needs immediate help—the adult obsessed with suicidal thoughts or threatened by losing his job or the imminent breakup of his marriage, the adolescent confused and frightened by a bad drug trip, or the child panicked about entering kindergarten and separating from his mother. Moreover, during their crisis they may be unusually receptive to psychotherapy if the traditional techniques can be modified to their needs.

CRISIS THEORY

As Gerald Caplan, a pioneer in community mental health, defines it:

> A crisis is provoked when a person faces an obstacle to important life goals that is, for a time, insurmountable through the utilization of customary methods of problem-solving [Caplan, 1961, p. 18].

Typically, the crisis situation is followed by a period of disorganization and emotional upset, during which the individual makes various abortive attempts at solution. Eventually some adaptation is achieved for better or worse, usually in four to six weeks according to Caplan's observations. The outcome of the crisis is frequently governed by the nature of the interaction taking place during the crisis period between the individual and key figures in his environment.

Crisis theory is based on the concept of homeostatic balance. It assumes that the individual is ordinarily in a state of relative equilibrium. That is, he has learned certain coping techniques that permit him to deal successfully with most common, everyday problems. Should certain problems prove to be somewhat out of the ordinary, leading to frustration or temporary emotional upset, he generally is able to apply his previously learned coping techniques to tolerate the frustration, resolve the problem, and successfully discharge any accumulated tension. However, when those problems persist, when they touch significant vulnerable areas in his personality, when his previous coping mechanisms cannot resolve the problem, or perhaps when several problems impinge on him at once, then the individual finds himself in a crisis situation.

An *emotionally hazardous situation* occurs when the individual perceives an obstacle or situation as a threat, loss, or challenge. Examples of such hazards might be a prolonged physical illness in a breadwinner that prevents him from supporting his family, the birth of a deformed or stillborn child, hospitalization of a young child, or perhaps an unmarried woman's discovery that she is pregnant. A *crisis* refers to the internal, acute, prolonged disturbance that may occur as the result of the individual's emotional reaction to the hazardous situation. Not all individuals faced by the identical hazardous situation will experience a crisis; some may have adequate coping techniques. However, certain common hazardous events, such as the death of a loved one, are likely to induce crisis states of varying intensity and duration in almost all people. An *emotional predicament* encompasses the entire crisis situation, including the distressed individual, the crisis itself, and the emotional hazard (Morley, 1970).

The crisis period typically has four phases (Caplan, 1964). In the first phase, tension rises, emotional discomfort occurs, and some disorganization of behavior follows the impact of a hazardous situation as the individual summons his habitual problem-solving responses in order to return to his previous state of equilibrium. In phase two, as these coping mechanisms fail to resolve the problem and the hazardous situation continues, tension and ineffectual behavior continue to rise. In the third phase, the tension level reaches the point where additional internal and external resources are mobilized. After calling on these resources, the individual's problem may abate in intensity to the extent that he can redefine the problem or perhaps give up certain goals as unattainable. If none of these measures successfully lowers his tension, he enters phase four, characterized by major disorganization and a possible emotional breakdown.

At this point, crisis theory remains largely descriptive although the overall conceptual framework has been developed. In terms of community mental health concerns, at least three general kinds of predictive indices are needed:

1. What kinds of events can be predicted to evoke crises in large numbers of persons?
2. What kinds of populations-at-risk can be identified, by reason of special vulnerability, in relation to events?
3. What kinds of interventions are specific for the favorable resolution of what kinds of crises [Kalis, 1970, p. 73]?[1]

Although these questions have not yet been settled, existing crisis theory does present a set of assumptions which can guide both research and crisis intervention:

[1] From Adelson and Kalis, *Community Psychology and Mental Health.* Copyright 1970 by Chandler Publishing Company. Reprinted by permission.

1. That human functioning requires the maintenance of an ongoing homeostatis or equilibrium not only within the organism but in relationship to the environment.
2. That any disruption of this equilibrium is followed by attempts to restore it or to achieve a new adaptive balance.
3. That certain disruptive periods, can, by their characteristics, be identified as crisis states.
4. That behaving organisms are more susceptible to external influence during a period of disruption than during a period of stable equilibrium.
5. That the period of disruption is self-limited and may be followed by a new adaptation which is qualitatively different from the one which preceded the disruption.
6. That equilibrium can be restored by changing features of the environment, changing modes of coping, or both [Kalis, 1970, p. 73].

CRISIS INTERVENTION

Crisis intervention is a psychotherapeutic approach which is prompt, brief, here-and-now, and action-oriented. As part of a community mental health effort, it contains features of both primary prevention (reducing the hazard as well as the person's vulnerability) and secondary prevention (early intervention at the beginning of a crisis or shortly thereafter). For example, Signell (1969) has pointed out that pregnancy outside of marriage is usually regarded as a hazardous event likely to result in a state of crisis in many women. Both that hazard and the individual's emotional vulnerability to such a pregnancy could be reduced by sex education, including information regarding the various means of contraception, reducing the stigma attached to such pregnancies, or liberalizing state abortion laws. Another hazardous situation involves the development of suicidal thoughts and life-threatening behavior in people. Primary prevention might aim at forestalling the suicidal crisis by: (1) developing an early case-finding technique or national data bank which could quickly identify individuals in the community who are members of high-suicide risk groups (for example, the elderly, the lonely, the chronically ill, and particularly those who have made prior suicide attempts); and (2) specifying, on the basis of research, those precipitating events (loss of a significant person leading to excessive guilt feelings, a depressive episode, irreparable body injury, chronic alcoholism) that are particularly hazardous and may lead to self-destructive behavior (Shneidman & Farberow, 1957). Today's suicide prevention centers, however, usually operate at the secondary prevention level, hoping to reach the potential suicide when his self-destructive behavior is in open expression but he is not yet so far into his crisis that he is unable to consider alternative ways of calling out for help.

The theoretical foundation for crisis intervention came from Lindemann's work on acute grief and bereavement and Bowlby's work on separation anxiety in children. Lindemann (1944), in a classic paper, first reported his observations of the bereavement reactions of families of victims who had died in the Coconut Grove nightclub fire in Boston in 1943. He compared brief and abnormally prolonged grief reactions in different individuals as a result of losing a significant person in their lives, concluding that the duration of the grief reaction depended on the success with which the person did his "grief work." Lindemann also outlined the distinct phases through which one passed in this "grief work" as he emancipated himself from the deceased individual, readjusted to an environment in which the deceased was missing, and began to form new relationships.

Bowlby (1960), a British psychoanalyst long interested in studying the effects of mother–child separations, observed three distinct phases in a young child after his mother left him in a hospital: (1) protest; (2) despair; and (3) detachment. During the first phase, the child protests the separation loudly and exhibits much outward distress, apparently maintaining the hope that his mother will return. In the second phase, he begins to exhibit signs of despair—inactivity, increased hopelessness and depression, withdrawal behavior. By the third phase, the child is resigned to the loss, becoming self-absorbed or attached to material objects and unable or unwilling to form attachments to surrounding nurturing adults.[2]

Lindemann's theoretical framework in particular, plus his suggestion that individuals could be helped through the stages of the normal course of grief, led to the development of crisis intervention techniques. Joined by Gerald Caplan in 1946, they together established a community mental

---

[2] Recent practices in many children's wards reduce the probability of such a crisis, thus reducing the overall hazards involved in hospitalizing young children. Frequently the mother remains in the hospital overnight with the child. At the same time, the children's ward decor, the nonhospital dress of ward personnel, and the use of familiar toys and books make for a crisis-intervention approach now taken for granted in most pediatric services (Kalis, 1970).

health program in the Cambridge, Massachusetts, area called the Wellesley Project (Caplan, 1964). There, many of the current techniques of preventive intervention as well as mental health consultation were developed.

Today, a number of crisis intervention settings exist in various parts of the United States. They provide brief, open-door, low cost, day or night emergency psychotherapy for people in a crisis situation who can benefit from a maximum of four to six visits. Among the best known are the Walk-In Clinic of the Bronx Municipal Hospital (Coleman & Zwerling, 1959), the Trouble Shooting Clinic in New York City (Bellak & Small, 1965), and the Benjamin Rush Center for Problems in Living, in Los Angeles (Jacobson, Wilner, Morley, Schneider, Strickler, & Sommer, 1965).

TYPES OF CRISES

Crises occur not only to individuals but also to families (due to war separation, drug addiction, runaway children, alcoholism, divorce), groups (combat soldiers, racial minorities, the elderly), or even communities (natural disasters, housing relocations, school integration). Erikson (1963) has described the various *maturational crises* faced by each individual, particularly in Western society, throughout his life cycle, beginning with infancy. In particular he has stressed that each stage of life contains certain developmental tasks that must be mastered with the achieved solution applied to the subsequent stage. Erikson has placed his greatest emphasis on the *identity crisis* in adolescents as a normative stage in the human life cycle (Erikson, 1968).

Whereas maturational or developmental crises may be thought of as a normal part of human development, certain *situational or accidental crises* may also occur unexpectedly at any point in such development. When these are superimposed on the natural maturational crisis, the combination may lead to a far more serious crisis. For example, Klein and Ross (1958) have studied the impact of kindergarten entry on young children and their families as the child learns to make the necessary role transition. They found school entry to be an emotionally hazardous situation in a time-limited transition period and to be marked by increased tension in the entire family. Loss of appetite, fatigue, stomach upsets, a return to bed-wetting or thumbsucking, increased irritability, and increased signs of dependence on the mother were common in the child. In a short time, at times even simultaneously, certain growth signs also appeared: increased assertiveness, visiting neighbors more often, rejection of babyish pursuits, heightened awareness of own clothing and personal appearance, and the development of more grown-up interests and attitudes. Parents, too, showed certain anticipatory tensions regarding the child's physical safety, their own sense of loss at separation from the child, and frequently some expectation that they would be criticized by those who would now see how they had raised their child. Sometimes the child saw the teacher as rivaling his mother for authority or as a more adequate disciplinarian or motivator than his mother. Group meetings with parents helped them redefine their roles and reconstitute parent–child ties at a new level.

Role change frequently produces a situational crisis (Parad, 1965; Aguilera, Messick, & Farrell, 1970). Just as the child and his parents need to adapt to new roles as the child enters school, so the life cycle is filled with a series of leaving old roles and adapting to new ones. Since roles are closely related to the individual's self-concept, changes in roles frequently trigger self-doubts and increased tensions, leading to a state of disequilibrium. Thus, marriage, parenthood, the sudden death of a spouse, the loss of purpose when children grow up and become independent, the loss of status upon losing a job, prolonged unemployment, retirement, divorce, or the development of a chronic and degenerative physical illness are all examples of situations calling for abrupt role changes which may set off situational crises.

Caplan (1963) has attempted to differentiate the characteristics of effective and ineffective patterns of coping with crisis, regardless of its nature or origins. He has suggested that adaptive coping requires:

1. Active exploration of reality issues and search for information
2. Free expression of both positive and negative feelings and a tolerance for frustration
3. Actively seeking help from others
4. Breaking problems down into manageable bits and working through them one at a time
5. Awareness of fatigue and tendencies toward disorganization, pacing one's efforts and maintaining control in as many areas of functioning as possible
6. Active mastery of feelings when possible and acceptance of inevitability when not; flexibility and willingness to change
7. Basic trust in oneself and others and basic optimism about outcome.

Maladaptive coping, in contrast, has the following characteristics:

1. Avoidance or denial of problems with judgments based upon wish-fulfillment or fantasy rather than reality
2. Avoidance and denial of negative feelings, dealing with them by projection or blaming when they do break through
3. When denial and avoidance break down, massive and generalized disorganization of functioning involving most areas of living
4. Inability to pace oneself, either overactivity or underactivity
5. Inability to seek or accept help from others
6. Reacting globally or stereotypically to problems; feeling easily overwhelmed.

The crisis situation may result in solutions which are in varying degrees adaptive or maladaptive. Consequently, the crisis represents a transitional period from which may emerge increased psychological vulnerability or an opportunity for further personal growth.

TYPES OF CLIENTS

The so-called psychiatric emergency patient is by definition in a crisis situation. He may be brought involuntarily to a general hospital emergency room, a psychiatric hospital, or a crisis clinic because he has engaged in some socially disruptive or deviant behavior (perhaps assaultive or bizarre behavior, perhaps being in an agitated state or having a bad drug reaction). He may voluntarily present himself to one of these agencies because he feels personally overwhelmed by catastrophic feelings. Sometimes he may call a hot line number or a specialized agency such as a suicide prevention center to seek help. At times, psychiatric emergency teams may come to his home if he is unable or unwilling to leave home to receive aid (Wayne, 1966).

The suicidal situation is the epitome of crisis. Traditionally, such individuals have been hospitalized and treated with conventional psychotherapy. However, such an approach in many cases provides insufficient protection; indeed, suicide in psychiatric hospitals, particularly among those who have previously threatened or attempted suicide, is not uncommon (Stone & Shein, 1968). A more effective approach, begun about a decade ago, involves suicide prevention services either by independent agencies or by part of an overall psychiatric unit, such as a community mental health center. Seventy-four such centers were in operation in various sections of the United States alone by 1968, in addition to others all over the world. Probably twice that number are now in operation (Farberow, 1968).

Among those individuals classified as psychiatric emergencies are: (1) severe depressive reactions, including but not restricted to those having made suicide attempts; (2) acute psychotic states; (3) hyperactive excited states, sometimes including schizophrenic and manic conditions; (4) acute anxiety and panic reactions; (5) acute hysterical reactions; and (6) a miscellaneous group of intoxications due to alcohol and drugs (Wayne, 1966). To this list, Work (1966) has added the following psychiatric emergencies in childhood: (7) severe fear and hysterical manifestations as a result of sexual assault; (8) separation anxiety; (9) fire setting (a community crisis and therefore an emergency to the parents); and (10) grief and bereavement resulting from death of a parent, relative, or friend. Various situational crises, such as the recent earthquake in Los Angeles, have produced psychiatric emergencies in many children.

One consequence of the community mental health philosophy is the effort to extend clinical services to individuals and groups heretofore alienated from such programs. A walk-in, crisis-oriented clinic in the client's local community, offering immediate assessment and rapid treatment, often attracts different people than those who typically seek psychotherapy in a traditional clinic. Efforts of such clinics as Los Angeles' Benjamin Rush Center for Problems in Living are directed toward breaking down the structure of conventional treatment facilities as well as overcoming cultural obstacles in order to make clinical services available in ways clients can accept, without a connotation of illness or pathology. The Rush Center's potential consumers reportedly see it as offering help with problems of living (not psychotherapy) by consultants (not doctors or therapists) (Morley, 1965). Morley's data indicate that while these clients were judged to be genuinely in need of psychotherapy, they would not ordinarily have sought such treatment because of a reluctance to consider themselves "sick" or to assume the role (and bear the stigma) of "patient." A large proportion of such clients are reported to be older, less well educated, and without the usual motivations for psychiatric help found in their traditional clinic counterparts.

Meeting the needs of such a population requires mental health professionals to develop new programs and services appropriate to the needs and life styles of these clients, and offer them in a way that will encourage use of the services (Reiff, 1966). Members of lower socioeconomic classes are a special target for such services. Clinicians must enlarge their understanding of the poor and examine their own biases in choosing clients with whom to work. The traditional clinic serving lower-income groups—with a crowded waiting room, long periods of waiting, endless forms to be filled out, impersonal, brief treatment usually by the least experienced clinician—is not conducive to effective delivery of treatment to anyone. Also, the traditional clinic is generally open only during daytime hours so the client must leave work or arrange for a baby-sitter, and treatment is often highly verbal; both of these factors are additional drawbacks for lower socioeconomic groups. These conditions may account for the high dropout rate after a few sessions at such clinics.

It is not surprising that Gardner (1967) has concluded that despite the overrepresentation of the lower class in all reported psychiatric illnesses (see p. 316), the rate of outpatient psychotherapy received by such individuals is about one-third the rate of the rest of the population. Aside from those diagnosed as psychotic, members of the lower socioeconomic classes experienced mainly diagnostic contact, while other clients frequently received therapeutic services.

The poor live with crisis always nearby. They are most likely to use crisis intervention services if: (1) these services are immediately available—in practice, for the poor, waiting lists mean no treatment; (2) facilities are easily accessible in evenings and on weekends and are close to their homes; (3) cost is reasonable; (4) those services are action-oriented and help them to resolve their immediate problems rather than merely encouraging the expression of feelings; (5) the therapist speaks their language (sometimes literally a foreign language) and understands their values; and (6) their suspicions, reservations, and misconceptions about psychotherapy are reduced.

THERAPEUTIC APPROACH

Although crisis intervention is not based on any single system of psychotherapy, its here-and-now, action-oriented efforts to mobilize the growth-directed forces within an individual are most consistent with the phenomenological therapies (see Chapter 7). Crisis intervention is not second-class psychotherapy but a unique form of intervention based on several assumptions: (1) the crisis is a self-contained situation of limited duration, with its own particular characteristics; (2) the person in a crisis is in a state of flux and therefore is unusually receptive to help, capable of being influenced in a brief period of time; and (3) to be most effective, intervention should be directed specifically at those aspects of the personality involved in the crisis itself, not at the precrisis personality, long-standing psychopathology, or the client's character structure as it developed in his early relationship with his parents.

Diagnosis, in the sense of arriving at a psychiatric classification, is not a significant part of this approach. Instead, the crisis therapist focuses on assessing: (1) the nature and severity of the immediate emotional hazard; (2) the acuteness of the crisis; and (3) the nature of the person's coping mechanisms. At this point, adjunctive drug treatment by a physician may help bolster the person's ordinary defenses. Occasionally, the crisis may continue to be so intense that the individual must be confined to a hospital or day-care unit, particularly if he is judged to represent a serious danger to himself or others or appears unable to function or make rational plans. Jacobson (1970) has estimated that approximately five percent of clients seen at a large crisis clinic are hospitalized, usually after a trial of crisis intervention. However, most clients are likely to continue in crisis therapy, usually up to a limit of six sessions.

Crisis intervention aims to influence the course of the crisis so that positive changes will follow the resolution of the crisis, and further, that the individual will have strengthened his coping mechanisms, his reality testing, and his self-esteem so that his long-range functioning is improved. There are at least two approaches to crisis intervention: the generic and the individual approach (Jacobson, Strickler, & Morley, 1968). The main thesis in the *generic approach* is that certain identifiable patterns occur in most crises, some of which result in adaptive and others in maladaptive outcomes. Several examples of predictable patterns have already been given in this chapter, such as the "grief work" in bereavement, the impact of kindergarten entry, or the typical pattern following hospitalization of a young child. The generic approach focuses on the characteristic course of a particular kind of crisis rather than on the specific psychodynamics of the individual involved in the crisis. Intervention is aimed at specific measures useful to anyone undergoing such a crisis without regard to individual differences. Mental health professionals and especially nonprofessionals may be trained in this technique of intervention. The clinician needs to understand the nature of crisis in general, specific crises in particular, and which approaches are especially effective in helping resolve certain crises. For example, he should know that the expression of grief following the death of a loved one is essential to the full resolution of the crisis; furthermore, he must understand that the accompanying depression is frequently based on guilt and anger directed toward the deceased (Morley, 1970).

The generic approach includes the direct encouragement of adaptive behavior, general support, environmental manipulation (such as referring the client to an appropriate resource—a physician, a social welfare agency, or an employment agency), and anticipatory guidance. Jacobson et al. (1968) provide the following example of the generic approach to crisis intervention:

A public health nurse visited the home of a couple in their early 30s, both high school teachers, who had one week earlier brought home their newborn and first baby. The baby boy was grossly deformed and diagnosed immediately by the obstetrician and pediatrician as almost certainly severely mentally impaired.

The nurse found the mother alone with the baby and in a highly lethargic and depressed state. The mother managed to communicate that she was "just waiting" for the state hospital to contact her and take "it" into permanent placement. She was vague about any details of arranging the placement and indicated that she and her husband found it very hard to talk to each other. Before the baby's birth she felt that there was very good communication between them. Her mother called her frequently to caution her about getting involved with the baby and to remind her that the physician had told her in the hospital to handle the baby as little as possible—that is, to just care for its physical needs so as not to get emotionally attached to the baby.

The nurse noted that the mother constantly referred to the baby as "it" and kept a physical distance from the baby's crib. She said to the mother, "Look, this is your baby. It came out of you and you have a right to hold it and cuddle it." Thereupon, the nurse picked up the baby and put it in the mother's trembling hands. The nurse stayed for another half-hour while the mother looked at and stroked the baby.

On the next visit, several days later, there was a dramatic change in the mother's appearance, for she was quite alert, active, and talkative. In response to the nurse's comments on this change, the mother said that a lot had happened since she had last seen her. She had been crying on and off for the first time since the baby's birth, had displayed anger at her husband's passivity in planning for the baby's hospitalization, and now they were talking to each other again. The husband had set up appointments with the state hospital staff for conferences on the consideration of placement.

The nurse asked what caused such changes in such a short period. The mother stated that it started when the nurse put the baby into her arms and encouraged her to look at it and recognize that it was her baby. The nurse had been the only person who had not cautioned her about thinking of the baby as a "real living thing." Although she now feels the terrible pain of her disappointment and the loss over the prospect of giving up her baby, she herself feels more alive again.

The nurse encouraged her in this and in subsequent visits to talk about her feelings, her disappointment, shame, and guilt, as well as her sorrow about the impending loss of the baby.

This illustrates a case of preventive help where the individual diagnoses of the mother and father were not known or explored, but where the necessary grief work was permitted to emerge and take a healthier course. The training and experience of the public health nurse in crisis situations involving separations or loss were instrumental in her approach to this family [Jacobson et al., 1968, p. 340–341].[3]

The *individual approach* to crisis intervention necessitates understanding the characteristics and natural course of crisis, but goes beyond the generic approach to attempt to understand how the crisis is related to the individual's intrapsychic and interpersonal conflicts. It is the preferred treatment when the individual is in a type of crisis whose adaptive and maladaptive solutions have not yet been identified. In addition, the individual approach is used with a client who fails to respond to a generic approach, thus necessitating a deeper study of the individual psychological processes involved. With this approach, intervention aims at helping the client achieve the optimal solution, considering the unique characteristics of his crisis situation as well as his personality. While such an approach is more likely to resemble conventional psychotherapy than the generic approach does, it is relatively unconcerned with the past except to determine why and how a previous equilibrium has been disturbed. The emphasis is on the here and now and on the processes involved in reaching a new equilibrium. In addition, Jacobson et al. (1968) urge including family members or other important persons in helping resolve the individual's crisis.

[3] From Jacobson, Strickler, and Morley, "Generic and Individual Approaches to Crisis Intervention," *American Journal of Public Health,* 1968.

Morley (1965) has described intervention techniques to use once the individual's emotional hazards and state of crisis have been identified, and the reasons why his usual coping mechanisms have not been effective under the current stress have been assessed: (1) describe to the client how the clinician sees the relationship of the present crisis to the client's life pattern, without losing the here-and-now orientation; (2) help him gain a cognitive grasp of the issues while bringing into the open the client's present feelings to which the client may not have access; (3) bring into play previously learned behavior patterns the client is not using at present; (4) explore with the client alternate coping mechanisms and alternate ways of viewing the problem; (5) help the client reorganize his social world; and (6) clarify and reemphasize the client's responsibility for his own decisions and behavior. Morley also helps his client make realistic future plans, including the possibility of long-range psychotherapy, in the minority of cases where this seems needed. Before termination, he explores with the client specific ways that future crises may be dealt with more effectively.

An example of the individual approach to crisis intervention lasting six sessions is presented by Morley:

> The consultee was a 22-year-old single girl who had until about four months prior to the contact been successfully employed as a secretary. The name Ruth will be used for the purpose of this presentation. Her general life situation at the time she was first seen was chaotic. She had made occasional ventures into prostitution, was quite confused in her speech and thinking, was [taking] narcotics, was completely unable to work, was having a tumultuous lesbian relationship of about six months' duration, was in generally poor health, had just made an unsuccessful suicide attempt, and based on a psychological test of suicide potential was considered to be a high risk. She came to the Center on an emergency basis because of the extreme distress she was experiencing in the relationship with her girl friend, who was also an addict, alcoholic, and probably psychotic.
>
> Ruth expressed her problem as centering around wanting to break the relationship with the other girl because of feeling she "would be destroyed or die" if she remained in it, but felt that the loss she would experience if she did leave would force her to kill herself.
>
> Because of the recent suicide attempt and the depression and suicidal ideation which was apparent clinically, the consultee was considered for hospitalization. She was strongly opposed to entering a hospital, and the examining physician felt that she could be treated on an outpatient basis.

Having ruled out the necessity of hospitalization, the assessment period was begun. Her clinical behavior at the outset left little doubt of the presence of a genuine crisis state, and the tentative working diagnostic impression was that of a depressive reaction in a basically passive–aggressive personality with significant sociopathic features. A minimum of early history taking was done. Clearly the key interpersonal relationship in the picture was that with her girl friend. She will be called Jane. Although [Ruth] had had a series of lesbian affairs in the past, this particular one seemed especially upsetting to her because of Jane's infidelity, open hostility, apparently psychotic-like behavior, and alcoholism.

Following this brief assessment, the consultation proceeded to the second stage, that of planning the nature of the intervention. Although there were certainly characterological problems in evidence, the present crisis appeared clearly to lie in her relationship with Jane, and in the context of crisis-oriented therapy it was this that was chosen to work with. She perceived herself to be in an insoluble situation whether she chose either to remain with or leave her partner. The working goal was thus set as helping her to work out a more tolerable relationship with Jane or to enable her to make the break from it without severe personality disruption. This crisis was apparently a relatively unique one in her life, and she had not developed tools with which to cope with it. In assessing Ruth's strengths, of primary importance appeared to be the fact that she had previously functioned on quite an adequate level, that she was well above average intelligence, that she was actively motivated to resolve her situation, and seemed capable of gaining insight into the nature of her difficulties. Less in the way of strength and support could be found among the meaningful persons in her environment—Jane could apparently be counted on for little, and the patient's mother also seemed quite unstable.

The active intervention itself was then begun in this case during the second hour. The consultant's initial major confrontation was in response to the way in which Ruth had described her living situation with Jane, which involved fights, jealous scenes, and an attempt by Jane to intensify Ruth's use of narcotics by bringing home a hypodermic needle. He stated that she seemed to be asking him to tell her that she could break up with Jane, and pointed out to her that only she could take responsibility for this decision. Ruth also made a request that he see Jane, [which, it turned out] was prompted by a wish on her part for him to judge Jane as "schizophrenic" and thus give Ruth support for the decision to leave. Following the pointing out of this to the patient, she appeared to take increased responsibility in making her own decisions.

The following hour [the third] was devoted to allowing her to recount in detail the events of the week, enabling her to clarify her perceptions of the problem and to explore her feelings about it.

Ruth was unable, it developed, to mention any specific characteristics of her relationship with Jane that she felt to be positive. She also announced at the end of the session that she had moved her furniture out of the apartment that she shared with Jane. She did not at this time intend to move out of the apartment, but felt that taking her possessions would enable her not to feel so tied down. At the same time she made several references to becoming more active in her social life, meeting new people and taking part in new kinds of activities. In this phase the therapist supported the adaptive coping mechanisms which were developing. This in effect seemed to bring into play both previously used behavior patterns and to an extent re-people the social world with significant individuals.

At the end of the third session, the consultant felt there had been another significant precipitating factor in the crisis which had emerged during the course of the meetings, and he chose to deal with this during the following hour. He continued on this tack even after the patient had begun to leave Jane. It developed that Ruth had become involved with an actor shortly before meeting Jane, and had felt a strong attraction toward him. This had apparently stirred up a considerable amount of panic about heterosexual relationships within Ruth, and she moved directly into the lesbian relationship with Jane. The threatened loss of Jane resulted in a rearousal of this panic. This interpretation was suggested to her, and after considerable resistance she accepted it and began to discuss her fears of becoming involved with men. She began to see her episodes of prostitution as geared to put her in a position where she could be contemptuous of men.

This session had apparently been quite upsetting for her, because she failed to appear for the fifth interview. She called later, however, and arranged for an appointment toward the end of the week. Another reason for missing the hour was that she had tried to make the break from Jane, had found herself unable to do so, and was afraid that the consultant would be critical of her because of this. She said that she had decided, however, that her relationship with Jane from here on would be on a totally different basis. She put this in terms of "living on my own life," refusing to be "overwhelmed" by Jane, and taking concrete action in finding other friends and becoming involved in a variety of other activities.

The final phase, that of final resolution of the crisis and anticipatory planning, became somewhat complicated by the fact that Ruth brought Jane with her to the final session. Her motivation for so doing was explored, and it appeared that the factors involved were to attempt to prolong the treatment in this manner, to recruit the therapist on her side against Jane, and to give herself the feeling that she was really able to "call the shots" in her life and demonstrate to herself that she did have control over what happened to her. All of the persons involved seemed to see Ruth as much improved from the condition she was in at the outset of the treatment. She appeared for the last hour attractively and appropriately dressed, showed no disorganization in her thinking, and her speech was clear and to the point, something which had certainly not characterized her at the beginning. Jane also made it a point to tell how she felt Ruth had benefitted. Ruth said she felt she had been helped considerably, and that she was [not] nearly so worried about her relationship with Jane. At her request she was given names of therapists whom she could contact in the future if she felt the need to do so. The final anticipatory planning consisted around having opened the channel for referral to another therapist if she felt the need, and leaving the door open for her to recontact the consultant if another crisis arose. Much of the anticipatory planning stage was already in operation with this patient prior to the final hour, as was reflected in some of the changes in her life style described above.

As can be seen from this case, the consultee had achieved significant gains during her period of treatment in crisis therapy, especially as reflected in the fact that she was no longer suicidal, in her improved physical appearance, in the decrease of confusion in thinking and speech, in a broadening of social activities and interests, in an increase in the number of friends, in an apparently less tumultuous relationship with her girl friend, in the fact that she was no longer taking narcotics, and in her expressed desire to give up her homosexual pattern. Equally apparent is the fact that there had been no "cure" or major characterological change—she was still involved in a nonadaptive lesbian relationship and was still not employed [Morley, 1965, p. 83–86].[4]

Although this chapter has mainly discussed development and resolution of individual crises, some clinicians (Hill, 1958; Parad & Caplan, 1960) have studied families in crisis—in particular, the family's crisis-meeting resources and the effect of the family life style on anticipating and dealing with crises.

In the same way, this chapter has emphasized the one-to-one relationships in working with clients in crisis, but a recent trend has been to work

[4] Morley, "Treatment of the patient in crisis," *Western Medicine,* 1965.

therapeutically with crisis groups. Morley and Brown (1969) have described such a crisis-intervention group. In keeping with Caplan's crisis orientation, group work includes a maximum of six weekly visits—one individual pre-group interview and five group sessions. Serious suicidal or homicidal risks or those judged to be psychotic are usually not placed in a group, but are seen in individual crisis intervention. Crisis groups appear to have the advantage for the individual participants of: (1) group support; (2) increased understanding and sensitivity because of the universality of crisis among the members; (3) a greater likelihood of accepting suggested alternate coping mechanisms when they are offered by a peer, particularly someone who has experienced various mechanisms in coping with his own crisis; and (4) encouragement to express significant feelings openly through observing other members expressing their feelings and gaining relief and other long-range benefits. This last point is one of the main benefits from all forms of group therapy (see Chapter 10).

SETTINGS FOR CRISIS SERVICES

A great many innovative therapeutic programs in new settings have developed in the last decade in order to reach the community and provide clinical services where they are directly needed. The following is far from an exhaustive description of such types of settings, since new programs are started in various parts of the country with great frequency in response to the needs of particular communities. However, five types of settings are described below as representative of such an approach:

1. **A walk-in clinic or crisis clinic.** This is an emergency-oriented, immediately accessible center operating in a traditional outpatient psychiatric clinic, a community mental health center, or a psychiatric hospital. It is usually manned by mental health professionals (psychiatrists, psychologists, social workers, public health nurses) aided by nonprofessionals generally trained in intake and evaluation procedures and possibly intervention techniques. It is likely to be centrally located, inexpensive, and open evenings and weekends. Its unique feature is its open-door policy for people in crisis, eliminating waiting lists, proper referral sources, and lengthy intake procedures. Such clinics generally attract people who find themselves in an emotional crisis but who ordinarily would not contact the usual outpatient psychiatric clinics or private practitioners for psy-

chotherapy. These clinics offer brief, highly focused therapeutic intervention for resolving immediate problems. Walk-in clinics tend to serve all who seek help, including those considered unsuitable for psychotherapy by other outpatient clinics. Walk-in clinics, thus, are meant to supplement, rather than replace such outpatient clinics. If the crisis remains acute after the six sessions, clients usually are referred to other mental health agencies. The operation of such clinics is described by Bellak and Small (1965) and Jacobson et al. (1965).

2. A suicide prevention center. This is an easily accessible, emergency, crisis-centered community agency, open around-the-clock daily, whose aim is to help prevent suicide. The first such agency, the Los Angeles Suicide Prevention Center, was established in 1958 (Farberow & Shneidman, 1961) and now provides clinical services to potential suicides, training and education regarding suicide prevention, and research into the burgeoning area called suicidology (Farberow, 1968). Clinical services rely heavily on the telephone as the initial means of establishing and maintaining contact with a potential suicide who calls for help while in a suicide crisis. Suicide potential is evaluated during such telephone contact and, when possible, callers are referred to appropriate community treatment agencies. An important part of suicide prevention centers' work is to train professionals, nonprofessional students, and volunteers to provide direct telephone contact with potential suicides, as well as to educate ancillary groups (police, physicians, lawyers) in the community. Research on suicide, once considered a taboo subject, has been stimulated by such an agency. Dozens of books on the clinical problems of identifying, assessing, predicting, and treating the potential suicide now exist. A Center for Studies of Suicide Prevention is now part of the National Institute of Mental Health. In 1971, the recently formed American Association of Suicidology began to publish its own journal, *Life-Threatening Behavior*, devoted to research on suicide and other self-destructive behavior.

3. A hot-line telephone service. This service is usually meant to serve adolescents and young adults who wish to discuss personal problems with a trained and understanding listener. Using the telephone as suicide prevention centers do, the hot line is meant to provide emergency counseling services, only by telephone and without follow-up face-to-face meetings, to individuals who find themselves in emotional crises requiring immediate intervention. Hot lines are frequently divisions of large hospital units, although some are part of city or county agencies, churches, service clubs, or civic organizations. Usually they are manned by volunteers who have been trained and continue to be supervised by a mental health professional. Although some hot lines provide around-the-clock service, most are open early afternoons until very late in the evening. The contact between caller and listener is usually on a simple first-name basis, without further identifying information on either part. Callers may call only once or may call repeatedly as the crisis is being resolved. The function of the counselor may range from simply listening to directing the caller to established agencies if more intensive or specialized help is indicated.

4. A free clinic. A free clinic is a combination medical–psychological–social service community-based agency offering free services to the indigent. Its clientele consists primarily of adolescents and young adults who seek help for infections (such as hepatitis), drug abuse, venereal disease, addictions, pregnancies, information on birth control devices, dental problems, and more strictly psychological problems. The first free clinic began in the Haight–Ashbury district in San Francisco to provide services to the local hippie population, who could not afford or did not choose to seek treatment from established clinics. The concept quickly caught on, and numerous free clinics now serve various parts of the United States and Canada, particularly hippie communities. There are two basic kinds of free clinics: (1) an independent clinic, established and underwritten by volunteer professionals (physicians, dentists, psychologists, social workers, nurses); and (2) a youth-oriented city- or county-supported clinic offering similar services as part of a municipal health department program. Free clinics tend to be located in the area of greatest need, either in a ghetto or in a known drug population area. Frequently, a store-front, an empty building or garage, or even a mobile unit serves as the clinic office. Staff, particularly at the independent free clinics, is all volunteer and would include professionals and perhaps indigenous nonprofessional volunteers (such as former addicts), students, or simply young people who have intimate knowledge of the "street scene." Medical and dental equipment is usually donated, as are the necessary drugs supplied by hospitals and pharmaceutical houses and administered by volunteer physicians. Free clinics are easily accessible, have no waiting lists or other red tape, are usually open at least five nights a week, and appear to be widely accepted by the population served. Psychological counseling, individually or in groups, is usually an important part of free clinic services and tends to be informal, with a sense of equality between staff and clientele. Freudenberger (1971) has recently described the operation of St. Mark's Free Clinic in New York City; it is located in two apartments and serves the medical, dental, and psychological needs of clients mostly between the ages of 16 and 25.

5. A psychiatric emergency team or crisis team. A mobile group able to provide emergency clinical services at the client's home is usually composed of some combination of psychiatrists, clinical psychologists, psychiatric social workers, public health nurses, and psychiatric technicians. The team is capable of a rapid and flexible response to individuals too emotionally distressed to come to existing out-patient facilities. Such teams are usually called on only under urgent conditions when other available community mental health services are unable to help. Early intervention is an important aspect of a psychiatric emergency team's work, since such intervention may provide an alternative to hospitalization or, in less extreme cases, prevent dangerously developing situations from reaching the point of desperation. Crisis teams are often part of a state hospital or county mental health agency. Their function is to be on call around-the-clock to respond to their supporting agencies' request to make an emergency home visit to evaluate the nature of an immediate stress situation and the individual or family's ability to handle it, and to develop an appropriate follow-up action plan in response to each situation for which they are summoned. While such action may include bringing an emotionally disturbed individual to a hospital for a more extensive evaluation, the purpose of such teams is generally to prevent progression of emotional disturbances, avoid long-term hospitalization whenever possible, and to help resolve the crisis while keeping the disturbed individual in the community where he can begin to receive appropriate help.

BRIEF PSYCHOTHERAPIES

To reach the goals of community mental health programs, mental health services must be extended beyond the one or two percent of the population who usually receive such services (Caplan, 1961). As indicated by the success of crisis intervention programs, large numbers of people are anxious for help in solving their emotional problems if that help is perceived by them as being relevant to their problems, within their financial means, available when needed, and does not include indefinite long-term commitment. In addition to those seeking help with crises resolutions, many others are beginning to seek out clinical services, particularly as such services become a part of Medicare and Medicaid benefits, labor-negotiated contracts, and health insurance benefits. A third new group of individuals seeking help in the community are those who ordinarily might have been hospitalized but by using psychoactive drugs are able to remain in their communities and use local alternate treatment programs. According to NIMH estimates, by 1973 the resident population of mental hospitals will be two-thirds smaller than in 1963 when the Community Mental Health Act was passed (Yolles, 1969); phasing out this traditional source of help adds greatly to the need to develop new therapeutic programs and train more mental health personnel to help the groups formerly served by hospitals (see Figure 12).

Figure 12. An aerial view of Camarillo State Hospital, outside Los Angeles, California. While turnover of patients in such hospitals has traditionally been slow, the use of psychoactive drugs plus efforts to provide local community care have now increased turnover rates dramatically. (Photo courtesy of California State Department of Public Works.)

There is still a great disparity between demand and supply of therapeutic services. Mental health practitioners tend to congregate in large metropolitan areas in large states. Five states (New York, California, Pennsylvania, Massachusetts, and Illinois) have more than one-half of all the practicing psychiatrists in the United States (Lewin, 1970). In contrast, 10 states have fewer than 50 psychiatrists, and many communities have no psychiatrists at all. Similar statistics apply to clinical psychologists and psychiatric social workers (Wolberg, 1965).

Efforts to correct this situation include: (1) establishing federally funded community mental health centers in rural and suburban areas as well as in metropolitan centers (500 such centers were expected to be in operation by 1970—Yolles, 1969); (2) focusing on prevention programs, particularly primary prevention, to improve the mental health of the community in general and reduce the need to treat specific individuals; (3) training more mental health personnel, both professional and nonprofessional, to use a variety of techniques that can be adapted to fit the mental health needs of different communities; and (4) developing brief psychotherapy procedures with limited objectives that are sufficient to supplement the more conventional but time-consuming psychotherapy. Since the first three points were discussed in Chapter 8, the remainder of this chapter will deal with the fourth point, brief psychotherapy.

Brief psychotherapy is not a new idea, although the community mental health movement has revived interest in it and encouraged its widespread application. Freud originally conceived of psychoanalysis as a brief procedure and saw many of his early patients for only a short time.[5] Only when the interest in repressed memories and analyzing the patient's character structure evolved did psychoanalysis become the lengthy procedure it is today. At first, Freud saw psychoanalysis primarily as a research tool to help conceptualize human personality; he anticipated that some day more efficient therapeutic techniques would supersede psychoanalysis as a form of treatment.[6]

---

[5] Freud is reported to have needed only five or six sessions to successfully treat Bruno Walter, the famous symphony conductor, for the partial paralysis of his conducting arm following the birth of Walter's first child. Rather than following classical psychoanalytic procedures, Freud was direct, supportive, gave advice (including a suggestion that Walter take a vacation), and urged Walter to continue conducting as best he could even with the disability. Walter reportedly followed Freud's advice, and his affliction disappeared shortly thereafter (Sterba, 1951).

[6] The reader may wish to review the more classical psychoanalytic approach at this time (see pp. 226–231) to clarify the modifications to be described.

Perhaps the most influential book on modifying psychoanalysis into briefer psychotherapy was *Psychoanalytic Therapy,* written in 1946 by Franz Alexander and Thomas French, leaders of the Chicago Institute for Psychoanalysis. They conceived of psychoanalytic therapy as providing a corrective emotional experience because the therapist deliberately creates a climate that contrasts with that of the patient's childhood. The key to briefer therapy, according to Alexander and French, lies in the therapist's manipulating therapy to take a different direction from psychoanalysis, especially preventing an intense transference neurosis from developing; briefer therapies therefore resemble the phenomenological therapies more than psychoanalysis in that they focus more on the present and deemphasize the reconstruction of the past. Psychoanalytic therapy also calls for analytic sessions of varying length and frequency during different phases of the therapy to reduce overdependency, and temporary interruptions at various points to test the patient's ability to cope with new experiences. They saw regression and overdependency on the analyst as common consequences of prolonged psychoanalysis. In the cases they presented in their book, therapy was frequently completed in between 10 and 65 sessions, in contrast to the minimum of 500 sessions most classical psychoanalysis requires.

Despite initial resistance, particularly by psychoanalysts, to Alexander and French's proposals, postwar demands forced many mental health workers to reassess the feasibility of brief therapy techniques. As a result, many clinicians began to practice psychoanalytic psychotherapy based on psychoanalytic principles but applied in a more flexible way in order to speed up the therapeutic process. Variations from classical psychoanalysis, in addition to those described by Alexander and French, have included: (1) abandoning free association as the primary source of data concerning the patient's thoughts; (2) fewer sessions per week, extending them over a shorter period of time; (3) shorter sessions; (4) abandoning the couch; (5) greater activity by the therapist beyond the interpretation of transference and resistance; (6) emphasis on what is happening in the patient's daily life; and (7) the therapist behaving as more of a real person than the neutral blank screen of psychoanalysis. Aguilera, Messick, and Farrell (1970) have compared the major differences between psychoanalysis, crisis intervention, and brief psychotherapy along several key dimensions (see Table 15).

The expansion of community mental health services in the 1960s led many clinicians to search for other effective briefer methods of therapy so they could serve more people. The preventive role of brief psychotherapy is increasingly acknowledged: (1) in preventing a minor, temporary problem from becoming a major disability (primary prevention); (2) in reducing the duration of an existing disorder (secondary prevention); and (3) in limiting the long-term effect of a chronic disability (tertiary prevention).

BRIEF THERAPY VERSUS LONG-TERM THERAPY

Brief psychotherapy is more than a truncated version of the more traditional long-term psychotherapy. Actually it has many advantages of its own beyond expediency. The major differences between brief and long-term therapy concern: (1) goals; (2) time factors; and (3) methods (Bellak & Small, 1965).

Table 15. Comparisons between psychoanalysis, brief psychotherapy, and crisis intervention methods*

	PSYCHOANALYSIS	CRISIS INTERVENTION	BRIEF PSYCHO-THERAPY
Goals of therapy	Restructuring the personality	Resolving immediate crisis	Removing specific symptoms
Focus of treatment	1. Genetic past	1. Genetic present	1. Genetic past as it relates to present situation
	2. Freeing the unconscious	2. Restoring to level of functioning prior to crisis	2. Repressing unconscious and restraining drives
Usual activity of therapist	1. Exploratory 2. Passive observer 3. Nondirective	1. Suppressive 2. Active participant 3. Direct	1. Suppressive 2. Participant observer 3. Indirect
Indications	Neurotic personality patterns	Sudden loss of ability to cope with a life situation	Acutely disruptive emotional pain and severely disruptive circumstances
Average length of treatment	Indefinite	From one to six sessions	From one to 20 sessions

* From Aguilera, Donna C., Messick, Janice M., and Farrell, Marlene S.: *Crisis Intervention,* St. Louis: The C. V. Mosby Co., 1970.

1. Goals. Generally speaking, brief psychotherapy is the preferred treatment for individuals undergoing either: (1) acute neurotic conflicts resulting in intense anxiety, panic states, or depression, or (2) incipient and acute psychotic states if the client indicates inner resources and past adaptability in problem-solving. Capitalizing on each individual's inherent potential for growth as well as his receptivity to help at these times, brief therapy may help reduce symptoms and help restore at least the previous level of functioning. In contrast to long-term psychotherapy, where a more extensive modification of the patient's personality might be attempted, the major goal of brief therapy is to help achieve symptom relief and provide him with sufficient understanding to recognize and cope with future conflicts. Thus, brief therapy has more limited goals but serves an important function in preventing more serious emotional disturbances in the future.

2. Time factors. Brief therapy is a relative term. Psychoanalytically oriented psychotherapy has reduced the length of psychoanalysis considerably, but it may still be longer than other approaches such as crisis intervention or behavior therapy. Small (1971) has suggested the generic term *briefer psychotherapies* to indicate that there are a variety of time-condensed techniques now being practiced. He has determined that the range of session contacts defined as brief by different clinicians may vary from one to over 200. However, brief therapy is commonly thought to comprise less than 20 sessions. In contrast to the regularity of long-term psychotherapy, brief therapy techniques are more flexible regarding time. In some cases, there may be a considerable length of time between sessions while the patient engages in various new activities. On the other hand, in a crisis situation, he may be seen intensively over several days. In addition, the length of individual sessions may vary, sometimes being as short as 15 minutes (Barten, 1965). Brief therapy is frequently undertaken with a predetermined idea of when it will end, again quite different from the open-endedness of long-term psychotherapy.

3. Methods. The briefer therapies encompass many techniques and take a variety of forms. Wolberg (1965) acknowledges that there is yet no adequate methodological model for brief therapy. However, he cautions against using the familiar therapeutic tactics of long-term therapy: relaxed listening, waiting for the patient to acquire motivation, and so on. Instead, he urges a quick focus on the target symptoms. Behavior therapists, too, concentrate on observable behavior (a symptom) that needs to be extinguished.

In recent years brief therapy has benefited by the advances in drug therapy. Combining psychological techniques having specific, limited goals with a variety of tranquilizing and antidepressant drugs administered by a physician, therapists have been able to focus on early secondary prevention and rehabilitation instead of long-term treatment and possibly institutionalization. When an individual is so anxious or depressed that he cannot cope with the usual process of verbal psychotherapy or cannot practice what he has learned in psychotherapy, certain drugs can provide an important adjunct to treatment. The use of the more potent tranquilizers has resulted in avoiding lengthy hospitalization for many acutely psychotic patients.

In addition to using drugs, many therapists engaged in brief psychotherapy rely heavily on direct intervention in the patient's life situation. Through such environmental manipulation, the patient may be helped to see that certain changes in his life circumstances (such as change of job, different housing, decision regarding hospitalization for a retarded child) may reduce the stress on himself and others considerably. Frequently the entire family may be seen, bringing specific family conflicts into the open. Travel and vacations—those traditional recommendations of general practitioners—may also be advised in certain cases, as Freud advised Bruno Walter. In extreme cases, therapists may urge brief hospitalization, perhaps for suicidal patients or those borderline psychotic individuals who are in an acute delusional state of recent precipitation (Bellak & Small, 1965).

THE CHARACTERISTICS OF BRIEF PSYCHOTHERAPIES

All forms of brief therapy appear to have the following elements in common:

1. Time-limited orientation, with the total length of treatment frequently predetermined during the initial interview
2. Early identification of specific problems to be dealt with, with little or no deviation thereafter
3. Rapid assessment of the individual in terms of (a) his personal strengths and weaknesses, (b) environmental stresses, and (c) the appropriateness of drugs or brief hospitalization in conjunction with therapy

4. Goal-directed, highly focused set of therapeutic procedures with specific, but limited, treatment objectives.

5. A directive approach by the therapist, who is active, supportive, and tries to work with the constructive qualities in the patient

6. Therapeutic efforts directed at symptom removal rather than searching for causes.

7. Considerable flexibility regarding frequency and length of individual therapeutic sessions

8. Little or no probing for early memories; the past is dealt with only if immediately and directly related to present difficulties

9. Termination according to schedule, at which time the possibility of future referral for help may be discussed, including the possibility of group therapy.

Short-term group psychotherapy, like its counterpart in short-term individual psychotherapy, has had the effect of accelerating the therapeutic process. Frequently such short-term groups are composed of parents who desire guidance with such common problems of child rearing as how to handle aggression, sex education, or discipline (Wolf, 1965). Sometimes groups of parents of exceptional children (the cerebral palsied, for example) may join together in a brief therapeutic experience. Occasionally, children with common problems (such as institutionalized delinquents) may be seen in a short-term group arrangement. It is becoming more common for emotionally disturbed children and their families to be seen for short-term family therapy (Kaffman, 1963). Another popular approach in recent years has been weekend marathon groups; they are composed of people with no previous contact who come together for one or perhaps several continuous, but time-limited, group sessions.

Brief therapy with children is usually the preferred treatment, being far more common than long-term, intensive psychotherapy (Koegler, 1966). For one thing, the young child's character structure is still forming; principal benefit may accrue from brief, directed efforts toward positive growth. For another, the child rarely seeks psychotherapy himself to resolve his inner conflicts (see pp. 195–198), but is more likely responding to environmental pressures from home or school. For this reason, the therapist, having gauged what is taking place, can intervene to reduce the stress on the child as well as on other family members. Considerable environmental manipulation is frequently possible in working with children. The child with learning difficulties and/or behavior problems in school can be helped as the therapist consults with the parents (to hire tutors, lower their academic expectations, discourage intellectual competition between siblings, and so on) as well as the school (to change the child's class placement, help teachers better understand the child's problems and needs).

THE EFFECTIVENESS OF BRIEF PSYCHOTHERAPIES

Two major stumbling blocks to the more extensive use of the briefer psychotherapies are: (1) the tradition among most clinicians that the more therapy the better, and (2) the belief that good, long-lasting results from psychotherapy are possible only after protracted treatment. Actually, no research supports the notion that 50-minute hours produce more positive results than shorter interviews or that several years of psychotherapy are necessarily superior to several weeks of intensive, highly focused intervention. Some therapists have begun to experiment with a 15-minute hour with selected patients (Barten, 1965), assuming that some patients can benefit from brief, regular contact during which the therapist can support limited objectives, monitor "acting out" tendencies or dangerous or self-destructive behavior, and support emerging adaptive attitudes. This forces both therapist and patient to be succinct and avoid the digressions that often fill the 50-minute hour. If this method proves successful, an obvious further advantage would be that more clients could be treated per hour. For some individuals, such as those recently discharged from a hospital, weekly contact, no matter how brief, may help provide the support necessary to function in their home communities.

Few adequate research studies on the effectiveness of brief psychotherapy have been carried out. One reason is the relative newness of the approach; another is the difficulty in tackling some of the problems inherent in all outcome research, where so many variables must be considered and a control-group baseline used (see pp. 24–25). Perhaps the most adequate attempt to evaluate short-term therapy has come from the research project undertaken by Group Health Insurance on the feasibility of providing insurance coverage for brief outpatient psychotherapy (Avnet, 1962). About 10 percent of this company's insurance subscribers (76,000) were told their policies entitled them to 15 office visits to a psychiatrist, for which they would pay only a modest fee as their share. Twelve hundred psychiatrists participated in the project over a period of two and one-half years. In that time, over 1100 men, women, and children received treatment of 15 sessions or less for a wide range of psychiatric disorders, almost all on an individual, private, outpatient basis.

Conclusions from the study were based on psychiatrist judgments on termination of psychotherapy and on the follow-up self-reports of patients two years or more after treatment. Over 75 percent of the patients were judged by their psychiatrists to be improved after the brief therapeutic experience (although objective criteria for their judgments is lacking). Over 80 percent of the patients reported improvement in themselves (Avnet, 1965). While the subjective nature of such evaluations in measuring change makes the study open to criticism, the high degree of agreement regarding improvement suggests something very positive resulted from such short-term help. Considering the improvement or recovery rates reported by practitioners of long-term psychotherapy, these findings are impressive indeed in underscoring the possible benefits and need for continued research into the development of brief psychotherapy methods.

CHAPTER 10 *Family Therapy, Group Therapy, and the Encounter Movement*

People participate in groups all their lives. At birth, entry into the family marks the first experience of being part of a social system and being shaped by group membership. Many other interpersonal experiences follow—at school, with friends and neighbors, in marriage, at work—all influencing personality formation. More and more clinicians are beginning to consider just how much these experiences help regulate and set the pattern for individual behavior, including the development of psychopathology. Such psychopathology has traditionally been regarded as the result of intrapsychic conflict; the newer, broader view is that it also evolves from disturbed interpersonal transactions.

This broader view has many implications for psychotherapeutic intervention. Instead of the somewhat artificial setting of individual therapy, family therapy and various forms of group therapy are thought to simulate real life more closely. Since much disordered behavior stems from and is reinforced by disturbed relationships with others, therapeutic experiences with groups may help work through such problems. In addition, certain kinds of group experiences are thought to benefit anyone who wishes to gain further self-awareness as well as heightened sensitivity to the feelings of others as well as feedback about himself. Encounter groups, sensitivity training groups, weekend marathon groups, and others are becoming a more common experience for many people who feel it helps overcome the loneliness and loss of meaning in their lives but who do not see themselves as "sick" and needing treatment.

FAMILY THERAPY

Psychologists have always been interested in their clients' early family relationships. Since Freud's early psychoanalytic formulations, family conflicts and alliances (the Oedipus complex, for example) have been commonly accepted as important factors in an individual's character formation and particularly in the development of neurotic behavior. However until recently, most psychotherapy, influenced by psychoanalysis, involved working with individuals alone to resolve their personal, intrapsychic conflicts. Family therapy, on the other hand, shifts the perspective to the family itself as a functional unit requiring study and treatment; the individual with the emotional problem or psychological symptoms is merely the *identified patient.* His problem may be etiologically and dynamically obscure from the standpoint of individual study, but can often be made intelligible when viewed in the matrix of a family social system in disequilibrium.

Beginning in the 1950s, a group of behavioral scientists under the leadership of anthropologist Gregory Bateson began to study the communication patterns between schizophrenic patients and their family members (Bateson, Jackson, Haley, & Weakland, 1956). In their paper, they proposed a double-bind theory to help account for the development of schizophrenia in some individuals. A double-bind situation is one in which the victim cannot succeed, no matter what responses he makes. According to the theory, a mother, made anxious and hostile when threatened by too close contact with her child but at the same time unable to accept these feelings in herself, communicates a double-bind message to the child. For example, she may overtly simulate affection, persuading the child to respond to her as a loving mother, only to withdraw from him whenever he approaches her. The child becomes confused when confronted by contradictory messages of love and hate, approach and avoidance, both emanating from the same person. Responding to her overture leads to rejection; failing to respond leads to the loss of possible love from her. The mother's denial of her contradictory messages adds to the child's confusion. At the same time, there is usually no strong or insightful father or other family member to intervene and support the child in the face of his contradictory experiences. Under these circumstances, the mother is considered to be schizophrenogenic—that is, her behavior fosters schizophrenic reactions in the child. The child may take refuge from all this confusion and incongruence by withdrawing from reality into a fantasy world, a precursor to schizophrenia.

The double-bind theory of the etiology of schizophrenia remains controversial. Critics have argued that similar double-bind situations are likely to exist in families that do not produce a schizophrenic child. Nevertheless, what concerns us here is the application of communications theory to studying what takes place in a family. Further study has clarified that there rarely are "binders" (such as schizophrenogenic mothers) versus "victims." Instead, the family as a whole is caught up in an ongoing system that requires therapeutic intervention. Each individual is part of a system that is malfunctioning as a whole. The breakdown of any one part —for example, the development of symptoms in one family member—may simply signal that the entire family unit needs treatment.

The work on a communication approach to the study of family behavior was carried on into the 1960s by a number of West coast behavioral scientists such as Don Jackson (1957), Jay Haley (1959), John Bell (1961), and Virginia Satir (1964). In 1958, the Mental Research Institute in Palo Alto, California, was formed, remaining today an outstanding center for research on family processes and family therapy.

At about the same time on the East coast, New York psychoanalyst Nathan Ackerman independently began to develop a philosophy as well as a set of techniques for family diagnosis and treatment (Ackerman, 1958). He saw the family as "a kind of carrier of elements predisposing to both mental illness and mental health [p. 104]." Psychiatric patients, according to Ackerman, come from disordered families. The family member who develops psychiatric symptoms may often prove to be the emissary in disguise for the whole disturbed family in need of treatment. He may simply be the scapegoat behind whom the family hides its own dysfunction. Typically, a therapist who begins to see a child with learning or behavior problems quickly realizes that those problems are part of a larger canvas involving many more people than the child himself. Ackerman views the identified patient (or *primary patient,* as he prefers to call him) as both an individual in distress and as a symptomatic expression of family pathology. Through a series of office interviews and home visits with the whole family, Ackerman is able to obtain a first-hand diagnostic impression of the dynamic relationships among family members and to institute family therapy for the entire group.

A prolific writer and editor, Ackerman (1966, 1970; Ackerman, Beatman, & Sherman, 1961, 1967) helped organize the Family Institute in New York City. Together with the Mental Research Institute in Palo Alto, both family-oriented centers have sponsored a multidisciplinary journal, *Family Process.* Today, a number of such centers exist in the United States (in Philadelphia, Washington, D. C., Galveston, Los Angeles). In England, John Howells (1971) has developed his own system of family psychiatry, and R. D. Laing (1967) has been in the forefront of work on schizophrenia and the family. Laing, showing some affinity to the studies on double-bind theory (Bateson et al., 1956) sees schizophrenic symptoms as a strategy invented by a person to live in what, to him, has become an unlivable world.

FORMS OF FAMILY THERAPY

Family therapy is practiced in a variety of ways; there is no agreed upon set of procedures yet. At least the following three forms may be differentiated:

1. Conjoint family therapy. This approach means one therapist simultaneously treats a nuclear family (parents, children, other significant relatives). Virginia Satir (1964), a social worker long associated with the Mental Research Institute, has written extensively on this approach and has presented numerous demonstration workshops in various parts of the country. Satir's approach is direct, simple, and straightforward. She sees her role as that of a resource person, an experienced observer from outside the family who herself is a model of clear, open, and simple communication. Her purpose is to show family members how to correct discrepancies in their communications and thereby achieve more mutually satisfying outcomes. A particularly illuminating verbatim transcript of a family session, along with a running account of the rationale for her therapeutic interventions, can be found in Satir (1967).

Ackerman also sees the family as a unit from the first interview. His technique is to focus on the immediate problems facing the family rather than delving into past events and relationships. His strategy is to be totally forthright, direct, and confronting, forcing family members to be more open to him and ultimately to each other. Sex, aggression, and dependency—the content of much family conflict—are all dealt with directly by cutting through the usual defenses against exposure.

2. Concurrent family therapy. This approach, less commonly used than conjoint sessions, means one therapist simultaneously treats various family members in separate sessions. The therapist pieces together a picture of how the family functions by hearing several sides of the same events and transactions. A variation of this approach is to work primarily with the identified patient—for example, a hospitalized individual—but also to see family members occasionally. The purpose here would be to elicit their aid at crucial times, to explain what is happening to the patient, to gauge their involvement in maintaining his psychopathology, or perhaps to alert them to customary patterns in the family that tend to interfere with the progress of the patient as well as being detrimental to the entire family.

3. Collaborative family therapy. In this approach, various family members are treated separately by different therapists. By collaborating with one another, each therapist can compare how his patient sees the situation with what another family member has reported to his colleague. Marriage therapy is frequently conducted this way. Martin and Bird (1963) call such an approach "stereoscopic therapy" to emphasize each therapist's double view of his patient. Child guidance clinics usually operate on this principle. Recognizing that treating the child one or two hours per week may be insufficient if he must return to the household from which his problems sprang, the general approach is to have different therapists see the mother and child separately, but work collaboratively. Unfortunately, fathers are frequently absent.

A variation of the collaborative approach is for co-therapists to work together with a family (Whitaker, 1965). In addition, each therapist can provide some objective reactions to the other's possible subjective over-involvement. When the co-therapists are male and female, there is the further possibility of providing the family with new parental models.

A therapist's approach may vary from family to family and will depend on his orientation, skill, and training and his perception of how best to intervene therapeutically. Since techniques of family therapy are not yet highly formalized, therapists commonly experiment with various combinations and shift from one approach to another at different phases of therapy. Thus, many therapists see whole families first and then shift to the parents, the siblings, one individual, or any combination that seems appropriate for the problem involved. Or, they might start with the individual and later bring in his family. Some therapists are beginning to see families together, either in married couples groups or multiple family group therapy, although this is not yet common (Group for the Advancement of Psychiatry, 1970).

INDIVIDUAL THERAPY OR FAMILY THERAPY?

There are at least two situations in which the clinician is likely to deal therapeutically with the entire family rather than with one of its members: (1) when individual therapy has failed or been very slow, with frequent relapses due to the family's resistance to any attempted change in the individual; and (2) when individual improvement due to individual therapy has led to considerable distress and the appearance of symptoms in one or more of the other family members. In addition, family therapy would seem to be preferred for: (1) marital problems; (2) generation conflicts between parents and children, especially adolescents; and (3) various family crises. Therapy for schizophrenics that includes their families has become more common and has been somewhat more successful than individual psychotherapy.

Family therapy is not simply treating individuals in a family context; the disordered family process must be changed. However, since most family therapists were trained as individual therapists, many continue to perceive individual psychopathology as their central concern while acknowledging the context of family life in which such psychopathology developed. Others focus on the disequilibrium in a family, considering individual intrapsychic conflicts to be secondary to improving the family's functioning as a more effective unit. Table 16 compares two kinds of family therapy. The individual-oriented therapist is likely to work with families but retain his focus on the individual. In effect, he attempts to adapt individual therapy to the family situation. The family-oriented therapist is interested in the family as a system. He believes his approach is a more realistic way to understand family psychopathology and a more efficient way to treat it in individual family members. To him, the traditional psychotherapeutic focus on the separateness and autonomy of the individual has made treatment difficult and prevention all but impossible. Family-oriented therapy can strengthen the family by helping it achieve a stronger sense of unity, an ability to communicate, and to work together constructively in realistic, mutually accepting, satisfying ways.

Table 16. Comparisons between individual-oriented and family-oriented family therapy*

INDIVIDUAL-ORIENTED	FAMILY-ORIENTED
1. Family therapy is one of many methods of treatment.	1. Family therapy is a new orientation to viewing human problems.
2. The individual's psychopathology is the focus of study and treatment; the family is seen as a stress factor.	2. The disordered family system needs some family member to express its psychopathology.
3. The identified patient is the victim of family strife.	3. The identified patient contributes to and is an essential part of family strife.
4. The family is a collection of individuals behaving on the basis of past experiences with each other.	4. The present situation is the major causal factor, since current problems must be currently reinforced if they continue to exist.
5. Diagnosis and evaluation of the family problem should precede intervention.	5. Immediate action-oriented intervention takes place at the first session, which is usually a time of family crisis, when the family is ripe for change.
6. The therapist is an observer evaluating the family's problems.	6. The therapist is himself a part of the context of treatment; his active participation affects the family system.
7. The therapist brings out clients' feelings and attitudes toward each other; he uses interpretation to show them what they are expressing.	7. The therapist uses fewer interpretations; he is interested in enhancing positive aspects of the relationships.
8. The therapist talks to one person at a time; family members talk largely to him rather than to each other.	8. Family members talk to each other, not to the therapist; all members are urged to participate.
9. The therapist takes sides in family conflict, supporting one member (for example, a child, a schizophrenic).	9. The therapist avoids being caught up in factional struggles in the family.
10. Family therapy is a technique for gathering additional information about individuals in the family.	10. Individual psychological problems are social problems involving the total ecological system, including the social institutions in which the family is embedded.

* Adapted from Haley (1970).

CONTRAINDICATIONS FOR FAMILY THERAPY

Not all disturbed families necessarily benefit from family therapy. For some families it may be too late to reverse the forces of fragmentation. In other families, it may be difficult to get a working relationship with the family started because key members are unavailable (children away at school, parent dead or hospitalized, family member refuses to attend family sessions). Sometimes one family member may so dominate the group with his malignant, destructive motivation (for example, because of a paranoid state or deteriorating organic brain-damaged condition) that the family therapy approach is unworkable (Ackerman, 1970). While conjoint family therapy may often be useful in treating schizophrenia in a family member (Jackson, 1961), sometimes acute schizophrenics are so panicked that, without the prior benefit of an established relationship with a therapist, they cannot tolerate the complexity and stress of family interviews (Wynne, 1965).

Family therapy demands open communication and the courage to risk exposing the truth. Sometimes parents, unaccustomed to sharing personal or marital secrets with their children (or family secrets with their therapist) balk at family sessions.[1] Ackerman (1970) has noted that some family members have such extremely rigid defenses that breaking through them may induce an acute depression, psychosis, or psychosomatic crisis. On the other hand, if the rigid defenses remain impenetrable, the individual remains walled off from his own feelings and inaccessible to the rest of the family, rendering intervention by family therapy ineffective.

None of these arguments necessarily rules out using family therapy. Instead, they indicate that certain family circumstances or characteristics may excessively handicap the potential benefits of therapeutic intervention on a family level.

GOALS OF FAMILY THERAPY

The major purpose in therapeutic work with a family is to improve its function as a working, interdependent group. This goal has important consequences for those individuals who make up the family. As all family

---

[1] Handling secrets or other confidential items presents a special ethical problem in family therapy. In individual psychotherapy, the patient's privacy is protected; his trust in the therapist maximizes his openness. In family therapy, the situation is more complicated, with different family members feeling varying degrees of trust or openness in front of the rest of the family and the therapist. Many family therapists consider secrets to be part of the family's problems in communication. Consequently, they may announce at the start that they will not keep secrets of one family member from the whole family in an effort to facilitate more open communication.

members are able to communicate better and remove obstacles to their overall functioning as a unit, each member is in a better position to grow and become better differentiated as an individual. Children are helped to make the ultimate separation from what Bowen (1966) calls the "undifferentiated family ego mass."

A useful distinction may be made between such long-term goals and other more immediate, short-term goals. Short-term goals vary, depending on the phase of therapy and the therapist's technique. Typically, the family therapist's initial goal is to discover if and how the identified patient's problem is linked to a definable system of family relationships (Group for the Advancement of Psychiatry, 1970). He explores with the family the various ways family members are emotionally and behaviorally involved with each other. A second initial goal may involve assessing what combination of family members (if not all) should continue to undergo family therapy at this time. Various combinations may be seen at different points over the course of therapy. A third short-term goal, once therapy is underway, is to sensitize the family members, through their participation, to the way they currently communicate with each other, solve problems, resolve differences, or deal with family crises. One overall goal, undertaken from the start by all family therapists, is to involve all family members in the therapeutic process. This is especially important for those individuals who are resistant and deny they have problems but come for therapy reluctantly and allegedly only for the sake of the identified patient.

A recent survey of family therapist practices by the Group for the Advancement of Psychiatry (1970) asked what these practitioners considered to be their primary and secondary goals for all families or certain families. Tables 17 and 18 reveal the goals reported by the 290 respondents. The overwhelming majority, about 90 percent, indicated that all eight of the listed objectives were either their primary or secondary goals with at least some families. Not a single respondent answered that improved communication was rarely or never a goal. Over half of the respondents had as a primary goal, either with all or certain families, all eight of the stated goals. However, improvement in individual task performance or in individual symptomatic improvement was more likely to be secondary goals for this sample of family therapists. This indicates that these goals had by no means been abandoned, but that change in only part of a family was given less emphasis than such family-wide change as improved communication.

Table 17. Primary goals stated by therapists with families actually in treatment ($N = 290$)*

PRIMARY GOALS	PERCENT OF ALL FAMILIES	PERCENT OF CERTAIN FAMILIES	TOTAL PERCENT
1. Improved communication	85	5	90
2. Improved autonomy and individuation	56	31	87
3. Improved empathy	56	15	71
4. More flexible leadership	34	32	66
5. Improved role agreement	32	32	64
6. Reduced conflict	23	37	60
7. Individual symptomatic improvement	23	33	56
8. Improved individual task performance	12	38	50

* From *The Field of Family Therapy*, GAP report No. 78. Copyright 1970 by the Group for the Advancement of Psychiatry, Inc. Reprinted by permission of the Committee on the Family, Group for the Advancement of Psychiatry.

TECHNIQUES OF FAMILY THERAPY

There is no single prevailing theory or single set of procedures followed by all family therapists. The psychoanalytically oriented therapist is likely to see the family constellation as the dynamic field from which individual intrapsychic conflicts emerge. Following Freud, however, most

Table 18. Secondary goals stated by therapists with families actually in treatment ($N = 290$)*

SECONDARY GOALS	PERCENT OF ALL FAMILIES	PERCENT OF CERTAIN FAMILIES	TOTAL PERCENT
1. Improved individual task performance	16	29	45
2. Individual symptomatic improvement	23	15	38
3. Reduced conflict	17	18	35
4. Improved role agreement	17	15	32
5. More flexible leadership	11	19	30
6. Improved empathy	17	8	25
7. Improved autonomy and individuation	7	5	12
8. Improved communication	8	1	9

* From *The Field of Family Therapy*, GAP report No. 78. Copyright 1970 by the Group for the Advancement of Psychiatry, Inc. Reprinted by permission of the Committee on the Family, Group for the Advancement of Psychiatry.

psychoanalysts, particularly those working with adults, have until recently dealt only with individual patients, refusing to work or consult with other family members. This situation is changing for some analysts, such as Grotjahn (1960), who has proposed a technique for the psychoanalytic treatment of families in which the whole family could be described as neurotic. Grotjahn maintains that certain complementary neuroses in a family can be treated through psychoanalysis. While concentrating his efforts on the psychoanalysis of the identified patient, Grotjahn occasionally uses conjoint and concurrent family therapy sessions to facilitate growth in all the family members.

The behavior-oriented therapist sees the family therapy situation as an opportunity to induce significant behavioral changes in the family members by restructuring their interpersonal environments (Liberman, 1970). Instead of being caught up in and rewarding maladaptive behavior with attention responses that socially reinforce the undesirable behavior (perhaps nagging, sympathy, babying, anger, or irritation), family members learn to recognize and approve only each other's desired behavior. The deviant member continues with his manipulative behavior or set of symptoms so long as the family expresses interest and concern, even if intermittently. The behaviorally oriented family therapist makes a behavioral analysis of the problems in the family, determining what behavior patterns in others each member would like to see increased or decreased. At the same time, he focuses on what environmental or interpersonal contingencies currently support the problem behavior. Once identified, the family is guided to change the contingencies of their social reinforcement patterns from maladaptive to adaptive target behavior. Sometimes modeling and imitation (see pp. 252–253) facilitates change, as the therapist or a family member exhibits desired, adaptive behavior. From this point of view, family therapy is viewed as a learning experience, with the therapist as an educator, model, "shaper," and himself a social reinforcer.

Perhaps the most significant contribution to understanding human interactions in a family has come from the development of a theory of communication applied to family therapy. Emerging from the work of Bateson et al. (1956) at the Mental Research Institute in Palo Alto, California, the approach is best described by Haley (1963) and Watzlawick, Beavin, and Jackson (1967). The family therapist is seen as a communication analyst who helps the family understand the communication pattern of their interactions. Like the phenomenologist, his interest is the here-and-now pattern of behavior, not inferred (and therefore less reliable) past causes. There is less speculation about why some behavior or symptom appears and more on how such behavior affects the client's surroundings. Disturbed behavior, according to this viewpoint, represents a communicative reaction to a particular untenable situation rather than the inexplicable reactions of a "sick" individual.

Communication theory contributes certain basic premises regarding human behavior:

1. All behavior is communication. Just as one cannot avoid behavior, so he cannot avoid communication. The wife who complains that her husband wants only to read the newspaper or watch television in the evening and "refuses to communicate" with her is nevertheless receiving his message of rejection or withdrawal as clearly as if he had stated it directly. In a family therapy setting, the therapist focuses on verbal communication between family members and also helps the family become aware of their nonverbal communications—gestures, posture, speaking order, seating arrangements, interruptions, and so on. One of the important advantages of family therapy is that the therapist sees the action played out in front of him, rather than relying on an individual patient's verbal report, which may be distorted.

2. Any communication does more than convey information; it also defines the relationship between communicants. The wife who greets her husband returning from work with "I'm tired" may be really asking him to take her out to dinner, to be especially kind and considerate, to take care of the children, not to be angry that the house is in disarray, not to expect sexual intercourse that night. Thus, all communication has both a report and command function.

3. The response to a communication offers feedback which confirms, rejects, or modifies the original communication. Communication is a system of exchange in which the message's intent must be clear. The husband in the previous example, by his response, may indicate which of the possibilities he believes his wife intended, and how he feels on the basis of his perception. If there is a discrepancy between her intention and his perception, she provides him with feedback ("I want to rest before dinner, which will be later than usual; however, I'm sure I will not be too tired for sexual relations later; I look forward to them.") The family therapist can help each family member be more open and direct instead of camouflaging his real messages.

4. The way a communication sequence is perceived by the participants is at the root of many relationship struggles. A couple coming for marriage therapy may begin to recognize that the husband communicates passive withdrawal and the wife, nagging criticism. The husband is likely to claim that his withdrawal is a defense against her nagging. The wife claims to be increasingly critical the further he withdraws. Their messages of "I withdraw because you nag" and "I nag because you withdraw" may become a circular, monotonous series, unbroken until each can recognize that he has perceived the oscillating behavioral events differently and has reacted to what he perceives as originating in the other. The therapist may help them see that it matters little who is correct, that the beginning point is arbitrary, and that both must recognize that they determine, as well as react to, the other's behavior.

5. Families establish their rules on the basis of command messages. Families are rule-governed systems. Many of these rules are so subtle and ingrained by time that they are taken for granted by family members. When someone exceeds the limits expected of him, negative feedback from others helps bring his behavior back into an acceptable range. Parents who scold an adolescent for staying out late appear to be concerned about his health, lack of sleep, or possible danger, but they may also be expressing the command message that they set the rules, he is still a child in their eyes, or they are not ready to abdicate control over his curfew.

6. A flexible family system permits negotiated rule changes; a pathological system adheres rigidly to fixed rules. Children, particularly adolescents, are frequently demanding family rule changes regarding bedtime, financial allowances, selection of clothes, and other matters. A flexible set of rules in a family allows negotiation. The family therapist may help a disordered family change their rules by acting as a go-between, mediating a conflict. Zuk (1969) believes family therapy provides a unique situation for examining destructive coalitions, alliances, and cliques in the family, which involve at least two persons joined against at least one other. His technique of triadic-based family therapy is to act as a mediator in order to apply leverage against the pathogenic ways in which certain families relate. In Zuk's view, changes in the family may result from the bargaining and negotiation that goes on between therapist and family members. The go-between process is aimed at reducing and replacing pathogenic relating.

INNOVATIONS IN FAMILY THERAPY

In addition to those methods of family therapy already described, certain recently attempted procedures point to new directions in psychotherapy in general. Several of these new techniques will be described below.

1. Multiple-impact therapy. In an effort to provide therapeutic intervention for a family with a disturbed adolescent in crisis, MacGregor, Ritchie, Serrano, and Schuster (1964) at the University of Texas in Galveston have developed a unique, intensive, crisis-focused approach to family therapy. An entire family comes for two days of continuing interaction with a team of mental health professionals. Beginning with a brief, initial team–family conference, various combinations of team members and family members split up into separate conferences: therapists overlap in working with different individuals or combinations; multiple therapists work with the same individuals or pair of family members; team–family conferences are held periodically; and occasionally two family members (perhaps father and son) may be left alone to work out certain problems themselves. Before leaving, follow-ups are arranged, varying from six weekly visits by the parents, to a half-day session three months later. Multiple Impact Therapy aims less to provide family members with insight than to change the family from a relatively closed system to an open system conducive to growth. Open communication, mutual acceptance, clear role differentiation between members, flexibility to attempt new ways of relating—especially to and by the disturbed adolescent—are all encouraged so family members can give up playing their repetitive roles in a reverberating system and begin to explore new ways of growth.

2. Multiple-family group therapy. Several clinicians (Berman, 1966; Laqueur, 1970) have recently begun to treat several families simultaneously. Usually used in a hospital situation where there rarely are enough therapists for individual patients or individual families, multiple-family therapy makes it possible to treat up to six hospitalized patients and their families in a group. In addition to increased efficiency, such an approach has proven useful in helping the patient adjust from a structured hospital milieu into an unstructured home situation. Berman has reported promising preliminary data, based on a year's operation of such a program in a Veterans Administration hospital. The readmission rate of past patients in such a program has been zero, compared to 30 to 40 percent of comparable patients ordinarily readmitted within a year of hospital discharge. Apparently the increased awareness and resolution of interpersonal difficulties in the family have been the most beneficial factors. In general, the benefits of such an approach accrue from the combined benefits of family and group therapy. Group identification and support, easy recognition of and quick involvement with each other's problems, seeing one family's communication problems portrayed by another family, and learning how other families solve their relationship problems appear to be particularly valuable. A corollary of this approach, gaining popularity outside hospitals, is for groups of married couples to participate in a group therapy arrangement, which is expected to lead to many of the same benefits.

3. Family therapy in the home.   As family therapists have shifted from the medical model, some have begun to explore the possibility of intervention techniques in nonmedical settings. With the growing emphasis on conceptualizing an individual's emotional disturbance as an expression of a family's disordered relationships, it seems clearer that such underlying conflicts might perhaps best be studied in their natural habitat, the home. Occasional or regular home visits by one or more therapists have the following advantages: (1) the total functioning of the family is more evident, with less opportunity to disguise or deny behavior or be on best behavior; (2) each family member is more apt to play his everyday role, forcing the therapist to undergo an unnatural role shift, rather than vice versa; (3) there is less chance of absenteeism by a family member, a common phenomenon in the office practice of family therapy; (4) there is more likely to be tacit recognition that the entire family has problems, rather than that a single family member requires psychotherapy in or out of a mental hospital; (5) there is apt to be less anxiety in familiar surroundings, encouraging more open communication and less artificial role playing to impress the therapist; and (6) the therapist is less likely to be treated with the stereotyped deference inherent in the patient–doctor relationship (Speck, 1964; Friedman et al., 1965). Social workers and public health nurses have long practiced family therapy in the home; now other mental health professionals are following their examples, either on a regular basis or on specifically chosen occasions. Ackerman (1958) has found that the home visit is especially useful for diagnosis. He has found the best time to visit is at the evening meal-time when the family is normally together. Arriving before the father returns from work, the therapist is in a better position to evaluate changes in the family organization, attitudes, and feelings with the arrival of the father. Ackerman is particularly interested in gauging the family interaction patterns, the emotional climate of the home, specific conflicts between family members, and patterns of restitution after conflict in the family. While Ackerman's efforts in the home are directed primarily at family diagnosis, Friedman et al. (1965) are interested in the possibility of treating schizophrenic individuals in their home settings as an integral part of the group treatment of the entire family. Rather than hospitalize a young schizophrenic, particularly when his family is living together, Friedman has conducted regular family therapy in the home. A number of detailed case studies show this method as modifying the schizophrenic's disturbance as well as creating more effective group functioning and a more satisfactory life for the entire family.

4. Network therapy. Some therapists have begun to extend the concept of family treatment of schizophrenics in the home by including all members of the identified patient's "social network." By this they mean that home treatment might be aimed not only at the schizophrenic and his family, but also might involve members of his extended family, friends, neighbors, and all others who play a significant role in his life. Network therapy is based on the assumption that there is significant pathology in the schizophrenic's communication patterns with all members of his social network, not just with his nuclear family. This approach works at tightening the network of relationships, making the entire group as intimately involved as possible in each other's lives. Speck and Rueveni (1969), developers of this method, see such networks as analogous to clans or tribal units; their major benefit is in offering support, reassurance, and solidarity to its members. In practice, members of the network gather in the home of the schizophrenic patient and his family, much as a tribe in a crisis situation might assemble. Thus, family, relatives, and friends are mobilized into a potent social force, particularly appealing in an age of increasing depersonalization and alienation. Such intervention aims to create a climate of trust and openness among all members as a prelude to constructive emotional encounters between them. Ultimately it is hoped that bonds between people will be strengthened, overt communication increased, and double-bind messages removed. Usually a team of professionals is present at six weekly four-hour sessions; some networks continue meeting on their own for varying periods of time thereafter. This approach seems promising, although it is still so new that few research results are available.

5. Conjoint sexual therapy. A significant form of marriage counseling, focusing on sexual dysfunction, has emerged from the research by Masters and Johnson (1966) on the anatomy and physiology of the human sexual response. These researchers have recently (Masters & Johnson, 1970) proposed a rapid treatment program for overcoming various forms of human sexual inadequacy, based on some of the findings in their original preclinical investigations. A basic premise in this approach is that both marital partners are involved whenever there is some form of sexual inadequacy, such as impotence or premature ejaculation in a man or a nonorgasmic response in a women. That is, sexual dysfunction is seen as a marital-unit problem, not the problem of one partner alone. Consequently, both partners participate in the treatment program. While it is understood that sexual functioning is not the total of any marital relationship, Masters and Johnson contend that very few marriages can exist as effective, complete, and ongoing entities if the sexual exchange is not comfortable and satisfactory to both partners.

The technique requires that the husband and wife spend a maximum of two weeks at a center away from home. The isolation from children, friends, business and professional demands, and time commitments is believed to be necessary for an effective treatment program. Each couple is seen by co-therapists, one man and one woman, preferably one each from the biological and behavioral disciplines. The dual-sex team is thought to avoid potential therapist misinterpretation due to male or female bias, perhaps because Masters and Johnson believe that neither sex can ever fully understand the other's sexual experiences. Couples are seen daily, separately at first, in order to do an individual sex-history taking (not only of chronological sexual experiences, but more importantly of sexually oriented attitudes, feelings, expectations, and so on). By the third day, co-therapists and marital partners meet to review accrued clinical material and to begin to relate individual and marital histories to present sexual dysfunctions. An educational process is begun at this point, teaching effective sexual functioning and attempting to overcome sexual myths, un-realistic sexual expectations, misunderstandings, and communication failures between the partners. Specific instructions for increasing sexual responsiveness are given. Husbands and wives are taught to share physical pleasure-giving without anxiety about sexual performance. By the fifth day, the couple is believed to be ready to begin to receive instructions in the physical and psychological techniques for overcoming the specific sexual dysfunctions which brought them for treatment. Long-term results are still inconclusive, although certain forms of dysfunction, such as premature ejaculation, appear to respond very positively to this method. Particularly important in evaluating this type of counseling is accurate follow-up research to determine the extent to which any gains made during the acute treatment phase can be retained. Masters and Johnson plan five-year follow-up studies.

THE EFFECTIVENESS OF FAMILY THERAPY

While family therapy during the last 20 years has developed into an orientation to changing human behavior that has attracted an ever-growing number of practitioners, relatively little objective research data have appeared. Family therapists are particularly enthusiastic about their methods' potential on the basis of seeing changes in previously unreachable patients or in families previously in the process of disorganization. As in the case of individual psychotherapy, each method has adherents who claim successes and know subjectively that "it works." However, changes in feelings, attitudes, or in the openness of communication between family members is difficult to measure. Increased self-esteem or the reduction of symptoms in the identified patient, desirable as that may be, sometimes is at the expense of lowered self-esteem or the development of symptoms in another family member. In any event, criteria for what constitutes a good family life is far from settled, particularly at a time when many are questioning the need for a conventional family life at all.

Clinical impressions of improvement in families remain, at this time, a substitute for controlled studies of the effects of family therapy. Framo (1965) has described some concrete, operational ways of estimating family improvement: (1) greater continuity in communication during sessions; (2) more conflicts resolved at home rather than brought to the therapist to solve; (3) increased likelihood of seeing one another as real people, rather than attributing to them characteristics they do not have; (4) more enjoyment of each other as a family; (5) greater individuation among the different family members, with greater tolerance for each member to separate from the family system; (6) less satisfaction from participating in family conflicts; (7) emotional forces become directed outside the family rather than remaining directed to one another; (8) increased and improved communication between parents, who usually end up more sympathetic to each other and with an increased chance for a meaningful relationship; and (9) perhaps most important, the family members discover that there are other ways of behaving toward each other and still remaining a family.

GROUP THERAPY AND THE ENCOUNTER MOVEMENT

In one form or another, group therapy has been practiced since early in the twentieth century, although the impetus for its major expansion came from the pressures for clinical services during World War II. Because of the limited number of trained therapists and the sudden influx of psychiatric casualties during wartime, new, briefer treatment methods were sought. In response, many therapists of various orientations began to modify their techniques, and by 1945 every school of psychotherapy was involved in group therapy (Rosenbaum & Berger, 1963). However, for many years group therapy did not have the status of individual therapy for many practitioners, who either refused to do group work or did so only as a concession in order to treat many patients simultaneously. This situation began to change during the last decade as more and more clinicians began to see that group therapy offered certain advantages not possible in individual therapy. Interestingly, having so recently won scientific and professional respectability as a method of treating emotional problems, it already has been called traditional by some clinicians (for example, Ruitenbeek, 1970) who see the field expanding into encounter groups and what is sometimes called the human growth-potential movement.

A BRIEF HISTORY OF THERAPY GROUPS
AND T (TRAINING) GROUPS

Most observers agree that the technique of group therapy was introduced in 1905 by Joseph Pratt, a Boston internist. Pratt developed a method of treating tuberculosis patients that included home visits and weekly meetings of approximately 25 patients. At such meetings Pratt would lecture, offer support and encouragement, and would lead a group discussion of their emotional problems, which he recognized as related to the physical course of the tuberculosis (Hadden, 1955). Pratt's approach received little attention from American psychiatrists of his day: However, at about the same time, in 1910, and without any knowledge of Pratt's work, Austrian psychiatrist Jacob Moreno began to use some techniques of the theater, such as role-playing, to encourage his patients to develop spontaneity and thereby work out their problems in a group setting. Moreno emigrated to the United States in 1925, where he soon introduced the technique of psychodrama. He is said to have coined the term group therapy in 1931 (Gazda, 1968).

During the 1930s, Samuel Slavson, an engineer by training, began to do group work at the Jewish Board of Guardians in New York City, from which emerged his activity-group therapy techniques (using play groups) with children and moderately disturbed adolescents (Slavson, 1964). Slavson's approach was based on concepts from psychoanalysis, group work, and progressive education. He organized the American Group Psychotherapy Association in 1943 and for many years was editor of its journal, *The International Journal of Group Psychotherapy.* Just prior to World War II and for two decades thereafter, Slavson was the outstanding spokesman for group therapy as an effective psychotherapeutic approach.

During the past decade, group therapy has expanded from a method of treatment to an increasingly popular means for learning how to relate more openly and honestly to people. Today, every large city and many medium-sized cities in the United States have growth centers or at least some sort of intensive group experience easily available to the public. Usually such experiences involve participation in encounter groups (or T groups or sensitivity groups[2]) in which 10 to 20 individuals, often strangers before the group meeting, meet for an intensive weekend session or periodically over several months to explore and exchange feelings and attitudes, gain awareness, and learn to deal with others in new, more fulfilling ways. Probably the best known growth center is Esalen in Big Sur, California; by 1970 it was reported to have had 50,000 participants in its

---

[2] There now are such a variety of these groups that one literally needs a scorecard to tell them apart. The various types of groups are described and differentiated on pp. 396–405.

various programs. At least 75 other growth centers in the United States were reported in 1969 (Yalom, 1970). Many fictional or autobiographical accounts of experiences at such centers have recently been published. Jane Howard's (1970) *Please Touch* provides a personal guided tour of various centers around the United States.

Encounter groups represent an amalgam of the theories and methodology of group therapy and the so-called human relations training groups. Whereas the former arose as a form of treatment for emotional problems, the latter derived from an educational tradition and is based on social psychological principles of group dynamics. Curiously, therapy groups and training groups (or T groups) have existed side by side since immediately after World War II, although there was little contact between the two until the middle 1960s. One notable exception was Bach's 1954 publication of *Intensive Group Psychotherapy,* which attempted to apply group dynamics principles to group therapy.

The first T groups were organized in 1946 under the direction of Kurt Lewin, a social psychologist and head of the Massachusetts Institute of Technology's new Research Center for Group Dynamics. Their original purpose was to train community leaders to facilitate understanding of and compliance with recently adopted Fair Employment Practices Acts (Benne, 1964). The first such group experience involved three small groups of 10 members each who held group discussions and participated in role-playing techniques to reenact their home community problems and practice alternate solutions to such problems. Evening staff meetings, analyzing the participants as well as the day's events were originally closed to the participants. However, as these participants learned of the staff meetings and began to take part, Lewin and his training leaders realized they had inadvertently discovered an effective method for human relations education —that is, that the participants could benefit most if they were confronted with observations regarding their behavior and the effects of such behavior on others. In this way, they could learn about themselves, about group behavior, and how to facilitate behavior changes in others.

Based on the success of the workshop, various T-group sessions began to be held every summer at Bethel, Maine. Inspired by Lewin's theoretical formulations, Leland Bradford (an educator), Kenneth Beane (a philosopher), and Ronald Lippitt (a social psychologist) founded the National Training Laboratories (NTL) in 1950. Originally a division of the National Education Association, NTL was created as a means of reeducating people's attitudes, values, and behavior through the group process. Now an independent organization, the NTL Institute for Applied Behavioral Science continues to offer training at Bethel and various other places throughout the world. Increasingly over the years, the purposes of T groups have shifted toward building self-awareness by understanding one's own inter-personal behavior. T groups are sometimes thought of as therapy for normals, since the focus is not on emotional disturbances but rather on improving human relations skills. Accordingly, T groups have become very popular among progressive business organizations, many government agencies, and school systems. (Some of the techniques and procedures of T groups are discussed on pp. 398–399.)

As T groups have become better known, many clinicians have become aware of their techniques and have adapted them to group therapy. At the same time, as the T group movement has attracted many clinicians to its ranks, it too has shifted its emphasis from a social psychological analysis of an individual's group behavior to a more clinical psychological study of him as an individual. Encounter groups in their various forms are a direct result of such a merger of concepts and procedures. Encounter groups typically use such innovations as: (1) increased emphasis on the here and now; (2) the concept of feedback in interpersonal communica-tion; (3) greater self-disclosure by the group leader (or *facilitator,* a term used to underscore the fact that his function is more to assist than to lead); (4) techniques such as verbal and nonverbal exercises to facilitate self-exploration, group interaction, and release human potential; and (5) time-extended meetings, as in group marathon sessions. As Yalom (1970) has noted, all these innovations have in part been adapted from the T group to group therapy.

THE PRACTICE OF GROUP THERAPY

While the practice of group therapy is characterized by considerable diversity depending on the theoretical orientation and personal skills of the group therapist, there nevertheless are certain similarities between all forms of group therapy. Typically, groups are comprised of five to 10 individuals who meet with a leader at least once a week for one and one-half-hour to two-hour sessions. The seating arrangement is usually circular so each group member can see and readily talk to every other member including the therapist. Usually groups are fairly heterogeneous, with members having a variety of occupations, a wide range of educational levels, a moderate range of age differences, and varying degrees of sophistication. Sometimes homogeneous groups are arranged (for example, composed of drug addicts, stutterers, or hospitalized patients with the same diagnosis), although even in such groups there is considerable heterogeneity in terms of personality characteristics, economic background, motivation, intelligence, and other factors. Actually, the stimulation of contrasting personalities, pathologies, and problems tends to facilitate group interaction and movement (Kadis, Krasner, Winick, & Foulkes, 1963). While some clinicians tend to exclude certain types of individuals (such as the brain-damaged, acutely psychotic, suicidal) from out-patient intensive group therapy, most follow a more pragmatic approach to patient selection, asking if a particular patient will help or interfere with communication in a particular group (Kadis et al., 1963).

Many therapists insist on seeing patients concurrently in individual as well as in group sessions, while others may work with a patient individually for a considerable period of time before placing him in a group. Patients are sometimes seen only in groups, without individual treatment, although most therapists prefer to learn something about the person through individual interviews before placing him in a group. Some therapists prefer to work alone with a group, while others prefer to work with a co-therapist. A male–female co-therapist team is likely to evoke a family situation feeling among group members, providing valuable material to be worked through. Co-therapists also have the advantage of providing useful feedback concerning each other's behavior. Some therapists, such as Wolf (1949), schedule periodic leaderless group sessions (called the *alternate session technique*) as a supplement to regular weekly group sessions. Wolf and others (Mullan & Rosenbaum, 1962) feel such meetings permit the group members to experience themselves as less dependent on the therapist, to develop a greater sense of personal responsibility, and to foster group organization. Other therapists forbid patients to contact one another between sessions for fear that they will form subgroups and possibly act out[3] feelings evoked by the group experience (perhaps sexual or aggressive impulses). More realistically, Yalom (1970) believes it may be useless to prohibit extragroup socializing, since invariably some such contact will occur dur-

---

[3] Acting out is a way of avoiding experiencing feelings by taking some action that reduces tension and avoids anxiety or discomfort.

ing the course of outpatient therapy and cannot be avoided for patients hospitalized in the same psychiatric ward. Instead Yalom considers any such contact to be less harmful, ultimately, to therapeutic progress than the harm of secret contact cloaked in a conspiracy of silence.

Groups may be either open or closed. *Open groups* maintain their constant size by replacing members who leave the group. Such groups may continue indefinitely, sometimes having a complete turnover of members before their ultimate termination. In certain training situations, group leaders finish their internships and are replaced by other leaders. *Closed groups* maintain a constant membership, accepting no new members for the duration of the group's existence, which is usually stipulated at the outset. Closed groups are most likely to exist in such settings as hospitals or prisons where the members are under some enforced stay. Occasionally parent groups meet for a fixed number of sessions to deal with their common problems regarding children. Closed groups are usually not feasible on an outpatient, voluntary basis. However, when they are feasible, they lend themselves more easily to research studies than do open groups.

THE UNIQUE ADVANTAGES OF GROUP THERAPY

In contrast to individual psychotherapy in which the therapist is the major change agent, changes in an individual as a result of a group experience come from the impact of the entire group. As group members begin to explore their problems in the presence of others, learning how they react to each other's behavior, sharing experiences, feelings, attitudes, and motives with each other, each member usually begins to obtain some sense of relief and feeling of well being. Different members profit in different degrees from the experience, based to a large extent on their willingness to disclose previously withheld or denied feelings. In addition, different members may benefit from different aspects of the same group experience. Finally, each member may benefit for different reasons at different stages of his therapy. The following advantages of group therapy distinguish it from individual therapy:

1. A group resembles everyday reality more closely than does the situation of talking individually to a therapist. A patient in a one-to-one relationship is less likely to role-play a relationship with a therapist; he usually simply describes his problems. The group adds another dimension, allowing the therapist to see the patient's actual behavior and customary way of interacting with people.

2. Each patient becomes aware that his problems are not unique. Frequently, group members have previously been social isolates particularly because they believed their thoughts, fantasies, feelings, or impulses made them different from other people. As social isolates. they have denied themselves the opportunity to discover the universality of what they had considered only personal difficulties. Group discussion, usually quite early in therapy, provides relief when each member learns he is not unique. Accordingly, he is encouraged to give up feelings of isolation and self-consciousness.

3. Group cohesiveness (or "we-ness") leads to increased acceptance, trust, caring, and support of one another. Self-acceptance is likely to increase when bolstered by the acceptance of a group of people who, unlike the therapist, are not required to care about him as part of their role. As a result, the individual may begin to reexamine and reevaluate his previous low level of self-esteem.

4. Each patient is encouraged to experiment with new coping techniques by imitating other members who improve. Particularly in open groups, new members have an opportunity to observe older members and their more successful ways of coping with problems.

5. Catharsis, reducing tension by ventilating feelings, is especially significant in group therapy. Rather than talking privately with a therapist about feelings toward people, the group situation demands the expression of feelings—both positive and negative—directly at other group members who evoke love, frustration, tears, or rage. Not only does the patient experience some sense of relief, but he also learns that intense affect does not destroy anyone, as he might have feared or fantasied. Consequently, he is encouraged to explore and express his feelings more openly in the future.

6. Self-esteem is increased by helping others. In individual therapy, the therapist alone offers help, which the patient receives but has no opportunity to reciprocate. In group therapy, empathy, warmth, acceptance, support, genuineness—usually the helping qualities of a therapist—may be received and given by any group member. In particular, patients with a feeling of low self-worth may benefit greatly from the experience of being important and helpful to another human being.

7. Insight and understanding of human motives and behavior helps many patients both during and after group therapy. Not only are they likely to be more attuned to their own feelings, but many report an entirely new way of understanding others after the group experience. As a result, social

sensitivity is increased, as are social skills, inevitably resulting in increased self-confidence with others.

VARIETIES OF GROUP THERAPY

1. Psychoanalytic groups. The classical psychoanalytic concepts and methods have been translated into a group setting by Wolf (1949) and Slavson (1964). Wolf meets with his groups, composed of four or five men and an equivalent number of women, for 90-minute sessions, usually three times per week. In addition, the group meets for an alternate session without the parental analyst figure one or two nights per week, in order to function more independently and work through their peer relationships. Wolf conceives of a group as a re-creation of the primary family, encouraging his patients to work through their unresolved conflicts in this simulated family situation. Group members are urged to engage in free associations about each other and to report their dreams. Resistances and transference feelings (developed toward all group members, not the analyst alone) are analyzed, usually by other group members. Interpretations by the analyst are kept to a minimum. Wolf and Schwartz (1962) maintain that unconscious material is worked through even more rapidly in analytic groups than in individual analysis. Slavson (1964) also uses the classical psychoanalytic concepts, although he opposes the alternate session because he believes the absence of the parental authority figures encourages uncontrolled and potentially destructive behavior, such as acting out sexual impulses. For Slavson, the focus of attention is on the individual rather than the group process. The group is merely a means of stimulating each of the members to act out his instinctual drives in the group setting. Much of Slavson's work has been with children; he has attempted to create a substitute family with the group leader as a permissive parent substitute.

2. Psychodrama. As developed by its founder Jacob Moreno (1946), psychodrama involves role-playing procedures in a group setting, which are intended to encourage catharsis, spontaneity, and self-understanding among the participants. Five instruments are used in psychodrama: (1) the protagonist—the patient; (2) a stage; (3) a director—equivalent to the therapist; (4) "auxiliary egos"—aides to the therapist or other patients; and (5) an audience. The situation to be dramatized on stage may involve an actual event from the protagonist's past life, a hypothetical event suggested by the therapist or patient, or a future event about which the patient anticipates distress. The plot provides merely the general background against which the patient may spontaneously act out the deep-seated feelings he could not express as easily in real life. When the patient is directed to portray himself, auxiliary egos are assigned supporting roles, playing significant people in the patient's life. Their purpose is to keep the action flowing, acting as catalysts to help the patient bring out his feelings. At various junctions, the director may suggest that the patient reverse roles with one of the players in order to interact with someone who now plays him. This is done in order to give him greater awareness of how another person sees him through his portrayal. In addition, role reversal lets the patient gain some understanding and feeling of how others in real life might react to him. Role reversal is just one of many techniques described by Moreno (1959) for helping the patient achieve greater spontaneity as well as greater understanding of his disturbed interpersonal behavior. Since all the action takes place in front of an audience, they may provide acceptance and understanding, or may themselves participate extemporaneously and thus benefit from the action taking place on stage. According to Moreno's conceptions, acting out rather than talking out feelings leads to deeper catharsis and helps free the patient's creativity. As in other forms of group therapy, each patient serves as a therapeutic agent for every other patient. By working through old situations and by learning to express oneself more spontaneously in new situations, the patient can develop more flexible social skills. The technique is thus particularly useful with patients who find it difficult to get in touch with their feelings or express them in words easily. Psychodrama's emphasis on both verbal and nonverbal techniques and the acting out of feelings has been influential in the development of many group training approaches, such as Gestalt groups, encounter groups, and group marathons.

3. Transactional analysis. Eric Berne, the originator of the psychotherapeutic method of transactional analysis (Berne, 1961) sees each individual as having three ego states at his disposal: child, adult, and parent. (An ego state is a consistent pattern of feelings and experiences related to a corresponding pattern of behavior.) The child ego states are relics from his childhood, reproducing in his behavior the reactive patterns of childhood. The adult ego states are concerned with collecting and processing data and planning action. The parental ego states are learned from parental figures and reproduce the feelings and behavioral responses of those figures. Transactional analysis involves determining which ego state is active at any given moment in an individual's transaction with another person. A game (Berne, 1964) is a series of ulterior transactions with a set of concealed but well-defined pay-offs. Games are common rituals of everyday living that provide an escape from intimacy. When transactional analysis is conducted in groups, most of the proceedings consist of discovering and analyzing the games played by the various group members (Berne, 1966). According to Berne, real intimacy rarely occurs in groups; all that can be expected for the most part is a kind of pseudo-intimacy, with emotion expressed without necessarily being authentic. That is, the affective expression is itself part of an externally programmed game in which the patient compliantly participates. Real intimacy, a game-free exchange of internally programmed affective expression, occasionally occurs, but generally only covered, socialized feelings are exchanged. The transactional analyst uses various techniques—such as interrogation, confrontation, and interpretation—in order to bring the group member to a position where he can exercise an adult option to choose more internally satisfying, game-free behavior. The analyst is essentially a teacher, helping group members understand and attempt to break through their games. Group treatment is the preferred method for most transactional analysts (Harris, 1967).

4. T (Training) groups or sensitivity training groups. A T group or sensitivity training group[4] is a learning laboratory for gaining greater awareness of self and others. The group usually consists of 10 to 15 people who meet in a residential setting (over a single weekend or for a fixed number of weeks) in order to learn from the laboratory experience how they and others interact in a group. The group is led by a trainer who imposes no structure or agenda but helps the group choose its own goals and directions and learn from its own experiences (Seashore, 1970). As the group process develops, each participant is encouraged to expose his feelings, thoughts, and behavior, give and receive feedback information, experiment with new behaviors, gain some awareness of his impact on others, and

---

[4] The T group experience is more commonly called "sensitivity training" on the West coast; the term was coined in 1954 at UCLA's Industrial Relations Institute, where such programs were developed to help selected industrial personnel become more effective managers and executives.

develop greater acceptance of self and others. The T group is essentially an educational experience, with the trainers likely to come from academic rather than clinical settings. The emphasis is on the here and now, as group members confront themselves as well as each other in the present. That is, sensitivity training is a particular kind of laboratory learning in which personal as well as interpersonal issues are the direct focus of the group (Egan, 1970). The goal is to open previously closed areas of thought and feeling, allowing the participant to experience deeper personal feelings and closer relationships with others after the laboratory experience is over.

While sharing some similarities with group therapy, there nevertheless are certain fundamental theoretical differences between therapy and T groups: (1) members of therapy groups seek treatment to relieve suffering, while members come to T groups to learn new interpersonal skills; (2) correspondingly, while the primary goal of therapy is to promote the individual's well-being, the goal of T groups is to improve the functioning of groups—industry, schools—to which the participant will return; (3) therapy groups accentuate the differences between therapist and patient, while in T groups the trainer differs from the other members only in possessing skill in a particular area; (4) the T group is of shorter duration and has more limited goals; (5) a therapy group is more likely to continue some dependence on the therapist, while the T group may develop with the trainer in a relatively less potent role (Frank, 1964; Kaplan, 1967); (6) T groups tend to operate in more informal settings such as resorts or retreats, and usually go on for one or two weeks for several hours each day, thus emphasizing the learning and group living aspect rather than the therapeutic one; (7) T groups end for all members at a prearranged time, while therapy groups continue for each member until he has reached his personal goals; and (8) T groups have always emphasized research, introducing new techniques developed by various human relations laboratories, while therapy groups have developed primarily on the basis of clinical experiences, often of a personal, intuitive nature. Despite these differences, therapy groups and T groups overlap in goals and share many of the same concepts and techniques for producing personal growth. As noted earlier, part of the appeal of T groups may be that they offer therapeutic benefits without the stigma of being considered treatment for emotional problems.

5. Basic encounter groups. Developed by Carl Rogers (1970) in the early 1960s and based in part on the process of traditional T groups and

in part on Rogers' own client-centered therapy (see pp. 267–270), basic encounter groups have enjoyed enormous popularity in the last decade. So enthusiastic has Rogers himself become about the therapeutic value of the group experience that he considers the encounter movement as "perhaps the most significant social invention of this century [Rogers, 1968]."
As in client-centered therapy, Rogers believes that therapeutic gain can occur after the group leader or facilitator creates the proper psychological climate of acceptance, nonjudgment, and empathy toward the group and its individual members. In the intensive group experience, as in a weekend workshop, particularly when there is much freedom and little structure, Rogers believes the individual will gradually feel safe enough to drop some of his defenses and begin to relate more directly on a feeling basis (that is, come into a basic encounter) with the other group members. Ultimately he will come to understand himself and his relationships with others more accurately, will change some of his unproductive attitudes and behavior, and subsequently will relate to others more effectively once he returns to his everyday life.

As Rogers describes the typical sequence of events, the refusal on the part of the facilitator to take directional responsibility leads to initial confusion, awkward silence, polite surface interaction, and frustration. During this "milling around period," some members begin to reveal personal attitudes, although others tend to ignore them and avoid any exposure themselves. Those who do develop the courage to express their feelings usually do little more than describe past feelings outside of the group. Slowly, here-and-now feelings, usually negative, begin to be expressed toward group members or the group leader, as individual members begin to test the freedom and trustworthiness of the group. As feelings of trust and group belongingness develop, certain members take the chance of letting the group know deeper facets of themselves. Currently experienced personal feelings toward one another are expressed in the increasing climate of trust. The group begins to develop a "healing capacity" as members exhibit a sensitive capacity to listen to, understand, and care about each other. As self-examination continues and social facades are dropped, the group seems to demand that each person be himself without hiding his feelings as he experiences them. In a free exchange, each member receives feedback information regarding how he appears to others. Individuals confront each other with positive as well as negative feelings in a way that involves closer and more direct contact than is usual in everyday life. The result of such a basic encounter often produces behavioral changes in the group (in gestures, tone of voice, spontaneity of feelings), leading ultimately to a more open, spontaneous, self-accepting person after the group experience is over. Rogers' naturalistic description of the basic encounter group process is based on the analysis of hundreds of tape-recorded sessions. In addition, he has used follow-up questionnaires for participants, the overwhelming majority of whom reported that the encounter group was a constructive, deeply meaningful, positive experience that has continued to make a positive difference in their lives months later.

6. Gestalt groups. Virtually unknown a decade ago, Gestalt groups today are developing at an unprecedented rate in the United States and Canada. This is due partly to the charismatic personality of Frederick (Fritz) Perls, the founder of Gestalt therapy. Also, the emergence of the Esalen Institute in Big Sur, California, with Perls in residence conducting seminars and weekend workshops, helped popularize the Gestalt therapy method of getting the individual in touch with his feelings of the immediate moment (see pp. 277–282). The focus of Gestalt therapy is always to help the individual gain awareness of himself in the "now," to be aware of what is —now—rather than what was, what should be, or what might be. The Gestalt technique of group therapy, patterned after Perls' method, is to disregard the group as such and to concentrate on each individual in the group in rotation. Usually beginning with a volunteer, the Gestalt therapist devotes his full attention to this individual as long as necessary, with the rest of the group observing. Perls will frequently ask each volunteer to become aware of his feelings and behavior (gestures, voice, an inappropriate smile canceling out an angry statement). In particular, the individual is to become aware of his sensations; in Perls' words, the patient needs "to lose his mind and find his senses." With the patient in the "hot seat" and Perls in close proximity, both in front of the group, the patient is pressed to tell what he sees and hears rather than what he is thinking. At times, the patient is directed to engage in a role-playing dialogue with different facets of himself (represented by an empty adjacent chair) or to report a dream and then let each part of the dream talk for itself, like objects in a fairy tale. Occasionally the Gestalt therapist will direct the individual in the "hot seat" to talk in turn to every other group member, who may reply as he chooses. Cohn (1970), an experienced group therapist who has taught various group techniques, finds that participants in Gestalt therapy workshops report the greatest personal involvement, despite the fact that each is a spectator rather than participant most of the time. She characterizes Perls as a Zen master who guides his apprentices, or group members, toward self-mastery, discipline, and freedom.

7. Synanon games.   A Synanon game is a leaderless group encounter that creates aggressive and provocative interchange (Casriel, 1971). The technique was first developed and has been practiced since the late 1950s at Synanon, a self-help organization in California for former drug addicts. Essentially, the game involves an intense, direct, verbal confrontation between participants with no holds barred. Shunning professional therapists (who are dismissed as passive, evasive, easily conned "shrinks," afraid of anger) (Enright, 1970), the game is played by 10 to 15 participants with varying degrees of experience. Only two rules are followed: (1) no physical violence or threat of violence; and (2) no consciousness-distorting drugs. Meeting on Synanon property, most groups are composed of ex-addicts who reside at Synanon, other nonaddict residents who have chosen the Synanon life style, plus nonresidents who come to participate in the game. Games usually last from two and one-half to three and one-half hours, although the length of time is flexible, depending on the group and a particular evening's game. The composition of any one group varies from meeting to meeting, so that the same people rarely meet in a game, although they may find themselves together in some other group in the future. A Synanon game has sometimes been referred to as "verbal attack therapy." Players are urged to tell the truth about themselves and others bluntly, without conforming to the customary social rules of conduct. Consequently, hostility in the form of ridicule, sarcasm, and viciousness is often the medium of exchange. An attempt is made to strip away every participant's social mask, to expose the fears, frustrations, and hostilities underneath. An important function of the game is to help the residents work through their disagreements, express and discharge their negative feelings, let off steam, and work through any quarrels or dominance struggles so they can function more positively in the Synanon community. The violent exchanges are assumed to deepen the emotional involvement among group members, helping create a community of mutual personal concern. Enright (1970) believes that without the game, the Synanon organization would probably cease to exist in a couple of months. While apparently effective as a drug rehabilitation program, many clinicians feel that this approach is dangerous if practiced by untrained group leaders or without leaders.

8. Marathon groups. A marathon group is a time-extended, uninterrupted group session designed to intensify and accelerate a therapeutic encounter by building up group pressure over time. Precedents for such groups, sometimes extending up to four days, come from: (1) the changing view of psychiatric hospitals as therapeutic communities (see p. 336), where in-patients are considered to be in 24-hour per day treatment; (2) recent innovations in family therapy, such as multiple-impact therapy (p. 384), where entire families are seen together over several days by members of a psychiatric team; (3) T group workshops, in which participants spend up to two weeks together in a residential setting; and (4) recent social experiments in group living in so-called communes, where members attempt to work out their personal problems and live together in an intensive, shared, group living arrangement. Stoller (1968a), an early practitioner of what he termed "accelerated interaction," first used the technique with chronic adult patients at Camarillo State Hospital in California with encouraging results. Bach (1966), a prominent group therapist, adapted the technique to his clinical practice, coining the term "marathon group therapy." Perhaps the most dramatic innovation in group therapy in recent years and one of the most highly publicized, a marathon group of 12 to 15 members typically begins on a Friday evening or Saturday morning and runs through Sunday. Participants are expected to remain together throughout the prolonged session, eating when they choose from a nearby buffet table, and sleeping, if absolutely necessary, in short naps or brief scheduled sleep breaks. Subgroups are discouraged. Physical threats or assaults are not permitted, nor is alcohol or drugs. Such a pressure-cooker atmosphere, aided by fatigue, is assumed to make participants lower their social masks and defenses and begin to engage more quickly on a more open, honest, and intensive basis. Individuals resistant to change are thought to be especially responsive to the pressures of time and the heightened intensity of the process (Bach, 1966).

Stoller (1968b) has described typical phases a marathon group undergoes. At the start, the participants are likely to present a static, formalized style of relating, taking turns telling their stories. After some conventional interpretation by more sophisticated members, usually unproductive, the group relationships begin to take on meaning and immediacy. Clashes between individuals occur frequently as the general formality drops. Heightened tension and a series of personal and interpersonal crises characterize most of the session. The tempo of the group quickens as the marathon draws to a close, with bolder interactions more common than at any previous time. The final phase usually results in an overall feeling of relaxation and informality, with the members reluctant to part. While sharing many aspects of encounter therapy with other groups, the marathon differs primarily in its greater compression and intensity, perhaps explaining why it is sometimes called "the 300-year weekend."

9. Nude marathon groups. Perhaps the most controversial of the new group therapies (Ruitenbeek, 1970) are nude marathon groups. Partly related to the general sexual revolution in the United States and partly related to the underlying goal of all therapy groups—to establish greater transparency and authenticity—nude marathons are a recent phenomenon, having first been described by Bindrim in 1968. They follow the same format and ground rules as marathon groups, but Bindrim feels that physical disrobing hastens emotional disrobing. Nakedness tends to erase the usual social and economic distinctions and makes it difficult to maintain a false or pretentious public image. Once the initial embarrassment or shame is overcome, participants are reported to shed their inhibitions rapidly and consequently to quickly decrease their sense of personal isolation and estrangement. Nude marathons, extending over 24 hours, are conducted either in isolated private homes with adjacent swimming pools or in nudist camps. Participants are expected: (1) to be known by first names only, if desired; (2) to refrain from using alcoholic beverages and drugs; and (3) to refrain from any overt sexual expression, although touching and hugging are permitted. (Overt sexual expression is defined as any activity which would be socially inappropriate in a similar group wearing clothes.) Generally, a brief period of nudity in the pool is used at the start in order to ease participants into later interpersonal experiences in the nude. Bindrim claims the nude marathon experience is especially useful with individuals who have symptoms of sexual problems, such as frigidity in women and impotence in men. Greater self-acceptance, in many cases associated with body image, is said to result from body exposure. Nude marathons are difficult to evaluate objectively because they are still too new and they evoke emotional reactions in researchers which cloud the issue. At present, they constitute perhaps less than one-tenth of one percent of intensive group experience (Rogers, 1970).

THE EFFECTIVENESS OF GROUP THERAPY

In the last decade, public enthusiasm for group therapy has created a groundswell. Thus, the focus of much psychotherapy has shifted from the individual patient to the group experience. Several factors probably account for this phenomenon: (1) the considerable dissatisfaction with the slow pace and dubious results of a great deal of individual psychotherapy; (2) the manpower shortage of trained therapists; (3) the high cost of psychotherapy; (4) the rejection of the medical model, which assumes that recipients of therapy are "sick"; (5) the artificiality of the one-to-one relationship; and (6) perhaps more significantly, in a period of rapid national social change, the confusion, loneliness, sense of alienation, and dehumanization which lead people to turn to others for support, understanding, and acceptance. Encounter groups are most likely to be sought out by middle-class people who have satisfied their physical needs and are now focusing on their psychological wants (Rogers, 1970). Accordingly, such groups have increasingly provided personal, meaningful, authentic human relationships that are unavailable for many in any other way.

Is group therapy effective? There is still a woeful lack of adequate research. Effective for what purpose? Each participant may enter a group with different goals. It is not at all clear yet whether group therapy alone, in conjunction with, preceding, or following individual therapy is most effective. Comparing matched groups, some of whom are undergoing the group experience and some of whom are not, would be desirable but is difficult to carry out. Few therapists would agree on the criteria for improvement. Although greater access to one's feelings, more open ways of relating to others, more growth-directed coping styles, greater self-awareness, greater sensitivity to others, and greater self-esteem all are important, these goals are often difficult if not impossible to measure. Too often, the criteria for success in individual psychotherapy are applied to group therapy, where they may be inappropriate.

Encounter groups in particular present a problem in evaluation. They probably produce fewer short-cut, magical, permanent solutions than their overenthusiastic adherents claim. On the other hand, they are far from the brainwashing and thought control conspiracies feared by various politically reactionary groups. Gibb (1970) has recently surveyed over 100 research studies related to encounter groups, concluding that for the most part such experiences produce therapeutic effects—changes in sensitivity, the ability to experience and express feelings, and a more positive set of attitudes toward self and others. In a carefully designed study, Lieberman, Yalom, and Miles (1971) compared the self-reports and other ratings of students who participated in various group encounter experiences with a matched group of students who acted as a control group. The results indicated that 75 percent of those in encounter groups reported positive changes in themselves, particularly in increased self-esteem. However, to a considerable extent the value of the experience depended on the skill and leadership style of the group facilitator. On the average, about 10 percent of the participants (or about one subject in each of the 10 groups in the study) may have been affected adversely enough to warrant psychiatric follow-up treatment.

These data suggest that encounter groups, while on the whole beneficial, must meet certain minimum requirements to improve their overall effectiveness. The following criticisms have been voiced by a number of clinicians regarding the current practices of encounter groups:

1. Their long-term benefits may be more apparent than real; that is, the participant may leave a weekend marathon group with a "high," experiencing a glow that gradually dissipates, leaving few tangible positive results.

2. An increasing number of untrained, unsupervised group leaders are offering their services to an unsuspecting public. Such "turn-on" specialists may give the illusion of help, particularly as they encourage heightened sensory awareness and the direct and immediate gratification of impulses through touching, hugging, stroking, pushing, hitting, or kicking. However dramatic it may be, such behavior does not necessarily produce long-term personality and behavior change, as any experienced clinician knows.

3. "Instant intimacy," the criterion for success in some encounter groups, is difficult to achieve for most people in a group setting with strangers, despite the appearance of meeting this criterion. Intimacy involves commitment to another person and cannot be genuinely accomplished in a brief period. In its place in many such groups is a more superficial emotional investment which, in the excitement of the moment, passes as intimacy.

4. Applicants frequently are inadequately screened before participation. Consequently, seriously disturbed people, unusually vulnerable people, people whose only contribution is of a destructive nature, or professional "circuit riders" of encounter groups may abound, detracting from the potential benefits that may accrue to others and sometimes inflicting considerable damage.

5. Deviant behavior is sometimes encouraged in a group through the social approval of its members. People who need psychotherapy may be misled into thinking their behavior is not disturbed or that they do not need a professional therapist but only periodic encounter experiences in which they can release their tensions.

6. Some individuals may be precipitated into a psychotic break, a serious depression, or suicide as a result of the intensive emotional experience. Despite this fact, few weekend workshops make follow-up studies to determine what has happened to participants. Serious ethical questions arise when a facilitator arrives in a new city, carries on a weekend group workshop with people he has never met nor will ever see again, and then leaves. While the freedom to experiment with new techniques must not be denied, responsibility must accompany such freedom.

7. Advertisements for encounter groups are becoming commonplace, a violation of APA Ethical Standards for Psychologists. While brochures announcing services to colleagues may be desirable, advertisements in newspapers must be discouraged.

8. Encounter groups tend to be anti-intellectual. Gut-level feelings are in, while head trips are out. The intellect is frequently scapegoated as the enemy of all that is natural, human, or fun. Yet lasting change probably requires some integration of the intellect with the senses.

Despite these objections, of which all responsible clinicians in the encounter movement are aware, there is much that is useful in an approach that aims at maximizing the human potential through expanded awareness and the development of peak experiences of joy (Shutz, 1967). The encounter movement is more than a passing fad; it appears to have developed spontaneously in response to the needs of many people, most of whom would ordinarily not have had any contact with mental health professionals.

In a sense, all the new techniques described in Part III of this book—group techniques, family therapy, brief psychotherapy, crisis intervention, community mental health efforts—underscore both the promise and potential of clinical psychology as well as the inadequacies of available techniques at this point in their development. The service needs of the community demand that the clinician develop techniques faster than he scientifically can. This book ends as it began, with a call for relevant research to advance knowledge concerning human behavior as well as to advance the development of psychological techniques to help alleviate unhappiness and bring about constructive personality and behavioral change.

References

Ackerman, N. W. Psychiatric disorders in children—Diagnosis and etiology in our time. In P. H. Hoch & J. Zubin (Eds.), *Current problems in psychiatric diagnosis.* New York: Grune & Stratton, 1953.

Ackerman, N. W. *The psychodynamics of family life.* New York: Basic Books, 1958.

Ackerman, N. W. *Treating the troubled family.* New York: Basic Books, 1966.

Ackerman, N. W. (Ed.) *Family therapy in transition.* Boston: Little, Brown, 1970.

Ackerman, N. W., Beatman, F. L., & Sherman, S. N. (Eds.) *Exploring the base for family therapy.* New York: Family Service Association of America, 1961.

Ackerman, N. W., Beatman, F. L., & Sherman, S. N. (Eds.) *Expanding theory and practice in family therapy.* New York: Family Service Association of America, 1967.

Adler, A. *The practice and theory of individual psychology.* London: Kegan Paul, Treuch, Trubner, 1925.

Aguilera, D. C., Messick, J. M., & Farrell, M. S. *Crisis intervention: Theory and methodology.* St. Louis: C. V. Mosby, 1970.

Albee, G. W. The dark at the top of the agenda. *The Clinical Psychologist Newsletter,* 1966, **20,** 7–9.

Albee, G. W. A declaration of independence for psychology. In B. Lubin and E. E. Levitt (Eds.), *The clinical psychologist.* Chicago: Aldine, 1967.

Albee, G. W. Conceptual models and manpower requirements in psychology. *American Psychologist,* 1968, **23,** 317–320.

Albee, G. W. Emerging concepts of mental illness and models of treatment: A psychological point of view. *American Journal of Psychiatry,* 1969, **125,** 870–876.

Albee, G. W. The short, unhappy life of clinical psychology. *Psychology Today,* 1970, **4** (4), 42–74.

Alexander, F. G., & French, T. M. *Psychoanalytic therapy.* New York: Ronald Press, 1946.

Alexander, F. G., & Selesnick, S. *The history of psychiatry.* New York: Harper & Row, 1966.

Allison, J., Blatt, S. J., & Zimet, C. *The interpretations of psychological tests.* New York: Harper & Row, 1968.

Allport, G. W. *Personality: A psychological interpetation.* New York: Holt, Rinehart & Winston, 1937.

Allport, G. W. The use of personal documents in psychological science. *Social Science Research Council Bulletin,* 1942 (Whole No. 49).

Allport, G. W. *Becoming.* New Haven: Yale University Press, 1955.

American Medical Association. Report of committee on mental health. *Journal of the American Medical Association,* 1954, **156** (1), 72.

American Psychiatric Association. *Diagnostic and statistical manual: Mental disorders (DSM-1).* Washington, D.C.: American Psychiatric Association, 1952.

American Psychiatric Association. *Diagnostic and statistical manual of mental disorders (DSM-II).* (2nd ed). Washington, D.C.: American Psychiatric Association, 1968.

American Psychological Association. *Ethical standards of psychologists.* Washington, D.C.: American Psychological Association, 1953.

American Psychological Association. *Psychology and its relations with other professions.* Washington, D.C.: American Psychological Association, 1954.

American Psychological Association, Committee on Relations with Psychiatry. 1958 Annual Report. *American Psychologist,* 1958, **13,** 761–763.

American Psychological Association. Ethical standards of psychologists. *American Psychologist,* 1963, **18,** 56–60.

American Psychological Association, Committee on the Scientific and Professional Aims of Psychology. Preliminary report. *American Psychologist,* 1965, **20,** 95–100.

American Psychological Association. *Standards for educational and psychological tests and manuals.* Washington, D.C.: American Psychological Association, 1966.

American Psychological Association, ad hoc Committee on Ethical Standards in Psychological Research. Ethical issues in psychological research—Forthcoming survey of APA members. *American Psychologist,* 1968, **23,** 689–690.

American Psychological Association, Education and Training Board. APA approved doctoral programs in clinical and in counseling psychology: 1969. *American Psychologist,* 1970, **25,** 1049–1050.

Ames, L. B., Leonard, J., Métraux, R. W., & Walker, R. N. *Child Rorschach responses: Developmental trends from two to ten years.* New York: Hoeber-Harper, 1952.

Ames, L. B., Leonard, J., Métraux, R. W., & Walker, R. N. *Rorschach responses in old age.* New York: Hoeber-Harper, 1954.

Ames, L. B., Leonard, J., Métraux, R. W., & Walker, R. N. *Adolescent Rorschach responses: Developmental trends from ten to sixteen years.* New York: Hoeber-Harper, 1959.

Anastasi, A. *Psychological testing.* (3rd ed.) New York: Macmillan, 1968.

Andrews, T. G., & Dreese, M. Military utilization of psychologists during World War II. *American Psychologist,* 1948, **3,** 533–538.

Ash, P. The reliability of psychiatric diagnosis. *Journal of Abnormal and Social Psychology,* 1949, **44,** 272–277.

Atkinson, J. W. (Ed.) *Motives in fantasy, action, and society.* Princeton, N. J.: Van Nostrand, 1958.

Atthowe, J. M., Jr., & Krasner, L. A preliminary report on the application of contingent reinforcement procedures: Token economy on a "chronic" psychiatric ward. *Journal of Abnormal Psychology,* 1968, **73,** 37–43.

Ausubel, D. P. Personality disorder is disease. *American Psychologist,* 1961, **16,** 69–74.

Avnet, H. H. *Psychiatric insurance: Financing short-term ambulatory treatment.* New York: Group Health Insurance, 1962.

Avnet, H. H. How effective is short-term therapy? In L. R. Wolberg (Ed.), *Short-term psychotherapy.* New York: Grune & Stratton, 1965.

Axline, V. *Play therapy.* Boston: Houghton Mifflin, 1947.

Axline, V. *Dibs: In search of self.* Boston: Houghton Mifflin, 1966.

Ayllon, T., & Azrin, N. H. *The token economy: A motivational system for therapy and rehabilitation.* New York: Appleton-Century-Crofts, 1968.

Bach, G. R. *Intensive group psychotherapy.* New York: Ronald Press, 1954.

Bach, G. R. The marathon group: Intensive practice of intimate interaction. *Psychological Reports,* 1966, **18,** 995–1002.

Bahn, A. K. An outline of community mental health research. *Community Mental Health Journal,* 1965, **1,** 23–28.

Baker, B. L. Symptom treatment and symptom substitution in enuresis. *Journal of Abnormal Psychology,* 1969, **74,** 42–49.

Balance, W. D. G., Hirschfield, P. P., & Bringmann, W. G. Mental illness: Myth, metaphor, or model. *Professional Psychology,* 1970, **1,** 133–138.

Bandura, A. *Principles of behavior modification.* New York: Holt, Rinehart & Winston, 1969.

Bandura, A., Blanchard, E. B., & Ritter, B. The relative efficacy of desensitization and modeling approaches for inducing behavioral, affective, and attitudinal changes. *Journal of Personality and Social Psychology,* 1969, **13,** 173–199.

Barbigan, M. M., Gardner, E., Miles, M. C., & Romano, J. Diagnostic consistency and change in a follow-up study of 1215 patients. *American Journal of Psychiatry,* 1965, **121,** 895–901.

Bard, M. Extending psychology's impact through existing community institutions. *American Psychologist,* 1969, **24,** 610–612.

Bard, M. Relevancy in clinical training. *Professional Psychology,* 1970, **1,** 263–264.

Bard, M., & Berkowitz, B. Training police as specialists in family crisis intervention: A community psychology action program. *Community Mental Health Journal,* 1967, **3,** 315–317.

Barker, R. G. *Ecological psychology.* Stanford, Calif.: Stanford University Press, 1968.

Barker, R. G., & Gump, P. V. *Big school, small school.* Stanford, Calif.: Stanford University Press, 1964.

Barker, R. G., & Wright, H. F. *Midwest and its children: The psychological ecology of an American town.* New York: Harper & Row, 1955.

Barten, H. H. The 15-minute hour: Brief therapy in a military setting. *American Journal of Psychiatry,* 1965, **122,** 565–567.

Bateson, G., Jackson, D. D., Haley, J., & Weakland, J. H. Toward a theory of schizophrenia. *Behavioral Science,* 1956, **1,** 251–264.

Bayley, N. Individual patterns of development. *Child Development,* 1956, **27,** 45–74.

Bayley, N. Comparisons of mental and motor test scores for ages 1–15 months by sex, birth order, race, geographic location, and education of parents. *Child Development,* 1965, **36,** 379–411.

Beck, A. T., Ward, C. H., Mendelson, M., Mock, J. E., & Erbaugh, J. K. Reliability of psychiatric diagnoses. *American Journal of Psychiatry,* 1962, **119,** 351–357.

Beck, S. J. The Rorschach Test and personality diagnosis. I. The feebleminded. *American Journal of Psychiatry,* 1930, **10,** 19–52.

Beck, S. J. *Rorschach's test.* Vol. I. *Basic processes.* New York: Grune & Stratton, 1944.

Beck, S. J., & Molish, H. B. (Eds.) *Reflexes to intelligence.* Glencoe, Ill.: Free Press, 1959.

Beers, C. W. *A mind that found itself.* New York: Longmans Green, 1908.

Bell, J. E. *Family group therapy.* Washington, D. C.: Department of Health, Education, and Welfare, 1961, No. 64.

Bellak, L. *The Thematic Apperception Test and the Children's Apperception Test in clinical use.* New York: Grune & Stratton, 1954.

Bellak, L. Community psychiatry: The third psychiatric revolution. In L. Bellak (Ed.), *Handbook of community psychiatry and community mental health.* New York: Grune & Stratton, 1964.

Bellak, L., & Small, L. *Emergency psychotherapy and brief psychotherapy.* New York: Grune & Stratton, 1965.

Beller, E. K. *Clinical process.* New York: Free Press, 1962.

Bender, L. A visual-motor test and its clinical use. *American Journal of Orthopsychiatry,* 1938, No. 3.

Benne, K. D. History of the T-group in the laboratory setting. In L. P. Bradford, J. R. Gibb, & K. D. Benne (Eds.), *T-group theory and the laboratory method.* New York: Wiley, 1964.

Bennett, C. C., Anderson, L. S., Cooper, S., Hassol, L., Klein, D. C., & Rosenblum, G. (Eds.) *Community psychology: A report on the Boston conference on the education of psychologists for community mental health.* Boston: Boston University Press, 1966.

Benton, A. L. *Revised visual retention test: Manual.* New York: Psychological Corporation, 1963.

Berenda, C. W. Is clinical psychology a science? *American Psychologist,* 1957, **12,** 725–729.

Berger, M. M. (Ed.) *Videotape techniques in psychiatric training and treatment.* New York: Brunner/Mazel, 1970.

Bergin, A. E. The deterioration effect: A reply to Braucht. *Journal of Abnormal Psychology,* 1970, **75,** 300–302.

Berman, K. K. Multiple family therapy. *Mental Hygiene,* 1966, **50,** 367–370.

Berne, E. *Transactional analysis in psychotherapy.* New York: Grove Press, 1961.

Berne, E. *Games people play.* New York: Grove Press, 1964.

Berne, E. *Principles of group treatment.* New York: Oxford University Press, 1966.

Bieri, J., Atkins, A. L., Briar, S., Leaman, R. L., Miller, H., & Tripodi, T. *Clinical and social judgment: The discrimination of behavioral information.* New York: Wiley, 1966.

Billingslea, F. Y. The Bender-Gestalt: A review and a perspective. *Psychological Bulletin,* 1963, **60,** 233–251.

Bindman, A. J., & Spiegel, A. D. (Eds.) *Perspectives in community mental health.* Chicago: Aldine, 1969.

Bindrim, P. A report on a nude marathon. *Psychotherapy: Theory, Research, and Practice,* 1968, **5,** 180–188.

Binswanger, L. *Being in the world.* New York: Basic Books, 1963.

Bloom, B. L. The evaluation of primary prevention programs. In L. M. Roberts, N. S. Greenfield, & M. H. Miller (Eds.), *Comprehensive mental health.* Madison, Wis.: University of Wisconsin Press, 1968.

Blum, G. A study of the psychoanalytic theory of psychosexual development. *Genetic Psychology Monographs,* 1949, **30,** 3–99.

Bolles, M., & Goldstein, K. A study of impairment of "abstract behavior" in schizophrenic patients. *Psychiatric Quarterly,* 1939, **12,** 42–65.

Bordin, E. S. Inside the therapeutic hour. In E. A. Rubinstein & M. B. Parloff (Eds.), *Research in psychotherapy.* Washington, D. C.: American Psychological Association, 1959.

Boring, E. G. Current trends in psychology: A special review. *Psychological Bulletin,* 1948, **45,** 75–84.

Boring, E. G. *A history of experimental psychology.* New York: Appleton-Century-Crofts, 1950.

Boss, M. *Psychoanalysis and dasein analysis.* New York: Basic Books, 1963.

Bowen, M. The use of family theory in clinical practice. *Comprehensive Psychiatry,* 1966, **7,** 345–374.

Bower, E. M. Primary prevention of mental and emotional disorders. A conceptual framework and action possibilities. *American Journal of Orthopsychiatry,* 1963, **33,** 832–848.

Bowlby, J. Separation anxiety. *International Journal of Psychoanalysis,* 1960, **41,** 89–113.

Breuer, J., & Freud, S. *Studies on hysteria* (1895). New York: Basic Books, 1957.

Brilliant, P. J., & Gynther, M. D. Relationships between performance on three tests for organicity and selected patient variables. *Journal of Consulting Psychology,* 1963, **27,** 474–479.

Bromberg, W. *The mind of man: A history of psychotherapy and psychoanalysis.* New York: Harper & Row, 1959.

Buck, J. N. The H-T-P test. *Journal of Clinical Psychology,* 1948, **4,** 151–159.

Bugental, J. F. T. Humanistic psychology: A new breakthrough. *American Psychologist,* 1963, **18,** 563–567.

Bugental, J. F. T. *The search for authenticity.* New York: Holt, Rinehart & Winston, 1965.

Bugental, J. F. T. The challenge that is man. In J.F.T. Bugental (Ed.), *Challenges of humanistic psychology.* New York: McGraw-Hill, 1967.

Buhler, C. *The human course of life as a psychological problem.* Leipzig: S. Hirzel, 1933.

Buhler, C. The general structure of the human life cycle. In C. Buhler & F. Massarik (Eds.), *The course of human life.* New York: Springer, 1968.

Buros, O.K. (Ed.) *Tests in print.* Highland Park, N.J.: Gryphon Press, 1961.

Butcher, J. N. (Ed.) *MMPI: Research developments and clinical applications.* New York: McGraw-Hill, 1969.

Butler, J. M., Rice, L. N., & Wagstaff, A. K. On the naturalistic definition of variables: An analogue of clinical analysis. In L. Luborsky & H. Strupp (Eds.), *Research in psychotherapy.* Washington, D. C.: American Psychological Association, 1962.

California School of Professional Psychology. *Catalogue, 1970–1971.* San Francisco: Author, 1970.

Caplan, G. *An approach to community mental health.* New York: Grune & Stratton, 1961.

Caplan, G. Emotional crises. In A. Deutsch (Ed.), *The encyclopedia of mental health.* Vol. 2. New York: Franklin Watts, 1963.

Caplan, G. *Principles of preventive psychiatry.* New York: Basic Books, 1964.

Caplan, G. The nature and problems of evaluation in community mental health. In L. M. Roberts, N. S. Greenfield, & M. H. Miller (Eds.), *Comprehensive mental health.* Madison, Wis.: University of Wisconsin Press, 1968.

Caplan, G. *The theory and practice of mental health consultation.* New York: Basic Books, 1970.

Carkhuff, R. R., & Berenson, B. G. *Beyond counseling and therapy.* New York: Holt, Rinehart & Winston, 1967.

Carson, R. C. The status of diagnostic testing. *American Psychologist,* 1958, **13,** 79.

Carson, R. C. A and B therapist "types": A possible critical variable in psychotherapy. *Journal of Nervous and Mental Disease,* 1967, **144,** 47–54.

Casriel, D. The dynamics of Synanon. In R. W. Siroka, E. K. Siroka, & G. A. Schloss (Eds.), *Sensitivity training and group encounter.* New York: Grosset & Dunlap, 1971.

Cattell, J. McK., & Ferrand, L. Physical and mental measurements of the students of Columbia University. *Psychological Review,* 1896, **3,** 618–648.

Cattell, P. *The measurement of intelligence of infants and young children.* New York: Psychological Corporation, 1947.

Coffey, H. S. The school of psychology model. *American Psychologist,* 1970, **25,** 434–436.

Cohn, R. C. Therapy in groups: Psychoanalytic, experiential, and gestalt. In J. Fagan & I. L. Shepherd (Eds.), *Gestalt therapy now.* Palo Alto, Calif.: Science and Behavior Books, 1970.

Coleman, M. D., & Zwerling, I. The psychiatric emergency clinic: A flexible way of treating community mental health needs. *American Journal of Psychiatry,* 1959, **115,** 980–984.

Combs, A. W., & Snygg, D. *Individual behavior.* New York: Harper & Row, 1959.

Cook, S. W. The psychologist of the future: Scientist, professional, or both. *American Psychologist,* 1958, **13,** 635–644.

Cook, S. W. The scientist–profesional: Can psychology carry it off? *The Canadian Psychologist,* 1965, **6,** 93–109.

Cooper, J. E. Diagnostic change in a longitudinal study of psychiatric patients. *British Journal of Psychiatry,* 1967, **113,** 129–142.

Cowen, E. L., & Zax, M. The mental health field today: Issues and problems. In E. L. Cowen, E. A. Gardner, & M. Zax (Eds.), *Emergent approaches to mental health problems.* New York: Appleton-Century-Crofts, 1967.

Cronbach, L. J. *Essentials of psychological testing.* (3rd ed.) New York: Harper & Row, 1970.

Cronbach, L. J., & Gleser, G. C. *Psychological tests and personnel decisions.* (2nd ed.) Urbana: University of Illinois Press, 1965.

Dahlstrom, W. G., & Welsh, G. S. *An MMPI handbook: A guide for use in clinical practice and research.* Minneapolis: University of Minnesota Press, 1960.

David, H. P. A Szondi Test bibliography, 1939–1953. *Journal of Projective Techniques,* 1954, **18,** 17–32.

Deri, S. *Introduction to the Szondi Test: Theory and practice.* New York: Grune & Stratton, 1949.

Dollard, J., & Miller, N. E. *Personality and psychotherapy.* New York: McGraw-Hill, 1950.

Dollard, J., & Mowrer, O. H. A method of measuring tension in written documents *Journal of Abnormal and Social Psychology,* 1947, **42,** 3–32.

Dreger, R. M. Objective tests and computer processing of personality test data. In I. A. Berg & L. A. Pennington (Eds.), *An introduction to clinical psychology.* (3rd ed.) New York: Ronald Press, 1966.

Dreger, R. M., Lewis, P. M., Rich, T. A., Miller, K. S., Reid, M. P., Overlade, D. C., Taffel, C., & Flemming, E. L. Behavioral classification project. *Journal of Consulting Psychology,* 1964, **28,** 1–13.

Dreikurs, R. The Adlerian approach to therapy. In M. I. Stein (Ed.), *Contemporary psychotherapies.* New York: Free Press, 1961.

Dunham, H. W. Community psychiatry: The newest therapeutic bandwagon. *Archives of General Psychiatry,* 1965, **12,** 303–313.

Dunn, L. M. *Peabody Picture Vocabulary Test.* Minneapolis: American Guidance Services, 1965.

Durell, J., & Schildkraut, J. J. Biochemical studies of the schizophrenic and affective disorders: In S. Arieti (Ed.), *American Handbook of Psychiatry.* Vol. 3. New York: Basic Books, 1966.

Egan, G. *Encounter: Group processes for interpersonal growth.* Belmont, Calif.: Brooks/Cole, 1970.

Eisenberg, L. The fathers of autistic children. *American Journal of Orthopsychiatry,* 1957, **27,** 715–724.

Eisenberg, L., & Greenberg, E. M. The current status of secondary prevention in child psychiatry. *American Journal of Orthopsychiatry,* 1961, **31,** 355–367.

Eisenberg, L., & Kanner, L. Early infantile autism, 1943–1955. *American Journal of Orthopsychiatry,* 1956, **26,** 556–566.

Ellis, A. *Reason and emotion in psychotherapy.* New York: Lyle Stuart, 1962.

Enright, J. B. Synanon: A challenge to middle-class views of mental health. In D. Adelson & B. L. Kadis (Eds.), *Community psychology and mental health.* Scranton, Pa.: Chandler, 1970.

Erikson, E. H. *Childhood and society.* (2nd ed.) New York: W. W. Norton, 1963.

Erikson, E. H. *Identity: Youth and crisis.* New York: W. W. Norton, 1968.

Eron, L. D. A normative study of the Thematic Apperception Test. *Psychological Monographs,* 1950, **64** (Whole No. 315).

Eron, L. D., & Chertkoff, S. O. Psychological tests in clinical practice. In L. E. Abt & B. F. Riess (Eds.), *Progress in clinical psychology.* Vol. VII. New York: Grune & Stratton, 1966.

Escalona, S. K. *The roots of individuality.* Chicago: Aldine, 1968.

Evans, J. *Three men: An experiment in the biography of emotion.* New York: Grove Press, 1950.

Ewalt, J. R., & Ewalt, P. L. History of the community psychiatry movement. *American Journal of Psychiatry,* 1969, **126** (1), 43–52.

Eysenck, H. J. The effects of psychotherapy: An evaluation. *Journal of Consulting Psychology,* 1952, **16,** 319–324.

Eysenck, H. J. Learning theory and behaviour therapy. *Journal of Mental Science,* 1959, **105,** 61–75.

Eysenck, H. J. Classification and the problem of diagnosis. In H. J. Eysenck (Ed.), *Handbook of abnormal psychology.* New York: Basic Books, 1961.

Eysenck, H. J. The effects of psychotherapy. *International Journal of Psychiatry,* 1965, **1,** 99–178.

Farberow, N. L. Suicide prevention: A view from the bridge. *Community Mental Health Journal,* 1968, **4,** 469–474.

Farberow, N. L., & Shneidman, E. S. (Eds.) *The cry for help.* New York: McGraw-Hill, 1961.

Faris, R., & Dunham, H. *Mental disorders in urban areas.* Chicago: University of Chicago Press, 1939.

Feldman, M. P., & MacCulloch, M. J. The application of anticipatory learning to the treatment of homosexuality. I. Theory, technique, and preliminary results. *Behavior Research and Therapy,* 1965, **2,** 165–183.

Fenichel, O. *The psychoanalytic theory of neurosis.* New York: W. W. Norton, 1945.

Fiedler, F. E. A comparison of therapeutic relations in psychoanalysis, nondirective and Adlerian therapy. *Journal of Consulting Psychology,* 1950, **14,** 436–445.

Fiske, D. W., Luborsky, L., Parloff, M. B., Hunt, H. F., Orne, M. T., Reiser, M. F., & Tuma, A. H. Planning of research on effectiveness of psychotherapy. *American Psychologist,* 1970, **25,** 727–737.

Ford, D. H., & Urban, H. B. *Systems of psychotherapy.* New York: Wiley, 1963.

Forer, B. R. A structured sentence completion test. *Journal of Projective Techniques,* 1950, **14,** 15–29.

Fowler, R. D. Automated interpretation of personality test data. In J. N. Butcher (Ed.), *MMPI: Research developments and clinical applications.* New York: McGraw-Hill, 1969.

Fowler, R. D., & Miller, M. L. Computer interpretation of the MMPI. *Archives of General Psychiatry,* 1969, **21,** 502–508.

Framo, S. L. Rationale and technique of intensive family therapy. In I. Boszor-menyi–Nagy & S. L. Framo (Eds.), *Intensive family therapy.* New York: Harper & Row, 1965.

Frank, G. H. Psychiatric diagnosis: A review of research. *Journal of General Psychology,* 1969, **81,** 157–176.

Frank, J. D. *Persuasion and healing.* New York: Schocken Books, 1963.

Frank, J. D. Training and therapy. In L. P. Bradford, J. R. Gibb, & K. D. Benne (Eds.), *T-group theory and the laboratory method.* New York: Wiley, 1964.

Frank, L. K. Projective methods for the study of personality. *Journal of Psychology,* 1939, **8,** 389–413.

Franks, C. M. Behavior therapy, the principles of conditioning, and the treatment of the alcoholic. *Quarterly Journal for the Study of Alcoholism,* 1963, **24,** 511–529.

Freud, A. *The ego and the mechanisms of defense.* New York: International Universities Press, 1946.

Freud, S. On the psychical mechanism of hysterical phenomena (1893). In S. Freud (Ed.), *Collected papers.* Vol. I. London: Hogarth Press, 1949.

Freud, S. The interpretation of dreams (1900). In *The basic writings of Sigmund Freud.* New York: Random House, 1938.

Freud, S. The psychopathology of everyday life (1901). In *The basic writings of Sigmund Freud.* New York: Random House, 1938.

Freud, S. Three essays on the theory of sexuality (1905). *The standard edition of the complete psychological works of Sigmund Freud.* Vol. 7. London: Hogarth Press, 1953.

Freud, S. Totem and taboo (1913). *The standard edition of the complete psychological works of Sigmund Freud.* Vol. 13. London: Hogarth Press, 1955.

Freud, S. *The problem of lay analysis.* New York: Brentano, 1927.

Freud, S. *Basic writings.* New York: Random House, 1938.

Freudenberger, H. J. Free clinics: What they are and how you start one. *Professional Psychology,* 1971, **2,** 169–173.

Friedman, A. S., Boszormenyi–Nagy, I., Jungreis, J. E., Lincoln, G., Mitchell, H. E., Sonne, J. C., Speck, R. V., & Spivack, G. *Psychotherapy for the whole family.* New York: Springer, 1965.

Fromm, E. *Man for himself.* New York: Rinehart, 1947.

Fromm, E. *The sane society.* New York: Rinehart, 1955.

Fromm, E. *The art of loving.* New York: Harpers, 1956.

Fromm–Reichmann, F. A preliminary note on the emotional significance of stereotypes in schizophrenics (1942). In F. Fromm–Reichmann (Ed.), *Psychoanalysis and psychotherapy.* Chicago: University of Chicago Press, 1959.

Frostig, M. *The Frostig Developmental Test of Visual Perception.* (3rd ed.) Palo Alto, Calif.: Consulting Psychologists Press, 1964.

Gardner, E. A. Psychological care for the poor. In E. L. Cowen, E. A. Gardner, & M. Zax (Eds.), *Emergent approaches to mental health problems.* New York: Appleton-Century-Crofts, 1967.

Garfield, S. L. Clinical psychology and the search for identity. *American Psychologist,* 1966, **21,** 353–362.

Garmezy, N. Vulnerability research and the issue of primary prevention. *American Journal of Orthopsychiatry,* 1971, **41,** 101–116.

Garvey, W., & Hegrenes, S. R. Desensitization techniques in the treatment of school phobia. *American Journal of Orthopsychiatry,* 1966, **36,** 147–152.

Gazda, G. M. Group psychotherapy: Its definition and history. In G. M. Gazda (Ed.), *Innovations to group psychotherapy.* Springfield, Ill.: Charles C. Thomas, 1968.

Gelfand, S., & Kelly, J. G. The psychologist in community mental health: Scientist and professional. *American Psychologist,* 1960, **15,** 223–226.

Gesell, A. L., & Amatruda, C. S. *Developmental diagnosis.* New York: Hoeber, 1947.

Gesell, A. L., Amatruda, C. S., Castner, B. M., & Thompson, H. *Biographies of child development: The mental growth of careers of 84 infants and children.* New York: Hoeber, 1939.

Gibb, J. R. The effects of human relations training. In A. E. Bergin & S. L. Garfield (Eds.), *Handbook of psychotherapy and behavior change.* New York: Wiley, 1970.

Gibson, R. W., Cohen, M. B., & Cohen, R. A. On the dynamics of the manic–depressive personality. *American Journal of Psychiatry,* 1959, **115,** 1101–1107.

Giedt, F. H. Comparison of visual, content, and auditory cues in interviewing. *Journal of Consulting Psychology,* 1955, **19,** 407–416.

Girardeau, F. L., & Spradlin, J. E. Token rewards on a cottage program. *Mental Retardation,* 1964, **2,** 345–351.

Glasser, W. *Reality therapy.* New York: Harper & Row, 1965.

Glidewell, J. C. Perspectives in community health. In C. C. Bennett, L. S. Anderson, S. Cooper, L. Hassol, D. C. Klein, & G. Rosenblum (Eds.), *Community psychology: A report of the Boston Conference on the education of psychologists for community mental health.* Boston: Boston University Press, 1966.

Goddard, H. H. A measuring scale for intelligence. *Training School,* 1910, **6,** 146–154.

Goldberg, L. R. Simple models or simple processes? Some research on clinical judgments. *American Psychologist,* 1968, **23,** 483–496.

Goldberg, P. A. A review of sentence completion methods in personality assessment. *Journal of Projective Techniques and Personality Assessment,* 1965, **29,** 12–45.

Goldenberg, H., & Goldenberg, I. School phobia: Childhood neurosis or learned maladaptive behavior? *Exceptional Children,* 1970, **37,** 220–226.

Goldfarb, A. Reliability of diagnostic judgments made by psychologists. *Journal of Clinical Psychology,* 1959, **15,** 292–296.

Goldschmid, M. L., Stein, D. D., Weissman, H., & Sorrells, J. A survey of the training and practices of clinical psychologists. *The Clinical Psychologist Newsletter,* 1969, **22,** 89–107.

Goldstein, A. P., Heller, K., & Sechrest, L. B. *Psychotherapy and the psychology of behavior change.* New York: Wiley, 1966.

Goldstein, K., & Scheerer, M. Abstract and concrete behavior. *Psychological Monographs,* 1941, **53,** No. 2.

Gorham, D. R. Validity and reliability studies of a computer-based scoring system for inkblot responses. *Journal of Consulting Psychology,* 1967, **31,** 65–70.

Gough, H. G. Clinical versus statistical prediction in psychology. In L. Postman (Ed.), *Psychology in the making.* New York: Knopf, 1962.

Gough, H. G. Some reflections on the meaning of psychodiagnosis. *American Psychologist,* 1971, **26,** 160–167.

Graham, F. K., & Kendall, B. S. Memory-for-Designs Test: Revised general manual. *Perceptual and Motor Skills,* 1960, **11,** 147–188.

Greenblatt, M., & Levinson, D. J. The goals and responsibilities of the psychotherapist: Some problematic issues. In A. R. Mahrer (Ed.), *The goals of psychotherapy.* New York: Appleton-Century-Crofts, 1967.

Greenson, R. R. *The technique and practice of psychoanalysis.* Vol. I. New York: International Universities Press, 1967.

Greenspoon, J. The reinforcing effect of two spoken sounds on the frequency of two responses. *American Journal of Psychology,* 1955, **68,** 409–416.

Greenwald, J. A. An introduction to the philosophy and techniques of Gestalt therapy. Unpublished manuscript, 1969.

Gross, M. L. *The brain watchers.* New York: Random House, 1962.

Grossberg, J. M. Behavior therapy: A review. *Psychological Bulletin,* 1964, **62,** 73–88.

Grosser, C., Henry, W. E., & Kelly, J. G. *Nonprofessionals in the human services.* San Francisco: Jossey-Bass, 1969.

Grotjahn, M. *Psychoanalysis and family neurosis.* New York: W. W. Norton, 1960.

Group for the Advancement of Psychiatry. *Report #62. Psychopathological disorders in childhood: Theoretical considerations and a proposed classification.* New York: Group for the Advancement of Psychiatry, 1966.

Group for the Advancement of Psychiatry. *Report #78. The field of family therapy.* New York: Group for the Advancement of Psychiatry, 1970.

Guerney, B., Jr. *Psychotherapeutic agents: New roles for nonprofessionals, parents, and teachers.* New York: Holt, Rinehart & Winston, 1969.

Guilford, J. P. *The nature of human intelligence.* New York: McGraw-Hill, 1967.

Gurin, G., Veroff, J., & Feld, S. *Americans view their mental health.* New York: Basic Books, 1960.

Gursslin, O. R., Hunt, R. G., & Roach, J. L. Social class and the mental health movement. In F. Riessman, J. Cohen, & A. Pearl (Eds.), *Mental health of the poor.* New York: Free Press, 1964.

Hadden, S. B. Historic background of group psychotherapy. *International Journal of Group Psychotherapy,* 1955, **5,** 162–168.

Haley, J. Family of the schizophrenic: A model system. *Journal of Nervous and Mental Disease,* 1959, **129,** 357–374.

Haley, J. *Strategies of psychotherapy.* New York: Grune & Stratton, 1963.

Haley, J. Family therapy. *International Journal of Psychiatry,* 1970, **9,** 233–242.

Hall, C. S., & Lindzey, G. *Theories of personality.* New York: Wiley, 1957.

Halpern, F. The Rorschach test with children. In A. I. Rabin & M. R. Haworth (Eds.), *Projective techniques with children.* New York: Grune & Stratton, 1960.

Hammer, E. F. (Ed.) *The clinical application of projective drawings.* Springfield, Ill.: Charles C. Thomas, 1958.

Hammer, E. F. Projective drawings. In A. I. Rabin (Ed.), *Projective techniques in personality assessment.* New York: Springer, 1968.

Hammer, M., & Kaplan, A. M. Theoretical considerations in the practice of psychotherapy with children. In M. Hammer & A. M. Kaplan (Eds.), *The practice of psychotherapy with children.* Homewood, Ill.: Dorsey Press, 1967.

Hanfmann, E., & Kasanin, J. Conceptual thinking in schizophrenia. *Nervous and Mental Disease Monographs,* 1942, No. 67.

Harper, R. A. *Psychoanalysis and psychotherapy: 36 systems.* Englewood Cliffs, N. J.: Prentice-Hall, 1959.

Harris, T. *I'm O.K., You're O.K.: A practical guide to transactional analysis.* New York: Harper & Row, 1967.

Harrison, R. Thematic apperceptive methods. In B. B. Wolman (Ed.), *Handbook of clinical psychology.* New York: McGraw-Hill, 1965.

Harrower, M. Differential diagnosis. In B. B. Wolman (Ed.), *Handbook of clinical psychology.* New York: McGraw-Hill, 1965.

Hartmann, H. *Essays on ego psychology: Selected problems in psychoanalytic theory.* New York: International Universities Press, 1964.

Hathaway, S. R., & McKinley, J. C. *Minnesota Multiphasic Personality Inventory.* Minneapolis: University of Minnesota Press, 1942.

Hathaway, S. R., & Meehl, P. E. *An atlas for the clinical use of the MMPI.* Minneapolis: University of Minnesota Press, 1951.

Hayes, S. P. Alternate scales for the mental measurement of the visually handicapped. *Outlook for the Blind,* 1942, **36,** 225–230.

Heine, R. W. A comparison of patients' reports on psychotherapeutic experience with psychoanalytic, nondirective, and Adlerian therapists. *American Journal of Psychotherapy,* 1953, **7,** 16–23.

Henderson, N. B., & Hildreth, J. D. Certification, licensing, and the movement of psychologists from state to state. *American Psychologist,* 1965, **20,** 418–421.

Henry, W. E., Sims, J. H., & Spray, S. L. *The fifth profession.* San Francisco: Jossey-Bass, 1971.

Hersch, C. The discontent explosion in mental health. *American Psychologist,* 1968, **23,** 497–506.

Hersch, C. From mental health to social action: Clinical psychology in historical perspective. *American Psychologist,* 1969, **24,** 909–915.

Hewett, P., & Massey, J. O. *Clinical clues from the WISC with special sections on testing black and Spanish-speaking children.* Palo Alto, Calif.: Consulting Psychologists Press, 1969.

Hildreth, J. D. Psychology's relations with psychiatry: A summary report. In B. Lubin & E. E. Levitt (Eds.), *The clinical psychologist.* Chicago: Aldine, 1967.

Hill, R. Generic features of families under stress. *Social Casework,* 1958, **39,** Nos. 2–3.

Himelstein, P. Research with the Stanford–Binet, form L-M. *Psychological Bulletin,* 1966, **65,** 156–164.

Hiskey, M. S. *Hiskey–Nebraska test of learning aptitude: Manual.* Lincoln, Neb.: Union College Press, 1966.

Hobbs, N. Sources of gain in psychotherapy. *American Psychologist,* 1962, **17,** 741–747.

Hobbs, N. Strategies for the development of clinical psychology. *The Clinical Psychologist Newsletter,* 1963, **16,** 3–5.

Hobbs, N. Mental health's third revolution. *American Journal of Orthopsychiatry,* 1964, **34,** 822–833.

Hobbs, N. Helping disturbed children: Psychological and ecological strategies. *American Psychologist,* 1966, **21,** 1105–1115.

Hoch, E. L., Ross, A. O., & Winder, C. L. (Eds.) *Professional preparation of clinical psychologists.* Washington, D. C.: American Psychological Association, 1966.

Hollingshead, A. B., & Redlich, F. C. *Social class and mental illness: A community study.* New York: Wiley, 1958.

Holt, R. R. Clinical and statistical prediction: A reformulation and some new data. *Journal of Abnormal and Social Psychology,* 1958, **56,** 1–12.

Holt, R. R. Clinical judgment as a disciplined inquiry. *Journal of Nervous and Mental Disease,* 1961, **133,** 369–382.

Holt, R. R. Experimental methods in clinical psychology. In B. B. Wolman (Ed.), *Handbook of clinical psychology.* New York: McGraw-Hill, 1965.

Holt, R. R. Diagnostic status and future prospects. *Journal of Nervous and Mental Disease,* 1967, **144,** 444–465.

Holt, R. R. The evaluation of personality assessment. In I. L. Janis, G. F. Mahl, J. Kagan, & R. R. Holt (Eds.), *Personality: Dynamics, development, and assessment.* New York: Harcourt Brace Jovanovich, 1969. (a)

Holt, R. R. Kubie's dream and its impact upon reality: Psychotherapy as an autonomous profession. *Journal of Nervous and Mental Disease,* 1969, **149,** 186–207. (b)

Holt, R. R., & Luborsky, L. *Personality patterns of psychiatrists.* New York: Basic Books, 1958.

Holtzman, W. H. Holtzman inkblot technique. In A. I. Rabin (Ed.), *Projective techniques in personality assessment.* New York: Springer, 1968.

Holtzman, W. H., Thorpe, J. S., Swartz, J. D., & Herron, E. W. *Inkblot perception and personality: Holtzman inkblot technique.* Austin: University of Texas Press, 1961.

Horney, K. *The neurotic personality of our time.* New York: W. W. Norton, 1937.

Horney, K. *Neurosis and human growth.* New York: W. W. Norton, 1950.

Howard, J. *Please touch: A guided tour of the human potential movement.* New York: McGraw-Hill, 1970.

Howells, J. G. (Ed.) *Theory and practice of family psychiatry.* New York: Brunner/Mazel, 1971.

Hunt, W. A. An actuarial approach to clinical judgment. In B. Bass & I. A. Berg (Eds.), *Objective approaches to personality assessment.* New York: Van Nostrand, 1959.

Hunt, W. A., & Jones, N. F. The experimental investigation of clinical judgment. In A. J. Bachrach (Ed.), *Experimental foundations of clinical psychology.* New York: Basic Books, 1962.

Hunt, W. A., Wittson, C. L., & Hunt, E. B. A theoretical and practical analysis of the diagnostic process. In P. H. Hoch & J. Zubin (Eds.), *Current problems in psychiatric diagnosis.* New York: Grune & Stratton, 1953.

Hutt, M. L. Revised Bender visual motor Gestalt test. In A. Weider (Ed.), *Contributions toward medical psychology.* Vol. 2. New York: Ronald Press, 1953.

Isaacs, W., Thomas, J., & Goldiamond, I. Application of operant conditioning to reinstate verbal behavior in psychotics. *Journal of Speech and Hearing Disorders,* 1960, **25,** 8–12.

Iscoe, I., & Spielberger, C. D. *Community psychology: Perspectives in training and research.* New York: Appleton-Century-Crofts, 1970.

Jackson, B. Reflections on DSM-II. *International Journal of Psychiatry,* 1969, **7,** 385–392.

Jackson, D. D. The question of family homeostasis. *Psychiatric Quarterly Supplement,* 1957, **31,** 79–90.

Jackson, D. D. Family therapy in the family of the schizophrenic. In M. I. Stein (Ed.), *Contemporary psychotherapies.* New York: Free Press, 1961.

Jacobson, G. F. Crisis intervention from the viewpoint of the mental health professional. *Pastoral Psychology,* 1970, **21,** 21–28.

Jacobson, G. F., Strickler, M., & Morley, W. E. Generic and individual approaches to crisis intervention. *American Journal of Public Health,* 1968, **58,** 338–343.

Jacobson, G. F., Wilner, D. M., Morley, W. E., Schneider, S., Strickler, M., & Sommer, G. J. The scope and practice of an early-access brief treatment psychiatric center. *American Journal of Psychiatry,* 1965, **121,** 1176–1182.

James, W. *Principles of psychology.* New York: Holt, 1890.

Janis, I., Mahl, G. F., Kagan, J., & Holt, R. R. *Personality: Dynamics, development, and assessment.* New York: Harcourt Brace Jovanovich, 1969.

Joint Commission on Mental Health of Children. *Crisis in child mental health: Challenge for the 1970s.* New York: Harper & Row, 1970.

Joint Commission on Mental Illness and Health. *Action for mental health.* New York: Basic Books, 1961.

Jones, E. *The life and work of Sigmund Freud.* New York: Basic Books, 1953 1955, 1957. Vols. 1–3.

Jones, M. *The therapeutic community.* New York: Basic Books, 1953.

Jones, M. C. A laboratory study of fear: The case of Peter. *Pediatrics Seminar,* 1924, **31,** 308–315.

Jung, C. G. *Studies in word association* (English translation). London: Heinemann, 1918.

Jung, C. G. *Contributions to analytical psychology.* London: Routledge and Kegan Paul Ltd., 1928.

Kadis, A. L., Krasner, J. D., Winick, C., & Foulkes, S. H. *A practicum of group psychotherapy.* New York: Harper & Row, 1963.

Kaffman, M. Short-term family therapy. *Family Process,* 1963, **2,** 216–234.

Kahn, M. W. Clinical and statistical prediction revisited. *Journal of Clinical Psychology,* 1960, **16,** 115–118.

Kalis, B. L. Crisis theory: Its relevance for community psychology and directions for development. In D. Adelson & B. L. Kalis (Eds.), *Community psychology and mental health.* Scranton, Pa.: Chandler, 1970.

Kaplan, S. R. Therapy groups and training groups: Similarities and differences. *The International Journal of Group Psychotherapy,* 1967, **17,** 473–504.

Karnosh, L. J., & Zucker, E. M. *Handbook of psychiatry.* St. Louis: C. V. Mosby, 1945.

Kelley, N. H., Sanford, F. H., & Clark, K. E. The meaning of the ABEPP diploma. *American Psychologist,* 1961, **16,** 132–141.

Kelly, E. L. Clinical psychology: 1960. *Newsletter of the Division of Clinical Psychology,* 1961, **14,** 1–11. (a)

Kelly, E. L. Clinical pyschology: The postwar decade. In W. Dennis (Ed.), *Current trends in psychological theory.* Pittsburgh: University of Pittsburgh Press, 1961. (b)

Kelly, E. L. *Assessment of human characteristics.* Belmont, Calif.: Brooks/Cole, 1967.

Kelly, E. L., & Fiske, D. W. *The prediction of performance in clinical psychology.* Ann Arbor: University of Michigan Press, 1951.

Kelly, G. A. *The psychology of personal constructs.* Vol. I. New York: Norton, 1955.

Kelly, G. A. The theory and technique of assessment. *Annual Review of Psychology,* 1958, **9,** 323–352.

Kelly, J. G. Ecological constraints on mental health services. *American Psychologist,* 1966, **21,** 535–539.

Kelly, J. G. Naturalistic observations and theory confirmation. *Human Development,* 1967, **10,** 212–222.

Kelly, J. G. Toward an ecological conception of preventive intervention. In D. Adelson & B. L. Kalis (Eds.), *Community psychology and mental health.* Scranton, Pa.: Chandler, 1970.

Kent, G. H., & Rosanoff, A. J. A study of association in insanity. *American Journal of Insanity,* 1910, **67,** 374–390.

Kety, S. S. Biochemical theories of schizophrenia. Parts I and II. *Science,* 1959, **129,** 1528–1532, 1590–1596.

Kety, S. S., Rosenthal, D., Wender, P. H., & Schulsinger, F. The types and prevalence of mental illness in the biological and adoptive families of adopted schizophrenics. In D. Rosenthal & S. S. Kety (Eds.), *The transmission of schizophrenia.* London: Pergamon Press, 1968.

Kirk, S. A., McCarthy, J. J., & Kirk, W. D. *The Illinois Test of Psycholinguistic Abilities.* (Rev. ed.) Urbana, Ill.: University of Illinois Press, 1968.

Klein, D. C. *Community dynamics and mental health.* New York: Wiley, 1968.

Klein, D. C., & Ross, A. Kindergarten entry: A study of role transition. In M. Krugman (Ed.), *Orthopsychiatry and the school.* New York: American Orthopsychiatric Association, 1958.

Klein, M. *The psychoanalysis of children.* London: Hogarth Press, 1932.

Klopfer, B., Ainsworth, M. D., Klopfer, W. G., & Holt, R. R. *Developments in the Rorschach technique.* Vol. I. *Technique and theory.* New York: Harcourt Brace Jovanovich, 1954.

Koegler, R. R. Brief therapy with children. In G. J. Wayne & R. R. Koegler (Eds.), *Emergency psychiatry and brief therapy.* Boston: Little, Brown, 1966.

Kogan, L. S. Research in clinical psychology. In I. A. Berg & L. A. Pennington (Eds.), *An introduction to clinical psychology.* (3rd ed.) New York: Ronald Press, 1966.

Koppitz, E. *The Bender–Gestalt test for young children.* New York: Grune & Stratton, 1964.

Krasner, L., & Ullmann, L. (Eds.) *Research in behavior modification.* New York: Holt, Rinehart & Winston, 1965.

Krutch, J. W. *The measure of man.* New York: Bobbs-Merrill, 1954.

Kubie, L. S. A program of training in psychiatry to break the bottleneck in rehabilitation. *American Journal of Orthopsychiatry,* 1946, **16,** 447–454.

Kubie, L. S. Medical responsibility for training in clinical psychology. *Journal of Clinical Psychology,* 1949, **5,** 94–100.

Kubie, L. S. The pros and cons of a new profession: A doctorate in medical psychology. *Texas Reports on Biology and Medicine,* 1954, **12,** 125–170.

Kubie, L. S. Pitfalls of community psychiatry. *Archives of General Psychiatry,* 1968, **18,** 257–266.

Kubie, L. S. A doctorate in psychotherapy: The reasons for a new profession. In R. R. Holt (Ed.), *New horizons for psychotherapy.* New York: International Universities Press, 1970.

Laing, R. D. *The politics of experience.* New York: Pantheon, 1967.

Landis, C. Statistical evaluation of psychotherapeutic methods. In S. E. Hinsie (Ed.), *Concepts and problems of psychotherapy.* London: Heinemann, 1938.

Langner, T. S., & Michael, S. T. *Life stress and mental health: The midtown Manhattan study.* New York: Free Press, 1963.

Laqueur, H. P. Multiple family therapy and general systems theory. In N. W. Ackerman (Ed.), *Family therapy in transition.* Boston: Little, Brown, 1970.

Lehner, G. F. J. Defining psychotherapy. *American Psychologist,* 1952, **7,** 547.

Levitt, E. E. The results of psychotherapy with children: An evaluation. *Journal of Consulting Psychology,* 1957, **21,** 189–196.

Levy, L. H. The skew in clinical psychology. *American Psychologist,* 1962, **17,** 244–249.

Levy, L. H. *Psychological interpretation.* New York: Holt, Rinehart & Winston, 1963.

Lewin, K. K. *Brief encounters: Brief psychotherapy.* St. Louis: Warren H. Green, 1970.

Lewis, N. D. C. American psychiatry from its beginnings to World War II. In S. Arieti (Ed.), *American handbook of psychiatry.* Vol. I. New York: Basic Books, 1959.

Liberman, R. Behavioral approaches to family and couple therapy. *American Journal of Orthopsychiatry,* 1970, **40,** 106–118.

Libo, L. M. Multiple functions for psychologists in community consultation. *American Psychologist,* 1966, **21,** 530–534.

Lieberman, M. A., Yalom, I. D., & Miles, M. B. The group experience project: A comparison of ten encounter technologies. In L. Blank, G. B. Gottsegen, &

M. G. Gottsegen (Eds.), *Confrontation: Encounters in self and interpersonal awareness.* New York: Macmillan, 1971.

Lindemann, E. Symptomatology and management of acute grief. *American Journal of Psychiatry,* 1944, **101,** 141–148.

Lindzey, G. *Projective techniques and cross-cultural research.* New York: Appleton-Century-Crofts, 1961.

Little, K. B., & Shneidman, E. S. Congruencies among interpretations of psychological test and anamnestic data. *Psychological Monographs,* 1959, **73** (6, Whole No. 476).

London, P. *The modes and morals of psychotherapy.* New York: Holt, Rinehart & Winston, 1964.

Los Angeles Society of Clinical Psychologists. Paradigm for the realization of a national conference on the professional preparation of clinical psychologists. Unpublished manuscript, 1964.

Louttit, C. M. The nature of clinical psychology. *Psychological Bulletin,* 1939, **36,** 361–389.

Louttit, C. M., & Browne, C. G. Psychometric instruments in psychological clinics. *Journal of Consulting Psychology,* 1947, **11,** 49–54.

Lovaas, O. I. Clinical implications of relationships between verbal and nonverbal operant behavior. In H. J. Eysenck (Ed.), *Experiments in behavior therapy.* New York: Macmillan, 1964.

Lovaas, O. I., Schaeffer, B., & Simmons, J. Q. Building social behavior in autistic children by use of electric shock. *Journal of Experimental Research in Personality,* 1965, **1,** 99–109.

Lowrey, L. G., & Smith, G. *The institute for child guidance: 1927–1933.* New York: Commonwealth Fund, 1933.

Lubin, B., Wallis, R. R., & Paine, C. Patterns of psychological test usage in the United States: 1935–1969. *Professional Psychology,* 1971, **2,** 70–74.

Lundin, R. W. *Personality: A behavioral analysis.* New York: Macmillan, 1969.

MacCorquodale, K., & Meehl, P. E. On a distinction between hypothetical constructs and intervening variables. *Psychological Review,* 1948, **55,** 95–107.

MacGregor, R., Ritchie, A. M., Serrano, A. C., & Schuster, F. P. *Multiple impact therapy with families.* New York: McGraw-Hill, 1964.

Machover, K. *Personality projection in the drawing of the human figure.* Springfield, Ill.: Charles C. Thomas, 1948.

Maddi, S. R. *Personality theories: A comparative analysis.* Homewood, Ill.: Dorsey Press, 1968.

Maher, B. *Introduction to research in psychopathology.* New York: McGraw-Hill, 1970.

Mahrer, A. R. *The goals of psychotherapy.* New York: Appleton-Century-Crofts, 1967.

Mariner, A. S. A critical look at professional education in the mental health field. *American Psychologist,* 1967, **22,** 271–281.

Marks, P. A., & Seeman, W. *The actuarial description of abnormal personality.* Baltimore: Williams & Wilkins, 1963.

Marmor, J. Social action and the mental health professional. *American Journal of Orthopsychiatry,* 1970, **40,** 373–374.

Marsden, G. Content analysis studies of psychotherapy. In A. E. Bergin & S. L. Garfield (Eds.), *Handbook of psychotherapy and behavior change.* New York: Wiley, 1970.

Martin, D. G. *Introduction to psychotherapy.* Belmont, Calif.: Brooks/Cole, 1971.

Martin, P. A., & Bird, W. H. An approach to the psychotherapy of marriage partners: The stereoscopic technique. *Psychiatry,* 1963, **16,** 123–127.

Maslow, A. H. *Motivation and personality.* New York: Harpers, 1954.

Maslow, A. H. *Toward a psychology of being.* Princeton, N. J.: D. van Nostrand, 1962.

Maslow, A. H. *Religions, values, and peak-experiences.* Columbus: Ohio State University Press, 1964.

Maslow, A. H. A philosophy of psychology: The need for a mature science of human nature. In F. T. Severin (Ed.), *Humanistic viewpoints in psychology.* New York: McGraw-Hill, 1965.

Maslow, A. H. Self-actualization and beyond. In J. F. T. Bugental (Ed.), *Challenges of humanistic psychology.* New York: McGraw-Hill, 1967.

Masserman, J. H. *Behavior and neurosis.* Chicago: University of Chicago Press, 1943.

Masserman, J. H., & Carmichael, H. Diagnosis and prognosis in psychiatry. *Journal of Mental Science,* 1938, **84,** 893–946.

Masters, W. H., & Johnson, V. E. *Human sexual response.* Boston: Little, Brown, 1966.

Masters, W. H., & Johnson, V. E. *Human sexual inadequacy.* Boston: Little, Brown, 1970.

Matarazzo, J. D., Saslow, G., & Matarazzo, R. G. The interaction chronograph as an instrument for objective measurement of interaction patterns during interviews. *Journal of Psychology,* 1956, **41,** 347–367.

Matson, F. W. What ever became of the third force? *Newsletter of the American Association for Humanistic Psychology,* 1969, **6** (1), 1–15.

Matulef, N. J., & Rothenberg, P. J. Toward new schools of professional psychology. *The Clinical Psychologist,* 1968, **22,** 16–19.

Matulef, N. J., & Rothenberg, P. J. Toward new schools of professional psychology. *National Council on Graduate Education in Psychology,* 1969, **3** (1), 8–23.

May, R., Angel, E., & Ellenberger, H. F. (Eds.) *Existence.* New York: Basic Books, 1958.

McMillan, J. J. Agenda for the '70s in professional affairs: Some first thoughts. *Professional Psychology,* 1970, **1,** 181–184.

McNair, D. M., Callahan, D. M., & Lorr, M. Therapist "type" and patient response to psychotherapy. *Journal of Consulting Psychology,* 1962, **26,** 425–429.

Mead, M. *From the South Seas.* New York: Morrow, 1939.

Mednick, S. A. Birth defects and schizophrenia. *Psychology Today,* 1971, **4** (11), 48–50, 80–81.

Mednick, S. A., & McNeil, T. F. Current methodology in research on the etiology of schizophrenia: Serious difficulties which suggest the use of the high-risk–group method. *Psychological Bulletin,* 1968, **70,** 681–693.

Mednick, S. A., & Schulsinger, F. A longitudinal study of children with a high risk for schizophrenia: A preliminary report. In S. Vandenberg (Ed.), *Methods and goals in human behavior genetics.* New York: Academic Press, 1965.

Meehl, P. E. *Clinical versus statistical prediction.* Minneapolis: University of Minnesota Press, 1954.

Meehl, P. E. Wanted—A good cookbook. *American Psychologist,* 1956, **11,** 263–272.

Meehl, P. E. Seer over sign: The first good example. *Journal of Experimental Research in Personality,* 1965, **1,** 27–32. (a)

Meehl, P. E. Discussion in H. J. Eysenck. The effects of psychotherapy. *International Journal of Psychiatry,* 1965, **1,** 156–157. (b)

Mehlman, B. The reliability of psychiatric diagnosis. *Journal of Abnormal and Social Psychology,* 1952, **47,** 577–578.

Meltzoff, J., & Kornreich, M. *Research in psychotherapy.* New York: Atherton, 1970.

Mendel, W. M., & Rapport, S. Determinants of the decision for psychiatric hospitalization. *Archives of General Psychiatry,* 1969, **20,** 321–328.

Menninger, K. *Theory of psychoanalytic technique.* New York: Basic Books, 1958.

Menninger, W. *Psychiatry in a troubled world.* New York: Macmillan, 1948.

Milgram, N. Children are waiting: Will clinical psychology go to school? *The Clinical Psychologist Newsletter,* 1970, **23** (3), 3.

Mittler, P. J. Assessment of handicapped children: Some common factors. In P. J. Mittler (Ed.), *The psychological assessment of mental and physical handicaps.* London: Methuen, 1970.

Moreno, J. L. *Psychodrama.* Vol. I. (2nd ed.) New York: Beacon House, 1946.

Moreno, J. L. Psychodrama. In S. Arieti (Ed.), *American handbook of psychiatry.* Vol. II. New York: Basic Books, 1959.

Morgan, C. D., & Murray, H. A. A method for investigating fantasies: The Thematic Apperception Test. *Archives of Neurology and Psychiatry,* 1935, **34,** 289–306.

Morley, W. E. Treatment of the patient in crisis. *Western Medicine,* 1965, **3,** 77–86.

Morley, W. E. Theory of crisis intervention. *Pastoral Psychology,* 1970, **21,** 14–20.

Morley, W. E., & Brown, V. B. The crisis-intervention group: A natural mating or a marriage of convenience? *Psychotherapy: Theory, Research, and Practice,* 1969, **6,** 30–36.

Morosco, T. E., & Baer, P. E. Avoidance conditioning of alcoholics. In R. Ulrich, T. Stachnik, & J. Mabry (Eds.), *Control of human behavior: From cure to prevention.* Vol. II. Glenview, Ill.: Scott Foresman, 1970.

Moustakas, C. (Ed.) *Existential child therapy.* New York: Basic Books, 1966.

Mowrer, O. H. What is normal behavior? In L. A. Pennington & I. A. Berg (Eds.), *An introduction to clinical psychology.* (2nd ed.) New York: Ronald Press, 1954.

Mowrer, O. H. "Sin," the lesser of two evils. *American Psychologist,* 1960, **15,** 301–304.

Mullan, H., & Rosenbaum, M. *Group psychotherapy: Theory and practice.* New York: Free Press, 1962.

Munroe, R. L. *Schools of psychoanalytic thought.* New York: Dryden Press, 1955.

Murphy, G. Psychological views of personality and contributions to its study. In E. Norbeck, D. Price-Williams, & W. M. McCord (Eds.), *The study of personality: An interdisciplinary appraisal.* New York: Holt, Rinehart & Winston, 1968.

Murray, H. A. *Explorations in personality.* New York: Oxford University Press, 1938.

Murray, H. A. *Assessment of men.* New York: Holt, Rinehart & Winston, 1948.

Myers, J. K., & Bean, L. L. *A decade later: A follow-up of social class and mental illness.* New York: Wiley, 1968.

Oppenheimer, J. R. Analogy in science. *American Psychologist,* 1956, **11,** 127–135.

Osgood, C. E., Suci, G. J., & Tannenbaum, B. H. *The measurement of meaning.* Urbana: University of Illinois Press, 1957.

Oskamp, S. The relationship of clinical experience and training methods to several criteria of clinical prediction. *Psychological Monographs,* 1962, **76** (28, Whole No. 547).

Oskamp, S. Overconfidence in case-study judgments. *Journal of Consulting Psychology,* 1965, **29,** 261–265.

Palmer, J. O., & Goldstein, M. J. (Eds.) *Perspectives in psychopathology.* New York: Oxford University Press, 1966.

Parad, H. J. (Ed.) *Crisis intervention: Selected readings.* New York: Family Service Association of America, 1965.

Parad, H. J., & Caplan, G. A framework for studying families in crisis. *Social Work,* 1960, **5,** 3–15.

Pasamanick, B. On the neglect of diagnosis. *American Journal of Orthopsychiatry,* 1963, **33,** 397–398.

Pasamanick, B., Dinitz, S., & Lefton, M. Psychiatric orientation and its relation to diagnosis and treatment in a mental hospital. *American Journal of Psychiatry,* 1959, **116,** 127–132.

Pascal, G. R., & Suttell, B. J. *The Bender–Gestalt Test: Quantification and validity for adults.* New York: Grune & Stratton, 1951.

Paul, G. L. *Insight versus desensitization in psychotherapy: An experiment in anxiety reduction.* Stanford, Calif.: Stanford University Press, 1966.

Paul, G. L. Strategy of outcome research in psychotherapy. *Journal of Consulting Psychology,* 1967, **31,** 109–118.

Pavlov, I. P. *Conditioned reflexes.* London: Oxford University Press, 1927.

Pearl, A., & Riessman, F. *New careers for the poor: The nonprofessional in human service.* New York: Free Press, 1965.

Perls, F. S. *Ego, hunger, and aggression* (1947). New York: Random House, 1969.

Perls, F. S. *Gestalt therapy verbatim.* Lafayette, Calif.: Real People Press, 1969. (a)

Perls, F. S. *In and out the garbage pail.* Palo Alto, Calif.: Science and Behavior Books, 1969. (b)

Perls, F. S. Four lectures. In J. Fagan & I. L. Shepherd (Eds.), *Gestalt therapy now.* Palo Alto, Calif.: Science and Behavior Books, 1970.

Perls, F. S., Hefferline, R. F., & Goodman, P. *Gestalt therapy.* New York: Julian Press, 1951.

Peterson, D. R. The doctor of psychology program at the University of Illinois. *American Psychologist,* 1968, **23,** 511–516.

Piotrowski, Z. Digital-computer interpretation of inkblot test data. *Psychiatric Quarterly,* 1964, **38,** 1–26.

Polanyi, M. *Personal knowledge.* Chicago: University of Chicago Press, 1958.

Pope, B., & Scott, W. H. *Psychological diagnosis in clinical practice.* New York: Oxford University Press, 1967.

Pottharst, K. E. To renew vitality and provide a challenge in training: The California School of Professional Psychology. *Professional Psychology,* 1970, **1,** 123–130.

Rabin, A. Diagnostic use of intelligence tests. In B. B. Wolman (Ed.), *Handbook of clinical psychology.* New York: McGraw-Hill, 1965.

Rachman, S., & Costello, C. G. The etiology and treatment of children's phobias: A review. *Journal of Child Psychology and Psychiatry,* 1962, **3,** 149–163.

Raimy, V. C. (Ed.) *Training in clinical psychology.* New York: Prentice-Hall, 1950.

Rapaport, D. *Diagnostic psychological testing.* Vols. I, II. Chicago: Year Book Publishers, 1946.

Reid, D. *Epidemiological methods in the study of mental disorders.* Geneva: World Health Organization, 1960.

Reiff, R. Mental health manpower and institutional change. *American Psychologist,* 1966, **21,** 540–548.

Reiff, R. The need for a body of knowledge in community psychology. In I. Iscoe & C. D. Spielberger (Eds.), *Community psychology: Perspectives in training and research.* New York: Appleton-Century-Crofts, 1970.

Reiff, R., & Riessman, F. The indigenous nonprofessional. *Community Mental Health Journal,* 1965, No. 1.

Reik, T. *Listening with the third ear.* New York: Farrar, Straus, 1948.

Reisman, J. R. *The development of clinical psychology.* New York: Appleton-Century-Crofts, 1966.

Reiss, M. Uses and abuses of statistics in biochemical investigations of psychotic patients. In M. Rinkel & H. C. B. Denber (Eds.), *Chemical concepts of psychosis.* New York: McDowell-Obolensky, 1958.

Rice, L. N., & Wagstaff, A. K. Client voice quality and expressive style as indexes of productive psychotherapy. *Journal of Consulting Psychology,* 1967, **31,** 557–563.

Riessman, C. K. The supply–demand dilemma in community mental health centers. *American Journal of Orthopsychiatry,* 1970, **40,** 858–869.

Rioch, M. J., Elkes, C., Flint, A. A., Usdansky, B. S., Newman, R. G., & Silber, E. National Institute of Mental Health pilot study in training mental health counselors. *American Journal of Orthopsychiatry,* 1963, **23,** 678–689.

Rodgers, D. A. In favor of separation of academic and professional training. *American Psychologist,* 1964, **19,** 675–680.

Roe, A. (Ed.) *Graduate education in psychology.* Washington, D. C.: American Psychological Association, 1959.

Rogers, C. R. *Counseling and psychotherapy.* Boston: Houghton Mifflin, 1942.

Rogers, C. R. *Client-centered therapy.* Boston: Houghton Mifflin, 1951.

Rogers, C. R. The necessary and sufficient conditions of therapeutic personality change. *Journal of Consulting Psychology,* 1957, **21,** 95–103.

Rogers, C. R. A theory of therapy, personality, and interpersonal relationships, as developed in the client-centered framework. In S. Koch (Ed.), *Psychology: A study of a science.* Vol. III. New York: McGraw-Hill, 1959.

Rogers, C. R. *On becoming a person.* Boston: Houghton Mifflin, 1961. (a)

Rogers, C. R. A tentative scale for the measurement of process in psychotherapy. In M. I. Stein (Ed.), *Contemporary psychotherapies.* New York: Free Press, 1961. (b)

Rogers, C. R. Toward a science of the person. *Journal of Humanistic Psychology,* 1963, **3,** 72–92.

Rogers, C. R. Client-centered therapy. In S. Arieti (Ed.), *American handbook of psychiatry.* Vol. III. New York: Basic Books, 1966.

Rogers, C. R. Interpersonal relationships: Year 2000. *Journal of Applied and Behavioral Science,* 1968, **4,** 265–280.

Rogers, C. R. *On encounter groups.* New York: Harper & Row, 1970.

Rogers, C. R., & Dymond, R. F. *Psychotherapy and personality change.* Chicago: University of Chicago Press, 1954.

Rogers, C. R., Gendlin, E. T., Kiesler, D. J., & Truax, C. B. *The therapeutic relationship and its impact: A study of psychotherapy with schizophrenics.* Madison: University of Wisconsin Press, 1967.

Rohde, A. R. *The sentence completion method.* New York: Ronald Press, 1957.

Rorschach, H. *Psychodiagnostik.* Bern: Huber, 1921.

Rosen, B. M., Barn, A. K., & Cramer, M. Demographic and diagnostic characteristics of psychiatric out-patient clinics in the U.S.A., 1961. *American Journal of Orthopsychiatry,* 1964, **34,** 455–468.

Rosenbaum, M., & Berger, M. (Eds.) *Group psychotherapy and group function.* New York: Basic Books, 1963.

Rosenblum, G. The new role of the clinical psychologist in a community mental health center. *Community Mental Health Journal,* 1968, **4,** 403–410.

Ross, A. O. General or special? *The Clinical Psychologist,* 1970, **23,** 4, 1–2. (a)

Ross, A. O. ABPP: In pursuit of excellence. *The Clinical Psychologist,* 1970, **23,** 3, 1–3. (b)

Rossi, A. Some pre-World War II antecedents of community mental health theory and practice. *Mental Hygiene,* 1962, **46,** 78–98.

Rossi, E. L. Game and growth: Two dimensions of our psychotherapeutic zeitgeist. *Journal of Humanistic Psychology,* 1967, **7,** 139–154.

Rotter, J. B. *Social learning and clinical psychology.* New York: Prentice-Hall, 1954.

Rotter, J. B., & Rafferty, J. E. *Manual: The Rotter incomplete sentences blank.* New York: Psychological Corporation, 1950.

Ruitenbeek, H. M. *The new group therapies.* New York: Avon Books, 1970.

Russell, R. W. Biochemical factors in mental disorders. In B. B. Wolman (Ed.), *Handbook of clinical psychology.* New York: McGraw-Hill, 1965.

Salter, A. *Conditioned reflex therapy.* New York: Creative Age Press, 1949.

Sanford, F. H. Annual report of the executive secretary. *American Psychologist,* 1951, **6,** 664–670.

Sarbin, T. R., Taft, R., & Bailey, D. E. *Clinical inference and cognitive theory.* New York: Holt, Rinehart & Winston, 1960.

Satir, V. *Conjoint family therapy.* Palo Alto, Calif.: Science and Behavior Books, 1964.

Satir, V. A family of angels. In J. Haley & L. Hoffman (Eds.), *Techniques of family therapy.* New York: Basic Books, 1967.

Sawyer, J. Measurement and prediction, clinical and statistical. *Psychological Bulletin,* 1966, **66,** 178–200.

Schafer, R. *The clinical application of psychological tests.* New York: International Universities Press, 1948.

Schafer, R. *Psychoanalytic interpretation in Rorschach testing.* New York: Grune & Stratton, 1954.

Schofield, W. *Psychotherapy: The purchase of friendship.* Englewood Cliffs, N. J.: Prentice-Hall, 1964.

Scott, W. A. Research definitions of mental health and mental illness. *Psychological Bulletin,* 1958, **55,** 29–45.

Seashore, C. What is sensitivity training? In R. T. Golembiewski & A. Blumberg (Eds.), *Sensitivity training and the laboratory approach.* Itasca, Ill.: Peacock, 1970.

Shakow, D. The training of the clinical psychologist. *Journal of Consulting Psychology,* 1942, **6,** 277–288.

Shakow, D. Clinical psychology: An evaluation. In L. G. Lowrey (Ed.), *Orthopsychiatry 1923–1948: Retrospect and prospect.* New York: American Orthopsychiatric Association, 1948.

Shakow, D. Psychological deficit in schizophrenia. *Behavioral Science,* 1963, **8,** 275–305.

Shakow, D. *Clinical psychology as science and profession.* Chicago: Aldine, 1969.

Shakow, D., Hilgard, E. R., Kelly, E. L., Luckey, B., Sanford, R. N., & Shaffer, L. F. Recommended graduate training program in clinical psychology. *American Psychologist,* 1947, **2,** 539–558.

Sharma, S. L. Clinical psychology: A social educational model. Unpublished manuscript, Sacramento State College, 1968.

Shatan, C. Community psychiatry: Stretcher bearer of the social order? *International Journal of Psychiatry,* 1969, **7,** 312–321.

Shaw, H. J., Matthews, C. G., & Klove, H. The equivalence of WISC and PPVT IQs. *American Journal of Mental Deficiency,* 1966, **70,** 601–606.

Shemberg, K., & Keeley, S. Psychodiagnostic training in the academic setting: Past and present. *Journal of Consulting and Clinical Psychology,* 1970, **34,** 205–211.

Sherif, M., & Hovland, C. J. *Social judgment: Assimilation and contrast effects in communication and attitude change.* New Haven: Yale University Press, 1961.

Shneidman, E. S. *Thematic test analysis.* New York: Grune & Stratton, 1951.

Shneidman, E. S. *The Make-A-Picture Story Test.* New York: Psychological Corporation, 1952.

Shneidman, E. S., & Farberow, N. L. (Eds.) *Clues to suicide.* New York: McGraw-Hill, 1957.

Shutz, W. C. *Joy.* New York: Grove Press, 1967.

Signell, K. A. The crisis of unwed motherhood: A consultation approach. *Community Mental Health Journal,* 1969, **5,** 304–313.

Skinner, B. F. *Walden Two.* New York: Macmillan, 1948.

Skinner, B. F. *Science and human behavior.* New York: Macmillan, 1953.

Skinner, B. F. Behaviorism at fifty. *Science,* 1963, **140,** 951–958.

Slavson, S. R. *A textbook in analytic group psychotherapy.* New York: International Universities Press, 1964.

Small, L. *The briefer psychotherapies.* New York: Brunner/Mazel, 1971.

Smith, M. B., & Hobbs, N. The community and the community mental health center. *American Psychologist,* 1966, **21,** 499–509.

Smith, W. L., & Philippus, M. J. (Eds.) *Neuropsychological testing in organic brain dysfunction.* Springfield, Ill.: Charles C. Thomas, 1969.

Snyder, W. V. *The psychotherapy relationship.* New York: Macmillan, 1961.

Sobey, F. *The nonprofessional revolution in mental health.* New York: Columbia University Press, 1970.

Speck, R. V. Family therapy in the home. *Journal of Marriage and the Family,* 1964, **26,** 72–76.

Speck, R. V., & Rueveni, U. Network therapy: A developing concept. *Family Process,* 1969, **8,** 182–191.

Spitzer, R. L., & Wilson, P. T. A guide to the American Psychiatric Association's new diagnostic nomenclature. *International Journal of Psychiatry,* 1969, **7,** 356–367.

Spradlin, J. E., & Girardeau, F. L. The behavior of moderately and severely retarded persons. In N. R. Ellis (Ed.), *International review of research in mental retardation.* Vol. I. New York: Academic Press, 1966.

Srole, L., Langner, T. S., Michael, S. T., Opler, M. K., & Rennie, T. A. C. *Mental health in the metropolis.* New York: McGraw-Hill, 1961.

Sterba, R. F. A case of brief psychotherapy by Sigmund Freud. *Psychoanalytic Review,* 1951, **38,** 75–80.

Sternbach, R. A., Abroms, G. M., & Rice, D. G. Clinical responsibility and the psychologist. *Psychiatry,* 1969, **32,** 165–173.

Stoller, F. Accelerated interaction: A time-limited approach based on the brief intensive group. *International Journal of Group Psychotherapy,* 1968, **18,** 220–235. (a)

Stoller, F. Marathon group therapy. In G. M. Gazda (Ed.), *Innovations to group psychotherapy.* Springfield, Ill.: Charles C. Thomas, 1968. (b)

Stone, A. A., & Shein, H. M. Psychotherapy of the hospitalized suicidal patient. *American Journal of Psychotherapy,* 1968, **22,** 15–25.

Stott, L. H., & Ball, R. S. Infant and preschool mental tests: Review and evaluation. *Monographs, Society for Research in Child Development,* 1965, **30,** No. 3.

Stretch, J. J. Community mental health: The evolution of a concept in social policy. *Community Mental Health Journal,* 1967, **3,** 5–12.

Strother, C. R. (Ed.) *Psychology and mental health.* Washington, D. C.: American Psychological Association, 1957.

Strupp, H. H. *Psychotherapists in action.* New York: Grune & Stratton, 1960.

Strupp, H. H. *Psychotherapy and the modification of abnormal behavior.* New York: McGraw-Hill, 1971.

Strupp, H. H., & Bergin, A. E. Some empirical and conceptual bases for coordinated research in psychotherapy: A critical review of issues, trends, and evidence. *International Journal of Psychiatry,* 1969, **7,** 18–90.

Sullivan, H. S. *The interpersonal theory of psychiatry.* New York: W. W. Norton, 1953.

Sullivan, H. S. *The psychiatric interview.* New York: W. W. Norton, 1954.

Sundberg, N. D. The practice of psychological testing in clinical services in the United States. *American Psychologist,* 1961, **16,** 79–83.

Sundberg, N. D., & Tyler, L. E. *Clinical psychology.* New York: Appleton-Century-Crofts, 1962.

Swensen, C. H. Empirical evaluations of human figure drawings. *Psychological Bulletin,* 1957, **54,** 431–466.

Symonds, J. P. Ten years of journalism in psychology, 1937–1946; First decade of the Journal of Consulting Psychology. *Journal of Consulting Psychology,* 1946, **10,** 335–374.

Szasz, T. S. Psychiatry, psychotherapy, and psychology. *Archives of General Psychiatry,* 1959, **1,** 455–463.

Szasz, T. S. The myth of mental illness. *American Psychologist,* 1960, **15,** 113–118.

Szasz, T. S. *The myth of mental illness: Foundations of a theory of personal conduct.* New York: Hoeber-Harper, 1961.

Szasz, T. S. *Law, liberty, and psychiatry.* New York: Macmillan, 1963.

Szasz, T. S. The psychiatric classification of behavior: A strategy of personal constraint. In L. D. Eron (Ed.), *The classification of behavior disorders.* Chicago: Aldine, 1966.

Szasz, T. S. Behavior therapy and psychoanalysis. *Medical Opinion and Review,* 1967, **3** (6), 24–29.

Talland, G. A. Psychology's concern with brain damage. *Journal of Nervous and Mental Disease,* 1963, **136,** 344–351.

Tallent, N. Clinical psychological testing: A review of premises, practices, and promises. *Journal of Projective Techniques and Personality Assessment,* 1965, **29,** 418–435.

Temerin, M. K. On choice and responsibility in a humanistic psychotherapy. *Journal of Humanistic Psychology,* 1963, **3,** 35–48.

Terman, L. M. *The measurement of intelligence.* Boston: Houghton Mifflin, 1916.

Terman, L. M., & Merrill, M. A. *Measuring intelligence.* Boston: Houghton Mifflin, 1937.

Terman, L. M., & Merrill, M. A. *Stanford–Binet intelligence scale.* Boston: Houghton Mifflin, 1960.

Thorndike, E. L. *Animal intelligence.* New York: Macmillan, 1911.

Thorne, F. C. Theoretical foundations of directive psychotherapy. *Current trends in clinical psychology, Annals of New York Academy of Science,* 1948, **49,** 867–928.

Thorne, F. C. *Clinical judgment: A study of errors.* Brandon, Vt.: Journal of Clinical Psychology, 1961.

Tomlinson, T. M. The psychotherapist as a codeterminant in client goal setting. In C. Buhler & F. Massarik (Eds.), *The course of human life.* New York: Springer, 1968.

Tripoldi, T., Epstein, I., & MacMurray, C. Dilemmas in evaluation: Implications for administrators of social action programs. *American Journal of Orthopsychiatry,* 1970, **40,** 850–857.

Truax, C. B., & Carkhuff, R. R. Significant developments in psychotherapy research. In L. E. Abt & B. F. Riess (Eds.), *Progress in clinical psychology.* Vol. VI. New York: Grune & Stratton, 1964.

Tryon, R. C. Psychology in flux: The academic–professional bipolarity. *American Psychologist,* 1963, **18,** 134–143.

Ullmann, L. P., & Krasner, L. (Eds.) *Case studies in behavior modification.* New York: Holt, Rinehart & Winston, 1966.

Ullmann, L. P., & Krasner, L. *A psychological approach to abnormal behavior.* Englewood Cliffs, N. J.: Prentice-Hall, 1969.

University of Michigan, Clinical Psychology Alumni. Clinical alumni statement on doctoral training. *Newsletter, Division of Clinical Psychology,* 1962, **15** (4), 7–10.

van Kaam, A. Counseling and psychotherapy from the viewpoint of existential psychology. In D. S. Arbuckle (Ed.), *Counseling and psychotherapy: An overview.* New York: McGraw-Hill, 1967.

Wallen, R. Gestalt therapy and Gestalt psychology. In J. Fagan & I. L. Shepherd (Eds.), *Gestalt therapy now.* Palo Alto, Calif.: Science and Behavior Books, 1970.

Wann, T. W. (Ed.) *Behaviorism and phenomenology.* Chicago: University of Chicago Press, 1964.

Ward, C. H., Beck, A. T., Mendelson, M., Mock, J. E., & Erbaugh, J. K. The psychiatric nomenclature. *Archives of General Psychiatry,* 1962, **7,** 198–205.

Watson, J. B. Psychology as the behaviorist views it. *Psychological Review,* 1913, **20,** 158–177.

Watson, J. B. *Behavior: An introduction to comparative psychology.* New York: Holt, 1914.

Watson, J. B. *Psychology from the standpoint of a behaviorist.* Philadelphia: Lippincott, 1919.

Watson, J. B. *Behaviorism.* New York: People's Institute, 1924.

Watson, J. B., & Rayner, R. Conditioned emotional reactions. *Journal of Experimental Psychology,* 1920, **3,** 1–14.

Watson, R. I. A brief history of clinical psychology. *Psychological Bulletin,* 1953, **50,** 321–346.

Watzlawick, P., Beavin, J. H., & Jackson, D. D. *Pragmatics of human communication.* New York: W. W. Norton, 1967.

Wayne, G. J. The psychiatric emergency: An overview. In G. J. Wayne & R. R. Koegler (Eds.), *Emergency psychiatry and brief therapy.* Boston: Little, Brown, 1966.

Wechsler, D. A standardized memory scale for clinical use. *Journal of Psychology,* 1945, **19,** 87–95.

Wechsler, D. *The measurement and appraisal of adult intelligence.* Baltimore: Williams and Wilkins, 1958.

Wertheimer, M. *A brief history of psychology.* New York: Holt, Rinehart & Winston, 1970.

Whitaker, C. A. Acting out in family psychotherapy. In L. E. Abt & S. L. Weissman (Eds.), *Acting out: Theoretical and clinical aspects.* New York: Grune & Stratton, 1965.

Whitaker, C. A., & Malone, T. P. *The roots of psychotherapy.* New York: Blakiston, 1953.

White, R. W. *Lives in progress: A study of the natural growth of personality.* New York: Dryden Press, 1952.

Whitehorn, J. C., & Betz, B. J. A study of psychotherapeutic relationships between physicians and schizophrenic patients. *American Journal of Psychiatry,* 1954, **111,** 321–331.

Whitehorn, J. C., & Betz, B. J. Further studies of the doctor as a crucial variable in the outcome of treatment with schizophrenic patients. *American Journal of Psychiatry,* 1960, **117,** 215–223.

Wiens, A. N. Scientist–professional: The appropriate training model for the mainstream of clinical psychology. *Professional Psychology,* 1969, **1,** 38–42.

Wilson, M. S., & Meyer, E. Diagnostic consistency in a psychiatric liaison service. *American Journal of Psychiatry,* 1962, **119,** 207–209.

Winder, C. L. Diversity for clinical training. *American Psychologist,* 1963, **18,** 69–70.

Witmer, L. Clinical psychology. *Psychological Clinic,* 1907, **1,** 1–9.

Wolberg, L. R. (Ed.) *Short-term psychotherapy.* New York: Grune & Stratton, 1965.

Wolberg, L. R. *The technique of psychotherapy.* Vol. I. (2nd ed.) New York: Grune & Stratton, 1967.

Wolf, A. The psychoanalysis of groups. *American Journal of Psychotherapy,* 1949, **3,** 529–557.

Wolf, A. Short-term group psychotherapy. In L. R. Wolberg (Ed.), *Short-term psychotherapy.* New York: Grune & Stratton, 1965.

Wolf, A., & Schwartz, E. K. *Psychoanalysis in groups.* New York: Grune & Stratton, 1962.

Wolman, B. B. Clinical psychology and the philosophy of science. In B. B. Wolman (Ed.), *Handbook of clinical psychology.* New York: McGraw-Hill, 1965.

Wolpe, J. *Psychotherapy by reciprocal inhibition.* Stanford, Calif.: Stanford University Press, 1958.

Wolpe, J. *The practice of behavior therapy.* New York: Pergamon Press, 1969.

Wolpe, J., & Lazarus, A. A. *Behavior therapy techniques.* London: Pergamon Press, 1966.

Work, H. H. Psychiatric emergencies in childhood. In G. J. Wayne & R. R. Koegler (Eds.), *Emergency psychiatry and brief therapy.* Boston: Little, Brown, 1966.

Wright, L. Symptoms: Is treatment mistreatment? *The Clinical Psychologist Newsletter,* 1970, **23** (3), 6–9.

Wynne, L. C. Some indications and contraindications for exploratory family therapy. In I. Boszormenyi-Nagy & J. L. Framo (Eds.), *Intensive family therapy.* New York: Harper & Row, 1965.

Yalom, I. D. *The theory and practice of group psychotherapy.* New York: Basic Books, 1970.

Yates, A. J. Symptoms and symptom substitution. *Psychological Review,* 1958, **65,** 371–374.

Yates, A. J. Psychological deficit. *Annual Review of Psychology,* 1966, **17,** 111–114.

Yolles, S. F. The role of the psychologist in comprehensive community mental health centers: The National Institute of Mental Health view. *American Psychologist,* 1966, **21,** 37–41.

Yolles, S. F. The comprehensive national mental health program: An evaluation. In L. M. Roberts, N. S. Greenfield, & M. H. Miller (Eds.), *Comprehensive mental health.* Madison, Wis.: University of Wisconsin Press, 1968.

Yolles, S. F. Past, present, and 1980: Trend projections. In L. Bellak & H. H. Barten (Eds.), *Progress in community mental health.* Vol. I. New York: Grune & Stratton, 1969.

Zigler, E., & Phillips, L. Psychiatric diagnosis and symptomatology. *Journal of Abnormal and Social Psychology,* 1961, **63,** 69–75.

Zimet, C. N. American Board of Professional Psychology and the changing nature of the profession of psychology. *Professional Psychology,* 1969, **1,** 48–51.

Zubin, J., Eron, L. D., & Schumer, F. *An experimental approach to projective techniques.* New York: Wiley, 1965.

Zuk, G. H. Triadic-based family therapy. *International Journal of Psychiatry,* 1969, **8,** 539–548.

Name Index

Abroms, G. M., 94
Ackerman, N. W., 116, 118, 373–374, 378, 386
Adelson, D., 343
Adler, A., 35, 194, 219
Aguilera, D. C., 347, 364–365
Ainsworth, M. D., 173
Albee, G. W., 38, 40–42, 73–74, 85, 102, 258, 302
Alexander, F. G., 49, 364
Allen, N., 297
Allison, J., 160
Allport, G. W., 7, 11, 270–271
Amatruda, C. S., 12, 161
Ames, L. B., 173
Anastasi, A., 149, 154, 156, 158
Anderson, L. S., 303
Andrews, T. G., 59
Angel, E., 35, 200
Ash, P., 123
Atkins, A. L., 143
Atkinson, J. W., 176–177
Atthowe, J. M., 255
Ausubel, D. P., 35
Avnet, H. H., 369–370
Axline, V., 197
Ayllon, T., 36, 255, 258, 263
Azrin, N. H., 36, 255, 258, 263

Bach, G. R., 391, 403
Baer, P. E., 251
Bahn, A. K., 319
Bailey, D. E., 136, 141, 143
Baker, B. L., 260
Balance, W. D. G., 42
Ball, R. S., 161

Bandura, A., 252–253
Barbigan, M. M., 125
Bard, M., 89, 339
Barker, R. G., 322–324
Barn, A. K., 117
Barten, H. H., 366, 369
Bateson, G., 372, 374, 381
Bayley, N., 12, 161
Bean, L. L., 14–15
Beane, K., 391
Beatman, F. L., 374
Beavin, J. H., 381
Beck, A. T., 123, 125
Beck, S. J., 47, 58, 171, 173
Beers, C. W., 51–52
Bell, J. E., 373
Bellak, L., 177, 295, 346, 359, 365, 367
Beller, E. K., 117–121
Bender, L. A., 167–168
Benne, K. D., 391
Bennett, C. C., 303
Benton, A. L., 168–169
Berenda, C. W., 28
Berenson, B. G., 203, 262, 312
Berger, M., 389
Berger, M. M., 209
Bergin, A. E., 205, 217
Berkowitz, B., 339
Berman, K. K., 384–385
Berne, E., 273, 397–398
Betz, B. J., 202–203
Bieri, J., 143
Billingslea, F. Y., 168
Bindman, A. J., 295
Bindrim, P., 404

Binet, A., 53
Binswanger, L., 274, 276–277
Bird, W. H., 375
Blanchard, E. B., 252–253
Blatt, S. J., 160
Bleuler, E., 108–109
Bloom, B. L., 305, 327
Blum, G., 177
Bolles, M., 169
Bordin, E. S., 207
Boring, E. G., 60, 61, 231
Boss, M., 274, 277
Boszormenyi–Nagy, I., 7, 385–386
Bowen, M., 379
Bower, E. M., 307–308
Bowlby, J., 345
Bradford, L., 391
Breuer, J., 220
Briar, S., 143
Brilliant, P. J., 169
Bringmann, W. G., 42
Bromberg, W., 52
Brown, V. B., 358
Browne, C. G., 145
Buck, J. N., 183–184
Bugental, J. F. T., 114, 266, 270, 275, 277,
    279, 289
Bühler, C., 271
Buros, O. K., 160
Butcher, J. N., 189
Butler, J. M., 208

Callahan, D. M., 203
Caplan, G., 305, 310, 328, 342–343, 345–
    347, 357–358, 361
Carkhuff, R. R., 22, 203–204, 262, 312
Carmichael, H., 125
Carson, R. C., 147, 203
Casriel, D., 402
Castner, B. M., 12
Cattell, J. McK., 53
Cattell, P., 161
Charcot, J., 49, 220–221
Chertkoff, S. O., 183
Clark, K. E., 77, 84, 100
Coffey, H. S., 85
Cohen, M. B., 205
Cohen, R. A., 205
Cohn, R. C., 401
Coleman, M. D., 346
Combs, A. W., 265
Cook, S. W., 72
Cooper, J. E., 125
Cooper, S., 303
Costello, C. G., 198
Cowen, E. L., 296
Cramer, M., 117
Cronbach, L. J., 134, 150–151, 159

Dahlstrom, W. G., 187–188
Darwin, C., 45–47, 57, 231
David, H. P., 180
Deri, S., 179–180
Dewey, J., 57
Dinitz, S., 122, 125
Dix, D., 51, 295
Dollard, J., 7
Dreese, M., 59
Dreger, R. M., 21, 117
Dreikurs, R., 208
Dunham, H. W., 316, 338
Dunn, L. M., 164
Durell, J., 17
Dymond, R. F., 23

Egan, G., 399
Eisenberg, L., 261, 307
Elkes, C., 62
Ellenberger, H. F., 35, 200
Ellis, A., 199
Enright, J. B., 402
Epstein, I., 326
Erbaugh, J. K., 123, 125
Erikson, E. H., 11, 35, 95, 197, 236, 346
Eron, L. D., 173–174, 176–178, 183
Escalona, S. K., 11, 161
Evans, J., 11
Ewalt, J. R., 297, 300
Ewalt, P. L., 297, 300
Eysenck, H. J., 114, 131, 215–218, 239, 261

Farberow, N. L., 345, 349, 359
Faris, R., 316
Farrell, M. S., 347, 364–365
Feld, S., 320–321
Feldman, M. P., 252
Fenichel, O., 225–226
Ferrand, L., 53
Fiedler, F. E., 194, 286
Fiske, D. W., 24, 128, 145, 148
Flemming, E. L., 117
Flint, A. A., 62
Ford, D. H., 198
Forer, B. R., 178–179
Foulkes, S. H., 393
Fowler, R. D., 146, 186, 189–190
Framo, S. L., 388
Frank, G. H., 126
Frank, J. D., 194, 203, 205–206, 399
Frank, L. K., 170
Franks, C. M., 251
French, T. M., 364
Freud, A., 95, 236
Freud, S., 11, 26, 35, 49, 52, 59, 171, 193–
    194, 200, 219–237, 276, 281, 285, 363,
    372, 380
Freudenberger, H. J., 361
Friedman, A. S., 7, 385–386

Fromm, E., 35, 95, 236, 271
Fromm–Reichmann, F., 49, 207
Frostig, M., 163
Galton, F., 47, 53, 171, 185
Gardner, E. A., 125, 350
Garfield, S. L., 29
Garmezy, N., 317
Garvey, W., 240, 243
Gazda, G. M., 390
Gelfand, S., 72
Gendlin, E. T., 23
Gesell, A. L., 12, 161
Gibb, J. R., 406
Gibson, R. W., 205
Giedt, F. H., 128
Girardeau, F. L., 255
Glasser, W., 273
Gleser, G. C., 150
Glidewell, J. C., 296
Goddard, H. H., 54
Goldberg, L. R., 131
Goldberg, P. A., 179
Goldenberg, H., 239
Goldenberg, I., 182, 239
Goldfarb, A., 122
Goldiamond, I., 254
Goldschmid, M. L., 27, 67, 192
Goldstein, A. P., 202, 208, 214
Goldstein, K., 169
Goldstein, M. J., 13
Goodenough, F., 181
Goodman, P., 277
Gorham, D. R., 188
Gough, H. G., 33, 132
Graham, F. K., 169
Greenberg, E. M., 307
Greenblatt, M., 34
Greenson, R. R., 221, 229
Greenspoon, J., 210
Greenwald, J. A., 280–281
Gross, M. L., 149
Grossberg, J. M., 260
Grosser, C., 312
Grotjahn, M., 381
Guerney, B., Jr., 312–313
Guilford. J. P., 160
Gump, P. V., 324
Gurin, G., 320–321
Gursslin, O. R., 293
Gynther, M. D., 169

Hadden, S. B., 390
Haley, J., 372–374, 377, 381
Hall, C. S., 234, 268
Hall, G. S., 52
Halpern, F., 173
Hammer, E. F., 183
Hammer, M., 196–197

Hanfmann, E., 169
Harper, R. A., 193
Harris, T., 398
Harrison, R., 176–177
Hartmann, H., 236
Hassol, L., 303
Hathaway, S. R., 188
Hayes, S. P., 163
Healy, W., 44, 54, 297
Hefferline, R. F., 277
Hegrenes, S. R., 240, 243
Heidigger, M., 273–274
Heine, R. W., 194, 286
Heller, K., 202, 208, 214
Henderson, N. B., 61, 98
Henry, W. E., 204, 312
Herron, E. W., 21, 174
Hersch, C., 103, 332
Hewett, P., 163
Hidreth, J. D., 61, 93, 98
Hilgard, E. R., 69
Hill, R., 357
Himelstein, P., 156
Hirschfield, P. P., 42
Hiskey, M. S., 162
Hobbs, N., 41, 259, 287, 295, 302, 329–330, 333
Hoch, E. L., 26, 78
Hollingshead, A. B., 14–16, 294, 316
Holt, R. R., 28, 133–134, 143, 148, 173, 202, 263
Holtzman, W. H., 21, 174
Horney, K., 35, 236
Hovland, C. J., 127
Howard, J., 391
Howells, J. G., 374
Hunt, E. B., 114
Hunt, H. F., 24
Hunt, R. G., 293
Hunt, W. A., 114, 127, 132, 142
Hutt, M. L., 168

Isaacs, W., 254
Iscoe, I., 304

Jackson, B., 109
Jackson, D. D., 372–374, 378, 381
Jacobson, G. F., 346, 351–353, 359
James, W., 52, 54, 57, 136
Janis, I., 263
Johnson, V. E., 387–388
Jones, E., 219
Jones, M., 336
Jones, M. C., 242
Jones, N. F., 132
Jung, C. G., 35, 171, 193, 200, 219
Jungreis, J. E., 7, 385–386

Kadis, A. L., 393

Kaffman, M., 368
Kagan, J., 263
Kahn, M. W., 132
Kalis, B. L., 343–345
Kanner, L., 261
Kaplan, A. M., 196–197
Kaplan, S. R., 399
Karnosh, L. J., 51
Kasanin, J., 169
Keeley, S., 147
Kelley, N. H., 100
Kelly, E. L., 27, 66–67, 73, 75, 128, 130, 145, 148
Kelly, G. A., 7, 143, 184
Kelly, J. G., 72, 312, 322, 325
Kendall, B. S., 169
Kennedy, J. F., 299, 312
Kent, G. H., 171
Kety, S. S., 16, 18
Kierkegaard, S., 273–274
Kiesler, D. J., 23
Kirk, S. A., 164
Kirk, W. D., 164
Klein, D. C., 303, 319, 346
Klein, M., 95, 197
Klopfer, B., 172–173
Klopfer, W. G., 173
Klove, H., 164
Koegler, R. R., 368
Koffka, K., 58, 278
Kogan, L. S., 12
Kohler, K., 58, 278
Koppitz, E., 168
Kornreich, M., 209, 217–218
Kraepelin, E., 48–49, 108–109, 171
Krasner, J. D., 393
Krasner, L., 239, 245–246, 255–256
Krutch, J. W., 271
Kubie, L. S., 79–81, 84, 339–340

Laing, R. D., 374
Landis, C., 22
Langner, T. S., 14, 316–317
Laqueur, H. P., 384
Leaman, R. L., 143
Lefton, M., 122, 125
Lehner, G. F. J., 71
Leonard, J., 173
Levinson, D. J., 34
Levitt, E. E., 215
Levy, L. H., 27, 72, 107–108
Lewin, K., 58, 391
Lewin, K. K., 363
Lewis, N. D. C., 48
Lewis, P. M., 117
Liberman, R., 381
Libo, L. M., 309
Lieberman, M. A., 406

Lincoln, G., 7, 385–386
Lindemann, E., 345
Lindzey, G., 170, 234, 268
Lippitt, R., 391
Little, K. B., 129, 148, 247
London, P., 201, 255
Lorr, M., 203
Louttit, C. M., 56, 145
Lovaas, O. I., 36, 198, 261, 263
Lowrey, L. G., 298
Lublin, B., 167, 180–181, 183
Luborsky, L., 24, 202
Luckey, B., 69
Lundin, R. W., 247

MacCorquodale, K., 256
MacCulloch, M. J., 252
MacGregor, R., 384
Machover, K., 181, 183
MacMurray, C., 326
Maddi, S. R., 267
Maher, B., 13, 31, 126
Mahl, G. F., 263
Mahrer, A. R., 201, 335
Malone, T. P., 200
Mariner, A. S., 94–95
Marks, P. A., 188
Marmor, J., 335
Marsden, G., 209
Martin, D. G., 210
Martin, P. A., 375
Maslow, A. H., 262, 264, 271–272, 275, 289
Masserman, J. H., 14, 125
Massey, J. O., 163
Masters, W. H., 387–388
Matarazzo, J. D., 209
Matarazzo, R. G., 209
Matson, F. W., 266
Matthews, C. G., 164
Matulef, N. J., 85–86
May, R., 35, 95, 200, 273–277, 286
McCarthy, J. J., 164
McKinley, J. C., 187
McMillan, J. J., 76
McNair, D. M., 203
McNeil, T. F., 18–19
Mead, M., 236
Mednick, S. A., 18–19, 317
Meehl, P. E., 20–21, 130–134, 136, 188, 214, 256
Mehlman, B., 122
Meltzoff, J., 209, 217–218
Mendel, W. M., 138–139
Mendelson, M., 123, 125
Menninger, K., 230
Menninger, W., 109, 298–299
Merrill, M. A., 54, 155–156
Messick, J. M., 347, 364–365

Metraux, R. W., 173
Meyer, A., 52
Meyer, E., 122
Michael, S. T., 14, 316–317
Miles, M. B., 406
Miles, M. C., 125
Milgram, N., 44
Miller, H., 143
Miller, K. S., 117
Miller, M. L., 186, 189–190
Miller, N. E., 9
Mitchell, H. E., 7, 385–386
Mittler, P. J., 162
Mock, J. E., 123, 125
Molish, H. B., 47
Moreno, J. L., 390, 396–397
Morgan, C. D., 58, 174
Morley, W. E., 343, 346, 349, 351–359
Morosco, T. E., 251
Moustakas, C., 197
Mowrer, O. H., 12, 38–39
Mullan, H., 393
Munroe, R. L., 227–228
Murphy, G., 11
Murray, H. A., 58, 144, 174, 176, 179, 285
Myers, J. K., 14, 15

Newman, R. G., 62

Opler, M. K., 14, 316
Oppenheimer, J. R., 3, 29
Orne, M. T., 24
Osgood, C. E., 143
Oskamp, S., 128
Overlade, D. C., 117

Paine, C., 167, 180–181, 183
Palmer, J. O., 13
Parad, H. J., 347, 357
Parloff, M. B., 24
Pasamanick, B., 115, 122, 125
Pascal, G. R., 168
Paul, G. L., 211–213
Pavlov, I. P., 45–46, 58, 240–241, 243
Pearl, A., 313
Perls, F. S., 200, 277–282, 401–402
Peterson, D. R., 82–83
Phillippus, M. J., 166
Phillips, L., 124–125
Pinel, P., 48, 295
Piotrowski, Z., 188
Polanyi, M., 266
Pope, B., 159
Pottharst, K. E., 86, 88
Pratt, J., 389–390

Rabin, A., 166
Rachman, S., 198
Rafferty, J. E., 178
Raimy, V. C., 60, 70

Rank, O., 95, 219
Rapaport, D., 146–147, 159, 171
Rapport, S., 138–139
Rayner, R., 57, 242
Redlich, F. C., 14–16, 294, 316
Reich, W., 219
Reid, D., 316
Reid, M. P., 117
Reiff, R., 207, 296, 307, 312, 337, 350
Reik, T., 95, 139–141
Reiser, M. F., 24
Reisman, J. R., 48, 50
Reiss, M., 17
Rennie, T. A. C., 14, 316
Rice, D. G., 94
Rice, L. N., 208
Rich, T. A., 117
Riessman, C. K., 315
Riessman, F., 312–313
Rioch, M. J., 62
Ritchie, A. M., 384
Ritter, B., 252–253
Roach, J. L., 293
Rodgers, D. A., 73–74
Roe, A., 75
Rogers, C. R., 22–23, 59, 69, 95, 114, 193–
    194, 197, 199–201, 262, 264, 266–270,
    275, 289, 399–401, 405
Rohde, A. R., 179
Romano, J., 125
Rorschach, H., 58, 171
Rosanoff, A. J., 171
Rosen, B. M., 177
Rosenbaum, M., 389, 393
Rosenblum, G., 296, 302–303
Rosenthal, D., 18
Ross, A., 346
Ross, A. O., 26, 78, 100, 333
Rossi, A., 297
Rossi, E. L., 273
Rothenberg, P. J., 85–86
Rotter, J. B., 10, 178
Rueveni, U., 386
Ruitenbeek, H. M., 389, 404
Rush, B., 48
Russell, B., 136
Russell, R. W., 17

Salter, A., 247
Sanford, F. H., 90, 100
Sanford, R. N., 69
Sarbin, T. R., 136–137, 141, 143
Saslow, G., 209
Satir, V., 373–374
Sawyer, J., 131
Schaeffer, B., 36, 198
Schafer, R., 148, 159
Scheerer, M., 169

Schildkraut, J. J., 17
Schneider, S., 346, 359
Schofield, W., 9, 206
Schulsinger, F., 18, 317
Schumer, F., 173–174, 178
Schuster, F. P., 384
Schwartz, E. K., 396
Scott, W. A., 12
Scott, W. H., 159
Seashore, C., 398
Sechrest, L. B., 202, 208, 214
Seeman, W., 188
Selesnick, S., 49
Serrano, A. C., 384
Shaffer, L. F., 69
Shakow, D., 13, 44, 68–70, 80
Sharma, S. L., 37
Shatan, C., 337, 340
Shaw, H. J., 164
Shein, H. M., 348
Shemberg, K., 147
Sherif, M., 127
Sherman, S. N., 374
Shneidman, E. S., 129, 148, 175–177, 247,
    345, 359
Shutz, W. C., 287, 407
Signell, K. A., 344
Silber, E., 62
Simmons, J. Q., 36, 198
Simon, T., 53
Sims, J. H., 204
Skinner, B. F., 243–244, 285
Slavson, S. R., 390, 396
Small, L., 346, 359, 365–367
Smith, G., 298
Smith, M. B., 302
Smith, W. L., 166
Snyder, W. V., 207
Snygg, D., 265
Sobey, F., 313–314
Sommer, G. J., 346, 359
Sonne, J. C., 7, 385–386
Sorrells, J., 27, 67, 192
Speck, R. V., 7, 385–386
Spiegel, A. D., 295
Spielberger, C. D., 304
Spitzer, R. L., 31, 109
Spivack, G., 7, 385–386
Spradlin, J. E., 255
Spray, S. L., 204
Srole, L., 14, 316
Stein, D. D., 27, 67, 192
Sterba, R. F., 363
Sternbach, R. A., 94
Stoller, F., 403
Stone, A. A., 348
Stott, L. H., 161
Stretch, J. J., 298

Strickler, M., 346, 351–353, 359
Strother, C. R., 75
Strupp, H. H., 203, 205, 208, 212–214
Suci, G. J., 143
Sullivan, H. S., 26, 35, 193, 200–201, 276
Sundberg, N. D., 135, 145, 180–181
Suttell, B. J., 168
Swartz, J. D., 21, 174
Swensen, C. H., 183
Symonds, J. P., 57, 60
Szasz, T. S., 38, 39, 94, 261

Taffel, C., 117
Taft, R., 136–137, 141, 143
Talland, G. A., 166
Tallent, N., 149
Tannenbaum, B. H., 143
Temerin, M. K., 272
Terman, L. M., 54, 56, 155–156
Thomas, J., 254
Thompson, H., 12
Thorndike, E. L., 45, 240–241, 243
Thorne, F. C., 34, 142, 143
Thorpe, J. S., 21, 174
Tillichi, P., 277
Titchener, E., 289
Tomlinson, T. M., 272
Tripoldi, T., 143, 326
Truax, C. B., 22–23, 204
Tryon, R. C., 66
Tuke, W., 50, 295
Tuma, A. H., 24
Tyler, L. E., 135

Ullmann, L. P., 239, 245–246, 255–256
Urban, H. B., 198
Usdansky, B. S., 62

Van Kaam, A., 274
Veroff, J., 320–321

Wagstaff, A. K., 208
Walker, R. N., 173
Wallen, R., 278
Wallis, R. R., 167, 180–181, 183
Walter, B., 363
Ward, C. H., 123, 125
Watson, J. B., 57, 241–243
Watson, R. I., 52, 54
Watzlawick, P., 381
Way, J. L., 167
Wayne, G. J., 348–349
Weakland, J. H., 372, 374, 381
Wechsler, D., 156–159, 166, 168
Weissman, H., 27, 67, 192
Welsh, G. S., 187–188
Wender, P. H., 18
Wertheimer, M., 58, 167, 278
Wertheimer, M. A., 241
Whitaker, C. A., 200, 375

White, R. W., 11
Whitehorn, J. C., 202–203
Wiens, A. N., 72
Wilner, D. M., 346, 359
Wilson, M. S., 122
Wilson, P. T., 31, 109
Winder, C. L., 26, 73, 78
Winick, C., 393
Witmer, L., 43–44, 52, 55, 297–298
Wittson, C. L., 114
Wolberg, L. R., 200, 229, 232, 363, 366
Wolf, A., 368, 393, 396
Wolman, B. B., 26
Wolpe, J., 35, 199, 242, 244–245, 247–251
Work, H. H., 349
Wright, H. F., 323

Wright, L., 260
Wundt, W., 44–45, 53, 57, 171, 289
Wynne, L. C., 378

Yalom, I. D., 391–393, 406
Yates, A. J., 165, 260
Yerkes, R., 56
Yolles, S. F., 37, 302, 319, 362–363

Zax, M., 296
Zigler, E., 124–125
Zimet, C. N., 101, 160
Zubin, J., 173–174, 178
Zucker, E. M., 51
Zuk, G. H., 383
Zwerling, I., 346

Subject Index

Abreaction, 220–221
Acting-out, 369, 396–397
Actuarial approach, 13, 34, 129–142, 319
Aftercare services, 297, 301, 309
Aggression, 198, 252, 257, 368
American Association of Applied Psychology, 60, 67
American Association of Clinical Psychologists, 57
American Association for Humanistic Psychology, 266, 271
American Association of Suicidology, 359
American Board of Professional Psychology, 37, 61, 69, 72, 93, 100–103
American Medical Association, 93
American Psychiatric Association, 31, 48, 57, 93–94, 96–97, 109–114
American Psychological Association, 37, 52, 57, 60–61, 63, 66–77, 84, 89–103, 302
Anamnesis, 5, 129
Anxiety hierarchy, 245, 247–251
Army Alpha Test, 56
Army Beta Test, 56, 163
Assertive training, 251
Assessment, 5, 19–21, 62, 79, 144–191, 245–247, 367
Austen Riggs Center, 36
Autism, 36, 198, 245, 261, 263

Babcock Story Recall Test, 146
Base rates, 136–139
Basic encounter groups (see also Encounter groups), 399–401
Bayley Infant Scale of Development, 161
Behavior modification, 10, 23, 36, 45, 63–64, 197, 200–201, 205, 210, 232, 238–264, 273, 282–283, 366–367, 381

Behavior therapy (see Behavior modification)
Behaviorism, 57–58, 241–242, 261–262
Bender-Gestalt Test, 167–169
Benton Visual Retention Test, 168–169
Binet-Simon Scale (see Stanford-Binet Intelligence Scales)
Biochemical factors in psychopathology, 15–17
Blacky Test, 177
Blind analysis, 129, 134, 174
Boulder Conference, 70–75, 79
Brain damage (see Organic brain dysfunction)
Brief psychotherapies, 361–370

California School of Professional Psychology, 86–89
Case history, 5, 19, 33, 48, 129, 188, 247
Cattell Infant Intelligence Scale, 161
Certification law, 61, 89, 94, 96–98
Chemotherapy (see Drugs)
Chicago Conference on Professional Preparation, 77–79, 82, 84
Child advocacy system, 333–334
Child guidance clinics (see Clinics)
Child rearing problems, 5, 8, 335, 372–373
Childhood disorders:
    classification, 116–121
    treatment, 195–198, 215, 368
Children's Apperception Test, 177
Classification system, psychiatric, 48–49, 108–126
Client-centered therapy, 23, 59, 194, 197, 199, 201, 267–270, 273, 400
Clinical psychology:
    activities, 4, 27, 66–67, 72–73, 145, 192–193
    definition, 3

history, 43–65
professional roles, 8, 9, 29
Clinical psychology division (Division 12) of APA, 60, 66–67, 69, 333
Clinics:
  child guidance, 4, 54, 57, 297–298, 375
  crisis or walk-in, 307, 346–350, 358–359
  outpatient psychiatric, 4, 15, 30, 40–41, 297, 341, 350
  psychological, 41, 44, 78, 297
Communication patterns, interpersonal, 372, 374, 378–384
Community Mental Health Act (1963), 299–300, 326, 362
Community Mental Health Centers, 4, 30, 36–37, 300–304, 363
Community psychology, 303–304, 307, 335
Computer, use of:
  in psychiatric case registers, 322
  in test interpretation, 20, 63, 130, 132, 142, 186–190
Conditioning, 23, 232, 239–245, 251–252, 261
Conference on the Education of Psychologists for Community Mental Health, 303
Consultation, mental health, 5, 27, 63, 301–302, 309–312, 335
Control groups, research, 12, 17, 23, 24, 146, 185, 216–217, 252–253, 369
Courts, 4, 54
Crisis:
  intervention, 201, 304, 341–361, 365–366
  theory, 342–344
  types, 11, 306, 346–347
Critical incident technique, 26

Day treatment center, 30, 40, 301, 309
Delinquency, 4, 54, 56, 298, 368
Demonology, 37, 47
Desensitization, systematic, 199, 205, 211–213, 240, 242, 244–245, 247–253, 263
Determinism, 219, 221, 233, 266, 272, 285
Diagnosis (see also Differential diagnosis), 6, 11, 12, 30, 32–34, 39, 43–44, 107–126, 146–147, 149–150, 185, 267–268, 306, 351, 373
Diagnostic nomenclature, 108, 121
Differential diagnosis, 71, 122–125, 149, 154
Division 12 (see Clinical psychology division of APA)
Doctor of psychology degree, 71–78, 82–85
Doctor of psychotherapy degree, 77, 79–82
Documents, personal, 7, 145
Double-bind theory, 372–373

Draw-A-Person Test, 21, 132, 145, 181–183
Dreams:
  in existential therapy, 276–277
  in Gestalt therapy, 281–282
  in psychoanalysis, 228–229
Drugs, 15, 22, 94–95, 232, 251, 295, 341, 351, 362, 367

Ecological research, 322–325, 329–331
Effectiveness of psychotherapy, 213–218, 294, 369–370, 388–389, 405–406
Ego psychologists, 236
Electroconvulsive shock treatment, 15, 94, 251–252, 294
Emergency care (see also Crisis), 301, 307, 348, 358–361
Encounter groups, 270, 288, 371, 391–392, 405
Epidemiology, 13, 305, 316–319, 322
Esalen, 273, 390–391, 401
Ethics:
  in professional practice, 37, 71, 76, 98–100, 102
  in research, 24, 99–100, 102, 210, 322
Etiology (see Psychopathology, etiology)
Existential therapy, 197, 200, 260, 273–277

Family:
  study, 13, 118, 308
  therapy, 7, 64, 201, 304, 368, 371–389
Fifth profession, 204–205
Free association, 47, 227–228, 364
Free clinic, 360–361
Frostig Developmental Test of Visual Perception, 163
Functional versus organic disorders, 34, 49, 108
Functionalism, 57

Genetic factors in psychopathology, 13, 17–19, 317–318
Gesell Developmental Schedules, 161
Gestalt psychology, 57–58, 278
Gestalt therapy, 200, 260, 277–282, 401–402
Goldstein-Scheerer Tests, 146, 169
Graham-Kendall Memory-for-Designs Test, 169
Group for the Advancement of Psychiatry, 116, 379–380
Group therapy, 58, 64, 389–408
Growth centers, 273, 288, 390–391, 401

Halfway house, 301, 309
Hanfmann-Kasanin Concept Formation Test, 146, 169
Hartford Retreat, 50
Hayes-Binet Scale, 162–163
Headstart Project, 5, 306, 326–327

High-risk conditions, 19, 305, 317–319, 322–323, 343–344
Hiskey-Nebraska Test of Learning Aptitude, 162
Holtzman Inkblot Test, 21, 174
Home visits, 7, 11, 352–353, 373, 385–387
Hospital, psychiatric:
  admissions, 13, 38, 137–139, 322
  discharge, 15, 322, 369
  population, 13, 40, 257, 324, 362
  research, 16, 22, 24, 323
  role of psychologist, 30, 41, 58, 94, 147
  treatment, 15, 36, 254–255, 384
Hot-line telephone service, 359–360
House-Tree-Person (H-T-P) Test, 183–184
Humanistic therapy, 199, 260, 270–273
Hypnosis, 49, 214, 220, 249–250
Hysteria, treatment of, 49, 220–222

Idiographic approach, 11, 139
Illinois Test of Psycholinguistic Abilities, 164
Individual differences, 11, 46–47, 53
Infantile autism (*see* Autism)
Infants, evaluation of, 5, 11, 47, 160–162
Inference, clinical, 134–143
Insurance companies, 37, 215–217, 369–370
Intelligence testing, 53–59, 154–164
Internal Revenue Service, 37
International Classification of Diseases (World Health Organization), 31, 109
Internships in clinical psychology, 56, 68, 93
Interviews, 5, 6, 11, 134, 145, 149, 246, 248, 318–321, 334, 341, 374
Intuition, clinical, 6, 20, 107, 127–142, 148, 181, 247, 256, 266

Joint Commission on Mental Health of Children, 333–334
Joint Commission on Mental Illness and Health, 61–62, 88, 299, 312, 321

Learning theory, 9, 23, 36, 41, 256, 263
Leiter International Performance Scale, 163
Licensure law, 61, 89, 94, 96–98
Los Angeles Society of Clinical Psychologists, 77, 91–92

Make-A-Picture Story Test, 129, 177–178
Manpower shortage (*see also* Nonprofessionals), 40–41, 62–63, 79, 294, 299, 307, 314–315, 334
Marathon groups, 368, 371, 403–405
Marital problems, 4, 376
Medical model, 30–42, 64, 102, 108, 236, 256, 302, 337

Medical school, 4, 74, 80, 94
Medicaid, 40, 362
Medicare, 35, 40, 362
Menninger Foundation and Clinic, 36, 133, 146, 202
Mental Health Study Act (1955), 61, 299
Mental hospital (*see* Hospital, psychiatric)
Mental hygiene, 51–52, 298
Mental illness (*see* Psychopathology)
Mental retardation, 4, 36, 43, 57, 147, 149, 154, 163, 254–255, 257, 299, 308
Miami Conference, 75
Michigan Clinical Psychology Assessment Project, 128, 148
Midtown Manhattan Study, 316–318, 322
Miller Analogies Test, 128
Minnesota Multiphasic Personality Inventory, 20, 63, 129, 131, 136, 152, 185–190
Modeling, 252–253, 381
Moral treatment, 50
Multiple-family therapy, 384
Multiple-impact therapy, 384

National Association for Mental Health, 52, 298–299
National Committee for Mental Hygiene (*see* National Association for Mental Health)
National Council on Graduate Education in Psychology, 85–86
National Institute of Mental Health, 37, 41, 52, 299–302, 318, 329, 359, 362
National Mental Health Act (1946), 299
National Training Laboratories, 391–392
Neo-Freudians, 236–237
Network therapy, 386–387
Neurologist, 165, 219
Neurosis:
  diagnosis, 15, 56
  experimental, 14, 45, 244
  treatment, 15, 194–195, 215–218, 226–231, 366
Neurosis, theories:
  behavioral, 239
  existential, 275
  Gestalt, 279
  humanistic, 271–272
  psychoanalytic, 225–226
Nomothetic approach, 11
Nondirective therapy (*see also* Client-centered therapy), 59, 267
Nonprofessionals, 5, 62, 64, 79, 296, 304, 307, 312–315, 334, 339, 358, 363
Normal behavior, 12
Norms, test, 20, 135, 150, 173, 176, 179, 183–184

Nude marathon groups (*see also* Marathon groups), 404–405
Nurses, public health, 7, 9, 27, 30, 62, 296, 301, 332, 352–353, 385

Objective tests, 20, 128, 147, 170, 184–190, 247
Observation, behavioral, 7, 11, 33, 145, 149, 161, 238–239, 241, 265, 325
Operant conditioning (*see* Conditioning)
Organic brain dysfunction, 4, 5, 34, 60, 147, 149, 158, 160–170, 174, 378, 393
Outcome research:
  in community mental health programs, 327–331
  in psychotherapy, 24, 210–218, 369

Paresis, 38, 49
Participant observation, 26, 200
Pattern analysis, test, 20, 159–160
Peabody Picture Vocabulary Test, 164
Peace Corps, 5, 83, 155
Pediatrician, 11, 137
Phenomenology, 170, 200, 232, 265–290
Phobia, treatment of, 58, 197, 205, 210, 239–245, 247–253, 263
Play therapy (*see also* Childhood disorders, treatment), 196–197, 259
Porteus Maze Test, 145, 163
Poverty, 207, 257, 293–295, 304, 312–315, 321, 335–337, 350
Prediction:
  clinical versus statistical, 129–134
  of response to psychotherapy, 60, 155
  of schizophrenia, 18
Prevention programs, 18, 30, 62, 64, 295, 298, 305–309, 316–317, 323, 363
Primary prevention, 305–308, 336, 344, 363, 365
Prisons, 4, 54, 56, 201
Private practice, 4, 27, 37, 55, 61, 63, 67, 71, 76, 92–96, 321
Privileged communication, 22, 37
Problems in living, 39
Process research, psychotherapy, 24, 208–210, 213
Professional school of psychology, 74, 78, 85–89
Prognosis, 13, 33–34, 108, 149, 152
Program evaluation research, 326–331
Progressive matrices, 163
Projective techniques, 21, 60, 62–63, 128–129, 134, 147, 150–151, 153–154, 170–185, 338
Psychiatric case registers, 322
Psychiatric social worker, 7, 9, 27, 30, 41, 201, 204, 301, 385
Psychiatric team, 30

Psychiatrist:
  judgments as validating criterion, 152
  as mental health professional, 9, 41, 148, 201–202, 204, 258, 301
  as practitioner, 15, 30, 321, 338–339
  relations with clinical psychologists, 60–61, 92–96
Psychoanalysis:
  of children, 197
  goals, 201, 283
  of students, 68
  technique of treatment, 9–10, 15, 34, 38, 49–50, 55, 59, 227–237, 257, 273, 283, 294, 363–365, 396
  theory, 32, 38, 49–50, 55, 58–59, 64, 146, 170, 199, 219–226, 239, 259, 270, 282–283, 293, 295, 338, 372
Psychoanalyst, 9, 38, 194, 198–201, 204, 219–237, 239, 258, 260, 274, 381
Psychodrama, 390, 396–397
Psychopathology:
  acute versus chronic, 12
  criteria, 12
  etiology, 5, 13–19, 50, 64, 108–121
  experimental, 14, 45
Psychopharmacology, 13
Psychosexual development, 11, 223–225, 236
Psychotherapy:
  analogue studies, 210–213
  definition, 191
  effectiveness, 24, 64, 131, 211–219, 294, 369–370
  patients, 15
  predicted response, 60
  research, 21–25, 202–219, 369–370
Public health orientation, 36, 295, 305–306, 316, 320

Q sort, 23, 129
Questionnaires, 11, 47, 145, 318–321, 325

Rational-emotive therapy, 199
Reality therapy, 273
Records, patient, 7, 11, 19, 48
Reciprocal inhibition, 244–245
Re-ED Project, 329–331
Rehabilitation services, 301, 304, 307, 309
Reliability:
  of clinical judgments, 127–134
  of psychiatric diagnosis, 121–126
  of scorers or judges, 154, 174, 176
  of tests, 21, 152–154, 161, 173, 176–177, 183
Research:
  animal, 14, 239–244, 263
  critique of model, 25–29

orientation, 3, 10, 72–73, 83, 256, 399
outcome studies, 24, 213–218
process studies, 24, 208–210, 213
Research areas:
  assessment, 19–21
  community mental health, 301, 315–331
  encounter groups, 405–406
  psychoanalysis, 234–235
  psychopathology, 12–19
  psychotherapy, 21–25, 202–219
Rorschach Inkblot Test, 21, 58, 129, 131–132, 145–146, 154, 171–174, 176, 247

St. Elizabeth's Hospital, Washington, D.C., 51
Schizophrenia:
  biochemical factors, 16
  definition, 7, 115
  double-bind hypothesis, 372–373
  experimental studies, 13–19
  family influence, 7, 19, 372, 374
  genetic factors, 17–19, 317–319
  heredity and incidence, 18
  prevention, 18–19
  prognosis, 49, 108, 138
  reactive versus process, 138
  social factors, 14–15, 294, 316
  treatment, 7, 23, 36, 49, 245, 254, 294, 386
School phobia, 182, 239, 260
School psychology, 44, 72, 145, 163–164, 324–325, 333
Scientist-professional model, 9, 60, 70–79, 83, 85, 102
Secondary prevention, 305, 307, 315, 344–345, 365
Self-actualization, 272–273
Sensitivity training, 58, 270, 371, 390, 398–399
Sentence Completion Test, 21, 178
Sexuality, 4, 198–199, 223–225, 232–234, 251–252, 387–388, 404
Shaping, behavior, 243, 253–254
Social worker (*see* Psychiatric social worker)
Speech pathology, 4, 44
Spontaneous recovery, 24, 215–218
Standards for Educational and Psychological Tests and Manuals, 151
Stanford Conference, 75
Stanford-Binet Intelligence Scales, 53, 145, 152, 155–156, 158, 161, 163, 181
Strong Vocational Interest Test, 128, 202

Suicide, 144, 306, 320, 341, 344–345, 348, 358–359, 407
Survey methods, research, 26, 319–322
Symptom substitution, 260
Synanon, 402–403
Szondi Test, 179–180

T groups (*see also* Sensitivity training), 270, 390–392, 398–399
Taxonomic sorting, 136–142
Tertiary prevention, 305, 307, 309, 365
Testing, psychological, 4, 5, 6, 7, 11, 19–21, 32, 53–65, 145–190, 193, 247, 331, 341
Thematic Apperception Test (TAT), 21, 58, 129, 132, 145–146, 154, 174–178, 247
Therapeutic community, 232, 304, 336
Therapy (*see* Psychotherapy)
Token economy programs, 36, 244, 254–256, 258
Training:
  graduate students, 27, 59–60, 66–89
  nonprofessionals, 5, 64, 79, 88–89, 304, 312–315, 339, 363
  psychoanalysts, 233
Transactional analysis, 273, 397–398
Type A therapists versus type B therapists, 202–203

Unconscious processes, 49, 141, 170, 200, 219, 221–223, 227–233, 239, 256, 263–264, 281, 290
U.S. Army, 56, 109, 185, 298
U.S. Public Health Service, 59, 70

Validity:
  of clinical judgments, 127–134
  of psychiatric diagnosis, 125–126
  of tests, 21, 126, 150–152, 161, 173–174
Veterans Administration, 59–60, 68, 70, 109, 203, 298, 302, 385

Walk-in clinic (*see* Clinics, crisis or walk-in)
Wechsler Adult Intelligence Scale, 156–158
Wechsler-Bellevue Intelligence Scale, 145–146, 156, 159
Wechsler Intelligence Scale for Children, 156–157, 164
Wechsler Memory Scale, 168
Wechsler Preschool and Primary Scale, 157
Word Association Test, 47, 146, 171, 178
YAVIS syndrome, 206